GEOFFREY WINTHROP YOUNG

GEOFFREY WINTHROP YOUNG

Poet, educator, mountaineer

Alan Hankinson

Hodder & Stoughton

Copyright © 1995 by Alan Hankinson
First published in 1995 by Hodder and Stoughton,
a division of Hodder Headline PLC

10 9 8 7 6 5 4 3 2 1

British Library Cataloguing in Publication Data

Hankinson, Alan
Geoffrey Winthorp Young: Poet, Educator, Mountaineer
I. Title
941.082092

ISBN 0 340 57609 X

Typeset by Hewer Text Composition Services, Edinburgh
Printed and bound in Great Britain by
Mackays of Chatham plc, Chatham, Kent

Hodder and Stoughton
A division of Hodder Headline PLC
338 Euston Road
London NW1 3BH

To Geoffrey's children,
Jocelin Winthrop Young
and Marcia Newbolt,
with thanks for their help.

I climbed all my life only for enjoyment, and abandoned myself to it.
G.W.Y. in *Mountains with a Difference*

Vitality is the only thing that counts!
G.W.Y. in a letter

CONTENTS

ACKNOWLEDGMENTS

Many people helped with the research for, and the writing of this book, most notably Geoffrey's children, Jocelin Winthrop Young and Marcia Newbolt. They talked to me about their father, gave me letters and diaries and other relevant papers, checked each chapter as it was written and sent me their comments and suggestions. Without their co-operation it would not have been possible to write the book. Marcia's husband, Peter Newbolt, was immensely helpful too.

Geoffrey's widow, Eleanor, died while this book was being written, but I had, fortunately, talked to her about Geoffrey and their lives together at length many years before, and kept my notes.

Other members of the family who gave generous help were: the daughters of Geoffrey's elder brother Georis, Virginia Lady Hutton and Mrs Robert Mathew; the son of Geoffrey's younger brother Hilton, Wayland Young (Lord Kennet of the Dene) and Lady Young; and Michael Gordon, a son of Eleanor's elder sister.

I am grateful, too, to many people who knew Geoffrey and were happy to pass on their memories and impressions. They are: Sir George Trevelyan and Mr Geoffrey Trevelyan; Claude and Peter Bicknell; Mrs Eva Chew; the late David Cox; Sid Cross and his wife; Robin Dower; Tony Dummett; A. B. Hargreaves; Robin Hodgkin; Bobby Files; John Kempe (former headmaster of Gordonstoun) and Roy McComish (also of Gordonstoun); J. H. Emlyn Jones; Scott Russell; and Ivan Waller.

My researches also owe much to the kindness of various archivists: Sophie Weidlich of Salem, Germany; Livia Gollancz of the Alpine Club; and the school archivists at Gordonstoun, Eton, and Marlborough College.

Dr C. T. Morley of Trinity College, Cambridge, and the secretary of the Donald Robertson Travel Fund, Miss Catherine Walters (also of Trinity College), sent me information about the Fund today. John Cleare/Mountain Camera supplied the modern photograph of the Täschhorn.

Finally, I have to thank four friends: Edgar Appleby of Keswick, who checked the war-time chapters for howlers; Jim Scott of Keswick, who gave expert help with the photographs; Walt Unsworth of Milnthorpe, who photocopied passages from his Alpine library; and, most important of all, Mrs Joan Alexander, again of Keswick, who scrutinised each chapter as it was completed and made many valuable suggestions.

AH

AUTHOR'S NOTE

This book relies heavily on quotations – from Geoffrey's published writings and also from his private letters and diaries and from a mass of unpublished papers. For the most part, even when writing in extremely difficult circumstances, Geoffrey was careful to write both legibly and grammatically, but very occasionally I have amended his punctuation in an effort to make his intended meaning as clear as possible. Within the quotations, I have used square brackets to enclose my own interpolations.

AH

1

Introduction

I NEVER MET GEOFFREY WINTHROP YOUNG. He was over seventy and very much the "Grand Old Man" of British mountaineering by the time, after the Second World War, that I started climbing – oddly enough, on a route that plays a recurring role in his story, Gashed Crag on Tryfan in North Wales.

As I grew more and more interested in mountaineering, I read his poems and books and derived excitement and pleasure and some instruction from his vivid, impressionistic accounts, the acute psychological observation and analysis, his already-dated but highly charged and romantic attitude towards mountains and what they could do for character and comradeship.

I read about him too, and learned about his war-work with the Friends' Ambulance Unit from 1914 to 1918, and his efforts to improve and broaden the British educational system which brought about, together with his friend Kurt Hahn, the establishment of Gordonstoun School and the Outward Bound movement and led to the Duke of Edinburgh's Award Scheme.

Geoffrey died in 1958. It was not until some twenty years later that I got to know his widow Eleanor, whom everybody called Len. I was writing a book about the pioneer climbers of Snowdonia. Geoffrey was one of the two key figures in that story, and Len, who soon became a friend, liked nothing better than to talk about Geoffrey and his formative parties at Pen-y-Pass. She sent me many passages transcribed from his pre-1914 Journals. But she did not let me see the Journals, for reasons that became clear when I did read them, researching for this book.

When I finished the Snowdonia book, I suggested a possible biography of Geoffrey, but Len was not encouraging.

A decade or so after that their son, Jocelin Winthrop Young, got in touch with me and raised the idea again. There was, he said, a mass of unpublished material: Geoffrey's private diaries from 1902 to 1914 and throughout the First World War, and again during the Second World War and on until May 1957; countless letters, mostly written by Geoffrey but also by family and friends; many autobiographical sketches he wrote in his later years, describing events and encounters long past; other documents and reports. Geoffrey was an assiduous collector and keeper of things, and his family have been the same. This book is very dependent on these primary documentary sources.

Jocelin said that he and his sister, Marcia Newbolt, would hand all the material over to me, give all the help they could, and not try to veto anything, however upsetting, that I felt ought to be said. They kept the promise.

My research – reading all the material and talking to Geoffrey's family and friends and surviving acquaintances – brought several surprises.

In the first place, I had always imagined Geoffrey as an almost wholly serious man. He could, indeed, be very serious about the things that mattered to him, such things as mountaineering and educational reform and the need to uphold civilised standards of behaviour. But he had a very lively sense of humour as well. Among his favourite words, recurring all the time in his diaries and letters, were "fun" and "jolly". He loved the playful and imaginative Irish way with words and ideas. Human quirks and quiddities and incongruities delighted him. He liked to read the Irish tales of Somerville and Ross aloud to the family, but there were some he could never finish for laughing. He disliked all kinds of pomposity and excessive piety, and enjoyed seeing them deflated. He was good at laughing at himself, seeing himself as others might be seeing him, mocking his own foibles and possible pretensions. On the Italian front, driving an ambulance up a mountain road and wondering why the Austrian gunners were not shelling him, he reflected: "Doubtless they only squinted at our car and said 'It's that old ass with his eyeglass again'." In old age, when he cut a distinguished figure and found himself widely lionised, he described himself in his diary as "an elderly celebrity, second-class".

He could, on the other hand, be fearsomely censorious when he felt the boundaries of decent conduct were being breached. His son Jocelin remembers a climbing club dinner, after the Second World War, at which a guest speaker ill-advisedly launched into a succession of risqué stories. Geoffrey swung round in his chair and fixed the offender with an unblinking glare of disapproval, made all the more effective by the monocle clenched and glittering in his eye. The effect was such that the speaker dried up in mid-sentence, then sat down unable to continue. In his diary entry for December 30, 1951, Geoffrey speaks of preparing a speech for the Rucksack Club, which included "a warning against the vulgar jokes they are dropping into in the speeches. Anything in the world can be put across if there is wit and art in the presentment. But crudeness is never worth hearing."

There is one important aspect of Geoffrey's life about which I knew nothing, had never heard a word, before I began to research this book. It is not mentioned in any of his published writings, and none of his obituarists referred to it. It happenened nonetheless. The evidence is there, in his unpublished papers and in official documents. Throughout the 1930s, up until the outbreak of the Second World War, he was a frequent visitor to Germany, and many of these journeys were to give help and encouragement to the liberal-minded and humane Germans – army officers, civic dignitaries, teachers, lawyers – who were opposed to everything that Hitler and the Nazi Party and the German government stood for. It was a dangerous thing to do. Very few of his German fellow-conspirators survived the war. Many were murdered in the blood-bath that followed the failed bomb plot against Hitler's life in July 1944.

Geoffrey was born into the English Liberal establishment and given the conventional and privileged upbringing of that class, but he did not become an establishment man. Although he met most of the leading figures of his time, he was not always impressed by them. He disliked and distrusted politicians, on the whole. He had no respect for careerists, people without true values or scruples, who measured success only in terms of income or power or status attained. His diaries and letters contain many explosions of disgust at the worldly go-getters around him, officials and bankers, MPs and press lords and others. In a letter to Jocelin in 1950 he wrote: "I do think sleek-haired, sleek-faced career diplomats the most contemptible class."

He valued his freedom and integrity more than worldly success, and, as a result, never became a rich man. He took a cavalier attitude towards money, with a positive aversion to studying accounts and totting up columns of figures.

There is a sense in which he could almost be described as "Bohemian". He admired adventurers and explorers, people of independent spirit who were not afraid to stand out from the herd and, if need be, stand against it. He enjoyed the company of artists and writers, dancers and wits and eccentrics. He travelled widely, especially in Europe, and learnt to speak colloquial Italian and reasonably good French and fluent German. At one period of his life, just before the First World War, he attended homosexual parties in Berlin, Paris and Soho.

There was a strong element of the actor in him. He dressed strikingly and could dominate a company, not in an assertive way but by the force of his personality and the quality of his discourse. He knew about this histrionic side to his character, and said it derived from his Irish ancestry, on his mother's side. Some folk suspected him of being a poseur, and some of the photographs of him suggest a man who knew how to strike an attitude. In my researches I must have talked to more than a score of people, all old folk now, and got them to remember him. Two women surprised me by saying his manner was always so smooth and courteous and considerate of others, they could not believe it was genuine.

But it was genuine. Most of those who knew him, and everyone who knew him closely, agree that one of his outstanding characteristics was his interest in the thoughts and feelings of other people. He was an excellent listener, good at getting people to talk. He studied himself and he studied others, not judgementally but out of concern and curiosity. He was exceptionally good with children, relishing their naturalness and playfulness and their unexpected responses. But he could talk to adult men and women too, not always of his own interests or class. As a result he made a multitude of friends, and he always followed Dr Johnson's injunction: "A man, Sir, must keep his friendship in constant repair."

Geoffrey sometimes regretted that his schooling, in the classics especially, had not been sufficiently rigorous. He was no subtle logician, never became the concentrated scholar that his father had been. It may have been an advantage. Certainly, it saved him from the dangers of settling for a narrow, cloistered, academic way of life. Geoffrey had an unusual mind, active and original and imaginative. His interests were wide-ranging, his sympathies broad. He was observant, sharp of eye and acute of ear. In the fields where he chiefly operated, in mountaineering and education, he was always looking for ways of improving things, livening them up, letting in more air and light. He was a compulsive reformer. He enjoyed argument, when conducted in a controlled and civilised manner, and he enjoyed a hard-fought campaign. He could be a formidable agitator and adversary, and it made him some enemies, among men of more entrenched, reactionary and conservative attitudes. It made him many more friends and disciples though. He was described as a "Pied Piper", a natural leader, a strong and beneficent influence on scores of young men. Before and after the First World War, he introduced many to the delights of climbing, at Pen-y-Pass in North Wales and in the Alps. His protégés included such leading figures as George Mallory of Everest, Siegfried Herford, Jack Longland and Wilfrid Noyce.

For Geoffrey, and for Len, the greatest quality of all was vitality. It is another word that recurs again and again in his letters and diaries. In his Journal, in 1914, he noted: "I believe in vitality first of all, and truth." To Len, in July 1917, he wrote: ". . . the thing is to live life out, and to have the joy of doing it, and to keep the capacity to enjoy. *Vitality* is the only thing that counts!" In 1938 he wrote to their son Jocelin: "It is a worthy and tremendous game this living, and it has to be lived and all one's force put into it." In 1951 he wrote a letter describing his first grandson and said: "Full of *vitality*, which to me means most." One of his pre-1914 poems "Motion" opens with the words: "Live life at the full; blend dream with the deed . . ." and more than forty years later he said those were the words he wanted on his memorial tablet in Cookham Church.

That was the core of his creed and for most of his life he lived by it. He had periods of near-despair and self-disgust, and his experiences in the First World War and in Hitler's Germany in the 1930s brought him very close to humanity at its most cruel and bestial, but that remained his faith and the basis of his hope. He was not a Christian in any conventional, church-going sense, but he had a powerful sense of awe in the contemplation of nature and human achievement. He loved mountains and weather and moving waters; he loved the colours and sounds of nature; above all, he loved humanity, family life, the comradeship and conversation of friends. He thought the human form, male and female, was beautiful, especially in graceful, athletic action, dancing or climbing, swimming and diving, fencing and boxing. Long after he died, Len said to their daughter Marcia: "I've often wondered what it was that made him so unusual, and I think it was chiefly his humanity. Anything human would interest him."

In many ways Geoffrey seems to have been greatly gifted by fate. He was the son of a baronet and grew up in a secure and comfortable home, looked after by parents, nanny and many servants, but also given freedom to explore and adventure. He had a happy childhood, an expensive if not very successful education, and a wonderful three years at Cambridge. He grew up to be fit, unusually strong, good-looking and graceful in movement. He was a man of thought, and feeling, and action, and the happy balance he struck between the three aspects gave him a poised and balanced personality.

Simply by his birth, Geoffrey was enlisted into a complex network of families and friends, acquaintances and contacts – the Trevelyans, Arnolds, Arnold-Forsters, Huxleys and many more – who held high moral and intellectual standards, but who saw nothing wrong in using their connections to further their causes and their careers. They exerted enormous influence over the political, social, artistic and academic life of the country. Geoffrey was implanted with these values as a boy.

Writing this book in an age that is less confident and much more cynical, I found it hard to believe at times that the things I was recounting had happened so recently. It is only a century, after all, since Geoffrey embarked on his student years at Cambridge; less than half a century since he died. Time and again, I thought of the famous opening sentence of L. P. Hartley's novel *The Go-Between*: "The past is a foreign country: they do things differently there."

2

Family Background

WHEN I READ BIOGRAPHIES, I usually skip rapidly through the pages that deal with the subject's family background. The relationships are complex and often hard to follow, and the characters and careers of remote progenitors seem to throw little light, for the most part, on the life I want to learn about. In the case of Geoffrey Winthrop Young, however, it is impossible to ignore his ancestors. In the first place, it was a comparatively distinguished family, and the three males of Geoffrey's generation – Georis and Geoffrey and Hilton, in order of appearance – all grew up to be remarkable men, though in very different ways and in widely varying fields of activity. In the second place, the matter of his genetic inheritance was important to Geoffrey. He found it fascinating and thought it could be instructive too.

Among his unpublished papers there are two long essays on the subject, both written during or just after the Second World War, in his mid-sixties. One is entitled "Family Failings" and in it he says:

> I have always wanted to know since I grew up, more about my own ancestors and where characteristics came from. And, in the case of bringing up our own children, I have often felt that it would have helped vastly if we could have "placed" traits as they appeared, and had some guidance as to their possible consequences, as evidenced by lives of those who had been made that way before in the family. But our last generations have been respectably secretive, and little has come down.

The other unpublished paper is called "Youngs" and he explained it with these words: "Before I get too old I must jot down something of my father and his brothers. For I believe that it is of use to know what to look out for, in family inheritance, of personal qualities. And good or bad."

His account of the family is far from being entirely congratulatory.

He acclaims their virtues and accomplishments but notices their shortcomings and failures too, and berates them with feeling. His strong moral sense is often offended and several ancestors are roundly condemned for narrow-mindedness and materialistic greed, "their middle-class piety, narrowness, obstinacy and selfish clan vanity".

He could be almost brutally blunt about some of them, but that was because he felt they had let the family down. He was, on balance, proud and happy to be a Young, and proud, too, that on his mother's side, the Kennedys, he could trace his descent as far back as the fourteenth century and to no less a figure than King Edward III.

The first notable figure in the story of the Youngs was Sir George Young, a successful naval officer in the second half of the eighteenth century, a time when the Royal Navy was more than usually active. He was a grandson of another George Young – George is the family's favourite name – who was born in 1669 and became a schoolmaster in Bere Regis, Dorset. By the time Sir George, the sailor, retired from the service he was an admiral. Geoffrey, who was his great-great-grandson, wrote: "The Admiral was clearly a man of fine personality and considerable distinction, a not unworthy founder of a family. A 'bigness' is evident in his character, even a certain nobility . . . Man of action, of enterprise, originality, great willpower, and fine taste. Clearly also of personal charm and social prominence." It is not clear what the evidence was for these judgements, probably no more than stories handed down from generation to generation and the trophies he brought back from his travels. But the bigness of the man, his imaginative and practical vigour, were demonstrated by the splendid house he built for his retirement years.

The Admiral bought a group of little islands in the River Thames, close to the village of Cookham and opposite the steep woods of Cliveden. It was here that Geoffrey and the other children spent their first and formative years, with the ever-present sounds and smells and sight of the passing water. In the opening chapter of his autobiographical book *The Grace of Forgetting* Geoffrey wrote:

> An Admiral ancestor piled chalk upon a group of Thames eyots, in a great angle of the river. He set upon it lawns and trees and bridges and trailing roses; and an eighteenth-century house that should still give him the feeling of his flag-ship, with central saloons that were oval and domed and excellent for music, and with side wings of large cabins. The walls were heart of oak, for he had a battleship towed up and broken up off the island, and the spaces between the walls were filled with chunks of oak. There were portholes for windows on the sea or land level . . .

The house was called Formosa, presumably for nostalgic reasons. Sadly, the striking and lovely Georgian building was demolished in the middle years of this century to make way for a modern house.

The Admiral's eldest son, Sir Samuel Young, was quite different from his father and, in Geoffrey's opinion, thoroughly deplorable. In "Family Failings" Geoffrey describes him as "Small, narrow, obstinate, quarrelsome, a hedonist, and with the one merit of artistic taste and connoisseurship, which led to his fine collection of stones, jewels, pictures, shells etc., and to his consorting with scientists such as Sir Joseph Banks". Geoffrey says his father always spoke of Sir Samuel, who was *his* grandfather, with contempt. Geoffrey believed that his father, "with his ultra Victorian prudery", had destroyed all the documents that might have thrown more and more unflattering light on Sir Samuel's character.

For all this, Sir Samuel did well for himself and the family. Born in 1764, he went out to work as an officer in the East India Company – there is a fleeting and unrevealing mention of him in the *Memoirs of William Hickey* – and married advantageously into the Baring family complex. The Barings sprang from a North German Lutheran family which had emigrated to Devon in the early eighteenth century and flourished as merchants and bankers. Sir Samuel became a wealthy man. He raised the family into the ranks of the minor nobility, becoming the first baronet of Formosa Place with the family motto "Be right and persist". And he did his dynastic duty assiduously, fathering six sons and three daughters.

The boys seem to have been a mixed bunch. One of them, according to Geoffrey's account, took horribly after his father, went into Baring's Bank and became a millionaire, was "narrow and mean and did nothing of import". Another joined the Plymouth Brethren and emigrated to Australia to found the antipodean branch of the Young family which has greatly flourished and multiplied, and which takes pride in the fact that their progenitor, the Admiral, was the first man to suggest the colonisation of Australia. Yet another son followed in his grandfather's footsteps, joined the Royal Navy and rose to the rank of Admiral. The youngest was drowned in the Thames, off the Formosa steps, as a child.

The eldest boy was called George. He, too, joined the Navy, and became a Captain. He was the second baronet, known to all as "The Captain". He was Geoffrey's grandfather, and Geoffrey, although he never knew him, approved:

He was not clever, or a man of great mark; not even a very outstanding seaman in those days of great seamen; but he clearly was well-loved, had charm, diligence, and his grandfather's humanity to his "young gentlemen", the midshipmen, and they were devoted to him. He had his own well-chosen seaman's library of small classics, studied and read, and was exquisitely neat with his hands, like his son, my father.

To Geoffrey's mind, perhaps the wisest decision his grandfather ever made was in his choice of a bride. In 1835 Captain Sir George married Susan Praed.

Geoffrey saw the Mackworth–Praeds as a valuable genetic acquisition. For generations they had beeen prominent in politics and the law as well as in the financial world, and Susan's brother, Winthrop Mackworth Praed, was a poet, still occasionally anthologised as the composer of elegant and witty verses, portraying society life in the years of George IV and William IV with sharp observation and affectionate, gentle mockery. He trained as a lawyer and practised briefly before going into politics and becoming a Conservative MP, on the reforming, non-reactionary wing of the party. There are parallels between Praed's life and that of Geoffrey Young. Both studied at Trinity College, Cambridge. While there, each won the Chancellor's Medal for English Verse two years running, and each worked briefly as a teacher at Eton. They both had a passion for dancing.

Geoffrey's belief that the injection of new blood could only improve the genetic strengths of the Young family was justified by the children born to the second baronet. There were five boys, all good-looking, each of them distinguished in one way or another, and one girl.

The eldest, another Sir George and Geoffrey's father, became an administrator and scholar and was a considerable athlete as a young man. The next, Edward Mallet Young, was a classicist and natural scholar; went to Trinity, Cambridge, where he was a member of the intellectually élitist discussion society, The Apostles; took holy orders, became a teacher, then a house-master at Harrow, and head-master of Sherborne. Geoffrey wrote of him: "For a man of charm, brilliance and a certain cultivated assertiveness, he was oddly unlovable – short in stature and protesting in manner." The middle brother, William Mackworth, was another all-rounder – athlete, musician and colonial administrator, who ended up as Lieutenant-Governor of the Punjab. The next, Albert Winthrop, became the rural dean in charge of the vast parish of Kingston-on-Thames, adored by his parishoners. "I heard him preach once or twice," Geoffrey said, "the voice deep and beautiful, the matter scholarly. But I think he was a sort of misfit – and lazy." The fifth and final boy was called Bulkeley Samuel. Like his brothers, he went to Eton and then to Cambridge. Unlike them, he had an open, out-going, cheerful personality. Geoffrey wrote of him: "He was the most likely of all to have reached high position because he had none of the inhibitions, reclusiveness, priggishness or religiosity that tied up his brothers in varying degrees."

The eldest of these brothers, Sir George, became the third baronet in 1848, when he was eleven years old. He was Geoffrey's father and he lived into great old age, until 1930, so he is a key figure in this story. In "Family Failings", Geoffrey said: "My father inherited the Praed powerful brain, with his father's diligence, neatness and natural virtue."

The dominant influence on Sir George's upbringing was his mother, Susan Praed, described by Geoffrey as "a woman of forceful personality, good brains, some musical and artistic gift, no taste, intense intellectual interests, severe piety, sterling conscience – an arrogant Victorian lady and a magnificent mother to her sons."

When she was widowed she took her five sons to live at Eton, so they could all go to the school there without excessive expense. The early promise shown by her eldest boy must have delighted her. Many years later, in the essay which he called "Youngs", Geoffrey wrote at length about the life and character of his father:

> George, in a fragment of autobiography I saw once at Formosa, wrote that he was "naturally good" – born with temperance in all his ways and desires. At two and a half he could read; at five, knew French. Before he went to school he had read all Gibbon, Shakespeare, and so on, aloud to his mother. He told me he was always and all his life more interested in books and what men wrote than in men. Ideas and literature absorbed him. To the end of life he remained a "Great Victorian", in the sense that he took all knowledge into his purview, and corresponded to the last with maths professors about the heresies of Einstein.

One of George's acquaintances at Eton was Algernon Charles Swinburne, some three years his senior. Apparently, Swinburne sometimes went to George's house to read old English ballads to the boys. A particularly grim poem, "The Old Woman of Barclay", would reduce Swinburne to paroxysms of delight, when he would coil up and "shriek with joy".

George was an earnest scholar, gifted with a marvellous memory, and he won a scholarship to Trinity College, Cambridge. There, Geoffrey says, "his real life began. Trinity turned him into one of the leading young men of the day, with a political future certain. He became President of the Union, following his uncle Praed; had the Macaulay rooms, and later the vast rooms over the Great Gate – where his immense sofa lasted to my time! – it could hold sixteen, he said."

He made good friends among the Liberal intelligentsia – among them, two eminent philosophers in later years, Henry Sidgwick and Henry Jackson; Lord Frederick Cavendish; and, most important of all, George Otto Trevelyan, a nephew of the great historian/states-man Macaulay. G. O. Trevelyan was to become a considerable historian and politician in his own right. For years he was Sir George's closest friend, until Gladstone's conversion to home rule for Ireland divided them as it divided the Liberal Party. Trevelyan followed Gladstone and Sir George went with the Liberal Unionists, and for a long time there was no contact between them – until their sons, the subject of this book and George Macaulay Trevelyan, yet another eminent historian, became close friends and brought their fathers together again.

Sir George studied classics, mathematics and philosophy at Cambridge and was disappointed when he failed, narrowly, to get a First Class degree in the final examinations. He went on to study law, qualified as a barrister and spent most of the 1870s working as secretary to a number of commissions of inquiry set up by Gladstone. He ran for Parliament several times under the Liberal banner but never succeeded; he was not really cut out for the rough-and-tumble of life in politics. In 1882 his Cambridge friend, Lord Frederick Cavendish, was appointed Chief Secretary to the Lord Lieutenant of Ireland, and it was arranged that Sir George should go to Dublin as his Political Secretary. But Sir George was still in England on May 6 that year when Lord Frederick, strolling across Phoenix Park, had been hacked to death by a gang of assassins. Geoffrey, a small boy at the time, said the arrival of the news at Formosa was "the most vivid memory of my childhood". It put an end to his father's political career.

Sir George was physically as well as intellectually vigorous. In 1870 he went to South America as secretary to the Demerara Commission, inquiring into the terms of coolie labour in British Guyana. He took the opportunity to explore the Essequibo and Potaro Rivers and to visit the Kaieteur Falls, famous for their clear drop of 740 feet. He was the first man to reach the side of the basin at the foot of the fall, and when he got there he dived in and fought his way through the turbulent water to clamber some way up the rock wall on the far side. The swim was not repeated for sixty years. Geoffrey described his father's daily swims in the Thames: "Bearded, tall, lean, with a powerful chest and long arms, he would sweep up-stream with the full breast-stroke. He continued the morning dip, even through winters, till after the eightieth year."

Sir George's mountaineering career was shorter-lived. In 1859, when he was twenty-one, he had several weeks of mountain walking in the eastern Alps, with his brother Edward and his Trinity friend, George Otto Trevelyan. In 1865 he was in the party that made the first ascent of the Jungfrau from the Wengen Alp. In August of the following year he took two of his brothers to the summit of Mont Blanc. They descended by the Mûr de la Côte and at some point one of the younger brothers slipped, pulling the others off and the three of them fell between fifteen and twenty feet. Two of them were only slightly injured but the youngest, Bulkeley, broke his neck and died soon after. They had been climbing without guides so Sir George counted himself responsible. He never got over it. Geoffrey wrote: "His brother's tragic death was such a frightful shock to his sensitive nature that he never alluded to climbing or the Alps for some sixty years. If the Alps were mentioned in his presence, inadvertently, by a visitor, he would rise quietly and leave the room." He maintained this practice even in the years before the outbreak of the First World War, when his son Geoffrey was the leading British Alpinist.

In 1882 Sir George was appointed a charity commissioner, becoming Chief Charity Commissioner in 1903. Geoffrey says his father was greatly liked and respected by those subordinate to him, but not by others:

> His equals were uneasy with him as he did not conciliate, and his Civil Service superiors were all afraid of him, or jealous – and them he was only ready to oppose. He cared for the causes, movements, principles above all; he was less concessive to humanity, in public relationships. He expected others to live and work by his standards. He was apart, not a "man of the world", and with no place in literary society or the social world equal to his personal claims – a Liberal, and Broad Church evangelical, strict, exclusive, formidable, a combination that fitted nowhere.

When he retired he became a force in local affairs – chairman of the Maidenhead bench, member of the Berkshire Education committee, influential in gaining recognition for Reading University. He was chairman of the Cookham parish council as well, and in this capacity was remembered by the youthful Stanley Spencer – whose paintings were to make the village and its churchyard known across the world. A biography of him, written by his brother Gilbert and published by Gollancz in 1961, gives a snap picture of Sir George in action in defence of ancient rights-of-way:

> On one of his summer evening walks a villager found that the footpath in Terrys Lane leading to the Basewall pit had been obstructed, and reported the facts to the Parish Council. The ceremony of removing the obstruction was in the nature of a big occasion which brought the villagers, including Father, Stan and me, in great numbers to the spot. In all matters of this kind, Sir George Young, the Chairman of the Council, assumed an air of lofty detachment and wore a black frock coat. Chopper in hand, he broke down the obstruction and, followed by the Council, proceeded along the path to the top of the hill, where from our position we could see, silhouetted on the horizon, Mr Parsons, the owner of the land, and the village policeman solemnly taking each of their names and addresses as they reached the top.

Some of Geoffrey's qualities were clearly derived from his father: respect for learning; hatred of vulgarity; the enjoyment of challenging physical exercise, in swimming especially. Both were gifted with strong constitutions, neat and dextrous hands, and pleasant, well-modulated speaking voices. Both believed, and acted on the belief, that people like them who had been lucky enough to be born at a privileged level of society were enjoined by that circumstance to do all they could to help others who had not been so fortunate. They shared a scathing contempt for those, particularly members of the family, whose sole concern was the extension of their own wealth and status and power.

But there were major differences between them too. Sir George was naturally academic, meticulous in research, anxious – above all else – for accuracy. Geoffrey's mind, by contrast, ran to the romantic and imaginative. He was not interested in detailed, factual precision. What mattered to him was the vividness and intensity of feeling, psychological perceptions, the great generalisations that might be drawn from observations. His style was impressionistic, not scholastic.

They were also very different in social attitudes. Sir George was reclusive, more at home with books than with people. Geoffrey, on the other hand, was out-going and convivial, affectionate and tolerant, genuinely interested in human nature, fond of wide-ranging conversation and all sorts of people. Fundamentally he was serious but he could also be light-hearted and playful, as many of his letters show.

Religion was another area of divergence. Sir George was a conventional church-going Anglican of rigid piety and propriety and some prudery. From his university days onwards, however, Geoffrey was coolly agnostic, largely indifferent to religious belief and with some distaste for those he considered over-pious.

These disparities between father and son may, perhaps, derive from the character of Geoffrey's mother, Lady Young. She was Irish, the daughter of a leading Dublin physician. Born Alice Eacy Kennedy, her first marriage was to Sir Alexander Lawrence, son of the famous soldier/statesman, Sir Henry Lawrence, hero and martyr of the siege of Lucknow. They had one child, but the marriage ended tragically and early, with the death of Sir Alexander in an accident in India. Lady Alice returned home to Britain and in 1871, at the age of thirty-one, married Sir George Young of Formosa Place.

She was a woman, judging from Geoffrey's accounts, of splendid presence and forceful character. Her appearances in the story of his life are occasional – the children were looked after by nannies – but striking, with something of the quality of a whirlwind fairy godmother. She bore Sir George four children. She was a great hostess. And she devoted a generous share of her fierce energies to social and charitable causes. When she died in 1922 the *Times* obituary described her as "one of the last of the *grandes dames*".

The Irish connection was precious to Geoffrey. As a child he enjoyed long summer holidays at Belgard Castle, the Kennedy family home near Dublin, in the enlivening company of his Irish cousins. He made many friends there and always loved going to Ireland, relishing the relaxed and amused approach to life, the fanciful and reflective style of talk. His son Jocelin says that as soon as Geoffrey arrived in Ireland, his voice would gradually take on a touch of the brogue. When he told his children stories they were usually old Irish tales. In a letter to his daughter Marcia, dated May 1942, he said: "The Irish have a lovelier manner in conversation than any other nation; because they never even say Yes or No but give the assenting half-sentence or the negative in its full echo. 'Did you see him?' 'I did' or 'I did not' – and what a far lovelier sound!"

Another side of the family, descendants of Geoffrey's younger brother Hilton, cherish a story from the childhood holidays at Belgard. There was an Irish nanny whose job it was to get the children to bed each evening. She would see them all safely tucked into their bunks in a dormitory room, then march to the door and switch the light off saying: "There you are then, all in the dark, like the Protestant bishops!"

In later life Geoffrey liked to make much of the fact that he greatly preferred the laid-back Irish manner to that of the Scots, whom he sometimes found over-intense and earnest and mercenary. It was not a serious prejudice though. Many of his friends and regular climbing companions were Scottish.

Nevertheless, Geoffrey was grateful for the Irish injection into the family. In "Family Failings" he wrote:

> There is a vein of the most unlikeable arrogance and gracelessness in the Youngs. We see it first in Samuel. By marrying an Irishwoman of a character even stronger than his own, and great gifts, my father saved most of us from the inheritance. But I can see warnings in the younger generation. They should marry Irish again, or something of strong personal strain. Self-righteous, complacent, virtuous-seeming, middle-class, obstinate "Youngism" is a fearful inheritance, and to be fought off like the plague.

3

The First Years

In one of his unpublished essays into autobiography, Geoffrey wrote:

> Probably my earliest memory is of my father, in an Indian dressing-gown and a beard, carrying me up and down the high night nursery on the top floor of the house in Hyde Park Gate where I was born, while I was coughing with the attacks of bronchitis I had as a baby, and smelling the hot linseed poultice and camphor, while he sang endlessly:
>   "Oh hush thee, my baby, thy sire was a Knight,
>   Thy mother a lady all beauteous and bright,
>   The woods and the hills and the flowers that we see
>   Are all of them coming, my baby, to thee . . ."
> with its crooning, sleepy refrain. I can hardly have been "out of arms" at that time.

This took place at Sir George's town house in London, but the strongest and most vivid memories of his early years, to judge from the opening pages of Geoffrey's retrospective book *The Grace of Forgetting*, sprang from life at their home on the Thames.

He was to achieve his fame as a mountaineer, but his first great passion was for water sports, swimming and diving and all kinds of boating. After all, the house was like a ship and their father loved the water, so it was inevitable that the children should grow up to be "water babies".

All round the house there were varied kinds of water to play and explore and adventure in – the softly flowing river, a swift mill stream, the pool at Odney where village boys from Cookham splashed and swam on summer afternoons:

> We ourselves bathed off the lawn in the early morning, where the main river ran deep between the house and the Cliveden woods opposite. There was a chill shudder in the air as the river mist lifted. The dew webs were cold

underfoot on the short lawn grass, and the crossing of the gravel path at the run was a mile of flinty points. On the high river bank behind the artfully ruined gothic arch, the lawn was still in shadow, and towels were hesitantly shed. But the shock of the plunge from above the old brick steps, and the resurgence into sunlight far out upon the open river, made an indescribable awakening into a changed and welcoming world. So young Adam must have felt as his eyes opened upon the dawn of his first day.

These memories were precious to Geoffrey. More than sixty years after the events, in a letter to his daughter Marcia that was written towards the end of the Second World War, he said:

> It's odd to wake up these fresh sunshine mornings, to bird song, and feel the stir to run out across the great Formosa meadow, and to the lock of the Odney pool, with the dew wet as rain wetting one's legs from the long buttercups, and the smell of wet reeds, the Thames' characteristic smell, drying a little in the first sun gleams . . . And, lordy-lord! – the incomparable shock of the water as one dived . . . the most memorable thrill in living. We must bathe again . . .

Geoffrey's growing-up was haunted and delighted by the river. When it was running full and strong, its song could be heard from the house. It was all about them, as companion and adventure playground. It did much, I believe, to create and condition the man – his love for natural beauty, his delight in physical movement that is both elegant and efficient, the urge to explore and adventure, his ability to analyse the special impact of sensations. "Much of the enchantment of a river," he wrote, "comes from its duplicating all the beauty near it or above it in its reflections, and preventing lines and colours that delight us from coming to abrupt endings."

Colour was important to him: "All my memories have always stayed for me only as pictures in colour. This has proved an inconvenience in humdrum competitive living and earning. Because examiners in exact sciences expect precise answers and memorised facts and dates; and they take a gloomy view of a memory – or for that matter a mind – that produces knowledge as a series in instantaneous lantern-slides, however true to colour and detail."

It is a sharp assessment of the nature of his own mental processes, their strengths and shortcomings. It was a continuing disappointment to his teachers, and sometimes to his father, that – although he had a mind that was lively and acute and that grew to be well-stocked – he took so cavalier an attitude towards prosaic facts.

Sir George and Lady Young had four children. The eldest, who had to wait a long time to succeed to the baronetcy, was christened George but everybody always called him Georis because it was felt there were already enough Georges in the family. Then came the only daughter, named Eacy, a popular name on Lady Young's Irish side of the family. Geoffrey was the third child, born on October 25, 1876. He was always proud of the fact that this was also the day of Agincourt and Balaclava. The last child, born in 1879, was named Hilton, after his godfather, an old friend of Sir George's. Another old friend was Geoffrey's godfather, Thomas Hughes, the author of *Tom Brown's Schooldays.*

Between the two youngest, Geoffrey and Hilton, there developed a very close and caring relationship, despite great differences in character and cast of mind. It survived into middle age.

Geoffrey had a very happy childhood, especially in the years before he had to go to school. They were privileged – a fine house and wonderful surroundings, servants to do the hard work, lots of freedom – but there was discipline too. The children had to learn good manners and self-control early, and quite soon they were doing lessons. Reading was important and it was customary, whenever possible, for the whole family to gather together in the evening to hear father or mother reading aloud or telling stories. "Our mother was not a fairy-story teller," Geoffrey remembered. "Her stories at evening were all of her life as a child in Ireland, gay and tragic and exciting, but factual; or of life in India. She never invented, and her clear, man-like brain and profound sense of artistic truth were foreign to imaginings."

There were grand visitors. Robert Baden-Powell, the national hero just home from Mafeking: "sat on the Formosa lawn with young ladies perching on the arms of his garden chair in a rapture of hero worship. He was full of plans for scouting for boys – to occupy them better – and asked me to take him out on the river so that I might describe to him our man-hunt on the fells . . ."

Earlier visitors had included the Poet Laureate, Tennyson. Geoffrey was fond of a story he must have heard from his mother or father: "Over the arching bridge ran the avenue to the island; and from it the vista of the mill stream either way, running between and under foliage golden in the afternoon sun, was magical. Here Alfred Tennyson stood at gaze, with his friends Leslie Stephen and Dickie Doyle, brought by the enthusiasm of Anne Thackeray, Lady Ritchie: 'Oh, Alfred! – isn't this Eden?'" According to family lore, at this moment an old lady from Cookham crept into view in a bath–chair, and Tennyson growled in reply: "Eden. And here's Eve!"

Later on, in the opening years of the twentieth century, Geoffrey took Roger Casement, home from Africa where he had been investigating Belgian misrule in the Congo, for a swim in the Thames: ". . . the memory of him, with long, dark wavy beard and hair and immense dark blue eyes, towering-tall, sun-scorched and ascetic as a Donatello statue on the grass of Odney bank before he dived, was never afterwards obscured. His dramatic adventures, recounted in a musically soft Irish voice, almost persuaded me to go back with him to Africa." Casement was knighted in 1911 and hanged for treason in 1916.

But most of the visitors, in the years when Geoffrey was growing up, were members of the Liberal establishment, serious and influential people, happy to relax in the ambience of Formosa but intent on earnest conversation – with Sir George about issues of political or social or educational concern – to Lady Young about plans for some charitable cause. Between the parents and their children, there was great respect and affection, but both parents had demanding interests in the world of affairs and were often either away or preoccupied. For the children, certainly for Geoffrey, the great sources of love and comfort were their nurses.

The first nurse that Geoffrey remembered was a big, strong, very upright Scotswoman, Catherine Fraser, who had worked for Lady Young in her days in India. She looked after Geoffrey the first year of his life, and was succeeded by a young woman of Prussian origin, whose full name was Olga Wanda Bertha Holtzmann but who was always known to the family simply as Frau. Geoffrey adored her as a child and went on loving her ever after. Among his unpublished papers are four large, closely typed pages, chronicling his debt and his devotion to her:

> She came back to my mother when I was about one year old, as nursery governess. Eacy was three and Georis already an old four, so I became "her boy". She laid her umbrella on the nursery Broadwood piano, and took possession. For over sixty years she remained the most devoted of all my friends. Not one birthday or Christmas passed, in all the years, without her long letter, with its even characters, and some small present, chosen with loving care. And when my children came, it was the same for them . . .

Frau had also worked for Lady Young before, looking after the only child of her first marriage. She came from an old East Prussian family but had none of the rigid austerity that is usually associated with that background. By Geoffrey's account, her great qualities were loving warmth and her sense of humour. He was, he says, a nervous child and a prey to night terrors, especially when they were staying in the London house:

> She had a bedroom always on the same floor and opening out of mine. I would listen in queer terror to the long, desolate shouting in the streets without, or wake fearful in the dark. Then would begin on a low note the cry "Frau-y! Frau-y!" and as soon as there might be a stir afar "Frau-y. May I come into your bed?" There was always "yes", however tired she might be. Then the fearsome rush through the dark and – oh, ecstatic relief and delight! – the warm cowering down in the bed beside her. And dreamless sleep.

His love for Frau was such as to present him with a searing dilemma: "I remember the terrible problem coming up irrepressibly into my mind, with a discomfortable feeling of disloyalty and doubt. If we fell into the river, which should I have to save first, Mother or Frau? – and knowing it ought to be Mother, and yet hardly letting myself realise it was Frau first."

Frau, after all, was always there and to be relied on: "We saw more of her than of Mother, who was in those days living a very full and brilliant social life." Frau was in charge of the nursery for the younger ones and gave lessons to the older, though Sir George would not let her try to teach them French, lest they grew up with a German accent. She did not enjoy teaching and, from Geoffrey's point of view, the things he learned from her were much more to do with her character, her example, than with any lessons.

It was from her, more than from his parents, that he learned to be demonstratively affectionate and to take an understanding interest in children. He grew up with much of her sense of humour, what he described as "Frau's glorious sense of fun, which invariably brought tears to her eyes that had to be wiped away". And from her example, he learned to be an understanding and tolerant European. Every two years, Frau went home to see her family and friends, returning full of toys and rich sweets and tales of German life and manners:

> . . . and the absurd way the Germans wanted to be offered things five times before they would accept; and Frau in her firm, head-shaking way would say to herself "Well, take it or leave it", and not offer it again – and

her sister would afterwards protest at her bad manners! – and Frau would explain how much more sensible was the direct English way. Frau had a marvellous way of drawing up and bridling back, not at others but at an idea, and lifting her circular, marked eyebrows over her long curved beak of a nose – that commented on the ludicrousness of things effectively.

It was her influence, more than any other single factor, that inspired his love for Germany, a love that survived the two world wars. He was ashamed at the way she was treated by some Englishmen when the First World War began:

She had never bothered to naturalise – no one did in those halcyon days! – so she was threatened with internment. Hilton stopped this, and she lived quietly, withdrawing from all society, with great dignity. The first, and, I think, the only person to "cut" her, after the war began, was the local vicar, whose church she attended!!!!!! She was entirely English, and Liberal, at heart by now. And had no respect for "the silly young emperor".

There was one family tragedy in Geoffrey's early years – the death at the age of fifteen of his sister Eacy. Geoffrey wrote: "She was a brilliant, clever, sensitive child, taking easily to scholarship and learning, and lively and long-limbed in the open." The loss was hardest, he thought, on Sir George. Their father had never got over the death of his brother Bulkeley in the Alps, for which he felt responsible, and now he was shattered by the death of his much-loved only daughter. Recalling it all, long after the event, Geoffrey said: "Eacy was the nearest of us to father, in mind and affection. After his death, I found dark locks of her beautiful hair in his cabinet."

Geoffrey's first years, though, were dominated by the all-pervading presence of the river. It gave early stimulus to three of his prime characteristics – love of hard physical effort, the pleasure he found in mastering skills, and his need for adventure. Encouraged by his father and even more by Georis, the elder brother who was even then showing signs of a strong and maverick temperament, Geoffrey soon became an expert at various kinds of watermanship – swimming and diving, canoeing and punting and riding white water. In *The Grace of Forgetting* he gives a vivid description of the thrills of shooting Odney weir in a Canadian canoe when the river is in flood:

. . . At the foot of the fall the face of the pool was churned up into a tossing hollow, with a return wave cresting viciously above it. The canoe, flung out upon the fall, came down upon hollow and wave with all its length at once, its nose high in the air, and with a back-wrenching crash. This was the crucial test of skill. The paddler, already sitting up and with paddle at the ready, had to make the immediate and mighty stroke that could alone keep the canoe straight and drive it up and over the smother of the returning wave.

There were rowing boats, too, and punts and it was not long before Georis had mastered the art of poling a canoe along, then passed it on to Geoffrey whose natural balance and co-ordination made him a quick learner. They invented canoeing games, including one where two canoes charged at each other, with two boys in each of them – one paddling hard, the other standing at the front with a punt-pole as a lance, a sort of water-borne jousting tournament. They even managed double-punting, two of them poling a canoe along in unison and at speed. When the youngest brother Hilton grew big enough, they took him on board as well and went triple-punting.

Hard winters, and there were several in the last decade of the nineteenth century, called for fresh adventures. They skated along the river and across frozen water meadows, tobogganed down snow-covered hills, and – another of Georis's inspirations – built themselves an ice-yacht and sailed across the marshes. Geoffrey loved the sensation of speed, and thought about it:

> It was exciting to me then first to discover, and I confirmed it in later years from glissading and other sports, that the sense of pace that all men seem to crave for, and that has upset the natural order of life on the globe, owes everything to the direct feel of the wind on the cheek, to the feel of the vibration just under the foot, to the sight of objects passing close before the eye, and to the sound in the ear of the nearby passing of the wind. I began to wonder why men try to go always faster upon engines, when the fun and pleasure of pace clearly depend only upon the nearness of our own sense – of touch, of sight, of hearing – to the object we are passing. I was almost anticipating the monotony or rather poverty of all sensation in an aeroplane.

It was on the river that Geoffrey first showed he had an aptitude for climbing. In the middle of Odney pool there was a stout, ten-foot-high mooring post, that leaned slightly down-stream. It made for a dramatic diving board, but hard to attain:

> The swarm up was strenuous. The post was old and water-worn below, and the flood had eaten away its seamed and weed-grown sides, leaving

downward spikes and jags to excoriate the up-cling of the thighs. At half height a rusted bolt-head gave a welcome finger pull. The top was four-sided and convex, curving up like a cardinal's cap, with a blunt apex. It had just room for my two feet clinging sideways on to the flanges. To straighten up on this stand after the last pull-up on clinging hands and feet was acrobatic, with the post leaning out giddily over the greenish-white bubbling of the eddies, fearsomely far below. The balance-up was seldom secure enough to give me time to get arms above head for a conventional header. As soon as I came erect enough to be in line with the leaning angle of the post, I dived off, with my hands clasped behind me.

4

School Life

LIFE AT FORMOSA WAS SO good and loving, secure but stimulating too, that it came as a great shock to Geoffrey when he had to go to boarding school. He was sent to Wymondley, a private prep school near Stevenage in Hertfordshire. In his unpublished papers, he describes this as "a horrible wrench to a very sensitive child", and says it was Frau who was deputed to take him to the railway station: "It was a wise choice, for I knew that she had not the ultimate decision and could not reverse the fate at the last. But as I went hopelessly up, in that far corner of the field under the Spanish chestnuts, I cannot forget her quiet strength and the tears slowly falling from her own eyes."

Once established, he got on reasonably well at the school. He was quick enough in the class-room and naturally good at games, but was never happy there: "Games were far too stressed at Wymondley, indeed at all schools at that date. We were very badly taught and grounded, and I missed this all my life." The headmaster, the Reverend F. J. Hall, had been a good cricketer and rugby player and had a lovely speaking voice (something that always impressed Geoffrey) but he was short-tempered and had, in Geoffrey's estimation, little understanding of small boys. The assistant master was another athlete, kindly but not very bright, whose interest in boys was not intellectual: "One of the memorable scenes was his sitting at the end of our weekly hot bath, correcting our small note-books and dictation and then, with one vast leg stuck up on our bath edge, feeling if our back was dry before we might stop rubbing, and our wriggle to escape the genial spank that followed."

Geoffrey was an unusually good-looking boy. The boys nick-named him "the Saint": "I resented the piety implied in the title; but in fact I shrank horribly from any vulgarity of word or touch. I hated even getting implicated in a wrestle. As a child, to be held down by the arms was literally torture, mad-driving. None of which in the least affected a luxuriant erotic imagination, entirely indefinite in its actualities." He was experiencing the first stirrings of his sexuality but it was given no physical expression. "Other people," he recalled, "had not the faintest effect on me in those years, sexually. Imagination was far away from reality in my case."

He made few friends at Wymondley, though an Irish cousin, Cyril Dickinson, soon turned up, and then his younger brother Hilton. He suffered from the bullying of older boys until his father complained, but found a Frau-like protective figure in the haven of the kitchen, with the "large, stout, Devonian cook, Joanna, a glorious soul . . . her kitchen was our warm and happy escape from every form of persecution or fear. And how many an evening in my first year did I sit safe on her large lap by the kitchen stove, while the other boys ramped in and out or about."

From time to time, his mother, Lady Young, would erupt into the school and do what she could to make his life more tolerable. She took Joanna and the house matron up to London for a treat, to show her appreciation for their kindnesses to Geoffrey. She once, "in her magnificent way", organised a London outing for the whole school, with special carriages up to town and a visit to the Military Exhibition. On another occasion, suspecting that Geoffrey's recurring bronchial troubles derived from his place near the door of the cold dormitory, "Mother swept in and my small iron bed grew into a four-poster, with great iron uprights and brass rods and four curtains of russet leaf-patterned linen. That it should have been done in a school of that period, and no opposition from school or boys, seems to me now amazing. But that was her way! and the world just accepted it."

He remembered one personal triumph from the prep school days. The first cricket eleven were playing against a bigger school at Stevenage:

Goodwin, a wild-haired rascal, was saving the game by hitting 60 or more in the last innings, and I went in as very last wicket, when there were over 12 runs still to make. Was there ever such an ordeal? For though I was a field, and could bowl a trifle, I could never bat. Gloriously I stuck and stone-walled, and the ball which had begun by looking a fierce, whirring, deadly canon-ball, grew larger and softer and easy to see. And I made 2! And I stayed in while Goodwin slogged – and we nobly won the match! Mr Hall gave me my cricket eleven colours immediately after – a dark blue and black striped silk scarf. I had it most of my life.

But he was never really reconciled to the place. Holidays were what mattered in those days and he was always in tears when the moment came to set off back to school:

School was never my real life and its folk were unreal fundamentally. I remember its grim, school smell, of yellow soaped floorboards and inky benches; and a few books in the small reading bookcase – the abiding, fascinating terror of *The Wandering Jew* that dug deep into imagination and memory; the attraction of *The Scottish Knights*, which I now find unreadable: the shaking sobs over the last fight in *Hereward the Wake*. Also Doré's illustrations to some story of the accident on the Matterhorn. All the rest belonged to home.

It was on summer holidays from prep school that Geoffrey was introduced to the mountains by his father. Sir George had renounced mountaineering but had not lost his taste for mountain walking. In August 1888 he took Geoffrey to Wales where, among other things, they climbed Cader Idris and Cynicht. Next year they walked extensively in South Wales. In 1890 they visited the Harz mountains in Germany and climbed the Brocken. The year after that Sir George took Geoffrey and Hilton to explore the hills of Killarney. Writing about it all some forty years on, Geoffrey could remember some of the meals they had eaten, encounters with local eccentrics, the Welsh rain, and some of his father's words of advice: "Never spring or stride uphill. Stick to it quietly"; "Never go on down where you have had to drop two or three times, close together, from your hands to your feet." In 1894 Sir George took Geoffrey – now at Marlborough – to Snowdonia where they ascended Snowdon, the Glydrs and Tryfan. They stayed at the Pen-y-Gwryd Hotel, the climbers' rendezvous in the heart of the mountains, where Geoffrey's godfather Thomas Hughes and a more famous novelist Charles Kingsley had lodged with Sir George more than thirty years before. Geoffrey later recalled:

On the gallant top of Tryfan we saw two men emerge from the cliffs, roped together, the first sight of the rope! I believe this was in truth the occasion of the first ascent of the North Gully of Tryfan, and the beginning of modern rock climbing in Wales. On to Snowdon we circled over the falling wave-crest of Lliwedd: most glorious of ridge walks, along which I have so often since raced the open sunset, after long enclosed hours of chilly shadows upon a Lliwedd rock climb.

Life at home at Formosa continued to be companionable, dinner-table conversation cultivated as a civilised art. "It was given an unchallengeable position in our family life, as being the most sociable of the arts, an art as essential for us to practise as good manners and morality." This training was important for Geoffrey. Throughout his life he valued good talk, conversation that was sometimes playful, often serious, always controlled and considerate to others.

There was time for reading, too. The great favourite of his early years was a book that was published when Geoffrey was six years old: "*Bevis*, in its first three-volumed green-and-gold edition, was the most companionable of all my early friends . . . Bevis and Mark, the two boys in the story, I lived with, and in their world. They were granted by their creator, Richard Jefferies, an undefined age that kept them always of my own age as I grew older, in a correspondence of likings, of growing ability to do things, and even of increasing freedom to adventure." When a new edition of *Bevis* was published in the early 1940s, Geoffrey complained that the map in the book did not correspond to the text, and spent many hours carefully re-drawing the map from internal evidence.

It was during the prep school years, but chiefly at home, that Geoffrey started to show an interest in, and some aptitude for the writing of verse. When he was about ten years old the boys were given a Christmas present of a small printing press, which was installed at their London home, now 115a, Sloane Street, and they used it to produce copies of their own works. Sir George, translator and prosodist, was no doubt proud of his son's precocious talent, and gave help that was not always welcome. When he was eleven or twelve Geoffrey wrote a poem in tribute to his mother, which came off the nursery press entitled "Mother o' Mine". In a later note Geoffrey commented: "I called it *To Mother*. Father supplied the present title which I deplored."

The question of which public school he should be sent to caused what Geoffrey described as an "almost mortal quarrel" between his parents. Eton was the family tradition, but out of the question at this moment because the elder brother Georis had just disgraced himself there in some way and been expelled. Sir George argued strongly that Geoffrey should be sent to Sherborne, where his brother Edward was headmaster. But Uncle Edward was in the middle of a tremendous row, with more than half his staff united against a decision of his, and soon after he had to resign. Sir George thought that sending Geoffrey there would be a pledge of support from the family. Lady Young insisted that the boy should not be used in this way. She prevailed. It was decided that Geoffrey should go to Marlborough College in Wiltshire.

He started there in September 1890, at the age of fourteen. His looks were immediately noticed and earned him a new nickname, "the cherub".

He went with reluctance and apprehension. In an unpublished essay written long after, he described his first hours there:

> That first awful night in dormitory, when I was brought in in pitch dark from the Master's Lodge where I left father, and crept into bed among unknown terrors and sleepers. And awoke with that indescribable shock to find myself at school . . . Beside me I found was another new boy, with kind face and big blue eyes. We whispered together and got some comfort in the cold dawn of autumn, in the cold panelled room, painted a chilly blue. And then, greatly daring, in the aching lonesomeness of my feelings, I whispered – "Shall we be friends?" And he whispered – "Yes". And I held out my left hand across the cold space, and he gripped it, and for two seconds we held fast.

It was a providential meeting. The other new boy was Christopher Andrews Wordsworth, unlike Geoffrey in many ways and very much more scholarly, but they became close friends for the rest of their lives. In 1910 when Wordsworth married one of Geoffrey's Irish cousins, Geoffrey was his best man.

None of the other Marlborough friends was of anything like the same importance. Vincent Baddeley, later to be private secretary to a succession of First Lords of the Admiralty, proved a good friend and useful contact later on in life. There was a boy called Borrodaile who, Geoffrey says, "became sentimentally devoted, being older but not far above me in school order. It was platonic but conspicuous. I was embarrassed once to be pointed out by his elder brother's blackguard friends as his young brother's 'tart' – the word alone offended me horribly." The atmosphere of the school, according to Geoffrey's account, was heavy with homosexual yearnings, sometimes repressed, sometimes not. Geoffrey, it seems, was one of the innocents, a romantic, confining his activities to long, companionable walks and earnest conversations. In his last terms, when his athletic achievements had made him a figure of some grandeur in the school, he fell heavily for a younger boy:

E. N. Bell: beloved Teddy Bell . . . I had never bothered about boys, and used all the school gossip and scandal without its meaning anything but jest. Suddenly I found the whole room or classroom glowing with sunshine if Teddy was in it, and lifeless without him. I was startled, for I shrank from any physical word or crudity. No use! I plunged deep into all the gold of pure, unselfish romance. It was *sheer* romance. I wanted to be near him, to talk, hear, even hold him. But with no other or more definite thought.

Geoffrey goes on to say that a year or so after he had left school, somewhat changed by his terms at Cambridge, he returned to Marlborough and took Bell for a drive on the Downs in a pony cart, and did make a physical advance. It was politely repulsed.

One other boy, older than Geoffrey, had a significant influence. This was A. M. Latter, who was generally unpopular because he was highly intelligent and cynical and outspokenly contemptuous of most of the school's shibboleths:

When Latter was specialising in history and working for the Balliol Brackenbury (which he got later), he was given a study to himself; and he exercised a privilege in putting me on a study list and giving me a free run of his study. A wonderful lightening, in that crowded noisy life. And there we talked, interminably. I recall fierce arguments about the Gadarene swine and Huxley, for he was an atheist and I a traditional Christian. I even remember saying with conviction that I could not conceive of being able to go on living if I did not believe in a future life and a God. He certainly made me think. In a way he was the only real education I got at Marlborough.

Life would undoubtedly have been more enjoyable had he been joined by his brother Hilton. But Hilton went to Eton. Geoffrey was more than a little put out that the family tradition, rejected in his own case, had been revived for Hilton, suspecting that the more rigorous, academic training of Eton would have injected some much-needed discipline into his mental activities. He also missed the range of contacts which Eton would have afforded him.

Two of Sir George's letters to his son have survived. When Geoffrey was made a prefect in 1894, his father wrote to him:

. . . you are now one of those who have influence to exercise, and responsibility for its right use . . . I think Marlborough society, while sound at core, perhaps is wanting in civilisation, to some extent. Anyhow, any when, there is always scope for improvement of the kind that comes from sympathy. Small boys have a great admiration for big ones. When they also are fond of them, the attachment becomes very close, and in after life it may produce much happiness.

And in June that year, when Geoffrey was awarded a poetry prize, Sir George wrote to the headmaster: "I hope this little ornamental success Geoffrey has obtained, which I think he thoroughly deserved, will prevent his being discouraged, and perhaps draw the attention of his master in school to the faculties of a mind which is not by any means commonplace, though of imperfect effectiveness as yet . . ."

The prize was awarded for a lengthy ode, grandly entitled: *The Death of Tennyson: a Monody*. It is a smooth and craftsmanlike piece of work very much in the late Poet Laureate's style, the first line running: "The Harp is still, the magic song is done".

Geoffrey's most acclaimed achievements at Marlborough, however, were athletic. He had good balance and quick reactions. He was an able fencer and good enough at hockey to play centre for his House, then for the school eleven. He also played, as scrum half, in the House and school rugger fifteens. *The Marlburian* for 1894, under the heading "Characters of the XV", sums up Geoffrey's rugger abilities in these words: "A somewhat small but plucky half. Marks his opponent well, but does not pass enough. Has always combined very well with his captain."

The game that stayed in his memory was an inter-House final. Their opponents had the stronger three-quarters so it was largely a question of defensive containment and hoping for a lucky break. The first encounter was scoreless. The replay looked to be going the same way when the other side at last succeeded in moving the ball out to their right wing, the fastest sprinter in the school. This was a boy called Goddard, later to become famous as a Lord Chief Justice of unfailing severity. Geoffrey remembered the moment:

> I was always fast to get under way, and for 50 yards was hard to catch or beat. Goddard took longer to work up to his maximum. In desperate resolution, I dashed across in pursuit. Inch by inch, I could feel I gained; but I knew it must be in the next few yards and he was visibly accelerating. He was not a swerver and not really a football player who knew how to hand-off; he was played for his pace alone. So, as we neared our corner flag, with a last leaping stride I caught his shoulder from behind and brought him down. It was the greatest run of my life!

So the second match was another scoreless draw. The game had been played so ferociously that the school doctor forbade a further replay and the honour had to be shared that year.

By his final year Geoffrey was something of a "swell" in the school. With two like-minded friends he used "to stroll down the town and breakfast at Arthur's together smartly, and we decorated our studies artistically, and were recognised to be something above the Marlborough philistine crowd". But writing about it many years later, he found little to praise:

> Curious, looking back, that though I was a high-spirited, athletic boy, with all types of success at the school, I recall no minutes of real pleasure there except on a few summer evenings, when we came down from the fields in whites at sunset, after tea, and suddenly the whole school would start a vast white circle of leap-frog round the Great Court, against the old, red-brick buildings, soaked with late golden sun. Though a small boy, I could leap-frog over the tallest boys, and exulted in the glorious feeling as I soared into the air, and in the muttered admiration this caused here and there from my elders and betters. At football, I could sometimes get something of the feeling in a good run, in a hard-fought match, with a shouting crowd round. But never the same delight in exalted movement, and supreme self-concentration of every fibre – I had to wait for climbing to renew the sensation, and improve upon it.

Most of his time at Marlborough Geoffrey thought of school as a prison. Occasionally he caught tantalising glimpses of a freer life beyond. He described one of these moments in the opening chapter of *On High Hills*:

> In Sixth Form Library, for me, the school curtains suddenly dragged apart. I came one day upon Whymper's *Scrambles*. With the first reading (of many – for I knew it in the end almost by heart) the horizon shifted. Peaks and skies and great spaces of adventure rolled upward and outward, smashing the walls of a small, eager, self-centred world. I wonder how many boys have owed the same debt to that great boy's book. Snows and glaciers began to "haunt me like a passion"; the delight in the thought of them always tempered by a little ache of unsatisfied longing . . . In our school hymn-books we, of the choir at least, were accustomed to scribble the date over the hymn of the day and add the record of any great event, such as our appearance in a school match of the winning of a school prize. It is curious now to read among these scrawls the first assertions of a new personality, less arrogant or, at all events, less priggish: "Shall I ever go to the Alps?" and "If I could only be a mountaineer."

5

Trinity, Cambridge: 1895–8

"TRINITY BEGAN A NEW WORLD, for at Marlborough I had never accepted the standards of value by which we were judged, physical or scholarship – they were not our home standards – and felt myself to belong to another order." It was with this sentence that Geoffrey opened an eighteen-page essay of reminiscences, written in the 1940s and called "Cambridge Friends".

If school had been a prison, Cambridge was freedom and Geoffrey made the most of it. It was there that he discovered and nurtured his gift for friendship. At school, games had been all-important, but at Cambridge – free at last to follow his own inclinations – he devoted the greater part of his great energies to clubs and societies, all-night conversations, and the cultivation of dozens of delightful friendships and acquaintances. It was during the three years at Trinity that he became a climber – on the crags of Cumberland, then on the college roofs and spires, then in the Alps.

Trinity was part of the Young family tradition. Sir George had been there forty years before, studying classics and becoming a Fellow. In early October 1895 he returned to see his son settled in: "At the Great Gate, as we entered, I for the first time, Father stopped and looked round. 'Geoffrey!' – he had a charming and impressive trick of only calling me by my name when he wished to be affectionately emphatic – 'Here I spent the happiest years of my life. It has been more home than any other house. I hope it may be the same to you!'"

Geoffrey started quite quietly, working hard, feeling lonely, occasionally seeing contemporaries from Marlborough. Christopher Wordsworth was at Clare, moving into the rowing world. Geoffrey had lodgings in Jesus Lane and his mother was quickly on the scene to make sure he settled in comfortably. He wrote to Sir George:

> Mother left me today in absolute luxury – quite like a fairy godmother – and I hardly know myself!! or the rooms! I hope she wasn't tired by it all . . . Mr Archer-Hind is directing my studies and looks over composition etc. – a rather dull, very ugly little man. I have one lecture every morning at 10 – Monday, Wednesday, Friday – on Thucydides with a Mr Wyatt, a very uninteresting lecturer. Tuesday, Thursday, Saturday on Lucretius with a delightful man, Mr Duff.

He was soon struggling, resentful of the fact that his grounding in Latin and Greek at school had been inadequate. In letters home he said he was working six hours each day but finding it very hard to memorise Latin verse: "A great difficulty I find is that I forget so soon after reading . . . I feel a little hopeless now and again, progress is so imperceptible." He was in the wrong discipline and he knew it: "I was no classical scholar. It was a mistake to have done Classics at all . . . Of course, I should have broken off into the new school of History or even the old type of English, but my father did not know of them as proper university studies – soft options he might have called them! – and I was very pliant as a boy and entirely guided by those who knew better." So he plugged on and worked enough to take a Second in the examinations at the end of the first year.

It was during his first long vacation, in the summer of 1896, that Geoffrey began real climbing, with a hemp rope and nailed boots. His friend from Marlborough, Vincent Baddeley, now studying at Oxford, organised a reading party at Watendlath near Borrowdale in Cumberland and invited Geoffrey to join them. More than sixty years later, after Geoffrey's death, Baddeley recalled: "None of us knew anything about climbing but Geoffrey arrived with Haskett Smith's recently published book on Lake District climbing and fired all with his enthusiasm. He had previously climbed in Wales but not in the Lake District. Thus inspired, we complete novices climbed the Broad Stand of Scafell, the Napes Needle and the Pillar Rock."

Back to Cambridge for his second year there, Geoffrey moved into rooms in Trinity, stopped worrying over-much about his studies, and concentrated instead on creating a full and varied social life for himself. Cambridge was a marvellous place, at that time, for a young man like Geoffrey. The university had a high reputation for intellectual vigour and openness. Trinity was by far the biggest and liveliest of the colleges, the country's leading training-ground for mathematicians and natural scientists. The generation just before Geoffrey had included the philosophers, G. E. Moore and Bertrand Russell. In 1893, it has been calculated, 195 members of Parliament were Cambridge men, and 68 of those were Trinity men. One-third of the members of Gladstone's last Cabinet, formed in August 1892, were Trinity men.

It was a very masculine society too. Cambridge had two colleges for women students Girton and Newnham, but women were going to have to wait more than half a century more before they were accepted as full members of the university. It was only recently that Fellows had been permitted to marry. Most were still bachelors, many of them highly misogynist and prepared to make it brutally apparent when women turned up to their lectures. Homosexuality was widespread and generally accepted, despite the fact that only a few months before Geoffrey arrived at Trinity, Oscar Wilde had been sent to prison for two years' hard labour for "committing acts of gross indecency with other male persons".

Nowhere in any of his writings does Geoffrey make mention of any homosexual affair while he was at Trinity. He does refer to one friend as "one of the few who gave my haughty sort of temperament a shock by a suggestion of physical emotion in his affection". He was still physically tentative. But he was also good-looking and fit, attractive in personality as well as in appearance. One of his friends, Frederick Pethwick Lawrence, a maths student who went on to become a Labour Minister, said to Geoffrey's wife many years later that Geoffrey, arriving in college as a freshman, had been "the most beautiful young man I have ever seen".

Judging from remarks in his unpublished papers, it seems that Geoffrey was physically shy when he went up to Cambridge. Almost certainly, he soon began to get over that. During his first year, as we have already seen, he returned to Marlborough to see Teddy Bell and make a pass at him. It seems more than likely that it was during his years at Cambridge that he became a practising homosexual – and more than likely, too, that he would be discreet and discriminating about it.

From the beginning of his second year, however, there was nothing hidden about his sociability:

I did not belong to the "talking lot" as I called them, the scholars and politicians and philosophers, but being intensely social I whirled round making my own friends in the most unlikely quarters and even in other colleges, a rare thing then . . . My rooms became a centre, and I never "sported the oak" day or night. In fact, I had a nervous dislike of not being in company, as soon as I moved into college, my second year.

The closely typed pages of "Cambridge Friends" name about fifty of his acquaintances at this period. Many became close and enduring friends. Some did not. He was not impressed, for example, by James Jeans, a maths student who was later to become famous as a popular astronomer: ". . . an insignificant personality, without real distinction . . . I felt he was one of the many who 'didn't count'." "Distinction" is a word Geoffrey used often. He admired good looks and style and wit and intellectual sharpness. But he was also looking for the unusual, the surprising, the entertaining, men of strong and distinctive personality, lively minded and widely cultured but not too serious, capable of fun and friendship, with an urge to adventure. He had no time for students who were totally immersed in their studies and conventional in attitude. He actively disliked those he found "pompous" or "priggish".

Although he admired high intellectual accomplishment, he was wary of it as well. He knew his own limitations and was aware that he could not hope to win admission to the company of "the Apostles". In his first year he had been elected to Trinity's leading debating club, the Decemviri, but he felt out of place with them: "I was terribly shy there, and spoke and went rarely. I had a strong inferiority sense, and no idea others could want to meet or hear me."

So he formed his own club which he called the Query Society. It was for debating and discussion but on a more light-hearted level than the other groups: "We did not take politics or clubs so seriously, and I rather enjoyed building up my own societies and cutting the established ones out, by sheer personal drive." The membership gradually grew to fourteen or fifteen, Trinity men predominating, though Geoffrey introduced friends from other colleges too. In debate they were not allowed to read their speeches. Geoffrey spoke one evening on "Tennyson and Browning from the philosophical point of view"; another member discoursed on "Positivism". The subject for debate on February 13, 1898 was "Is climbing folly?" Geoffrey's younger brother Hilton, who had arrived at Trinity in October the previous year, argued that it was, while Geoffrey defended his sport and carried the evening by six votes to five.

The next week the subject for consideration was "The position of man in the universe", and everyone was required to speak in the character of some famous person, real or fictional. Geoffrey chose the role of the Devil. His brother Hilton spoke for Paracelsus. Christopher Wordsworth was Lewis Carroll. A. W. ("Sandy") Mackay, who was reading classics and moral science and who went on to eminence at the Scottish bar, was Schopenhauer. The triumph of the evening, apparently, was the impersonation of Marie Corelli by C. K. Clague, a maths scholar with a fine whimsical wit.

Other members of the Query included John Talbot, a future headmaster of Haileybury and G. H. Hardy who later became Professor of Mathematics at Cambridge and the leader of the Trinity group that, in 1916, stood against the expulsion of Bertrand Russell from his Fellowship for his pacifist stand.

Sandy Mackay became a regular climbing companion of Geoffrey's, first on the roof-tops of Trinity, then on the crags of Cumberland and Snowdonia, then in the Alps where they did some guideless first ascents in the summer of 1898. Geoffrey wrote of him: "He was the best guideless companion I ever had; even better than H. O. Jones, I think. For his physique was magnificent and his agility unusual."

Their partnership was launched in darkness, on the roofs of their college, in a sport that Geoffrey organised.

One of their friends, John Talbot, had attic rooms in New Court, one of whose windows gave ready access to the leads. Talbot was no climber but he was a generous man and his rooms became a regular base camp for the more adventurous.

It had to be done at night because such activity was frowned upon by the authorities as possibly dangerous to the students and destructive to the aging fabric of their buildings. It also had to be done quietly for the same reason, particularly when the route ran close to a don's rooms. In his account of Route B, the complete circuit of Cloister Court, Geoffrey adds a note: "It is possible to gain this point by a most interesting little cross-route from the gyp-room window of a certain famous first-floor Historian." This was the great Lord Acton.

The quotation is from Geoffrey's first published work *The Roof-Climber's Guide to Trinity*, which came out as a May-Week joke in 1900. Geoffrey wrote the route descriptions entirely from memory when he was at Jena University. He then sent the script to Sandy Mackay for checking, and Mackay drew the illustrations. The little book was popular and sold out quickly and is now a rare item in the antiquarian book-shops.

It was written in parody of the pompous, mandarin, academic style of the early Alpine climbing guides – larded with learned quotations from Horace, Goethe, Shelley, Browning and others, and heavy with portentous words and detailed attention to the most trivial features. Here he is, in the Introduction, discussing the attitude of the college authorities to the sport:

Doubtless, the fact that a certain bashful conservatism has confined the excursions hitherto to hours of the night has done much to induce this orophismic philistinism, but Alpine ascents suffer under a similar disadvantage, and we confess that, however illogically, we should view with regret an alteration in the College regulations tending to soften the conditions. The darkness, besides comfortably concealing the accumulating soot on hands and person, surrounds the venture with an air of vague mystery, and lends a pleasing uncertainty to the handholds, a depth of impressive gloom to the courts and gutters, and a shadowy outline, fraught with terror, to the colossal-seeming towers, that could hardly be spared; while the recurring step of the night porter, heard when the climber hangs in literal suspense in some awkward lamp-glare, rouses thrills of the chase unknown to legalised stegophilism.

The publication of the booklet was probably one of the factors that prompted the college authorities to act. In the autumn of 1901 the Vice-Master, Aldis Wright, decided that it should be made clear whether or not roof-climbing was permitted. The College Council instructed two junior Fellows, G. M. Trevelyan and Gilbert Walker (who went on to be India's Hydrographer Royal), to investigate the matter and report back. They were given the power to co-opt Geoffrey to help them.

So the three of them solemnly repeated the classic routes in broad day-light, with the college porters in attendance, carrying fire-ropes in case they should be needed. Geoffrey enjoyed it greatly. They made their report and the sport was declared illegal. The idea spread quickly to Oxford where the early enthusiasts included Leo Amery and Julian Huxley. There was a very active period in Cambridge in the 1930s, delightfully chronicled in 1937 in a book called *The Night Climbers of Cambridge*, by a whimsically pseudonymous Whipplesnaith.

Geoffrey followed up his little *Guide* with another spoof volume that has become a collector's item, *Wall and Roof Climbing*, which came out in 1905. It is more substantial than its predecessor, a mock-learned dissertation on the history of the sport, illustrated by an astonishingly wide range of joke quotations from Greek and Latin, English, French and Italian literature. It makes a case for the sport: "Roof-climbing is no child's play, and the local mill chimney is not a fit practice ground for the novice. It is an art distinct in itself: that which gives it its chief charm, the variety of roof forms and the infinite number of materials employed, wood, brick, stone, concrete, iron, slate, chalk and lead, also constitutes the chief danger."

It is arguable whether or not Geoffrey actually invented roof-climbing. Like most such questions, it is a matter of definition. Cambridge and Oxford had been hosts to countless generations of young men, enjoying their first taste of freedom, vigorous and competitive and often wild. Thousands of them must have scaled walls and clambered up public monuments, in the heat of liquor or high spirits. Hundreds of thousands habitually climbed over college walls simply to get to their beds after the gates had been shut at 10 p.m. Ninety years before Geoffrey arrived at Trinity, Byron had been on the library roof and left decorations on the statues to prove it, but he gained access by way of a winding staircase inside the building. Geoffrey and his friends were the first to make a systematic exploration of the possible Trinity routes, and he was certainly the first to publish a guidebook to them.

The sport gave them a lot of excitement and fun. They wore their oldest clothes and rubber-soled tennis shoes. They took an "Alpine" hemp rope and made much use of what climbers call "combined operations", standing on each other's backs or shoulders to gain height and reach hand-holds. Several of them grew so fond of climbing that they went with Geoffrey to Cumberland and the Alps in the holidays.

His regular roof-top companions, between 1895 and 1899, were Sandy Mackay, Christopher Wordsworth, F. W. Dobbs and C. K. Clague, one of those whom Geoffrey introduced to climbing. "He first climbed Hall with me," Geoffrey wrote, "and left his handkerchief on the pinnacle, tearing off the name corner. But Parry, our tutor, identified it cleverly, and was so pleased that he forgot to gate Clague." Another of the climbers, A. Wedgwood, an engineer and adventurer, took four green-paper parasols to the library roof and left one in the hands of each of the statues.

One of Geoffrey's roof-climbing companions became a special

friend. This was Felix Martin Levi, a maths scholar. In "Cambridge Friends" Geoffrey wrote ecstatically about him:

> Small, black-curled, a pure oriental of the type of the ancient Egyptian pictures in the National Gallery, with pock-marks, sallow skin, the most fascinating and attractive ugly face I ever saw, and brown eyes of a lambency, glow, brilliance and soft splendour indescribable. A witty, cultivated, aristocratic Jew, son of a Brummagen jeweller. Never again did I meet such extraordinary sympathy and charm of mind, and affection, and humour of temperament. He would gleam and quiver all over with vital enjoyment of life and a joke or an adventure. No company could resist him . . . He joined me in everything, came to the hills, fell in love with mountains, shared every craze for adventure or speculation, and we passed days and nights alike in endless enchanting talk, covering the substance of the whole world . . . He was much at Formosa and everywhere accepted as the best of friends, the most sensitive and refined of natures. I never knew a finer gentleman, in the finest sense.

Levi's sudden death a few years later was to be a great shock and sorrow to Geoffrey, and so, too, was that of another young man whose friendship, born of Trinity and nurtured in mountain adventures, was to be of high importance. Donald Robertson was two years younger than Geoffrey, one of brother Hilton's contemporaries. But he soon became Geoffrey's friend as well, and no other Cambridge man followed Geoffrey so whole-heartedly into his distinctive approach to the mountains.

"Tall, powerful, blond, with round face and a jutting nose like Pitt's. Clever, friendly eyes, well in above rounded cheeks. A fine athlete and oar and a passionate mountaineer, one of the few I did not introduce to it. We clicked at once and in time he became my nearest intimate." Geoffrey goes on to say that though he could not hope to match Robertson intellectually, they came together "into the mountain romance".

It was during the years at Trinity that Geoffrey formed the habit of judging men by their response to mountains. "The truth was, men had to share my interest. I never believed in friendship only of the house. Every friend had to come to the hills and if possible be a climber." In the long summer vacations he went on reading parties to the Cumberland fells, took to wearing the heavily nailed boots of the pioneer rock climbers and, with the loan of a farmer's hay-rope, led his friends up the recently created classic routes on Pillar Rock and Napes Needle. On his second long vacation, in the summer of 1897, he spent a thrilling few days with his elder brother canoeing down the white waters of the River Tarn in the south of France, then took the train to Savoy for his first encounter with the Alps. It was the start of a lifelong passion.

Thirty years later, writing the opening chapters of *On High Hills*, he gave a rhapsodical description of those first days of discovery and revelation. The great peaks of the Alps had all been climbed by this time, but there were still many lesser summits and long ridges and remote regions where men had never been. Geoffrey loved everything about it: the other-worldliness of life in the high valleys and villages; the pre-dawn starts and the long, hard days under the sun; the majesty of ever-changing, far-ranging prospects; the variety of physical challenges, the hard ice of the glaciers, steep slopes of snow and steeper faces of warm rock, the airy ridges, rapid glissades down to the valley in the evening, the stunning plunge into a glacier pool. He was not a tall man, about five feet nine inches, but he was fit and strong and supple, with great stamina and an attitude towards the mountains that was bold as well as respectful. But it was more to him than a purely physical experience: "I felt that I belonged to these mountains," he wrote, "and that they belonged to me." His accounts of his climbs are alive with joy and a sense of communion with the mountains, a mystical, quasi-religious feeling in which his own separate identity evaporated and he felt himself part of a much greater, harmonious whole.

Very soon he was venturing on to untrodden ground, making new routes. Sometimes he climbed alone, sometimes with roped companions, Felix Levi or Sandy Mackay from Trinity, later on with professional guides like Clemenz Ruppen and Louis Theytaz. In one passage of *On High Hills* he discussed the contrasting appeals of solo climbing and climbing with a companion, and came to this conclusion:

In the end I was to find that my own road to satisfaction lay through a combination of the two. The gateway to the poetry of adventure opened for me not far short of the borders of physical possibility. The companionship that could bring me to that point in safety, and yet not jar with the pleasant world of feeling that lay beyond the gate, had to be at once technically expert and at least sympathetic enough to keep quiet. And then – that point safely reached and in harmonious company – sometimes even for long hours together when the machinery of the body was working at its best with the senses all in accord and alert, the vibrating cord would tighten or the gate open – whichever image you please – and through beauty of sight and sensation and through a delight in being alive almost painful in its vividness there would throb the conviction that all was very right with both worlds, all very right with myself, and that they were all one and the same thing, and indistinguishably happy.

True to form, Geoffrey gives no dates and few factual details. His first Alpine peak was the Aiguille de la Grande Motte. He made a solo ascent of the Pigne de l'Allée from Zinal. His first big mountain was the Aletschhorn in the Bernese Oberland, nearly 14,000 feet above sea level.

The world of Alpine climbing was a much smaller one in those days and word spread rapidly. Almost from the start Geoffrey was making a name for himself. Some of the older guides remembered his father. Before he set off on his first full season, Geoffrey sought the advice of the great Alpine expert, W. A. B. Coolidge, who had just moved into his house in Grindelwald, and got a generous response. In October 1897 Coolidge wrote again to congratulate Geoffrey on his climbs. During his second full season he made an impressive solo ascent, and described it in these words:

> On the col at daybreak I sighted a guided party ascending from the farther, Ferpècle side; and they hailed me anxiously and courteously to join their rope. But I was still timid of real mountaineers. And I dashed ahead of them, chipping steps up the sharp, hard snow to the summit, hurried down the far ridge on to the Moiry glacier, and so ran down and away round the Garde de Bordon and back to Zinal, in a fashion farouche enough to have started a new legend of the "wild boy of the mountains".

Back at Trinity, in his second year there, Geoffrey was reading widely, not so much in the classical texts he was supposed to be studying as across the range of English literature, especially poetry. He was writing poetry too, and this led to his greatest public success at the university, the winning of the Chancellor's Medal for English verse in successive years, 1897 and 1898. Winthrop Mackworth Praed, his great-uncle, had achieved the same feat in 1823 and '24.

Geoffrey's first medal-winning poem was on the subject of Sir Francis Drake – 166 lines of rhyming couplets, in iambic pentameters, full of patriotic spirit and admiration for the successful man of action. The second was about St Augustine of Canterbury, in the same metric form and much the same length, but gentler and more meditative in mood. Both are well-crafted and elegant, in the eighteenth-century Augustan manner. Neither gives any sign of strong feeling or hint of poetic originality. The distinctive tone of voice that was to raise Geoffrey's later poems above the level of the ordinary was still to be found.

A few of Geoffrey's letters home from Trinity have survived. At the start of his second term he wrote to his mother: "I find hardly any of my friends managed last term under £70!!!" A year later, in January 1897, he asks her to send his wooden skates, and adds, "Have you seen about Aconcagua? There'll soon be only Everest left for me." The summit of Aconcagua, the highest in South America, had been gained by an Alpine guide on January 14. To his father he wrote about his continuing struggles with the classics, especially Greek texts, asking for advice. At the beginning of his last year, with the final exams looming ever closer, he was in near-despair: "I am so growingly unsatisfied about my work: it gets harder and harder to put any interest into it, and I feel almost in the state Plato describes. If a man works on at work for which he has no taste or power, he grows to hate it – and himself."

One letter to his father records a minor triumph on the cricket pitch. He had played for the Old Marlburians against the old school: "It was awfully jolly; so many men I knew, and all so nice – even the 'Blues'. My batting was out of form, but I 'saved the match' by some marvellous fielding flukes that took them all by surprise." He did not take the organised team sports of Cambridge seriously, but even so he was the regular centre-forward for the Trinity hockey eleven and occasionally played for the university.

A Trinity friend, Francis M. Cornford, later to become Professor of Greek Philosophy, introduced him to the Shakespeare Reading Society and he enjoyed their meetings. He attended some debates at the Union but it was rare for him to speak. Articulate enough among friends, he remained shy about public speaking. At the Decemviri, he got to know Desmond McCarthy, a year or two his senior but a fellow-mountaineer, later to achieve fame as a literary critic and broadcaster, and he was taken up by G. M. Trevelyan, then a history student beginning his final year. Geoffrey wrote to his father:

Trevelyan is a dark, thin-nosed, keen-looking man, who seemed excessively nice and made me feel very much at home . . . The debating was not very much – Trevelyan had the most to say – and some speeches were very amusing. It was all very light and pleasant. I got up, as is the custom for new members, and spoke somehow, but of course was horribly nervous. However, I had plenty of flow of words, even if they were nonsense. We ended up about 11.45 and parted. Trevelyan has asked me to breakfast on Monday. I don't think he has connected me with you yet.

The final comment refers to the fact that their fathers had been Trinity contemporaries forty years before and remained friends until Gladstone split the Liberal Party by plumping for Home Rule for Ireland in 1885.

There is, at first glance, something odd about the close relationship that developed between Geoffrey and George Trevelyan. It was Trevelyan who made the initial running, Geoffrey who held back. The Trevelyans were infinitely grander than the Youngs. They originated in Cornwall but by this time had been long established at Wallington in Northumberland, at the centre of an estate of 22,000 acres. George Trevelyan's biographer, David Cannadine, says, "The history of the nation was but the history of the Trevelyans writ large." And there was a family tradition of intense intellectual power and competitiveness. George Trevelyan's great-uncle had been Lord Macaulay, the famous historian, statesman, consummate parliamentary orator and popular poet. His father, too, was a distinguished historian and had been a minister in successive Gladstone governments. And George himself was on his way to a First Class degree and a Fellowship, the first man ever to get a Trinity Fellowship for history. It was all rather high-powered for Geoffrey, who had an acute sense of his own intellectual shortcomings. Furthermore, as Geoffrey wrote, "the Trevvys were very rich and we were decidedly poor." And there were considerable character differences between the two young men. Trevelyan's attitude to life was generally serious and he made no effort to be charming. Geoffrey was the opposite, putting great stress on playfulness and the social graces. He also, as his descriptions of the Cambridge friends repeatedly show, thought it important to have a mellifluous and well-modulated speaking voice. Trevelyan's was harsh and barking.

But they had important things in common as well – privileged backgrounds, Cambridge and Trinity, family traditions of Liberal humanism, the sense of what they owed to society, a shared love of talking and walking. In 1897 Geoffrey wrote home: "I walked to the Marble Arch on Saturday week to clear the cobwebs. We did (Trevelyan and I) the 54 miles in 12.50 hours". So they averaged more than four miles an hour. Their fathers, Sir George Young and George Otto Trevelyan, had done the same walk in 1858 when they were students at Cambridge.

Geoffrey soon came to love not only George Trevelyan but the whole, wide-ranging family. He became a regular guest at Wallington and was made welcome by Sir George Otto, the second baronet, and his three sons, Charles who became an active Socialist and succeeded to the baronetcy, Robert who devoted himself to poetry, and George the historian.

In a way, and he certainly believed this, it may have been Geoffrey's differences from them that endeared him to the Trevelyans:

> There was something charming, but very formidable, in their standards of value. It was a very high-pressure atmosphere, among the family, of intellect and learning. And though I felt always woefully short of it, and was shown up all the time, I think that my sheer gaiety and romanticism and joy in moving, and unlikeness to anything else in their rarefied world, was the reason they all grew so fond of me.

Geoffrey and George, and sometimes Charles, went for long walks across the Northumberland moors, and Geoffrey found climbing routes on the small cliffs they came across and up the walls of the ruined folly above Cambo. George would struggle loyally up these but he was not a natural climber. Sir George Otto had never been a climber but he could appreciate its appeal. In one of his autobiographical essays, "Trevelyans and Ourselves", Geoffrey recalled an afternoon at Wallington when he was playing with Trevelyan grandchildren on the lawn and Sir George Otto had wandered out from his study to watch:

> I was sending up a mechanical aeroplane I had brought them. This got caught in a tree-top in mid-lawn. And I quickly swung up into the branches, and shot up the tree to the final top where it was caught. Sir George watched from below, delightedly. Then he shook me charmingly by the hand. "This climbing," he said, "is wonderful movement. And now I have seen the *very* best." And with that his voice died away, the light died formidably out of his attentive eyes, and he drifted silently back into the study.

Behind his abrupt, sometimes gruff manner George Trevelyan concealed a very ardent and affectionate nature. It shows strongly in all his many letters to Geoffrey, and the early ones bubble with an almost school-boyish enthusiasm and high spirits. He addresses him as "Geoff" and writes: "I am sure you know how deeply interested I am in you, and apart from you in your work." There is a shining, unaffected innocence in Trevelyan's protestations of friendship. In September 1898, for example, he wrote: "You remember our talks in Cornwall upon the windy highlands above the crags. Brief as that time was, it is to me a romance, as also that day on the Pillar. 'Oh the great days in the distance enchanted . . . forty years on?' – if it seems thus three months on, I hope we shall get many more such days together in the future. Your affectionate friend . . ."

During their Cornish walking tour in the spring of that year the two young men had discussed their delight in Robert Louis Stevenson's *Kidnapped*, published in 1886, and wondered if it might be possible to devise a game that would re-create the excitements of the great chase across the Highlands when David Balfour and Alan Breck were hunted by the English red-coat soldiers. It was a fruitful discussion. In June 1898 sixteen undergraduates from Cambridge, most of them Trinity men, spent a riotous week at Seatoller House at the head of Borrowdale in Cumberland, and on four consecutive days took part in a thrilling but entirely bloodless man-hunt over the fells. Twelve of them acted as the hounds and pursued the other four, the hares, across the rough, steep slopes of the central mountains of the Lake District from eight in the morning till ten o'clock each evening. The hares wore bright red sashes to make themselves identifiable and visible from a distance. A touch of the hand was a capture. One day George Trevelyan, one of the hares, was ferociously pursued by Geoffrey, and Trevelyan described it afterwards as "the most exciting five minutes I have ever had in my life. We both went as hard as we possibly could over a chaos of wet rocks, not looking where our feet were planted, but simply bounding by instinct . . . we both of us rolled over and over several times among the boulders." But Trevelyan was fast downhill, and escaped by crouching in a cave. Geoffrey said: "The whole hunt was full of incident and fun, and to many of us *Kidnapped* has now a new meaning."

That hunt was the beginning of a tradition which still survives. The rules have been slightly amended over the years but the enthusiasm has persisted. Nowadays, in fact, there are two man-hunts each year, almost always from Seatoller House – one of them for Cambridge, and chiefly Trinity students; the other for members of the Trevelyan family and their friends.

At one time or another many outstanding men have taken part. George Trevelyan's eldest brother Charles, who was a member of Britain's first Labour government, was Master of the hunt for thirty-three years and took part in thirty-seven meets. Other huntsmen and hares have included Herbert Samuel, the leader of the Liberal Party; Raymond Asquith, the brilliant son of the Liberal Prime Minister; Leopold Amery, a Conservative minister; Hugh Dalton, who was the Labour Chancellor from 1945 to 1947; Professor Cyril Joad, popular philosopher and *Brains Trust* pundit; and Sir David Wilson, who became Governor of Hong Kong. Geoffrey took part in ten hunts altogether, and always enjoyed it. In his diary in 1911 he wrote: "Lake Hunt a record. Gorgeous weather: bathed 3–7 times a day! went hare for two days and found I could still run them all out over rough country."

The year of the first man-hunt was also Geoffrey's last year at Cambridge. As he had long feared, he did badly in the final examinations. He wrote to his father when the results came out in June: "Parry has told me just now that I have only been allowed the Ordinary. I won't disguise that this is a great blow. I don't think I realise it yet quite. I don't mind saying now that I had sneaking hopes of a Second . . . It is a bitter pill, but I am not cast down; I almost feel stronger for a new fight."

But what was the new fight to be? He wanted to switch to modern languages, French and German, perhaps spending a further year in Cambridge, then a year or more in Europe. His father, disappointed but not too surprised, responded with a long, considerate letter which concluded: "I recommend you, after much thought, to plunge on modern languages." He advised against staying on in Cambridge. It would be better, he said, to go and spend a few months in France and Germany.

6

Europe and Eton: 1898–1905

GEOFFREY LEFT CAMBRIDGE IN THE summer of 1898 and for the next three years and more he was chiefly in Europe, gaining proficiency in French and German and beginning to build himself a reputation as an Alpine mountaineer.

He spent some time in Geneva but the dates are not known. Little is known, too, about his time in France. One letter has survived, from Geoffrey to his father and dated July 1900, describing life with a provincial French family: "I am getting a little more at home with the sound and often can get the drift of general conversation." He was in Paris for the Great Exhibition of 1901. And he spent some time at Blois in central France, possibly because it was there that the purest French was said to be spoken. In his unpublished notes about his "Cambridge Friends", he says that Felix Martin Levi did well in his exams for the Indian Civil Service and passed through Paris *en route* for India: "I was studying in France when he went out, and going up from Blois, walked the streets of Paris all night so as to be sure to meet his train in the early hours. We had coffee by the station, and a long gossip full of plans." Most likely, the plans were about Alpine routes they were to attempt when Levi came home on his first long leave.

More is recorded about Geoffrey's time in Germany. He studied at Jena University for almost a year, from the beginning of May 1899 until March 1900. His stay there was enlivened for him by the company of another Trinity friend, Hugh Tempest Sheringham, who later became known as the writer of articles and books about angling. In "Cambridge Friends" Geoffrey described Sheringham:

He had a glorious deep singing voice, of true bass quality, and was musical. We went down together, and arranged to share the same lodgings in Jena, where he went to study music. A delightful companion, our interests were so different and our instincts so much the same, that we never had any friction. His singing was glorious, especially of Schubert, and I have never again heard so royal a rendering of *Der Tod und das Mädchen*, with his superb compass. With my Swiss friend Zuberbühler's incomparable tenor, we had unforgettable evenings. Our humorous appreciation of the German was the same and we shared endless jokes and collected the things "*Verboten*" under the Empire. It was Hugh who found the unsurpassable specimen – a notice-board in the centre of a dried-up pond, with only upon it these words – "It is forbidden to throw stones at this notice!" He carried me off to learn to fish in the Thuringer Wald at Meyersgrund, I only conditioning that if I got too bored, I might learn the trumpet in the woods. I had one day's fishings, and then – learned the trumpet!

Geoffrey loved music and at various stages of his life tried to learn an instrument – the piano in childhood, later the trumpet, the accordion and the xylophone. He never grew proficient in any of them, lacking a true ear, he said, and the requisite co-ordination between ear and hand. But he had a pleasant light tenor voice and enjoyed singing. He was greatly moved by his Swiss friend, Werner Zuberbühler's singing in the St Matthew Passion in Jena. At Easter 1990 he went with Zuberbühler on a walking tour in Appenzellarland:

visiting the farms and hearing the marvellous voices of the women and the boys and men. They sang every evening, and at times a whole train-load, coming back from some pagan *festa* on the hills, would break out into yodelling songs all the length of the carriages . . . I lived for some days in a Swiss village with my many Swiss friends and again, after the public was shut out, we all joined in music and singing till late in the nights. The East Swiss were then still unspoiled and wore their beautiful and costly national *Tracht* or costumes naturally and on any day of holiday or Sunday.

A few years later when Geoffrey was in his climbing prime and making remarkable new routes in the Alps, he liked to round off long hard weeks of physical exertion and excitement with a few days in Vienna or Munich, enjoying the rich food and the music:

One great week or more I had at Munich, when the *Ring* moved down there. I'll not forget those four-hour performances, with a vast interval in which we all turned out into the restaurants to eat roast goose and duck and drink vats of dark brown beer, and then paced round the gardens before going in again for two more acts. The old mad king's brother used to play in the orchestra. He was mad too, but a fair musician; only, as they could not rely on him, he used only to be allowed to play on a muted violin. I was near him and it was pathetic to see the old gentleman's complete happiness and his rapture in the music, as he scraped away on his silent fiddle.

There was another strange and silent encounter in Geoffrey's time in Germany. He had been wandering in Appenzellarland and travelled by train via Munich and Dresden on to Berlin. He was in a third-class carriage, virtually alone, in tattered walking clothes:

> The train slid slowly into the Bahnhoff Friedrichstrasse. I got up, with rucksack slung over one shoulder, ready . . . Suddenly I saw that the great station was lined with troops, ranks of the magnificent Prussian Guards. I let down the glass, ready to watch, as it was clear someone was arriving by our train and was being received in state. We slid slowly on . . . and I saw there was a great red carpet and on it two figures, the nearest in a sort of Hussar kit, with a busby and an enormous plume to it, blazing with orders. I guessed it must be the Emperor even as we slid up, and the Crown Prince, in blue uniform, behind him. By some colossal error, my carriage stopped exactly at the red carpet and I, at my window, looked straight out at the Emperor, straight into his face – it was burned a deep brown, all covered and mapped with little lines and wrinkles. I had no hat to take off and my hair was a-tumble. So all I could do was draw up straight and smile, as it were inviting him to share our mutual appreciation of the mistake, one gentleman to another! For a long second he glared mask-like right into my eyes, then came an odd twinkle – he must have seen I was English by the clothes – and then a slight smile, which I feel certain he would never have conceded to a subject German! It had just the right shade of pleasant recognition that we were both in an embarrassing situation against our will, but that formalities must be observed all the same! Then the train slid on, and I bowed to the window. Someone probably caught it badly for the blunder; but few folk can ever have looked so close, and on a level, into that strange man's face.

Throughout his life, and despite the fact that this involved two long world wars in which the Germans were the chief enemy, Geoffrey's deeper attachment was to Germany rather than France. He mastered the German language, speaking it like an educated native and translating into English Schiller's ballads and some of the devotional poems of Dietrich Bonhoeffer. His French, on the other hand, although it was fluent, was never more than what a discriminating Frenchman might describe as "good – for an Englishman". He made many friends in Germany and showed the mettle of his friendship in the 1930s when he worked assiduously to rescue them from Hitler's brutal rule. Perhaps his affection for Frau prepared the ground for this special attachment. The happy months at Jena fostered it.

There was one brief period of trouble at Jena. The Boer War was still raging and most Europeans, the Germans particularly, condemned British policy and methods in South Africa. A weekly paper, *Simplicissimus*, made its feelings known by publishing a somewhat obscene cartoon of Queen Victoria. Geoffrey, who was a good Liberal and strongly opposed to the Boer War policies of the Conservative government, found his patriotism so offended that he got all the copies of the paper that he could and burned them publicly. As a result he was challenged to duels, then a standard practice among German students and military men. As an Englishman, Geoffrey was able to refuse to accept such challenges without loss of honour. On one occasion though, when he was travelling by train, he was challenged by a drunken student who happened to have a pair of duelling pistols with him. Geoffrey accepted this challenge, stipulating that each of them should stand at opposite ends of the corridor, with a third man in the centre compartment to signal by dropping a handkerchief. Geoffrey had opened his window and, when the signal was given, fired out of it. He never knew where the other man's shot went.

Throughout his European travels Geoffrey kept in touch with his family at home, taking particular interest and pride in the progress of his younger brother, Hilton. Hilton was at Trinity, reading Natural Sciences, until the summer of 1900 when he took a First Class degree. He was more academic than Geoffrey, and more politically ambitious. He became President of the Union, and then editor successively of *Granta* and the *Cambridge Review*. From Jena, Geoffrey sent some short poems for publication in *Granta*, most of them in mockery of Hilton's highly elaborate and artificial style of verse at that time. Another poem parodied the over-heated Jingoism of the British popular press over the Boer War. Geoffrey also wrote book reviews for the *Cambridge Review*, beginning a lifelong habit of occasional journalism.

His climbing skills were developing and his enthusiasm was undiminished. At Easter 1898 he was at Ogwen Cottage in Snowdonia, with Sandy Mackay and Felix Levi and other Trinity friends. In June that year he was in the Alps again, with Levi and George Trevelyan. He was back again in August, this time with his aunt, Mrs J. H. Tuke, his mother's sister who was about sixty years old but still game for mountain exploration. Together they clambered about the ice falls of the Great Aletsch Glacier and up one or two steep rock pinnacles.

He described the expedition in an ecstatic letter to his mother, dated September 11, 1898:

I had a perfect time at Bel Alp: the place was too lovely for words and the Miss Kinders wonderfully kind and look-afterish. I got a lot of jolly climbs there, several new ridges and a little peak, which I called Dame Alys, after you. Just before I left I had one perfect round. I left Bel Alp about 5 a.m., and, with my guide Clemenz, made a new and much-improved ascent of the Fasshorner. We descended by another unclimbed ridge to the hut on the Ober-Aletsch Glacier, and passed a lovely night there. The evening effects are marvellous, standing in one's shirt-sleeves at the door of the rough cabin, and seeing the great rivers of white ice rolling at one's feet and spreading up to the great circle of glorious peaks shutting in every side, while the colours were fading through every shade of red, purple and gold on the snow, until it settled into the final deep violet and pallid silver or starlight. And all in perfect stillness, except for the occasional boom of an avalanche.

In 1990 Geoffrey was elected a member of the Alpine Club, the world's senior mountaineering club. It was an important step. He quickly became an active and increasingly influential member, campaigning hard to make the club more sociable and welcoming and democratic. He wrote many articles for the annual *Journal*, was elected to the committee and finally, in 1941, became President.

Although he was mostly in Europe in the three and a half years after leaving Cambridge, he paid frequent visits home, walking and climbing with friends, and getting a preparatory taste of school teaching.

It seems to have been assumed, without any argument, that he was going to be a teacher. He liked the young. His academic record was not good enough to get him a university post, so it would have to be school teaching and he was happy with that. He had already done much thinking about what was wrong with the schooling he had undergone and how things might be improved and corrected. Immediately after leaving Trinity he had spent a few weeks at the Cambridge training school for secondary teachers. During his travels in Europe, especially in Germany, he had investigated the teaching methods and studied the educational theories that were being discussed.

In January 1900, back home from Germany, he began to use his countless contacts to get some teaching practice and earn a little money. Henry Hart paid him £5 for a week's teaching at

Sedbergh. Matthew Bayfield, a rock climber as well as an eminent Greek scholar, employed him at Eastbourne College. He spent a term at Haileybury, working under Edward Lyttelton, and some time also at Wellington College where the headmaster was Bertram Pollock who had been his house-master at Marlborough and who was later to become Bishop of Norwich. While at Wellington he got to know a governor of the school, Colonel Patrick Wellington Talbot, a godson of the first Duke of Wellington. The colonel, now over eighty years old, had been private secretary to the great man when he was Commander-in-Chief of the British army, post-Waterloo. He told Geoffrey this story: "The Duke wrote an infernal scrawl. On one occasion all the secretaries failed to read his script, and Talbot was sent in, as young and a favourite, to ask its meaning from the Duke. The Duke glared, took it, and looked at it fixedly. Then he growled, with his iron dignity and invisible humour, throwing the note back to Talbot: 'It's my damned business to write orders, my boy. And it's your damned business to read them!'"

Some time in 1901 Geoffrey received a summons from the headmaster of Eton:

Dr Warre was a vast, ruddy Devon yeoman and rowing Blue, immense in his authority and huge in a sort of scholarly stupidity. He sent for me and, in his great study, boomed at me, rather inarticulately, offering me one of the regular Classical Tutorships and teaching posts. I was *bouleversé*. Surely he knew I was no scholar? And yet, it was fascinatingly tempting! I had only to say yes and my whole future was secure and golden in prospect. Could I do it? Could I manage somehow to scrape through with Latin and Greek? My mind flashed to and fro. The Etonian level of Latin verse! Proses, daily supervisions . . . I knew I couldn't. I blundered out that I mustn't accept, I was no Classics scholar. He looked confused. I don't think Warre ever imagined an educated man could not write Latin and Greek prose and verse of some sort. He grubbed in the papers on his desk: "You have two Chancellor's Medals, I see!" he boomed. I saw it too! – he had never dreamed a University Medal could be for anything but Classics. And he was an Oxford man . . . My mind cleared. Of course I couldn't accept. "I should like a foreign language post, Headmaster, if one falls vacant," I said. "Ugh," he boomed, as much upset as I, that such things could exist as refusals of Eton masterships.

A few months after this Geoffrey received a letter from Dr Warre, offering him a post as usher, tutoring in modern languages. In January 1902 he went to Eton, took pleasant rooms in High Street, and began his working life.

At this stage a new and helpful factor enters the story – Geoffrey's Journal. It is possible that he kept diaries before this but if he did, the evidence has not survived. From the beginning of 1902 onwards, however, long periods of his life are recorded in his Journals, many hundreds of large, closely written pages, all clearly dated and crammed with detail, a particularly valuable source because he was writing without any thought of publication, simply to set the record down while the events and his responses to them were still fresh in his mind. He wrote in ink, sometimes red but mostly blue. The writing is small and neat and italic, and generally legible. In the first Journal, a big, black notebook with lined pages, he did not make daily entries, but every few weeks or so sat down to scribble out notes and descriptions of the more important events – where he had been, whom he had met, what his thoughts and feelings had been, occasionally launching into passages of serious introspection and self-examination. A note on the opening page says: "G.W.Y. A rough journal of doings between 1902 and 1914." The first entry is: "1902. January. Settled at Eton, with C. S. McDowell in No. 26." The final entry says: "1914. Summer. The Alps. Return from Monte Fiano via Alps. The War breaks out." There are then many blank pages but right at the back Geoffrey made a list of the books he was reading in the first months of 1904. It includes several plays and stories in German; some French memoirs; Moore's *Life of Byron* and Byron's poems; some histories and several novels in English. His favourite was Robert Louis Stevenson, who had died in Samoa ten years before. He read *The Suicide Club*, *The Master of Ballantrae*, *Three Merry Men*, *Memories and Portraits*, the letters, and Lloyd Osbourne's book about Stevenson's last years *Vailima Memories*.

Geoffrey had three and a half years at Eton and loved it. He hurled himself into the life of the school, taking the teaching duties seriously but finding time for a hectic extra-curricular life. He took to playing rugger and hockey again; also played fives and soccer occasionally; introduced fencing to the school; used the river for swimming and skating and boating; did much cycling and hard walking and, in the holidays, climbing. He was close enough to Formosa Place to be able to visit his parents frequently and share their social life. He developed a passion for dancing, and often escaped to London for the social whirl and some light flirtation. By the autumn of 1903 he felt so well settled into the Eton life that he could write in the Journal: "Feel that I am getting really into this place, and that the reserve barriers are breaking down." He was suggesting improvements to the school timetable. Before the end of 1904 he was vigorously involved in the politicking for the headmastership. Dr Warre was soon to retire and Geoffrey lobbied for his friend Edward Lyttelton, who had been a guest at Formosa Place and taught to punt by Geoffrey. Lyttelton was elected to the post at Easter 1905.

One of Geoffrey's pupils was a boy called L. E. Jones who half a century later published a book called *A Victorian Boyhood*, in which he paid tribute to Geoffrey:

> Another young Master with whom I sat, tête-à-tête, in his rooms in the High Street once a week my last Summer Half was Mr Geoffrey Winthrop Young. I had to write essays for him on general subjects; it is interesting to me to remember, having regard to his own flashing and jewelled sentences, that he made me cut and prune, and throw out the epithets . . . If only I had held the key that could have unlocked, on occasions, the casket of that ardent and distinguished mind! But I never did. With Renaissance good looks, reserved and patently dwelling in a different world from that of the ordinary run of the younger "beaks", he did not even let out to me that he was already, in those years, a giant among mountaineers and the maker of many a famous first ascent. I never remember him speaking of himself, or saying a word irrelevant to the matter in hand. He was grave and courteous and impersonal.

Eton's outstanding house-master at this time was Arthur C. Benson, an articulate and clever and highly sensitive man, very much at home in the exclusively male atmosphere of Eton, though soon to leave to become Master of Magdalene College, Cambridge. Geoffrey enjoyed Benson's hospitality and his conversation: ". . . he made a delightful host. His *cuisine* and wine were excellent, and he kept the talk going at a high level." Benson had been something of an Alpinist in his younger days, giving it up after a dangerous moment in 1895. It seems that, descending from some summit above Bel Alp, Benson had fallen into a deep crevasse and had been held, swinging in icy space, by the strength of his guide, Clemenz Ruppen. Benson afterwards wrote a dramatic account, never published, of the incident, praising Ruppen's courage and the remarkable strength that enabled him to haul Benson up by the rope, inch by inch, until he could reach over the edge and grab him by the hair and pull him to safety on the snow. Geoffrey read a copy of this account in Bel Alp, and added further information:

> Benson never knew the whole story! Clemenz told it me during our long talks in night bivouacs. With all his great strength he could only

just keep from being dragged in after Benson. Being the tough peasant he was, of the old tradition, he decided that as the father of a large family, it would do Benson no good if he followed him in and left his children to be supported by Benson's relations! So while he fought, inch by inch, to lift him, with one hand he reached into his jacket pocket, felt his knife and opened its large, easy blade, ready in the final issue to cut the rope and let Benson drop. Having resolved on this and got the knife ready, he fought on until he had drawn Benson so nearly up that he could reach over and grip him by the hair and haul directly on this, for the rope would be cutting deep into the snow edge and preventing a direct haul. Benson never knew of that open knife ready.

By far the cleverest pupil Geoffrey encountered at Eton was John Maynard Keynes, who would have been outstanding in any generation. Keynes was a mathematician and a sixth-former in 1902, sent to Geoffrey to polish his essay-writing skills with a view to the approaching scholarship examinations. He liked Geoffrey, describing him as "the first grown-up I really talked to easily". In return, Geoffrey liked the boy and formed an immediate admiration for the sharpness of his intelligence and the breadth of his knowledge and interests. They kept in touch when Keynes moved on to King's, Cambridge, and in the summer of 1905 Geoffrey persuaded him to join a climbing party in the Alps. He habitually tried to get the young men he was fond of to try the mountains, and he had a special reason in the case of Keynes because he thought he was in danger of becoming unbalanced, too intensely and exclusively concerned with the intellectual life. After the holiday he sincerely believed he had been successful. He wrote about Keynes: "Obviously he was revelling in every minute of it . . . I took him up the Aiguille d'Argentière and he went very well indeed. I watched him going up the final cone of hard snow, bent like a dark ray, swooping, and even so radiating vital awareness." There was probably a large element of wishful-thinking in this. Geoffrey always found it hard to accept that some of his friends were unable to share the joy he found in mountaineering. Certainly, Keynes' account of the trip was entirely different. On August 11, 1905 he wrote to Lytton Strachey:

We have made our way to Chamonix over passes; on Tuesday we climbed up to a hut (circ. 9,000 feet) to sleep. After 2½ hours sleep we set out in the dark with lanterns on to the glacier, crossed a pass, climbed a mountain and reached our destination after 19 hours. The expedition was lengthened out to this untoward length by the incompetence of the guides who took us wrong at every crucial point . . . We had to cross a beastly bit of glacier in the dark . . . What rot all this is about nature. I have seen the superbest views and the wildest and most desolate expanses of snow and ice; there was even danger: but not for one single moment have I been moved with anything I can call violence. Feelings of course one gets and a kind of passion of calmness but the whole is on an altogether lower scale of merit.

By his last remark, presumably, he meant "lower" than the intellectual plane.

Keynes' comments were no doubt coloured by the fact that he was writing to Lytton Strachey. Three years later Geoffrey happened to meet Strachey when he had just returned to London from a visit to the island of Skye. Geoffrey asked, hopefully, if he had not been impressed with the peaks of the great Cuillin Ridge. "I thought them simply absurd," Strachey replied.

It was naive, perhaps, of Geoffrey to suppose that some benign compromise might be forged between mountaineering and the claims of Bloomsbury and higher economics. Geoffrey regretted it but accepted it too, and the friendship with Keynes survived intact. They met only occasionally but always cordially. Just after the Second World War Geoffrey met Keynes in the hall of a London club, on his return from the international conference at Dumbarton Oaks. "Well, Maynard," he said, "is the world doing what you tell it to?" Keynes smiled and replied: "*Parts* of it, I assure you, are excellent." And in some unpublished notes on Keynes Geoffrey wrote: "I felt in the latter years that I had never known, or known of, a man of whom it could safely be said that he possessed genius, who remained in such complete control of his own gifts, and in whom the essential humanity always dominated the intellect and the senses. Human life and human beings remained the tests, and every idea and impulse had only validity in relation to them."

Geoffrey's mountaineering continued to develop during the Eton years. He was at Bel Alp for ten days in August 1902 and climbed three summits, including the Nesthorn. The next year was one of relentless bad weather and he did not go to the Alps. But 1904 made up for that with a will. Geoffrey made several first ascents and met Gertrude Bell, the formidable explorer and mountaineer. With the guide Louis Theytaz, he made his own first ascent of the Matterhorn. They did it by the Hörnli Ridge, the route created by Edmund Whymper's ill-fated party in 1865.

Geoffrey had arranged for another guide to leave food and fuel for them at the Hörnli but, but when they arrived there, late in the afternoon, there was nothing for them and the place was deserted. Bad weather was predicted. It was too late to go down to Zermatt for provisions so they spent a miserable night, cold and hungry and thirsty. In his book *On High Hills* Geoffrey described the next day:

> Day at last broke in upon us through the chinks, with the inverted glare that tells us, even before we look out, that it is shining upon new-fallen snow outside. We crept out into the sun-trickles, and felt cold; and we looked up at the enormous leaning peak with its night-wrap of fresh snow, and felt hungry. But there was a tingle of glowing anger inside us, and we fed with set teeth upon our resolve not to be baulked. I felt that Louis, as he puckered his eyes against the sunrise, was only waiting for a word. And at last I murmured to the wind generally that since we were both there for the first time it did seem a pity to go down without at least exploring the way on to the base of the peak. That was enough. We abandoned our sacks – they were empty – and all loose gear, tightened our belts, and trotted up into a glorious flashing morning, with the mountain before us, and all to ourselves! Louis had not been on the Matterhorn before; but he never made a mistake or halted for the route. We had started as late as the sunlight; and now it blazed torridly to recover its lead, clearing the snow off the slabs just ahead of us as quickly as we climbed. The icy wind lessened our thirst, and the exciting pace left us no time to realise the slower pangs of hunger.

The climb to the summit took them only a minute or two over three hours. Now they had time to rest and survey the panoramic view:

> The snowcrest between the summits had been frayed into a transparent comb, frigid with wind-whipped ice. From time to time the gusts crashed through the icicles, and scattered them in a metallic rattle down the southern precipices. We sat and sucked long ice-spillikins, and tried to take in the incomparable circle of conflicting view – sheer mountain form and mass, modelled only in planes of light and shadow, yet in hopeless agreement with the colour and atmosphere of valley and Italian distance. The Matterhorn view is more difficult to master than the Matterhorn. I have, on occasion, spent three hours alone with it on the summit; only to find myself at the end still wrestling with new and opposing impressions, and never even able to arrange them in orderly memory.

The Matterhorn was no great challenge to a climber of Geoffrey's ability but it meant a great deal to him. Gustave Doré's graphic illustrations of the 1865 disaster had printed themselves indelibly on his schoolboy mind; then, as a sixth-former, the reading of Whymper's *Scrambles Amongst the Alps*. More than twenty years after his first ascent, Geoffrey climbed the same route again and got himself on to the front pages of the British newspapers because by that time he had only one leg.

He was back in the Alps for the Christmas–New Year holiday 1903–4 with Marcus Heywood, one of his Eton essay pupils. From the Grand Hotel, Adelboden, he wrote to his father on January 10:

> We had two days good skating here, and then I got bored with the *table d'Hôte* and went off to Visp. I met my old guide Clemenz there and we tramped up the Zermatt valley to St Nicklaus, arriving about 4. The valley looked beautiful under snow, with all the torrents frozen into luminous green cascades, and the rocks covered with huge columnar icicles of a thousand shapes. We slept at a small inn – all the big ones are closed – and in the evening an assembly of the guides came in to see us, all the Pollingers, Imbodens, Lochmatters and Knubels of famous memory, and we sat round a long table and drank local vintage and talked shop. Two of the Seiler family arrived in the evening, so we took one of their sleighs in the morning, and after photographing some of the celebrities, started off on the iced roads, tremendously wrapped up! The drive became yet more beautiful as we got up into the sunlight, but was uneventful. We reached Zermatt about 2, to find one small inn open. We strolled after lunch and got a magnificent view of the Matterhorn, hung with ice, and the snow-covered valley with its big hotels and torrents all curiously silent and softened – infinitely more pleasing than I have ever known it in summer.

There was much climbing in Britain too in these years, in North Wales and the Lake District and Scotland.

In January 1903 he joined Sandy Mackay on the Isle of Arran and at their hotel met some of the leading mountaineers of the previous generation. They included Professor Norman Collie, a distinguished chemist and a passionate mountain man with many new routes to his credit, especially on Skye but also in the Scottish Highlands, the Lake District, the Rockies, the Lofoten Islands, the Alps and the Himalayas. Another member of the group was Charles Granville Bruce, then a major in the Fifth Royal Gurkha Rifles and already an experienced explorer in the Himalayas. Both Collie and Bruce had been on the Nanga Parbat expedition of 1895 in which A. F. Mummery was killed. Geoffrey made long-lasting friends with both of them, but it was another veteran mountaineer, William Cecil Slingsby, whose friendship was to be most important to him in the years to come. Slingsby was a Yorkshire squire, a clubbable and great-spirited man and a superb mountain explorer. He had done many hard routes in the Alps but his great claim to fame was as "the father of Norwegian mountaineering", with more than fifty first ascents to his credit. Nearly forty years after their meeting on Arran, Norman Collie wrote a friendly letter to Geoffrey and included his reflections on the climbing qualities of two eminent figures: "I enclose," he said, "some remarks of my own about Mummery and Slingsby – they are *for you only. Private and confidential. Most private and confidential.*"

The letter is in the Geoffrey Young collection in the archives of the Alpine Club in London. As far as I know, Collie's remarks have never been published. They were written in May 1942 – Collie died later the same year – and I think the passing of over half a century is enough to excuse publication now. This is what Collie wrote:

> I have always found that people considered Mummery a splendid *rock climber*, and they did not know that he was by far the finest *ice climber* amongst *all amateurs*. There have been many rock climbers better than Mummery, but no ice climbers who have come anywhere near him. Emil Rey said that he was better than all the Swiss guides. But Mummery was *not* a good mountaineer. He was not good in knowing what was the best way up a mountain or the safest. Once he was started on a route it was almost impossible to get him to turn back from the difficulties and dangers. Now Slingsby was a *magnificent mountaineer* . . . Slingsby was a *perfectly safe man to climb with*, and Mummery was not.

The importance of safety-consciousness in the mountains was underlined during that mid-winter Arran holiday. In his Journal Geoffrey simply noted: "Mackay broke his leg on Cir Mor, and it took until 2 a.m. to get him down, with 16 volunteers, in a storm." He gives a fuller and much more dramatic account in his book *Mountains with a Difference*. He and Mackay were attempting the ice-glazed walls of a steep buttress. Geoffrey led and the climbing was so delicate that his progress was very slow, and it became evident that they were going to be overtaken by darkness before they reached the top. The only quick way of escape was to descend into a snow-filled gully to their right. Mackay, the burlier and stronger of the two, paid out the rope as Geoffrey slithered down. Then Mackay jumped, relying upon the soft snow to break his fall, but there was rock just beneath the snow where he landed and one leg was broken in two places. Geoffrey fixed a splint as best he could with an ice axe, glissaded down the gully and then ran the length of Glen Sannox to summon help. It was dark by the time he gained the road, and there was another long run to reach the hotel. Once there, he organised a strong rescue party, seized some food and blankets and a lantern, and set off to run all the way back:

> It was rough going, and many miles of it, and all uphill. Surprisingly, and for the first time in my life, I began to feel exhausted as I ran. Alarmingly, as I forced the pace up the last long third of the valley, I felt a strange sensation, my legs crumpled, and I rolled over on the heather – in as near a faint as I had ever known. This would not do. I considered the odd happening as I lay, and remembered that I had not eaten since breakfast some 15 hours before . . . I chewed two large hard captain's biscuits. Instantaneously energy flowed back into every joint, like liquid life trickling through me. I raced on again, and scrambled up to the craggy and snowy mountain shoulder, hailing at times to cheer Sandy.

He found Mackay, fed him and kept him warm until the rescue party arrived with a cumbersome army stretcher. Then followed the laborious, interminable descent. Mackay was saved and his leg mended but that was the end of their Alpine partnership, the best of Geoffrey's early mountaineering years.

Towards the end of that year, 1903, Geoffrey himself suffered a fall. It was term-time but he paid a flying, weekend visit to Wasdale Head in the Lake District. The Journal says: "By night train to Seascale, bicycle to Great Screes Gully. I had bad fall at last pitch. Slept and went to little church at Wasdale ('The Lord upholdeth all such as fall' was sung!). Second day, scramble round Great Gable, bicycle to Seascale and back to early school on Monday!" The gullies above the Wastwater screes are notorious for their unreliability. Geoffrey, who was apparently climbing solo, was lucky he was not badly injured.

Two important events, for Geoffrey personally and for British climbing, took place in the summer of 1903.

The weather was too bad for his usual Alpine season, so he went instead to Ireland to visit cousins and go cycling and walking and climbing in County Donegal. He spent a few days with his parents at Formosa Place, then headed north to see Cecil Slingsby at his home at Carleton on the Yorkshire moors. His Journal says merely: ". . . delightful family and pretty children". He described it much more romantically in *Mountains with a Difference*, written many years later, when he recalled the visit and seeing Slingsby with his beautiful wife and "a sun-drift of wide-blue-eyed children with soft mischievous voices". One of these children was Eleanor, who was to become his wife sixteen years later. At this moment of their first meeting she was seven years old, nearly twenty years Geoffrey's junior.

From Carleton he crossed over to Snowdonia to join a group of friends at the new hotel, Gorphwysfa, at the top of Llanberis Pass, a place called Pen-y-Pass. Once again the Journal is terse: "Party met there – Chitty, Hope-Jones, Harry Baring Gould, Page Dickinson, George Trevelyan. Too cold and stormy, but climbed on Y Wyddfa, North and South Gully of Tryfan, Parson's Nose." They were only there briefly and there is nothing striking about the climbs they did, but this was a significant moment in the story of British climbing. It was the first Pen-y-Pass party, the start of a tradition that lasted some thirty years under Geoffrey's benign direction and that inspired and enthused many of the great men of the sport, Siegfried Herford and George Mallory, Jack Longland, Ivan Waller, Wilfrid Noyce, A. B. Hargreaves and many more.

Geoffrey was leading an intensely full, varied and satisfying life. Eton kept him busy in term-time, teaching fourth-form German and French and coaching some more senior boys in essay-writing, organising and playing games, campaigning with like-minded colleagues who wanted to reform the school system and break the autocratic and rigid rule of the classicists. He made many friends, but it was inevitable that he should also make some enemies. The Journal makes it clear that he knew about the enemies but he does not name them. In the spring of 1905 he noted: "I gather that I am thought stand-offish, but when one is so sensitive to opinion and slights, one must protect oneself – or rather one can't help doing so."

Towards the boys his manner was generally reserved, but a few would be invited to Formosa Place for weekends on the river. Among the favoured were Maynard Keynes; Harry Baring Gould, a distant cousin; and the charming and clever boy, Marcus Beresford Heywood, whom he had taken to the Matterhorn and who was to be one of his closest friends and mountaineering companions in later life.

Geoffrey used the holidays to the full. Summer was for the Alps, when the weather allowed. At Christmas he went climbing in the Lake District or Scotland or Snowdonia. Each Easter holiday was dedicated to more cultural and exotic explorations along the northern shores of the Mediterranean, in Italy and Greece and what used to be called Asia Minor and is now Turkey.

Half a century later Geoffrey described his journeys in the eastern Mediterranean in his book *The Grace of Forgetting*. The two chapters, "Mount Athos" and "Easter Journey", display his naturally high-flown style at its highest – vivid, colourful, allusive, excitable and packed with strong adjectives. His elder brother Georis had joined the diplomatic service and been sent to work as a secretary at the British embassy in what was then called Constantinople. Geoffrey wrote: "I used to race across Europe in my short Easter break to join him, and find myself launched upon an *Arabian Nights* adventure, unrolling itself like a magic carpet hazardously and entrancingly in continuous travel."

Georis organised and led the expeditions into remote regions. Geoffrey portrayed him in these words: "He himself, aquiline, monosyllabic, and compelling or persuasive as occasion served, rode ahead, a graceful and tireless horseman in brown riding-boots, a long Newmarket coat, the whip that signified authority in the East looped over his shoulder by its long lash, and a gold watch somewhere attached, for impressive production as a symbol of our wealth and dignity." Georis also carried a revolver, handy but out of sight, because much of their travelling was in lawless country. There were dangerous moments but he never had to fire it. Geoffrey carried a camera. He was a keen and competent photographer, and several of his pictures illustrate the two chapters.

In 1902 Geoffrey explored Constantinople and Scutari, then set off with Georis to study the excavations of Troy, after which they moved into wilder areas to enjoy the hospitality of ancient monasteries and suffer the squalor and privations of life in the villages. The rooms were often flea-ridden. Sometimes they were welcomed and fêted, at others they were obstructed by corrupt local officials, threatened by local villains, followed by importunate beggars and spies. Much of the travelling was in unpopulated mountain country. They finally reached Salonika where Geoffrey, already bound to be late for next term's opening day, leapt on to the train for Ostend and London. He passed the journey in typing out his recollections of the journey. The account of this first trip filled fifty-eight pages, and at the end he wrote: "Moral – A brother is after all the best companion."

The following Easter he went with two friends, Charles Trevelyan and J. F. Grace, to Milan and then on a tour of Greece – he was trying to learn modern Greek – then to Constantinople again for another adventurous foray into Asia Minor with brother Georis. Then he rushed home on the Orient Express, typing all the way.

The holiday was usually no more than three weeks and Geoffrey took it as a challenge to pack in as much as possible. He was always late getting back.

In 1904 he spent the whole time with Georis, visiting Troy once more, then many of the Aegean islands. The next year, sometimes alone and sometimes with friends, he covered northern Italy – Lake Como, Milan, Verona, Mantua, Padua and Venice.

If they passed a challenging mountain, they would climb it. When they came to water, they plunged in. He saw the journeys, especially those in Asia Minor, as "riding raids into the past". In *The Grace of Forgetting* he wrote:

> Around us as we rode was the present, mostly swamp, barrenness and barbarism. But everywhere through and behind this degradation, in fragmented beauty returning to dust, I was seeing the relics of the lost cultures of this coast, of the city ports, of art and luxury from which had been embarked for its cradle-time in Greece our infant Western civilisation, and with it our own standards of the worth-while in life.

On one of the eastern visits he saw the Dancing Dervishes in action and was impressed:

> Their movement, with the swirl of the loose eddying robes to the mystical reed-flute music, ending with an incredible velocity of spin, had a demonic beauty. Those were years when dancing was wholly fascinating; when it was the best of rests to waltz through the night hours in London, even at the price of catching the milk train down in time to take early school, with a lightning change of clothes in the guard's van.

His journal makes regular mention of dances, sometimes at Formosa Place, more often in London. Geoffrey was no socialite but he had a passion for dancing, especially waltzing.

In some unpublished pages about his early relationships with young women, he makes it apparent that he saw them primarily as dancing partners. The first one he mentions is Elska Ramsay, daughter of the chemist Sir James Ramsay:

> She was petite and trim, with fine eyes and complexion – pretty, not beautiful. But a lovely mover! Our steps fitted gorgeously. We arranged to meet at dances and when the first public rooms opened, the Empire Rooms in Kensington, with the first suspended floor, I used to come up regularly from Eton and dance half the night with Elska . . . Of course, it was the time when to dance often with a girl "meant something"; but as I was never flirtatious or indeed moved sentimentally at all by girls, I – and Elska – had no after-thought. So I was slightly shocked when Aunt Georgie Tuke approached me in the way ladies did then, wanting to know, on Lady Ramsay's behalf, whether I had "any intentions". I said emphatically no!

There were several scenes of this sort. Geoffrey, after all, was young and good-looking, vigorous and charming, and though he was not a rich man, his career prospects looked promising. To many mothers he must have seemed eligible enough. But marriage was not at the front of his mind. Writing it all up many years later, probably after the Second World War, he said: "My relations with girl friends were far more what they are at the present day, a comradeship, often individualised for a time. But such terms were not recognised then, and in each successive familiar friendship, the small world about us concluded that an Engagement must follow – or the friendship be ended."

Geoffrey's upbringing led him into great embarrassment on one of his trans-Europe journeys:

In the days before English women painted or powdered, a fantastically made-up and lovely Roumanian "lady" was on the same *train-de-luxe*, and periodically invaded my compartment, and languished. I was embarrassed because two of my senior Eton colleagues were travelling on the same train and were decorously amused and shocked at the affair. At last, being naturally shy, I had to complain to the guard, who warned the lady off, but obviously thought me a noodle! The lady beamed and misted in once again in a flourish of white powder, and said reproachfully: "*Que vous êtes timide, M'sieur, d'être si beau!*"

Geoffrey goes on to remark: "We were certainly handicapped in dealing with the larger and especially the foreign world in our travels, by our very strict and high-minded upbringing and home atmosphere. We had too little experience of how to steer clear *before* the storms were already upon us."

He did once propose marriage – to Rachel Lyttelton, the niece of his schoolmaster friend Edward Lyttelton. He was visiting the family at their holiday house on the Norfolk coast:

Tall, elegant, serene and ivory cool and lovable, we were friends in walks on the cliffs. For the first time since schooldays I fell "in love", and the whole world coloured into rose lights and romance. On the third day I proposed, with no definite rejection. Then I had to go off north, while she thought it over. I travelled in a glow, and from every halt sent back boxes of flowers, and on several nights love lyrics.

The affair was blocked by Rachel's mother, Lady Cobham, who thought her daughter could and should do a good deal better. Geoffrey was miffed: "I was not vain of myself, but I resented even

a younger son of my family being treated as not up to the Lytteltons."
But he soon got over any pain he may have felt: "I had been, perhaps,
more in love with feeling myself in love than with the girl."

During the winter of 1904–5 Geoffrey had a climbing holiday
in the Langdale valley with Vincent Baddeley and others. "We
collected a jolly party," he wrote in the Journal: "We ran over the
hills, sang all the evenings for ten days of beautiful soft weather."
Then the Journal says: "Returned to stay with the Edward Lytteltons
at their new cottage near Cromer; had very cold draughts and some
good walks. Talked over with E. L. his answers in applying
for the Headmastership here." Lyttelton was then headmaster of
Haileybury.

Dr Warre was retiring after twenty years as headmaster of Eton
and the battle for who should succeed was on. By Easter the result
was known. Lyttelton had won, and almost immediately he wrote
to Geoffrey saying it was for him "to keep the Head straight", a
joking reference to the time when Geoffrey taught him to punt on
the Thames at Formosa Place.

Things could hardly have looked better for Geoffrey. He was not
yet thirty but already very happily settled at Eton, now with every
prospect of early preferment. His little book *Wall and Roof Climbing*
was finished and about to be published. But the rest of the year, 1905,
brought two stunning blows. During the Easter holiday he received
news from India:

> Levi, my best Cambridge friend, companion in many wanderings and
> perfect nights and days, in laughter and danger, the subtlest brain ever
> encountered, was killed by the earthquake at Dharamsala, when just on
> his way home for his first leave after five years. A terrible shock, it has
> taken me down into depths and difficulties never before faced, and talked
> out now with Hilton and Mother. But one emerges with a clearer sight
> of one's own beliefs, if they are vaguer than one thought to find. I sent
> a short obituary to *The Times*.

He distracted himself with a hectic round of visits, then a trip across
northern Italy, admiring the landscapes, studying the architecture
and paintings, enjoying the company of friends. Then he returned
to Eton for the last term under the headmastership of Dr Warre. In
the Journal, in red ink, he wrote simply: "Back here. No change.
Perfect weather. Bathed already (May 8)."

The next entry, in blue ink, said:

August. Left Eton. Too happy to last, but a selfish happiness in a way; clouded with the fear of losing the one spring of freshness; and facing its loss too late to change horses on this queer rough path of the world. Well, it's worth playing the game through for its own sake, as well as for the family and those splendid friends. I don't think I feel bitterness towards one soul there. Just honestly sorry for their mistake that I think has lost the school something of future benefit, as I am sorry for my own frequent blunders, spoiling a good work that held the heart. At least I feel these four years have been full work, and helped many beginnings, some of which still cling round me, others are already off on the whirpool. I start life again with far more self-reliance, with a juster estimate of the worth of my work in life, and a deepened knowledge of myself and the values of life. Nothing in the circumstances has shaken me so deeply as F.M.L.'s death did. In a way that was, I think, a preparation. It cleared the sight, and I saw depths that these surface storms have never ruffled. Nobody can ever know what my Mother, Father and brothers have been to me. I feel like a child, dreadfully hurt and crying out, and at the same time with a security of touch and tread that I never dreamed to possess. We are far deeper *in* nature than we ever know. Our own depths swallow our own cares and leave no ripple but a strange surprise.

It is an odd statement but clearly from the heart. The Journal was for Geoffrey's eyes only. It seems that he wrote this when the initial shock of his dismissal was beginning to subside, writing to try to sort it all out in his mind, to get things into perspective. It is significant, I think, that in the passage quoted he does not say he had been sacked, and gives no hint of the reason why he was sacked.

Eton College archives, those that survive, give no clue either. All that can be found is a line in the minutes of a meeting of the Provost and Fellows that speaks of Young being allowed to surrender the lease of his house "following his departure in exceptional circumstances".

There is no definitive evidence then, but there can be little doubt, I think, that Geoffrey was dismissed because he had been found guilty of some homosexual activity. He talks of being "honestly sorry for their mistake", suggesting that the school authorities had misread the evidence and refused to accept his interpretation of it. Or perhaps he merely meant that it had been a mistake to sack him for something that was known to be widely practised. Homosexual acts were illegal, but, as all accounts of the period make apparent, in the English public schools and ancient universities the practice was not only widespread but also generally accepted. Some were promiscuously homosexual;

others, like Lytton Strachey, were flamboyantly so; Geoffrey, by contrast, would be restrained and discreet.

Family and friends rallied round. He was asked to go and stay with the Master of Trinity, Montagu Butler: "I shall not forget his pointed charm and hospitality to me, when I was deeply wounded at my retirement from Eton, and I was pressed to stay with him, and the episode dismissed with a grave, smiling understanding, and implied reproof of the Etonian precipitance and clumsiness."

And A. C. Benson, settling in as Master of Magdalene, sent Geoffrey a note of commiseration, saying ". . . my own experience is that nothing is *ever* as bad as one fears or indeed expects; and I believe it will be the same about the darkest things of all."

7

Alpine First Ascents

GEOFFREY WAS BADLY SHAKEN BY the sacking from Eton but he soon found solace in the mountains. His 1905 Alpine season was important for several reasons. He began to make impressive new routes. He started his partnership with the professional guide Josef Knubel, who was to be his companion on most of his great routes. And he met, and climbed with, the only other British mountaineer who was climbing at that time at his own level of enterprising excellence, V. J. E. Ryan.

Geoffrey's Journal gives no more than the skeleton of events. Under the heading "August Holidays" it says simply that he went to Switzerland with Robin Mayor, the philosopher and Fellow of King's College, Cambridge, and Will Slingsby, one of Cecil Slingsby's sons, and Maynard Keynes. This was the occasion, already described, when he tried, without success, to get Keynes interested in mountaineering. Josef Knubel, who was twenty-four years old, the son of a guide from St Nicklaus, was with them on the ascent of the Aiguille d'Argentière. A day or two after this Geoffrey and Knubel made their first big climb together, traversing the Charmoz and the Grépon in one day. It was an impressive beginning, and established the companionable fact that they matched each other closely in skill and boldness, speed and stamina, and also in the reflective quality of their enjoyment. They had perfect weather. This is how Geoffrey described the excitement of the climbing, once they had gained the first high pinnacle on the Charmoz Ridge:

> Beyond it the sheer, sharp-cut and crumpled horns along the narrow rock crest tossed us up and down through the fresh morning air with exhilarating vigour. Bent upon crossing all their storm-filed points, we hazarded several giddy and some probably novel swings and roundabouts, before we were flung up, from the wrong side, on to the summit rock. I recollect in particular a hand-hanging roundabout along the Mer de Glace face, with a swing up over an overhang on to the extreme edge of the Charmoz wall.

It was a stirring passage; which drew from Josef the whole chromatic scales of his little excited shrills – "Hjesas! Hjesas!! Hjesas!!!"

When he wrote that, Geoffrey was recalling the experience some twenty years after the event and it inspired him to one of his finer flights in praise of the sport:

> Mountain climbing is the supreme occasion of physical enjoyment. Even so, the days when the condition of the mountain, the condition of the weather and the condition of every member of the party are all perfect and working perfectly in accord can come but rarely. But when they do come, for their duration the delight of rhythmic movement dominates all our consciousness. It is not the ecstasy of the spinning Dervish, which is a stupor achieved by mechanical repetitions. It is a changing delight, based upon motion infinitely varying. Far from doping, it actually stimulates our senses and our intelligence. So that we see, feel, hear and appreciate through our trance with an almost unnatural intensity, and at the same time continue in alert control or our own spell-weaving.

The passage reminds me of something that Coleridge, who – among other achievements – invented the sport of fell walking in the Lake District and made the first recorded rock climb in England, wrote in a letter to a friend: "The farther I ascend from animated Nature, from men, and cattle, and the common birds of the woods and fields, the greater becomes in me the Intensity of the feeling of Life."

After the big traverse Geoffrey and Knubel made an attempt on the Dru but bad weather had come in and they were forced to retreat. So they moved across to Zermatt to try the Matterhorn and there met V. J. E. Ryan, one of the great eccentrics in the story of British mountaineering.

Ryan was only twenty-two – six years younger than Geoffrey – but already his austere, inflexible character seems to have been fully formed. He was not an easy man to get to know or to get on with. In the obituary which Geoffrey wrote for the 1949 edition of the *Climbers' Club Journal*, he said: "Ryan was an unusual but not unknown type of Irishman, reserved, proud, excitable, dissatisfied; without any share of the more sociable Celtic qualities, the wit, the humour or the ready human sympathy. The gods who showered on him all worldly gifts, withheld the power of ever appearing to be happy or even in harmony with his surroundings." Ryan was, in many ways, the antitheses of all that Geoffrey represented, and it is a tribute to Geoffrey's tolerance and charm and also to his relish for human oddities that he contrived to create a friendship with this very private and prickly man. The files of the Alpine Club archives in London hold several of Ryan's letters to Geoffrey, written between 1906 and 1912, all of them brisk but also, for Ryan, amiable in tone.

To some degree, Ryan's background explains his nature. He grew up in the Protestant landed ruling class of Ireland and his father was a major general. He went into the army himself, serving as an artillery officer in Malta and Ceylon, resigning his commission in 1905 when he inherited a large estate in County Cavan. He had begun climbing at the age of fifteen, showed a natural talent for it and, in 1903, hired the brilliant Lochmatter brothers, Josef and Franz, as his guides. It was with them that all his great, innovative climbing was done, always with a guide leading. Geoffrey wrote:

> He never carried a sack – his guides were there for that; and I never saw him carry an ice axe – the guides, he said, were there for that too, and it bored him. It was another idiosyncrasy that he never cared to lead on rocks himself, or to cut the steps. But he could walk up or down steps in ice or snow at any angle in balance. He had daring, initiative, endurance, and a bold eye for a new line.

Geoffrey recalled their first meeting, shortly after he and Knubel had checked into an almost empty hotel: "Round the Schwartzsee Hotel that evening Ryan strode to meet me. Rumour had told him of my coming, and his guides were already my friends. 'You're going for the Furggen Ridge, I suppose?' Ryan remarked at once conversationally – 'so am I'. There was satisfaction for both of us, in coming across someone else who was playing the rigour of the game in that slackwater period."

Once again Geoffrey's Journal is laconic, saying simply: "Climbed Furggen Ridge with Ryan and made new ascent of Weisshorn."

The first of these climbs, fully described in *On High Hills*, was done in two parties – Ryan and the Lochmatters first, Geoffrey and Knubel following. The intention was to gain the top of the ridge, then traverse left to the Italian Ridge and gain the summit that way. As they approached the high saddle, however, it became noisily clear that the cliffs on either side of them were under constant bombardment from falling stones. Ryan was all for pressing on and hoping for the best. The guides were unanimous in recommending the shorter traverse right to the Hörnli Ridge:

> The relationship between Ryan and his guides at once became plain, as I listened to Josef's responsible and anxious explanations of the dangers

in laboured English, to a Herr whose vexation he seemed more anxious to deprecate than to appeal to his mountaineering knowledge. Ryan's impatience with our hesitation to start up those bombarded shelflets over Italy had a rasp in it. He was very much the young officer ordering the charge. But in the end he accepted without resentment our unanimous opinion against the attempt.

The other ascent, by a new route on the south-east face of the Weisshorn, was less controversial and more impressive. The start was delayed by bad weather, so for twelve hours, while the snow fell outside the hut, Geoffrey and Ryan played chess. Ryan won two games to Geoffrey's one. When the weather relented the five of them set off in the same order as before but unroped, up the Schalliberg glacier, then on to the steeper rock of the face. They were within 1,000 feet of the summit when the cliff steepened abruptly and forced them to rope up:

I let Josef run out his full 70 feet of rope, before I followed him up its upward traverse. Minute holds there were, at inter-stellar distances; but at half the height one had been left out. I bungled here for some time, much puzzled how Josef, whose reach was considerably shorter than mine, could have passed the absence of hold seemingly without hesitation. At last I found it, a sole-supporting ledgeling on the underside of a glazed plate. Josef grinned down at me from above as I exclaimed, and used it.

The route took them directly to the summit, where they were greeted by an icy wind. Geoffrey always had a special affection for this mountain:

Of all mountains the Weisshorn, to me, promised the most; from all points of view – with one possible exception – fulfilling our ideal of a mountain. Three, and unlike, are the great edges of its glorious pyramid; and threefold, and strikingly dissimilar, are the aspects of its western, easterly and northerly faces . . . In all, I think, I stood upon the symmetrical summit eight times; reaching it by six different lines, four of them new, and leaving it again by four different lines, three of them first descents.

On this first occasion, they descended by way of the east ridge:

On the way down, again in unroped and sociable independence, Ryan and I examined and discussed the two great south faces of the Täschhorn and the Dom opposite, and we resolved we would try them together the next year, when they might be more free from snow. How ample then was the choice, when whole faces looked at us unclimbed, and we knew that even if we waited for years, there was no risk of any competitor entering the lists before us.

From the Alps Geoffrey crossed southern France to join his brothers and other friends in the Pyrenees. The diplomatic service had transferred Georis from Constantinople to Madrid, and he had acquired a villa at San Sebastian. There they were joined by the youngest brother Hilton, who had taken a First Class degree in Natural Sciences at Cambridge, studied law in London, and been called to the Bar in 1904. They were joined by Hilton's Cambridge friend, Charles Donald Robertson, and Geoffrey's friend, G. M. Trevelyan who had already published two history books and who was now teaching at a Working Men's College in London. They did the usual tourist things – watched the battle of flowers, went to a bull-fight – and some mountaineering too. The Journal records: "Tremendous expedition across Pigne de l'Aya, night out . . . With E. H. Y. [Hilton] and C. D. R. [Robertson] went to Burgos, wonderful place; rode south across deserts, stayed three days in beautiful and hospitable monastery . . . thence Madrid. Stayed Georis's beautiful flat. Amazed by Velasquez. Visited Toledo. Bought brass, which was recovered when stolen. Wrote several lyrics."

In October Geoffrey returned home to confront the big problem ahead, what his next job was to be. It was quickly solved. By this time he had a wide range of influential and well-disposed contacts, especially in the field of education, and no inhibitions about using them. The Journal says: "October. Returned Formosa. Began negotiations Education Office. Appointed November 25 in a hurry, because Conservatives just going out. Got in *first*, though Modern Languages were only wanted as third in order of choice. Began work Whitehall – Inspections at Eastbourne, Harley, Kidderminster etc. Most absorbing work."

It was a time of upheaval in Britain, in politics and in education. After almost twenty years of continuous rule, the Conservatives were on the way out. Faced with bitter divisions in his own party over empire trade and a rising national demand for social reform which he was unable to meet, Prime Minister Balfour resigned, and the general election of 1906 returned the Liberals to office with a landslide majority in the House of Commons and a richly talented cabinet under Sir Henry Campbell-Bannerman. Geoffrey and his family and most of their friends were delighted. They shared the widespread feeling that reforms were needed to make society more fair and democratic, that men were perfectible and that education was the way to bring it about.

It seems strange that, so soon after being sacked from his teaching job, Geoffrey should be appointed one of His Majesty's Inspectors for Secondary Schools, with considerable powers to investigate and pass judgement. It was an influential job and it came to him at a significant time. The great achievement of Balfour's government had been the Education Act of 1902 which brought all the primary and secondary schools of England and Wales under local government control, and made public money available to pay teachers properly and ensure a standardised level of quality. It inaugurated a period of rapid expansion, especially in secondary education.

So Geoffrey went to live in London. He moved into Hilton's house at 22, Launceston Place, Kensington, where he entertained his friends and did much dining out and dancing. The job meant a lot of travelling, which helped him to keep his country-wide friendships in trim and introduced him to a new delight, that of motoring. And it afforded him the generous holidays he had grown accustomed to.

He took his work seriously though. He had strong feelings about the importance of education and strong views about how it should be conducted. He disapproved of the worship of games, and at Eton had been a leading activist in the movement to break the traditional iron grip of the classicists in the class-rooms. Although he always regretted that his own training in Latin and Greek had been insufficiently rigorous, he believed that the way they were drilled into young Etonian minds was unnecessarily harsh and deadening. He thought the old-guard classicists were élitist, exclusive and blinkered, preoccupied to excess with literal precision and grammatical accuracy, killing the very things they loved by their rigidity and lack of imagination.

Before and during his years at Eton Geoffrey had written a number of reflective articles about education for the *Westminster Gazette* and another magazine called the *Pilot*. He was developing theories of his own, especially about the psychological aspects of the problem. In a long account of the development of his educational ideas, which he wrote after the Second World War, he recalled his thinking at this time:

> I was interesting myself in examining how far a teacher, when he dealt with the collective personality of a class, was forced to assume a different

personality himself. Something in the fashion of an actor who has to alter and emphasise, by technique, in order to convey a character across the footlights to a collective audience. The point had never been mentioned in any of my training schools; but it seemed to me fundamental if a man was to acquire a successful technique in teaching and in class discipline . . . It was becoming obvious to me, from many instances among my friends, that the sincere soul who held that the natural relationship which he had with Brown and Robinson unofficially out of class must also be the right behaviour with them when together in the classroom, failed, early and heavily, in class discipline. He failed because Brown and Robinson in class were absorbed into the collective personality. This is as distinct from that of the master in his chair opposite, as is that of the audience from the actor on the stage; as distinct, and in a way as opposed. To meet it, the master on his side must assume a presentation of himself that embodies also the authority of his position. He need not be false to his real self; but he must be more than "merely himself". The moment class is over, his natural relationship with each individual boy can, and ought to, be resumed.

He was already concerned at the number of English schools, the boarding schools especially, that formed enclosed and often embittered little societies with virtually no contacts with the world outside their walls:

The atmosphere in common rooms of such schools reflected the conditions of the monastic life. Men who had been selected for varied reasons and for unlike qualifications and interests were thrown together in an unavoidable and constant intimacy. They had not the privilege, which they had had at college, of selecting their own daily companions. Their profession, however, forced them to co-operate closely, however antipathetic their personalities. I never elsewhere met more petty quarrelling and undignified squabbling than in barrack-like, door-banging and jaded common-room life towards the end of term. Mr Perrin and Mr Trail were alarmingly true to the usher life of that period.
[*Mr Perrin and Mr Trail* was a public school novel recently published by the ever popular Hugh Walpole.]

Geoffrey believed that learning need not always be painful. Young minds would respond to beauty and excellence and knowledge if it were presented to them in a stimulating way. In his unpublished papers he tells two stories that illustrate this:

Inspecting Stratford-on-Avon Grammar School and sitting in the Armoury of the old Guildhall, where Shakespeare also probably was taught. A dull man was taking English and reading *Treasure Island*. And I sat with mind remote, thinking of what Shakespeare might have thought, there? Then I heard the dull voice: "The wake of the ship – what is the wake of a ship, boys?" I looked along the benches in front of me, of Warwickshire country boys. And then, from a sandy-haired, brown-faced, hazel-eyed boy, lolling on the desk in the back row, with a rather absorbed expression, I heard, in broad Warwickshire, and rather shyly, "The side of the ship on which the sun shines first, sir?" The dull teacher tried to cover up the answer from my notice with a loud "No, no!" But I literally exclaimed aloud in delight. Pure poetry! And what W. S. himself would have said as a boy!

The second story Geoffrey tells comes from the years before he became an Inspector, when he was visiting Edward Lyttelton at Haileybury. He was fond of Lyttelton but had no regard for his teaching:

He was taking the Sixth Form in English, on a hot lazy afternoon, and reading aloud the English poets. To keep the drowsy boys awake, he was using the bad device of leaving lines unfinished and pouncing on them to supply the rhyme. I heard him start the lovely *Aubade* [by Sir William Davenant]: "The lark now leaves etc.", and come to
"Awake, awake! break thro' your veils of lawn!
Then draw your curtains, and begin . . ."
He omitted "the dawn". "Begin . . . begin . . . begin . . .?" His deep resonant voice moved from boy to sleepy boy. No answer. Then, from a gay clever little scamp in a laughing voice: "Begin – to yawn!" Again I burst into a laugh. But Edward was without humour . . . "Oh, you *stupid* boy!"

At Christmas 1905 he went to Stool End Farm at the head of the Great Langdale valley in the Lake District, with brother Hilton and six or seven of their friends, including the painter William Arnold Forster. The weather was fine and they did much fell walking. Geoffrey hired the services of Gaspard, the professional guide at the Wastwater Hotel, and was introduced to several rock climbs – Slingsby's Chimney on Scafell Pinnacle (pioneered by Cecil Slingsby in 1888), the Arrowhead Ridge on Great Gable and the classic route, Kern Knott's Crack.

An annual pattern was set: British mountains at Christmas and Easter – the Alps in the summer – and during term-time a lively social life in London, together with a full and varied programme of school inspections. His special district was Norfolk and Lincoln and he enjoyed it:

Did a lot of inspection at Norwich and gained general experience and found my colleagues excellent fellows. The contact with the Democracy, with its different shibboleths and total unacquaintance with the genus "great", is very stimulating, and opens the eyes to the value of English small-town life, before only appreciated abroad . . . Really to work for oneself and be free of the sound of a bell is man's work. I think I could be content with this alone.

There is a revealing aside in the Journal notes about his London life in early 1906: "Conducted a pleasant flirtation, and many dances: all rather a disappointment, but it is pleasant to feel the capacity to love someone of the other sex growing, as the absorption in school-being fades, and the normal standards of life revive." He also records the receipt of a letter from V. J. E. Ryan, asking him to join him on a trip to the Himalayas that summer: "I am going to the Nubra district that Collie told me about. My party is Myself, Josef and Franz Lochmatter. *I do wish you could join me*; if you can manage to get away, come, only your personal expenses would fall upon you." It was a generous offer but Geoffrey's job made an absence from Britain from May to October impossible. In the event, Ryan did not go either, but it is interesting to reflect upon what that formidable foursome might have achieved in the days when vast regions of the Himalayas were open to exploration and conquest.

The Easter holiday was devoted to climbing. First he went to Wasdale Head in the Lakes to climb with H. V. Reade, squire of Ipsden in Oxfordshire and a distinguished civil servant, and with George Abraham of Keswick who was a pioneer of Lake District climbing and a professional photographer. "A jolly party," the Journal comments: "found I could go well still." Then he hurried down to explore the granite cliffs of Cornwall and climb with the leading pioneer of that area, A. W. Andrews.

In the spring Hilton Young went to Italy with George Trevelyan to accompany him on the trail of Garibaldi's marches, a journey that led to Trevelyan's first important work of history, the Garibaldi trilogy. At Whitsun Geoffrey was back at Stool End Farm for another man-hunt across the fells. During the summer term he worked hard, but found time for a half-hearted flirtation: "Thought myself in love with Rachel Kaye Shuttleworth, but was glad when we settled not to pursue the subject. *Sic transit!* Anyway, more time etc. for a motor car, which at least can travel about with me." Then came the summer holidays and the Alps again and a better, busier season than ever.

He summed it up in the Journal: "Unique season – new climbs on

Breithorn, Dom, Täschhorn, Weisshorn etc. Week at Montenvert; 21 hours on Requin by wrong route, two Drus, circuit of Grépon, Charmoz and Blaitières in one day. Täschhorn with Ryan, and did not expect for about six hours to get back alive. Had Knubel for the year."

They were all superb climbs but the outstanding one was the first ascent of the tremendous South Face of the Täschhorn. The story has become one of the legends of Alpine achievement – for the formidable nature of the route and also for the terrifying intensity of Geoffrey's account in *On High Hills*. He wrote it twenty years after the event, and it shows how vividly the details of that ordeal lodged in his memory – not only the nature of the terrain and the climbing and the weather but also the grim sensations that the climbers had to endure. The account, covering more than twenty printed pages, has a compelling, nightmarish quality, conveying – to my mind, more powerfully than any other passage of mountain writing – what it must feel like to be in a bad and dangerous place, in bad weather, fighting for apparently endless hours, always desperate and often close to despair, to force a way through. The man who led them through the crux section was Franz Lochmatter, and Geoffrey prefaced his description with a high tribute:

> Franz Lochmatter's mountaineering feat was the greatest I have witnessed, and after a number of years I can still say the greatest I can imagine. It is right that it should be recorded; for I do not suppose that in its mastery of natural difficulty, in its resistance to the effects of cold and fatigue and to the infections of depression and fear, it has often been equalled on any field of adventure or conflict.

The party was the same one that had climbed the Matterhorn and the Weisshorn the year before – Ryan with his two Lochmatter guides, Geoffrey with Knubel. The route was, indeed, the one that Ryan and Geoffrey had surveyed and discussed on their descent from the Weisshorn. Now they attempted it.

The weather was discouraging. After a night at the Täschalp hut, they set off before dawn in a cold drizzle which they withstood for a while before retreating "to a day of chess and wild-raspberry jam". They made an earlier start the next morning, in colder but clearer air, and raced up the snow slopes that led to the foot of the face. The western buttress above them was step and liberally plastered with fresh snow, but the holds were plentiful enough to allow them to climb unroped – Ryan's party first, with him between the two guides; Geoffrey and Knubel following.

At 7.30 a.m. they paused on a rock ledge to eat a quick breakfast, standing up. It was their last food and their last rest for many hours. The open face above them was steeper, so they roped up at this point – Josef Lochmatter, Ryan, then Franz – then Geoffrey, with Knubel bringing up the rear. They climbed on, finding no stances where they might rest a moment and no rocky knobs where they could hitch the rope and get some sense of protection. After a long time a rope was tied between Franz Lochmatter and Geoffrey, so that all five men were now linked together, none of them with any doubts that a fall by one of them would most likely bring all of them crashing down. Fingers and feet were numbed by the intense cold. It was snowing again. All of them were worrying about the situation they were in, and even more about the situation they would be in if they found there was no way up above them.

They spotted a gully high above and to one side, and thought it might make for easier progress, so they made a delicate, ascending traverse to gain it. But when they reached it, one glance was enough to know that there was no route there. So Josef Lochmatter climbed carefully down to the bed of the gully and inspected the snow-spattered wall beyond.

"It won't go," he shouted up to them.

"But it *must* go," Franz shouted back, and set off down to join his brother and take over the lead. At this point in his narrative, Geoffrey contrasted the climbing styles of the brothers:

> Josef, and other great guides, on slabs moved with the free poise of an athlete and the foot-cling of a chamois. Franz, in such case, had the habit and something of the appearance of a spider or crustacean. His curled head disappeared altogether. His body and square shoulders split and elongated into four steely tentacles, radiating from a small central core or hub of intelligence, which transmitted the messages between his tiny hands and boots as they clung attached and writhing at phenomenal angles and distances.

They resumed climbing, with Franz leading and Knubel, now carrying all the rucksacks and ice axes, in the rear. The weather had grown danker. "The fight went on doggedly," Geoffrey wrote, "with that determination to take no long views but to make just the next hold good and the one more step secure, which enables a human atom to achieve such heights of effort and to disregard such lengths of suffering."

They found their way into a narrow chimney which afforded some sense of protection. Josef Lochmatter took the lead again and for a while the climbing was easier. Their hopes rose that the chimney might signal the end of their struggle:

And then, it all ended! The chimney simply petered out: not under the south-east ridge, as we might have hoped, but in the very hard heart of the diamond precipice some six hundred feet below the final and still invisible summit. The vague exit from the chimney faded out against the base of a blank cliff. One of its side walls led on for a little, and up to the left. There it too vanished, under the lower rim of a big snowy slab, sloping up, and slightly conical, like a dish-cover. I have reason to remember that slab. It formed the repellent floor of a lofty, triangular recess. On its left side, and in front, there was space and ourselves. On its right, and at the back, a smooth leap of colossal cliff towered up for a hundred feet of crystallised shadow, and then arched out above our heads in a curve like the dark underside of a cathedral dome. A more appalling-looking finish to our grim battle of ascent could hardly have been dreamed in a "falling" nightmare; and we had not even standing room to appreciate it worthily! As I looked up and then down, I had an overpowering sense of the great grey wings behind us, shadowing suddenly close across the whole breadth of precipice, and folding us off finally from the world.

But our long apprenticeship to discouragement stood us in good stead. Muscles braced anew obstinately; determination quickened resentfully. The recess on whose lip we hung had been formed by the sliding of a great wedge of rock off the inclined, dish-cover slab, once its bed. But on our right the cliff continued the original line. My impression of this, therefore, was as of a high building viewed from under one corner. Its sheer front wall stretched away to the right, flush with the sill of our slab. The end wall of the building formed the right side of our recess, and over-hung the slab. The rectangular house-corner, where the two walls joined, rose immediately above us, vertical and iced, but a little chipped by the rending out of the wedge. Again, the front wall of this projecting house did not rise to the same height as the cliff that backed our recess. Forty feet up – my measures are merely impressions – the wall slanted steeply back in a roof, receding out of sight. Presumably another huge wedge had here slid from its bed, on a higher plane. Above and beyond this roof the precipices rose again into sight, in the same line and of the same height as the cliffs which backed our recess. Only, the cliff vertically above us was crowned by the great dome or overhang. There must be, therefore, invis-ible above, some rough junction or flaw where the line of cliffs above the receding house-roof linked on to the forward jut of our dome. Four vital questions suggested themselves: Could the house-corner be climbed? Was the roof, if attainable, too steep to crawl up? Might there be a flawed connexion where the precipice upon which the roof abutted joined on to the side of the dome? If there was such a flaw, would this yield us a passage out on to the face of the convex dome *above* its circle of largest dimension, on its retreating upper curve, or *below* it, under its hopeless arch? These details are tiresome, perhaps unintelligible. But they may help other climbers to a better understanding of Franz's remarkable feat.

Right up in the angle of the recess there was a rotund blister of rock modelled in low relief on the face of the slab; and round this a man, hunched on small nicks in the steep surface, could just belay the rope. Josef and Franz were crouching at this blister up in the recess. The rest of us were dispersed over freezing cling-holds along the lower rim of the slab. And the debate proceeded, broken by gusts of snow. The man to lead had clearly to run out a hundred to a hundred and fifty feet of rope. He could be given no protection. His most doubtful link would come some eighty feet up, above the roof. If he found a flaw there, and it served him favourably, he would be out on the convex of the dome fully a hundred feet above us, and outside us in a direct line above our heads. If, at this point, he could not proceed – well, it was equally unlikely that he could return!

Franz showed no hesitation. The hampered preparations for the attempt went on hurriedly. We had all to unrope as best we could, so as to arrange for the two hundred feet of possible run-out, and we hooked on to our holds with difficulty, while the snow-frozen rope kinked and banged venomously about us. In the end little J. and I had to remain off the rope, to leave enough free. Then –

> as a flame
> Stirred by the air, under a cavern gaunt –

Franz started up the corner, climbing with extraordinary nerve but advancing almost imperceptibly. It was much like swarming up the angle of a tower, rough-cast with ice. Ryan and little J. crept up near the blister; but as there was no more room I remained hanging on to the fractured sill of the slab. In this position I was farther out; and I could just see Franz's two feet scratting desperately for hold to propel him up the tilt of the roof above the corner. The rest of him was now out of sight. The minutes crawled like hours, and the rope hanging down to us over the gable-end hardly seemed to stir upwards. The snow gusts distracted us cruelly. A precipice in sunshine seems at least interested in our microscopic efforts. Its tranquillity even helps our movement by giving to it a conspicuous importance. But when the stable and the unstable forces of nature join in one of their ferocious, inconclusive conflicts, the little human struggle is carelessly swallowed up in uproar, and tosses unregarded and morally deflated, like a wet straw on a volcanic wave.

Suddenly I heard that unmistakable scrape and grit of sliding boot-nails and clothes. Above my head, over the edge of the roof to the right, I saw Franz's legs shoot out into space. Time stopped. A shiver, like expectancy, trembled across the feeling of unseen grey wings behind me, from end to end of the cliff. I realised impassively that the swirl of the rope must sweep me from my holds before it tightened on the doubtful belay of the blister. But fate was playing out the game in regions curiously remote. My mind watched the moves, itself absorbed into the same remote, dispassionate atmosphere. It seemed unwilling to disturb the issue by formulating a thought, or even a fear. The fact of the body seemed negligible; it had no part in the observant aloofness into which all consciousness had withdrawn. Something of the same feeling of separation between the body and the watching mind is the experience of men actually falling or drowning, when action is at an end and there is not even pain to reunite bodily and mental sensation. But during the crises of this day the condition lasted, with me certainly, for spaces that could only be measured by hours.

Franz's boots again disappeared above the edge. No one in the recess had known of the slip, out of their sight and lost in the gusts. He had stopped himself miraculously on the rim by crushing his hands on to ice-dimples in the slab. The hanging rope began again to travel up along the slanting gable-end of the roof. There was a long interval, and now and then the sound of a scratting boot or the scrabble of loose surface. Then the rope began, jerkily, to work out and across far above our heads. Franz had found a flaw in the join of the cliffs above the roof, and he was creeping out on to the projection of the dome. The lengthening rope now hung down well *outside* the men in the recess, and it might have hung outside me on the lower rim, had they not held in its end. Its weight upon Franz, as it swayed down through the snow, must have added to his immense difficulties. He was well out of sight, clinging somewhere above on the upper curve of the overhang.

An indistinct exchange of shouts began, half swallowed by echo, wind, and snow. Franz, it appeared, was still quite uncertain if he could get up any further. For the time he could hold on well enough to help one man with the rope; but he had not two hands free to pull. I could hear his little spurt of laughter at the question – "Could he return?" He suggested that Josef should join him, and the rest wait until they two might return with a rescue-party. Wait, there! – for at best fifteen hours, hanging on to the icy holds, in a snow wind! Well, then, what if we four tried to get down, and he would go on alone – if he could? "Get down? Ho, la, la!" – Josef was at his resourceful wits' end. I suggested, pacifyingly, that Ryan might join and reinforce Franz, and that we remaining three could attempt the descent together. This provoked the crisis, which had been long threatening. Josef's competence and control were second to none in the Alps; but the responsibility, the physical strain, and this last disappointment had overstrained the cord. It snapped; and in somewhat disconcerting fashion.

Harsh experience can teach us that when these accidiæ occur, as they may to the most courageous of men if tested unfairly, the only remedy is to soothe or to startle. The first was impracticable in our situation. I spoke sharply in reproach, but without raising my voice. The experiment succeeded surprisingly. Self-control returned upon the instant, and for the rest of the day Josef climbed and safeguarded us with all his own superb skill and chivalrous consideration.

He was right in so far that, at that hour of the day and upon those treacherous cliffs, now doubly dangerous under accumulating snow, all the odds were against any of us who turned back getting down alive. Franz in any case could not get back to us, and he might not be able to advance. We were committed, therefore, to the attempt to join him, however gloomy its outlook. As many as possible must be got up to him – and the rest must be left to chance.

Josef started his attempts on the corner. This left room for me to move up to Ryan on the slab. He asked me, I remember, what I thought were the chances of our escape. I remember, too, considering it seriously, and I can hear myself answering – "About one in five." As we talked fragmentarily, and listened to the distant scraping of Josef's feet up the roof, I recalled – with a grim appreciation of this new, first-hand example – having often remarked in the stories of shipwreck or other catastrophe how inevitably and usefully the "educated" man plays up to the occasion. For the audience of his own mind as much as for anybody else he sustains almost unconsciously the part which his training imposes upon him as alone consistent with his self-respect.

The end of the long rope hooted down past us. It hung outside the recess, dangling in air; and I could only recover it by climbing down again over the rim of the slab and reaching out for it one-handed with my axe. I passed it up; and then I stayed there, hanging on, because I could no longer trust hands or feet to get me up the slope again. Ryan began the corner; but if I have described the position at all intelligibly, it will be seen that while the corner rose vertically on our right, the long rope hung down on a parallel line from the dome directly above our heads. So it came that the higher we climbed up the corner the more horizontal became the slanting pull of the rope, and the more it tended to drag us sideways off the corner and back under the overhang. Very coolly, Ryan shouted a warning before he started of the insufficient power left in frozen hands. Some twenty feet up, the rope tore him from his inadequate, snowy holds. He swung across above our heads and hung suspended in mid-air. The rope was fixed round his chest. In a minute it began to suffocate him. He shouted once or twice to the men above to hurry. Then a fainter call, "I'm done," and he dangled to all appearance unconscious on the rope. Franz and Josef could only lift him half-inch by half-inch. For all this hour – probably it was longer – they were clamped one above the other on to the steep face of the dome, their feet on shallow but sound nicks, one hand clinging on, and only the other free to pull in. Any inch the one lifted, the other held. The rough curve of the rock, over which the higher portion of the rope descended, diminished by friction the effectiveness of each tug. The more one considers their situation, the more superhuman do the co-operation and power the two men displayed during this time, at the end of all those hours of effort, appear. Little J. and I had only the deadly anxiety of watching helplessly, staring upward into the dizzy snow and shadow: and that was enough. J. had followed silently and unselfishly the whole day; and even now he said nothing: crouching in unquestioning endurance beside the freezing blister on the slab.

Ryan was up at last, somehow, to the overhang; and being dragged up the rough curve above. A few small splinters were loosened, and fell, piping, past me and on to me. I remember calculating apathetically whether it was a greater risk to try and climb up again into the recess, unroped and without any feel in fingers and toes, or to stay where I was, hanging on to the sill, and chance being knocked off by a stone. It is significant of the condition of body and mind that I decided to stay where I was, where at least stiffened muscles and joints still availed to hold me mechanically fixed on to my group of rounded nicks.

Ryan was now out of sight and with the others. When the constriction of the rope was removed he must have recovered amazingly toughly, and at once; for down once more, after a short but anxious pause, whistled the snow-stiffened rope, so narrowly missing me that little J. cried out in alarm. I could not for a time hook it in with the axe; and while I stretched, frigidly and nervously, Josef hailed me from seemingly infinite height, his shouts travelling out on the snow eddies. They could not *possibly* pull up my greater weight. Unless I felt sure I could stick on to the corner and manage to climb round to them by Franz's route, it was useless my trying! At last I had fished in the rope, with a thrill of relief, and I set mental teeth. With those two tied on to the rope above, and myself tied on – in the way I meant to tie myself on – to the rope below, there were going to be no more single options. We were all in it together; and if I had still some faith in myself I had yet more in that margin of desperation strength which extends the possible indefinitely for such men as I knew to be linked on to me above. And if I were once up, well, there would be no question after that about little J. coming up too!

I gave hands and feet a last blue-beating against the rock to restore some feeling to them. Then I knotted the rope round my chest, made the loose end into a triple-bowline "chair" round the thighs, and began scratching rather futilely up the icy rectangular corner. For the first twenty-five feet – or was it much less? – I could just force upward. Then the rope began to drag me off inexorably. I clutched furiously up a few feet more; and then I felt I must let go, the drag was too strong for frozen fingers. As I had already resolved, at the last second I kicked off from the rock with all my strength. This sent me flying out on the rope, and across under the overhang, as if attached to a crazy pendulum. I could see J. crouching in the recess far below, instinctively protecting his head. The impetus jumped the upper part of the rope off its cling to the rock face of the dome above, and enabled the men to snatch in a foot or two. The return-swing brought me back, as I had half hoped, against the corner, a little higher up. I gripped it with fingers and teeth, and scrambled up another few feet. But the draw was now irresistible. I kicked off again; gained a foot or so, and spun back.

I was now up the corner proper, and I should have been by rights scrambling up the roof on the far side of my gable edge. But the rope, if nothing else, prevented any chance of my forcing myself over it and farther to the right. Another cling and scratch up the gable end, and I was not far below the level of the dome overhanging above and to my left. For the last time I fell off. This time the free length of the rope, below its hold upon the curve of the dome, was too short to allow of any return swing. So I shot out passively, to hang, revolving slowly, under the dome, with the feeling that my part was at an end. When I spun round inward, I looked up at the reddish, scarred wall freckled with snow, and at the tense rope, looking thin as a grey cobweb and disappearing frailly over the forespring of rock that arched greedily over my head. When I spun outward, I looked down – no matter how many thousand feet – to the dim, shifting lines of the glacier at the foot of the peak, hazy through the snowfall; and I could see, well inside my feet, upon the dark face of the precipice the little blanched triangle of the recess and the duller white dot of J.'s face as he crouched by the blister. It flashed across me, absurdly, that he ought to be more anxious about the effect of my gymnastics upon the fragile thread of alpine rope, his one link with hope, than about me!

I was quite comfortable in the chair; but the spinning had to be stopped. I reached out the axe at full stretch, and succeeded in touching the cliff, back under the overhang. This stopped me, face inward. I heard inarticulate shouting above, and guessed its meaning, although I was now too close under the dome to catch the words: – "They could not lift my dead weight!" I bethought me, and stretched out the axe again; got its point against a wrinkle of the wall, and pushed out. This started me swinging straight out and in below the dome. After two pokes I swung in near enough to be able to give a violent, short-armed thrust against the cliff. It carried me out far enough to jump quite a number of feet of rope clear of its cling down the rock above. The guides took advantage of the easing to haul in, and I pendulum'd back a good foot higher. The cliff facing me was now beginning to spring out in the Gothic arch of the overhang; so it could be reached more easily. I repeated the shove-out more desperately. Again they hauled in on the released rope. This time I came back close under the arch; and choosing a spot as I swung in, I lifted both feet, struck them at the wall, and gave a convulsive upward and outward spring. The rope shortened up; and as I banged back the cornice of the arch loomed very near above my head. But the free length of rope below it was now too short to let me again reach to the back of the arch with leg or axe. I hung, trying in vain to touch the lowest moulding of the cornice above with my hands. I heard gasps and grunts above quite distinctly now. The rope strained and creaked, gritting over the edge of the rock above me. I felt the tremor of the sinews heaving on it. But for all that, I did not move up. I reached up with the axe in both hands, just hooked the pick into a lucky chink of the under-moulding, and pulled, with a frantic wriggle of the whole body. It was a feeble lift, but enough for the sons of Anak above to convert into a valuable gain. The axe slipped down on to my shoulder, held there by its sling. I reached up and back with both arms, got hold of a finger-grip, and gained another inch. Infinitesimal inches they seemed, each a supreme effort, until my nose and chin scratched up against a fillet of the cornice. Then the arms gave out completely, so much at the end of their strength that they dropped lifeless. But the teeth of the upper jaw held on a broken spillikin and, with the stronger succour of the rope, supported me for the seconds while the blood was running back into my arms.

Wrestle by wrestle it went on. Every reserve of force seemed exhausted, but the impulse was now supplied by a flicker of hope. Until, at last, I felt my knee catch over a moulding on the edge, and I could sink forward for an instant's rest, with rucked clothes clinging over the rough, steep, upward but *backward* curving of the dome. It is impossible to suggest the relief of that feeling, the proof that the only solid surface which still kept me in touch with existence had ceased to thrust itself out for ever as a barrier overhead, and was actually giving back below me in semi-support.

But there was no time, or inclination, to indulge panting humanity with a rest or a realisation. I crept up a few feet, on to small, brittle, but sufficient crinkles. The dark figures of the three men above were visible now, clinging crab-like and exhausted on to similar nicks, indistinct in the snow dusk, but still human company.

The climb was still far from over. It was snowing more heavily now and there was a long wait while they got the rope down to Knubel and he struggled up, laden as he was, to join them. All were exhausted, unsure that they would find a way out but absolutely certain that they could never go back the way they had ascended.

Geoffrey's account devotes more than a page to his thoughts during the experience, the way in which his initial fears evaporated rapidly to be replaced by "the feeling of belonging to an impersonal, timeless existence".

It was late afternoon and the fight went on: "I can recall nothing but obscurity, steepness, and an endless driving of the muscles to their task. Still no message of hope reached us from above; and yet we must have left another 400 feet of rib and crack, snow-ice and equivocal holds below us. Even fancy dared not whisper to itself of the summit: the next five feet, and still the next five feet were the end of all effort and expectation."

At last the angle of the slope began to ease and suddenly Geoffrey found himself on summit ridge, close to the top. He halted there to protect Knubel's ascent, then the two of them trudged up to join the others: "We found them, relaxed in spent attitudes on the summit-slabs, swallowing sardines and snow, our first food since half past seven in the morning. It was now close upon six o'clock. Franz came across to meet me, and we shook hands. 'You will never do anything harder than that, Franz!' 'No,' he said reflectively, 'man could not do much more.'"

Then came the long descent to the valley. The three guides stopped at the hut at Randa to get some sleep. For Franz Lochmatter at least the sleep was fitful. In his obituary on him, written for the *Alpine Journal* of 1933, Geoffrey said that someone once asked him if he had slept soundly that night. "No," Lochmatter had replied, "he had waked himself up too often by falling between his bed and the wall, in trying to get the feel of something between his back and space."

Geoffrey and Ryan marched on in the darkness to reach the Monte Rosa Hotel in Zermatt some time after 3 a.m. They had been on the go for over twenty-four hours.

In his obituary of Ryan Geoffrey wrote:

The story of the Täschhorn is now known. Never can an experienced party have been more deceived by the look of a precipice from its foot. Ryan climbed throughout the long day with his usual intrepid precision and nerve. Apart from a few expressions of the ever-present and impatient urge which seemed to be driving him always upwards and on, and through him his guides, he took no part in the deliberations which took place as to our desperate line. In our worst dilemma, when Franz was starting to hazard his extraordinary ascent up the overhang, Ryan asked me what I thought were our chances of coming out of it alive. When I estimated the odds pessimistically, I remember that he remarked, in his ordinary staccato voice and manner, that the year before he would not have cared a damn which way it went, live or die, but that this year he had married, and he left it at that.

As soon as he had recovered, Geoffrey went on with Knubel to make the first ascent of the south-west face of the Dom. It was nothing like the Täschhorn experience – "sunny, straight-forward, and wholly pleasurable", in Geoffrey's words.

The route on the Täschhorn, the crux top part of it, was not repeated until 1943 when a powerful Swiss team did it and were mightily impressed. Their leader, Georges de Rham, hammered four pitons in to give them protection, and said that "even with all the resources of modern technique, pitons, clasp-rings and rubber shoes, I thought it was exceptionally severe."

Geoffrey never climbed with Ryan again, though they kept in occasional touch until 1914 when Ryan rejoined the army. He was severely injured in one hand in the war and did no further climbing. In 1921, according to Geoffrey's obituary, Ryan and his wife left Ireland because of the Troubles and never returned. She hated Ireland. Ryan hated England. So they lived in Jersey which, Geoffrey says, they both hated. Ryan died in 1947.

He had never been a member of the Alpine Club. He was up for election once but was black-balled "on the grounds of incivility in the Alps to some older members", in the words of Tom Longstaff.

Geoffrey, however, was a member and an increasingly active one. In January 1906 he had read a paper to the Club about his Weisshorn climb the season before. He was writing articles and book reviews for the *Alpine Journal*. And in his own private Journal, on his return to England from the 1906 season, he wrote: "Met many friends and began conspiracy to resocialise the Alpine Club, with Schuster, Wollaston, Mayor, Ellis etc." The next entry, dated "Autumn", speaks of a conspirators' dinner and a visit to Cecil Slingsby in Yorkshire: ". . . got him to propose Davidson as Vice-President for A.C."

Geofrey enjoyed politicking. He was by no means a compulsive trouble-maker, but he was prepared to pitch in when he thought reform was needed. He took pleasure in bringing his powers of persuasion to bear to win others round to his point of view. He and some like-minded members of the Alpine Club now formed an informal pressure-group which Geoffrey, in his Journal, calls the "IDC". It is not known what the initials stood for – possibly the Independents' Dining Club – but the group's objective was simply to let some fresh air into the musty corridors of the Club.

It was an overdue cause. As the world's senior mountaineering society, the Alpine Club still carried great prestige but by the opening years of the twentieth century it had become little more than a cosy sort of social club for aging Alpinists, a place where they could meet and reminisce and agree with each other's prejudices. There were enlightened Alpine men from earlier generations – men like Norman Collie and Cecil Slingsby – who took the broader view, but the majority of them had settled into the conviction that the only proper way to climb was the way they had done it in the Alps thirty or forty years before. They disapproved of climbing without professional guides. They were not particularly concerned with mountaineering in other great ranges, the Caucasus, the Rockies, the Himalayas. They dismissed the new breed of rock climbers in Cumberland and Snowdonia as "gymnasts" and "chimney sweeps". Some of them even held that everything worthwhile in the Alps had already been done and, in the words of the late David Cox in his article about Geoffrey in *Mountain* magazine in January – February 1976, "anything new could only be an inferior route or stunt variation."

In that article David Cox went on to say that Geoffrey had been a member, and a proud member of the Alpine Club since 1900. At first, he did not challenge the old-fashioned spirit of the place:

> Fairly soon, however, he began to work for practical reforms of a kind with which other clubs have later become familiar – increasing the proportion of elected to official members of the committee, tightening of the mountaineering qualifications for membership, modernising the standards and outlooks of the *Alpine Journal* (a much-needed step) . . . At the same time, his own climbs year after year were showing how antiquated some of the approved canons had become. He did not directly challenge these, but simply climbed in the way he enjoyed – which opened up new vistas to anyone who wanted to see them, as just a few of his contemporaries did.

Geoffrey persuaded some influential men to join the IDC: A. E. W. Mason, already a successful novelist as well as a keen mountaineer; John Buchan; Leo Amery, the Conservative politician; Maynard Keynes; and Percy Farrar who was soon to become editor of the *Alpine Journal*.

Early in 1907 Geoffrey just missed, by a single vote, getting himself elected on to the Club committee. He noted in his Journal: "The IDC dinners very successful; 'killed by success,' Schuster says. It is interesting to have a corner all to one's self where one counts just for what one *is* and social distinctions all disappear. A delightful set of men, these climbers, and now I have my foot on that Olympus, it makes a pleasant sidelight on life."

8

The Pen-y-Pass Parties

GEOFFREY'S RECORD IN THE ALPS gave him every right to be a member of the Alpine Club, but there was never any danger that he would be one of those who looked down on the emergent sport of rock climbing on British crags. His first mountain scrambling had been in Snowdonia; his first roped climbing in the Lake District; he had climbed in Scotland and Ireland. If his most impressive new routes were in the Alps, it is also arguable that this most telling contribution to mountaineering was in Britain and can be summed up in one phrase, the Pen-y-Pass parties.

He had been to the hotel at the top of the pass at least twice before, but the tradition of an annual gathering of friends there began at Easter 1907. His Journal tells the story:

> Arranged for a large party at Pen-y-Pass and Pen-y-Gwryd, and crossed England from Gainsborough in the car . . . Haddon, seen at sunset and in isolation, one of the most beautiful and appealing places I have ever seen. Next day to Stockport. Here I picked up Marcus Heywood, and then to Chester, Mold and Flint. Then in a lilac and gold sunset all along the coast road of North Wales to Carnarvon in the dark. A really poetically beautiful run that stirred even Marcus! He writes of this weekend as the pleasantest of his life. At Carnarvon met H. V. Reade, and next day up to Pen-y-Pass. Took Marcus up Lliwedd etc., then made two new ascents on the E. Buttress with H.V.R. and Andrews. Perfectly gorgeous weather, and never a cloud for weeks! Later the crowd came . . . My car joined up the two hotels and all made me welcome. Climbed the great Craig-yr-Ysfa Gully and led my rope. Also the Slanting Gully, the Horned Crag Route, Cyrn Las, and thoroughly explored the E. Buttress. Had a search party round to Ogwen in the dark for three incompetents. A glorious time.

The names Geoffrey mentions amount to a virtual catalogue of the pioneers of Snowdonia climbing. Some of them, with J. M. Archer Thomson at the head, were of the first generation, finding ways up the cliffs in the 1890s. Others, like Marcus Heywood and Page Dickinson (a cousin of Geoffrey's), were the vanguard of the new generation that Geoffrey was to bring into the sport in the next few years, until the outbreak of the First World War brought the parties to a temporary halt.

The hotel at Pen-y-Pass was a mile up the road from that at Pen-y-Gwryd, which had been the centre for the first explorers of Snowdonia. Pen-y-Pass was closer to the crags, especially Lliwedd, the favourite cliff in those days. It also had young and hospitable proprietors, the Rawson Owens. Rawson Owen had been a professional soldier, a Hussar with active service in the Boer War. He loved to reminisce about his days on campaign and to show off his horsemanship by his handling of "the smartest pair and brake in Wales". Mrs Owen was an excellent cook and organiser, inclined to drink rather too much at times. Geoffrey loved them both, and was particularly fond of telling a story against himself. Arriving at the hotel on one occasion, he told Rawson Owen to bring in his luggage from the brake. Owen had had a long wait at the railway station and a long drive back in the rain and was not in the best of tempers. He replied: "I'm the proprietor, not the bloody boots. Bring in your own damn luggage!"

The first party was, it seems, entirely male, but as the years went by Geoffrey saw to it that wives and girlfriends and children were welcomed. Soon they filled the hotel and its adjoining shacks and cottages – about fifty people altogether – out all day walking or climbing, assembling after dinner to talk and sing and enjoy impromptu entertainments, and for contests of strength and gymnastic ability. "With our coming together in that high air," Geoffrey wrote, in a chapter of Carr and Lister's *The Mountains of Snowdonia*, "all cares seemed to drop from us, like clouds sinking below us on that two-way view down the pass. A tradition of our best selves, of our best performances clothed each of us again, and the happy mantle seemed to fall as lightly and immediately upon all newcomers, with very few exceptions through the years."

Nearly fifty years later, writing about the early days at Pen-y-Pass in the opening chapter of *Mountains with a Difference*, Geoffrey gave full rein to his romantic, rhapsodical style:

Climbing then had the freshness of a dawn. Nobody was on the hills but the few farmers and herds and ourselves. Outside the initiate circle, no one bothered about us. The cliffs lay round us unvisited, with their

mystery of "climbs". For those first years we sped over fells and hills
alone or with the few, realising the glory of untrodden height and of the
movement and effort its steepness demanded. I came down at evening
generally with reluctance, because rest and reaction, sensations delightful
in proportion to the greatness of the effort which leads on to them, were
even better enjoyed among the heights themselves.

At the beginning of that chapter he described the special thrill of
making a new route:

On the first of the new rock climbs which I made in North Wales, a climb
up a square-cut chimney at the southern end of the Glyder Vach precipice,
I looked down the grey falls of scree on to the wide green Nant Francon
valley with its thin ribbon of winding road, and I thrilled suddenly with
a new feeling. For hundreds and thousands of years, high and close above
the passing and repassing of countless generations, this upright corner of
beautiful and solid England – or rather Wales – had been waiting unvisited,
untrodden, even unseen, until during the few days of my own short life,
the climbing enthusiasm had broken over us, and had set me, miraculously,
upon it. Here upon this ledge since earth took form out of chaos no one
before me had set foot. On that glister of crystal quartz under my hand no
eye before mine had ever rested. I tingled as I stood to the very boot-nails.
And an enchantment as secret and enthralling as first love seemed opening
behind and within all the unvisited cliffs and mountain walls in my sight.

The Pen-y-Pass parties were Geoffrey's creation, a practical expression of his urge to enthuse others and bring them into his "initiate
circle" of mountain lovers. He was the presiding spirit. He issued
the invitations and organised the daily expeditions, making sure
everyone had a rewarding time and no one was left out. His rule
was tolerant and benevolent; his manner of control was quiet and
considerate. Only two things upset him seriously: coarse behaviour
in company, and reckless conduct on the crags and mountains.
Although his disapproval was rarely roused, there was no mistaking
it when it happened. He once watched the young George Mallory
leading a party up a rock climb and was horrified to see him taking
quite unnecessary risks. The public ticking-off he delivered when
Mallory returned to ground level went into legend.

Geoffrey had many favourite stories from the early days at
Pen-y-Pass. He loved to tell how his Cambridge friend C. K.
Clague, a devotee of the stories of Lewis Carroll, once fell fifty
feet, was safely caught by the rope, and immediately quoted the Red
King: "I advise you fellows to come down the regular way and not

by the volcano!" He often quoted Claude Elliott's advice to a woman climber struggling on the Teryn Slab: "Better not put more than *one* foot on the same hold as your two hands." And he appreciated the speed of thought of the Oxford classicist A. D. Godley, who fell a few feet into the bed of a gully and said as he landed: "If I had been quicker I should have said I was going to jump."

It was during the Easter 1907 gathering that the Pen-y-Pass book was started, a large stout notebook. Any new routes made on the crags were briefly recorded, with an account of the problems to be overcome. The book also contains many pages of snap-shots of the party-goers, with captions by Geoffrey. On the front page he gave the chief dates: his first visit to Pen-y-Pass in 1901; the next, with friends, in 1903; the formal start of the parties proper in 1907; their resumption in 1919 after a four-year break during the First World War; their second resumption in 1946 after the interruption of the Second World War; the last, farewell gathering in 1947. A note below, in Geoffrey's hand, says: "I started this book about 1907, at Mrs H. V. Reade's request. It travelled every year to Pen-y-Pass, sometimes twice; and lay on the smoking-room table during the party. Some 600 persons in all attended the parties."

Early in 1907 Geoffrey was voted on to the committee of the Climbers' Club, the club for Snowdonia climbers, and immediately he was in action. His Journal notes: "Made a brilliant (!) speech at their dinner, with Charles Trevelyan and Francis Acland as my guests, who also spoke. Helped to settle the Eckenstein-Abraham climbing row over the Abrahams' North Wales book." Oscar Eckenstein was an impressive but odd man, one of the very few who could get along with "the great beast", Aleisteir Crowley. A railway engineer by profession, he was a veteran climber with an original and inventive mind, a pioneer exponent of balance climbing and a pioneer, too, of the use of crampons on snow and ice. Like many of the Snowdonia men, he hated publicity, believing that their sport should remain private and exclusive. The Abraham brothers of Keswick, George and Ashley, had grown up in a very different tradition. They were professional photographers and took the view of their Lake District mentor, O. G. Jones, that climbing was such fun that everybody should be told about it and encouraged to have a go. In 1906 the brothers published a book *Rock Climbing in North Wales*, crammed with accounts of adventures on the cliffs of Snowdonia and illustrated by their superb photographs. This would have been enough to upset Eckenstein but, compounding the offence, one passage in the book, about an early attempt on the Devil's Kitchen, vividly described his assault on the crux wall and "precipitate retreat". An incensed Eckenstein introduced a resolution at the Club's annual meeting, the exact terms of which have not been recorded. The tenor, however, is obvious. Ashley Abraham stood up to plead that he and his brother had intended no personal offence. Eckenstein was finally persuaded to withdraw his resolution. Geoffrey was one of those who poured oil on the stormy tea-cup waters. Such prickly sensitivity is, alas, not uncommon in the story of mountaineering. It is a measure of Geoffrey's amiability that he contrived to establish, and retain, the friendship of both parties to the dispute.

His schools inspection work was based in Lincolnshire at this time and he was enjoying it: "Hard work. All the Lincoln schools fully inspected. Pleasant colleagues. Beginning to find my métier as general flint for other men's ideas to strike on." He was also enjoying his new car, a Swift, and the freedom of movement it gave him. At Whitsun he drove to the Lake District for the Seatoller man-hunt on the fells, where he was joined by a group of nearly twenty including the Trevelyans and Herbert Samuel, later leader of the Liberal Party. He wrote in the Journal: "Good weather and very fine hunting. Went hare second day and was chased from Haystacks over Kirk Fell and in the evening all over Greystones. Took the car over the Honister! Jolly talk with G.M.T." George Trevelyan had married by this time – a daughter of the novelist Mrs Humphry Ward – and they were about to have their first child, a girl they called Mary. There is no hint that Geoffrey was thinking of marriage, though there is a cryptic line in the Journal for that summer: "Met the Shuttleworths at dances – why – *oh why?* – ever?" A few weeks later, at yet another dance, he noted: "Young Shuttleworth touchingly affectionate". This was Rachel Kaye Shuttleworth, the daughter of a Liberal peer. At Formosa once Geoffrey was so swept away by the summer heat and the music that he proposed to her and felt an instant terror that she might say yes. Luckily she did not. "I never forgot the lesson," he wrote later, "and never again let myself be carried away by circumstance and atmosphere."

Geoffrey was back in the Alps in the summer of 1907, this time with C. D. Robertson. The weather was generally poor but they managed some long, fast routes including the Midi-Plan traverse in fourteen and three-quarter hours, and some new routes too – a ridge on the Aiguille du Midi, and new ways up the Rimpfischhorn and the Zinal Rothorn. He noted in the Journal: "Going very strong and no signs of age yet! Find that in pace and last I can out-go all but (perhaps) two guides and all amateurs. Go better at end of long day than beginning. Took no unnecessary risks and met and made many friends. It is amusing to find oneself the mythical hero of a district, and to have an arête actually named after one! – on the Weisshorn, my favourite peak!" The ridge is still known as the Young-grat.

Josef Knubel was with them when they gained the Weisshorn hut at 7.30 p.m. to find it empty except for two young Swiss, who said they had failed to reach the summit that day and now planned a few hours' sleep and a return to the valley. Geoffrey's amazement when he heard this – he could not believe that anyone would give up when the Weisshorn summit lay so close – was later made famous by Robertson in a paper he read to the Alpine Club, which he called *Alpine Humour*. The only possible explanation Geoffrey could think of was that the two Swiss had run out of food, so he offered them half of his party's supplies. That was not the problem, they said, they were worried about the north wind. Geoffrey pointed out that the wind had subsided. In any case, they said, they did not want to cut steps. "We'll go first," Geoffrey said, "and you can follow in our steps." Finally they came clean; they were tired and did not want to bother. Geoffrey, completely baffled, admitted defeat at last.

In the autumn of 1907 Geoffrey was elected to the committee of the Alpine Club, top of the poll. He noted: "Poor things! they'll get gunpowdered a bit now, quite half a dozen plots ready for them. Started my scheme at Climbers' Club for combining English Club Journals and producing local 'Guides' to stop these terrible accidents." Rock climbing was growing more popular in Britain and there had been several fatal accidents in Wales and the Lake District. Geoffrey believed that the time had come to produce guidebooks to the different climbing areas, describing the established routes and indicating the degree of difficulty and danger involved in attempting them. In this way, newcomers to the sport would at least stand warned. He also thought the annual journals published by the various clubs should put more emphasis on security, explaining the correct ways to use the rope.

Geoffrey, as usual, was the arranger of the Christmas party that gathered at Wasdale Head and included Vincent Baddeley and Francis Acland, Cecil Slingsby and his fourteen-year-old son Laurence who was beginning his climbing career, Donald Robertson and many others. They did a lot of the classic routes and spent Christmas Day on Pillar Rock with champagne. Geoffrey met and made friends with some of the leading men of the Cumbrian climbing fraternity. He wrote in the Journal:

A grand party. Much singing and ragging and some talk: all write of "the happiest days" they have ever spent. On Xmas night the valley children gave us *Beauty and the Beast* in soft Cumbrian dialect. On New Year's Eve we had speeches and more songs. The car in great request . . . What views we had this year in the Lakes. Gorgeous sunsets of ochre and amethyst setting behind the blue-tinted front of the rocks, with darkness catching at our heels in the long ice gullies, and the lakes deep blue with all the distant hills . . . Called on the dear old parson and went to one evening service in the wee kirk; a large congregation of some 30! . . . If only Hilt had been with us! Read no papers – a real rest altogether.

Hilton had suffered a nervous breakdown earlier in the year, largely from over-work in his brother's view. He had also given up the bar for journalism and was an assistant editor on *The Economist*.

In the same passage of the Journal Geoffrey paused to take a longer look at the point his own life had reached: "Only 31, and most of the pleasures and reputation which my chosen lines of life can bring are already there! Well, I enjoyed more the early years of romance and effort, when no one knew one, and it all seemed a remote kingdom of coloured romance."

Early in 1908 Geoffrey found himself at an author's dinner, sitting opposite Winston Churchill: ". . . an unhappy man, I should say" was his Journal comment. Geoffrey was there as a guest of Donald Robertson, who was now at the Treasury and had also become secretary of the Authors' Club. In a typewritten account of the evening, written nearly forty years on by which time Churchill had made himself a legendary figure, Geoffrey made no mention of this apparent unhappiness:

He talked restlessly and cleverly, and it was the first I heard of his queer, unmistakable diction, with the "s" always sounded high in the palate, as if it were a half guttural. Not quite a lisp, but a "ch" sound in it. I also heard Antony Hope inviting him down to his bachelor house in the Isle of Wight, and describing their games there, and bathing, and some rag devised by A. E. W. Mason . . . and Winston accepting appreciatively. Then he got up to make a speech; and, addressing a literary audience perhaps for the first time, made a brilliant proposal for creating an Academy of Literature . . . Next, up got the long white-bearded Sir—, and proclaimed that such an academy had already existed for some years and that he himself was the president. Winston took it magnificently. He threw up his hand, like a fencer saluting a "hit", and in an audible aside wailed "Spare the unhappy son of a distinguished father!" I liked him, while I envied him.

A few weeks after this dinner Churchill became President of the Board of Trade in Mr Asquith's Liberal government.

Easter 1908 brought another Pen-y-Pass party, arranged by Geoffrey. The company included H. V. Reade, a senior civil servant, and his formidably charming wife who took over the running of the social side of things; Captain J. P. Farrar DSO, a man with an impressive Alpine record who was making his first acquaintance with British rocks and was impressed; an Irish contingent led by Geoffrey's cousin Page Dickinson; and Marcus Heywood. In his Journal Geoffrey lists those attending and concludes with the words: ". . . and above all Marcus Heywood, who promises to be a splendid man, and incidentally a fine climber. One of my real successes in boys, has taken to work, on fortune's changing, like a young hero, and is doing right well." Many Snowdonia regulars were there, including Archer Thomson and A. W. Andrews, and there was much hard climbing, including "a tremendous new climb on the Crib Goch Buttress arête".

There is an open, pre-lapsarian innocence in the way Geoffrey described it all in his Journal:

> . . . a lot of good talk and good going. We had the hut outside, four of us, and had a great time – much cold wind and water . . . Climbing well, but found I could easily overdo it . . . Such a really pleasant holiday, with so much youth, affection, good talk and sensation, that it is almost like getting back to school! – at my age! Somehow one feels that these good times and youthful "rags" must get rarer, and my "boys" are getting older – thank goodness they are not too old yet for good jokes and wild pillow fights. And the hills as lovely and varied as ever . . .

A few lines further on in the Journal Geoffrey wrote: "Life does not feel as if it is 'meant' for long. I should hate to be left alone or old. It must just go for all it can, while it lasts. It's all worth it; every child that laughs and every flower or rock that looks at one and is seen, if only once."

Geoffrey was at the Seatoller man-hunt on the fells at Whitsun: "The Lake Hunt delightful. More convivial than usual . . . The 10th anniversary of our old joke! Samuel [Herbert Samuel] read a delightful 'prophecy' paper on '40 years on', and I gave a song-poem with a 'What's that? What's that? Tally-ho!' chorus. Good weather and long hunts. George [Trevelyan] hunted me for three hours, and I got away; pleasant not to be too old yet."

The old Trinity friendship had been kept fresh by their annual meetings at the man-hunt and through Trevelyan's assiduous and affectionate correspondence. In 1903, writing to thank Geoffrey for his congratulations on his becoming engaged, Trevelyan said: "We are not lost to each other, Geoff." Two years later, on hearing of Geoffrey's sacking from Eton, he wrote: "Bitterly do I regret that I know no living Etonian on whom to disgorge my fury. It's not sympathy but knocking someone down that is needed to relieve my feelings . . ."

Early in 1908 Geoffrey wrote in his Journal: "The verse-making power has revived, and there has been a large output of lyrics: some I think very fair, but the vein is thin, and does not work easily for long." Despite his reservations, he now had enough poems to consider the publication of a slim volume. He showed them to brother Hilton who was encouraging. At the Seatoller meeting he showed them to George Trevelyan who was more than encouraging. At the end of June Trevelyan wrote to Geoffrey, praising his poems in general and describing one of them "The Wind" as "a great poem . . . the first which has ever sung the mountains from the climber's or modern point of view in a strain worthy of such a theme". And he added: "Please go on taking yourself seriously and work at the great gift you have, the noblest gift of man and the rarest."

Trevelyan must have taken a copy of the verses away with him, because he wrote again, on July 30, with his detailed and thoughtful comments. The letter was written at Robin Ghyll, Trevelyan's holiday cottage in the Great Langdale valley:

> I have given very careful attention to your poems during the last ten days holiday . . . My belief that "The Wind" is a great poem is stronger than ever. My belief that you may become a great poet is with me as before. But I also think you have got to round two or three important corners before you get there. I will tell you what I personally think these corners are: 1. Want of compression. 2. Want of contrast. 3. Obscurity.

It is perceptive criticism. He goes on to analyse "The Wind" and two other poems, "The Quest" and "Morning", in more detail. But the letter ends on a heartening note: "Now mind you, I see the real essence of poetry in lots and lots of lines in these poems that I criticise thus. If I did not I would not be at the trouble to criticise them, but would simply say 'Go and be a minor poet if it amuses your leisure'. But you have hit the real sound as none of these minor poets do . . ."

"G.M.T most helpful about the verses," Geoffrey noted, and set about revising them along the lines suggested.

He did not go to the Alps in the summer of 1908. On a visit to the Fens, he had contrived to contract malaria, and was still recovering from it when the holidays came. So it was arranged that he should go to stay with his brother Georis who was attached to the British Embassy in Washington. He crossed the Atlantic in a ship of the White Star line, with one of the Formosa valets to look after him, and recuperated in the handsome house on the coast of Massachusetts that Georis and his wife Helen had taken. Geoffrey spent long hours sunbathing and swimming, revising his poems, and building sand models of the Matterhorn and the Weisshorn. He rode a lot in the woods, often with Georis and sometimes with a beautiful young American called Martha Phillips. According to autobiographical notes he wrote many years later, Geoffrey suspected that Martha was in love with Georis at the time and that he was used to try to distract her from the embarrassing infatuation. If that was the plan, it did not work. Martha was well-connected and rich, charming and excellent company, but no relationship developed. In his Journal, back in England, Geoffrey said: "Cornford and others marrying – and I? They tried hard to bring it off in America, but the old impossibility always there."

He visited Boston and New York and Washington, where he was invited to the White House and had a ten-minute chat with President Theodore Roosevelt who was fond of talking to mountain men. Five years earlier he had camped in the Yosemite Valley, California, with John Muir, the prophet of wilderness conservation, and become enthused with the idea of protected national parks. Presumably Georis had set up the invitation by letting the White House know that his brother was a leading Alpinist.

Geoffrey gave an account of his meeting with the president in one of his unpublished papers, written long afterwards:

Short, sturdy, spectacled, tough, brusque . . . he seized my hand and started at once on his own feats in the White Mountains . . . He urged me to explore the White Mountains etc. and then went off on his latest hobby, the reformed spelling of English! – tragic, because I couldn't get him off it again, and I disliked the idea and knew it was impracticable over here at least . . . He was very like Marcia's Teddy Bear.

The great event of the holiday for Geoffrey, though, was the arrival of his first nephew. In the *Journal* he wrote:

Never was such a perfectly idle holiday, nothing but rest and enjoyment. Helen a perfect sister . . . Got infinite impressions and fun. And above all, the baby! That perfect moonlit evening together, then the mad hunt in the dark for the black, bolted pony, consulting of constables – final rush in a cold raw dawn on a wheezy motor to Beverley to fetch the nurse! And then the unspeakable joy and relief. Glorious.

It was a son, who was christened George Peregrine but known throughout his life as "Gerry" to distinguish him from all the other Georges. He became the fifth baronet when Georis died in 1952.

Back home again there is little mention of work in the Journal, whose entries deal with family affairs – Hilton was fully recovered and their father was off to America – and politicking in the climbing world. Geoffrey's campaign now was for climbers' guidebooks to the various crags and areas: "My plan for local guides, to check these accidents by information, adopted at the Climbers' Club, and the first to appear on Lliwedd shortly."

This was an important development in home climbing, predominantly the work of Geoffrey and carried out in the face of considerable opposition. There were already some pocket-sized climbers' guidebooks for some Alpine regions, but there was nothing of the kind for the British crags. Many of the old guard, men like Eckenstein, held that such publications would remove the uncertainties and delights of exploration. They would do everything for the climber, except the climbing itself.

Until this time it had been the custom, in the Lake District and Snowdonia, for the creators of a new route to write a descriptive paragraph or two in the hotel book, saying where it was to be found and where it went, what the special difficulties and dangers were. In addition, the annual journals of the clubs had started to give brief accounts of new routes made in the past year. Geoffrey was now convinced that something more comprehensive was needed, available to the general public and small enough to slip into the back pocket of the climbing breeches. He worked hard to convince his

fellow committee members of the Climbers' Club, then to persuade
the leading Snowdonia pioneer, Archer Thomson, to write the first
volume.

In a note he wrote many years later, opposite the title page in
his copy of *The Climbs on Lliwedd*, Geoffrey said: "This was the
first 'guide' of the pocket-type produced. We were opposed to the
idea of guides. But when the Abrahams began to issue their books
large and small, with much inaccurate description, we recognised
that we must give in. With difficulty I persuaded J.M.A.T. *He* only
gave in from irritation at the Abrahams claiming as 'first ascents'
many climbs he'd done!"

Archer Thomson had studied classics at Cambridge and by this
time had become headmaster of Llandudno County School, which
gave him ready weekend access to his favourite cliffs, those of
Lliwedd. He was a very reserved and introverted man, capable of
day-long silences, but a fine natural climber and a writer with a nice
line in spare, dry, academic wit. Geoffrey, perhaps characteristically,
saw him as a crypto-romantic. In a chapter he wrote in the early 1920s
for *The Mountains of Snowdonia*, describing the first twenty years of
Pen-y-Pass, Geoffrey had this to say about Archer Thomson:

> The Welsh hills are haunted by the thought of J.M.A.T., still in later
> middle life unsurpassed in the precision and grace of his methods, as we
> used to see him, poised on one foot on a Lliwedd slab, his statuesque
> head with its toss of grey curls thrown back, gazing intently upward
> for the next movement, or crouching solitary on some tiny bracket in
> space, smoking contemplatively. Always taciturn and mysterious, he
> regarded his relations with the hills, and with what they yielded him of
> success, as a romantic trust . . . It marked an epoch in mountaineering – a
> turning-point I always look back upon with personal satisfaction – when
> he at last consented to bring out the Lliwedd and Ogwen guidebooks (the
> first of them in conjunction with Andrews), the earliest venture of their
> kind; and when he agreed to adopt a form of description and graduation
> which became the model for our first textbooks.

Geoffrey worked hard on the Archer Thomson script, checking
for accuracy and correcting the proofs. He wrote a brief preface,
saying:

> The guides are in no way intended to compete with the many delightful
> volumes which have made literature of the climbing in this region. It is
> hoped, however, that a small portable guide, which can be consulted on

the spot, and which will tell the newcomer what he is in for before he starts a climb, and where he is and what he may expect at any point on his climb, may do something to avert in our own country the calamitous flood of catastrophe which in some neighbouring lands year by year more fatally pursues the achievements of ignorance and thoughtless enterprise.

Geoffrey was anxious, though, that the guidebooks should not be too detailed. They would indicate the location and line of a route, but it would be left to the climber on the spot to discover and to solve the problems. In this way, the spirit of individual exploration would be sustained.

The Lliwedd book came out in 1909, and was soon followed by Thomson's guide to the Ogwen District, then Tryfan. The little books were an immediate success. The club for Lake District climbers, the Fell and Rock, did not get round to producing guidebooks to its own crags until 1922. Since then, however, every climbing area in Britain has followed the Snowdonia example, generally along the lines laid down by Geoffrey, and new, updated editions appear regularly to keep pace with new discoveries and developments.

History, then, has entirely vindicated Geoffrey's persistence, though in one respect his wishes did not prevail. He was against the idea of categorising climbs according to their degree of difficulty. O. G. Jones, in his book *Rock Climbing in the English Lake District*, had listed the routes and divided them into four grades: Easy, Moderate, Difficult and Exceptionally Severe. The Abrahams, in their books, had done the same. Geoffrey wrote:

> I held and still hold that such lists are pernicious. They can rarely be true for more than a single climber; they reverse the natural mountaineering order in which climbs should be sought out and attempted; and they set a premium upon "stunting" and competitive climbing . . . such a list induces ambitious young climbers from the first to neglect the natural and sculptural lines up cliffs, the ridges and great gullies and rifts first seen and historically first climbed, in favour of sensational or arbitrary variants.

The earliest guidebooks deferred to Geoffrey's feelings but later editions, and all subsequent guides, have given the grades of every route listed. There are today something like twenty categories of difficulty, with another range of technical grades to categorise each part of each climb.

For the Christmas holiday at the end of 1908 Geoffrey was back at Wasdale Head with an even larger party that the year before. The regulars were all there – Donald Robertson and Page Dickinson, George and Charles Trevelyan, many climbing friends. But there were new faces too: Leonard Huxley (a school teacher who had switched to publishing) brought his two eldest sons, Trevenen and Julian, both at Oxford; Cecil Slingsby was there again with his son Laurence and two Norwegian mountaineers, Schelderup and Rubenson; and, most surprising of all, the eccentric Horace de Vere Cole, author of the great "Dreadnought Hoax", when he and fellow-Bloomsburyites, disguised as the Sultan of Zanzibar and his retinue, got themselves shown round the Royal Navy's top-secret battleship.

In his Journal Geoffrey wrote:

> The usual clear and good climbing up to Xmas Day, then fierce frost. Xmas Day gorgeous; 7 of us lunched in sun on the Scafell Pinnacle . . . Not climbing well myself: evidently not really back in form yet. Donald first class. The local children gave us Dick Whittington this year, and 4 of us sang a quartet. The next night Page and I wrote one of our operatic extravaganzas and acted it. Many witty songs . . . Page and I in good gagging form. Seldom heard such laughter. Should have beaten them all in Billiards Fives Tournament but for foul play (!).

This was a violent game the Lakeland climbers had invented, with two players in each team, stationed at one end of the billiard table and trying to project a ball into one of the pockets at the other end. Geoffrey and Cecil Slingsby reached the final, where they were beaten by George and Ashley Abraham.

At the beginning of 1909 all was going well for Geoffrey and his brothers. Georis got a story published in the *Cornhill* magazine. Hilton was working at *The Economist* and campaigning hard for free trade. Geoffrey continued working as a schools inspector, had his poem "Wind" published in the *Contemporary Review*, was elected to the Austrian and Italian Alpine Clubs, and contrived to get his friend J. P. Farrar appointed assistant editor on the *Alpine Journal*. The Liwedd guidebook came out and was well-received generally. Then on a trip to Cambridge for the Charles Lamb dinner he met two outstanding undergraduates – "George Mallory, beautiful and a brilliant climber, Rupert Brooke the 'poet'". Both were to become national heroes, in completely different ways.

Geoffrey met Mallory at the dinner and took to him immediately. Mallory was twenty-two and reading English at Magdalene College, a very handsome, well-mannered, serious-minded man who had climbed in North Wales, the Lake District and the Alps. A day or two later, in Mallory's rooms, Geoffrey was introduced to Rupert Brooke. In an unpublished note, written many years later, he contrasted the two young men:

> In looks and height and grace, Brooke was far less striking than Mallory, with his six feet of deer-like power concordant with the perfect oval of his face, the classic profile and long, oval, violet eyes. But the difference of the extent to which they used their advantages was conspicuous: Mallory seemed to do everything to prevent himself having to owe anything to externals. But Rupert gave the sense of someone using every charm and advantage to its full and honest limits to enhance his personality and its effect, under a surface of aloof unawareness.

Geoffrey was more than ten years older than Brooke and much more experienced in the ways of the world. Though he was impressed by the younger man's ebullience and gaiety, he was almost shocked by his calculating attitude:

> We had a lively talk. He was full of a visit he had just paid to London, to two well-known magazine editors, to whom he had been, he boasted charmingly, offering lyrics. I was amazed at his courage and sophistication.
> "Did they take any?" – this was in Mallory's gravely beautiful tenor voice, with a little mockery in it.
> "Yes, two – perhaps more later" – Rupert, gratified and serious.
> "Which? Have you read me them?"
> "No" – Rupert radiated a satisfied charm from his deep chair. "I haven't written them yet. I shall have to begin thinking about it . . ."
> It took my breath away, and I laughed out. Somehow, to be "placing" one's poems, which were to me a secretion of inner being which it took years before I could bring myself to give away to the public, in this frank and brazenly commercial way didn't belong to my world.

Geoffrey invited Mallory to join his Pen-y-Pass gathering that Easter. They arrived there before the others: "Alone with him for a week; had the shanty. At first bitter blizzard, and driven off Parson's Nose. Then perfect weather. Explored Craig-yr-Ysfa, 3 new climbs, bathing each time on way back. Then did his 'Slab' climb on East Buttress. The hardest rocks I have done." This was the route on

Lliwedd that Mallory was said to have first done the year before, taking a short cut because darkness was falling and he had left his pipe on the ledge above.

Then the usual party-goers arrived and there was more climbing: "Did Route One (variation), led up Slanting Gully (at last!), Central Chimney, part of Avalanche Route, West Buttress with Farrar and Sparrow – bathed in Llydaw three times. Climbed well but Mallory is a better man, wonderfully supple. Sang in the evenings, hot baths before fire in shanty, all very jolly."

In the closing days of the holiday he severely strained an abdominal muscle and made the injury worse by trying to disregard it. The doctors ordered him to spend three weeks in bed. He was staying, when in London, at Hilton's house at 22, Launceston Place, Kensington, and it was filled with friends of all kinds, bearing gifts and condolences. In the quiet periods he read Milton and Shakespeare. The moment he had recovered he went to Cambridge to see George Mallory and there met Geoffrey Keynes, Maynard's younger brother, who was to become a celebrated surgeon as well as a great bibliophile and protagonist of the long-neglected poet William Blake.

Life for Geoffrey was full and sweet, but he now got a sharp reminder that his old enemies – never named even in his private Journal – were still at his heels: "Hear I am to be opposed at the Savile Club. How these devils pursue with their filthy minds. It gives a physical pain round the heart, I find now, to feel that there is *anyone* attacking one in hate like this! Strange to feel oneself really loved by a large social world of two or three sets, and then come upon this hideous travesty of oneself in another."

A few lines further on in the Journal he reflects: "Is this really middle age? these muscles and health rather giving out? Or is it, as they all say, that 'you live too fast'. Sparrow called it 'overburning vitality'! Well, only active participation, change of place and interests, mental stimulus and new and old friends kept in touch, can keep off the greyness and aimlessness of it all: but these notes are *not* for meditations. Drive on!"

The book of poems was published, by Smith Elder, that summer: "Summer Vac. *Wind and Hill* appeared! Father did proofs. Great success. Splendid letters from John Bailey, Herbert Fisher, G.M.T. and the rest; also Desmond MacCarthy. *All* reviews good, even *The Times* and *Contemporary*."

It was a slim volume, twenty-eight poems in all, most of them in free verse, none of them very long. He dedicated it to his mother with this tribute:

> To Mountains, that have given me
> a kingdom of reality
> more rich than childhood's fairy trove,
> this be the token of my love;
>
> to icy steep and bracken slope,
> to every queenly height of hope,
> but chiefly to that most dear one
> was named 'Dame Alys' – by her son.

Geoffrey had, undoubtedly, been revising the poems in the light of George Trevelyan's criticism, but the faults Trevelyan indicated are still detectable, especially the unvaried elevated tone. They are clearly from the heart, emotion recollected in tranquillity, speaking of Geoffrey's great relish for life in many of its aspects – his love of nature and hard exertion, of cold water and plunging into it, comradeship and friendship, his love for children, above all his love for mountains and climbing them.

One of the poems "Mountain Playmates" opens with the declaration:

> Fire made them, earth clothed them, man found them,
> our playmates, the princes of hills . . .

Again and again he returns to the mountain theme, crafting variations on what is virtually the same message, very reminiscent of the message that Wordsworth proclaimed in so much of his poetry – the calming, consoling, healing powers of close communion with nature, of high endeavour in high places. Perhaps the best example, certainly the poem that is best-remembered now, is "A Hill". These are its first and final verses:

> Only a hill: earth set a little higher
>   above the face of earth: a larger view
> of little fields and roads: a little nigher
>   to clouds and silence: what is that to you?
> Only a hill; but all of life to me,
> up there, between the sunset and the sea . . .

Only a hill: yes, looked at from below:
   facing the usual sea, the frequent west.
Tighten the muscle, feel the strong blood flow,
   and set your foot upon the utmost crest!
There, where the realms of thought and effort cease,
wakes on your heart a world of dreams, and peace.

9

The Death of Friends: 1909–12

IN THE SUMMER OF 1909 Geoffrey was back in the Alps:

Off to Alps, taking and paying for Mallory, to get him back there. Donald joined a few days later, fagged from his Royal Commission on Proportional Representation. First to old Bel Alp: Closeny good as ever, great welcome, grand bathing. Climbed new S. Ridge of Unterbächhorn, naming subsidiary peak after Gerry: with M and D climbed S. E. Ridge of Nesthorn, a tremendous business: 22 hours, back at 12.30. Up Aletsch Glacier to Concordia: traversed Finsteraarhorn inter alia, long day; did Jungfrau in hail and snow, fine view from top: down difficult ice fall to Bel Alp: self worked that day like a hero! Over to Chamonix, joined by J. Knubel. Did Aiguille Verte descent by Moine Ridge, on separate rope with Mallory; came down last. Weather very uncertain . . . Traversed Aiguille Chardonnet (again last) from Lognan chalet. Did Grépon in icy conditions . . . Camped out three nights under Aiguille Charmoz with sacks; two nights rain, slept under great slabs. Explored Mer de Glace face of Grépon and nearly climbed Col de Blaitière, beaten 1½ hours from ridge by furious storm. Terrific crack climb (100 feet) at foot. Lived all the season on crampons . . . Grandes Jorasses ridges no go this year! Crossed to Zermatt. Awful weather. Dashed up to bivouac with Perry Smith and Knubel and comic porter and bagged the north face of the Weisshorn . . . Very jolly everywhere. Great fuss made all up the valley at my return. The "Young" myth as rampant as ever! . . . Came back in tremendous form. Climbed as well as ever. Did not slip hand or foot once all the season! Really do think I *know* more about it than most amateurs or professionals. The guides, I know, take it for granted that I'm "one of them". Safeness is what I hear them particularly commenting upon.

Crampons, now in universal use, were still considered outré by some of the old guard at this period who preferred the laborious business of cutting steps up endless slopes. Geoffrey had no such inhibition and much more fun.

The high point of the season's achievements was the unguided ascent of the Unterbächhorn, immediately followed by the South-East Ridge of the Nesthorn. In his book *On High Hills* Geoffrey gave an exciting account of the day's events and paid tribute to his two young companions:

> Charles Donald Robertson, urbane and accomplished in mind as he was strenuous upon the hills . . . George Leigh Mallory was conspicuous, strenuous and unsparing of himself in mind as he was superb in physique and accomplished in mountain action . . . To both of them life was a treasure of value; but it was also a talent to be reinvested for the profit of others. Neither hesitated to risk the loss of his share in it, if by doing so he could help to keep the great spirit of human adventure alive in the world.

The three of them set off from Bel Alp at 3 a.m. in foul weather, but at dawn they emerged above the clouds and into bright sunlight. At 7 p.m. they breakfasted at the foot of the steep ridge, and two hours later they were on the summit of the Unterbächhorn. All were going well, so they pushed rapidly on along the ridge leading towards the Nesthorn: "The muscular output was tremendous; for the continuity of the ridge, neither rising nor falling, nor growing harder nor easing off, was so persistent that we had never a reason for varying the pace or for slackening in our steady pursuit of the clock. I have not often traversed a ridge that put such a premium upon good combined climbing, or developed so much consciousness of a real rhythm of the rope."

At the foot of the South-East Ridge of the Nesthorn, they paused briefly to consider: "The grand Nesthorn arête, storming above us into the sky in sheer tower and step and brow, held all our eyes. Had it been past one o'clock we might have hesitated. But it was only half-past twelve. We had the whole afternoon before us, and a habit of elastic forward movement in our limbs and muscles that could not be gainsaid."

The chief problem was the four great towers that blocked the way up the ridge. The first two could be delicately by-passed, but the next two were formidable, very steep and plastered with uncertain ice:

> While traversing under the first tower I had to run out the whole of our rope before I could get footing sound enough to pause upon. The steps

were in any case no more than knife-scars on a fragile cake-icing; and during the passage under the dark overhang of the last tower the whole of our rope was not enough, and we were all three strung out airily on the faltering slabs at the same time. Our progress here was deliberate and very gentle. Our feet and axes brushed the ice-bloom on the rocks as lightly as a bee passing upon a flower.

It was 4 p.m. when they reached the foot of the overhang, the point of no return. Geoffrey had been leading for many hours. Now he handed over to the better cragsman, George Mallory, and paid the rope out cautiously, through a narrow nick in the rock slab, as Mallory inched his way delicately to the left, searching for a way up the fluted ice.

The crux move was about fifteen feet above the slab, where Geoffrey was watching breathlessly:

> I saw the boots flash from the wall without even a scrape; and, equally soundlessly, a grey streak flickered downward, and past me, and out of sight. So much did the wall, to which he had clung so long, overhang that from the instant he lost hold he touched nothing until the rope stopped him in mid-air over the glacier. I had had time to think, as I flung my body forward on to the belayed rope, grinding it and my hands against the slab, that no rope could stand such a jerk; and even to think out what our next action must be – so instantaneous is thought.

Miraculously, the rope held and Mallory was uninjured and soon rejoined Geoffrey on the slab, "apparently entirely undisturbed". Geoffrey now set off to force a route directly upwards:

> Not that I liked it. The crawl up and over the baffle of the snow-fungus was an anxious performance . . . Its protrusion pushed me out of balance; and I had to try for a pick-hold at arm's-length over its crest and trust to toe-holds kicked timorously up its indurating snow face. I heard myself grunt with relief as I got a friction arm-hold over the edge, on the sloping snow-shelf above. I wriggled my chest up on to the slant of the shelf, and then swung up my legs, so that they lay along the narrow snow. A few caterpillar coilings, and then at last I found a finger-hold on the smooth rock wall behind my snow-fungus.

They were all on the summit at seven that evening, twelve hours since they had started climbing and just in time to see a brilliant sunset.

Then they raced down the gentler slopes that lead to the Aletsch

Glacier, glissading part of the way. In the dying light they set about the long, laborious glacier trudge. Lower down, the snow was very soft and Geoffrey finally halted, "mentally and physically incapable of making one more step".

Mallory pressed on while Robertson searched his rucksack and found some old biscuits and cheese: "These acted at once like raw spirit. We had not stopped to eat for more hours than I can recall, certainly not since the morning; and now every mouthful trickled cordially to some separate languid extremity."

The moon had now risen and they struggled on to reach the hotel at Bel Alp after twenty-two hours' hard going.

Back in England after the holiday Geoffrey noted in his Journal: "Grateful for a splendid month of returned vigour, and splendid sights and days. Oh, this climbing, these hills; what a feeble creature I should have been but for them. To have found *oneself*, and known oneself strong."

He enjoyed climbing and all that it gave him, including the *réclame*: "Glorious to feel really fit, well and strong again, 'Middle age' gone for the time. The camping out did it! Those heights at 8,000 feet! The applause of the crowd is pleasant too. To be *the* man of the place, with whispers as you pass, and J. M. Barrie brought up to be introduced! Quaint and grotesque vanity!"

There was a strong element of Barrie's Peter Pan in Geoffrey's reluctance to admit to adulthood. Although he was still in his early thirties, he was already worrying about the possible waning of his youthful spirit and energy. He looked for signs of incipient baldness. In his Journal, he confessed: "Absurdly difficult to grow older at heart, but very old in head, I think, when it has a chance."

In autumn 1909 he plunged himself once more into club politics. He listed his achievements so far in the Journal. On the Alpine Club front, he claimed, he had started social evenings and dinners; begun the reform of the *Alpine Journal*, writing much for it and getting Farrar made sub-editor; introduced the idea of a distinguishing badge or colour; got the premises done up; launched plans to improve the library; and begun moves to reform the club's entrance qualifications and the selection of committee members. He felt he had enlivened the social spirit of the club and "Stirred them up generally!"

This was the year, 1909, when Mr Asquith's Liberal government came into head-on collision with the House of Lords, which refused to approve Lloyd George's radical budget. A general election was inevitable. Hilton Young, still working on *The Economist* and active in the Liberal cause, threw himself into the campaign, challenging no less a figure than Austen Chamberlain for a seat in his Birmingham stronghold. The Young family rallied. Geoffrey wrote in the Journal: "Hilton's great campaign against Austen Chamberlain at Birmingham. Went up there often: heard his magnificent speeches and gradual improvement, especially his magnetic power as a 'leader'. If only he gets the chance!" The election took place in early 1910 and Geoffrey was there again:

> Heard Hilton speak greatly, dominating his audiences. Mother up there in great form, captivating all the party. Met the George Cadburys, the Morpeths etc. Stuck to Hilton all through. Saw the counting and Austen's paper giving himself 7,500 majority! H was cross at only getting 5,000 odd! H magnificent, though his nerves went for ten minutes in his room after all was over . . . Mother marvellous and unfailing.

It was not surprising that Chamberlain retained his seat, although across the country the Conservative Unionist Party was heavily defeated.

At Christmas 1909 there was the usual happy gathering at Pen-y-Pass. Up to now Geoffrey's mountaineering had brought him nothing but excitement, fitness, fulfilment, comradeship and some renown. Now, out of the blue, in a period of little over two years, he was to suffer three hammer-blows from mountain accidents.

The first occurred at the Pen-y-Pass party at Easter 1910.

In *Mountains with a Difference*, published more than forty years later, Geoffrey recalled the day:

> Charles Donald Robertson's fall on Glydyr Vach, on the first day of the largest and most promising of the Welsh parties, darkened the hills with clouds that never again quite dispersed. I was climbing on Tryfan when the rumour reached me, and I ran across the cliffs and the Glydyr east crags winged by a desperate fear, until I found them. He was a giant in stature and in intellect, irreplaceable in the public service and among his friends. We erected the chapel and monument at Glansevern in sight of the cliffs in his memory, and founded the Trust that takes undergraduates to the hills under his name.

It happened on the morning of Good Friday. Donald Robertson had only just joined the party and the route he was attempting to lead, the eastern gully of Glydyr Fach, was well within his normal powers. But he had not climbed for months. His companions watched him ascend some twenty-five feet, then pause, apologising for keeping them waiting and saying that his fingers were out of practice. He then slowly gained a further ten feet. According to Geoffrey's report in the *Alpine Journal*, published in May 1910:

> He was then seen to get both hands over what appeared from below to be an excellent projecting hold. For a moment he hung, feeling with his feet for a foot-hold; then, after a second's pause, his hands quietly opened, and he dropped silently and without an effort. It is almost certain that the fall was due to the momentary suspension of consciousness, induced by the overtaxing of untrained muscles and nerve, which has been responsible for so many apparently unaccountable accidents. He cannot even have known that he fell.

He fell head-first into the gully bed and never regained consciousness. They got him to the hospital in Bangor by late afternoon and he died there soon after midnight. He was buried in the quarrymen's church at Bethesda.

Geoffrey was devastated. Some three years older than Robertson, he had long admired his superior intellect, his mountaineering prowess, his quiet and sensitive sympathy and his great gift of humour. No one, Geoffrey felt, had stood closer to him in the nature and depth of his passion for the mountains. In the previous *Alpine Journal* Robertson had written lines that might easily have come from Geoffrey's pen:

> High places are homes of ancient worship; ascent is a consecrated type of labour for an exceeding great reward . . . For some of us the most potent spell is not danger nor beauty, not fullness of life, but a simple call, a sense of craving when we are not with the mountains, of content when they stand about us. This peculiar joy and satisfaction is a proper stuff for poetry, an emotion with a mystic touch.

In his Journal, writing soon after the accident, Geoffrey said:

> All that he has been to us nothing can express . . . A man of mysterious mind and nameless charm . . . Terrible despair that first night: but for Baddeley nearly mad. He was wonderful in his extraordinary thought and care of me and all the details . . . After the beautiful funeral, which 20–30 of our boys and men attended in climbing clothes, I went back to Gorphwysfa for a week. The men were all extraordinarily *loving*. Page spoke of the feeling of brotherhood as being like being in heaven. Surely we are a wonderful brotherhood. After a few days reasoned myself into

quiet happiness; but O the loss to *us* . . . The mountains, strangely enough, only seem the dearer, and Don, as he lived, died without leaving a cloud . . . No one has ever understood *me* as he did . . ."

His father sent a letter of condolence and on April 6 Geoffrey replied:

Your letter is most helpful. A great nervous shock makes one's thought even more confused: and I feel always that the precise form of belief varies strongly with mood. I think I get nearest it in saying that while, at the moment, I cannot accept any definite interpretation of what must be beyond finite thought to understand, I rely ultimately on what Donald called "Faith", the belief in ultimate God, in a determining intelligence that controls all existence on a principle of unity . . . Donald's perfect close to a singularly perfect life leaves no cloud, not even a shadow on our beloved hills. The thought of such an end was always with him . . .

Robertson's death prompted a concerned letter from George Trevelyan:

. . . He had one fault, only one that I know of, and this one I only gather from your letter – he did not value his own life enough for others' sake. It is the last generous infirmity of noble minds, but alas what loss and misery and waste it causes. And, Geoffrey, I am bound to tell you that from your letter, beautiful as it is, deeply as you sympathise with it – from your letter I fear that you, too, perhaps do not enough value *your* life . . . Geoffrey, do you know that if you get killed climbing, you will break *many* hearts, and take the sunshine out of many lives . . .

Back to London and work, the sheer busyness of his life helped the healing process. He saw a good deal of his political boss, Walter Runciman, President of the Board of Education. He also saw much of Marcus Heywood, and helped to fix him up with a partnership in an engineering firm in Newcastle-upon-Tyne. That year's *Alpine Journal* was dominated by the loss of Donald Robertson; Geoffrey wrote a memorial tribute and an account of the fatal accident. His own Journal recorded a little success at the Alpine Club: "At AC triumphantly carried through the emblem and colour, 2–1 majority: fine debate and much intrigue." He had been campaigning for the introduction of a Club badge, an idea that caused fierce controversy. He later remarked that if it were necessary to liven the Club up, he would cheerfully propose the badge's abolition. The Climbers' Club offered him their presidency, but he turned it down, saying

Professor Farmer should take priority. Brother Georis and his wife were in Europe on embassy business, and Geoffrey often saw them at Formosa weekends. But the Journal paragraph describing all this activity ends with the words: "Donald always there in thought."

At Whitsun he took part in the Seatoller man-hunt, and in the summer holidays he went again to the Alps, this time with Marcus Heywood.

The weather was variable but they managed to get a lot done: "On the whole," Geoffrey noted in his Journal," grand peak-bagging season, spite of bad weather: 11 peaks in 12 days! a record first season for Marcus. I am going first rate, safer and faster than ever, though never going all out." They slept out some nights, glissaded down the snow slopes and, whenever they could, plunged into the icy glacier pools. Heywood shared Geoffrey's relish for cold water.

One of their routes, the west face of the Zinal Rothorn, was another first ascent. Geoffrey was proud of this for an unusual reason, as he later wrote in *On High Hills*:

> For the attempt was based, without reconnoitring, upon a flattering chain of reasoning. We found one day that an unusual coating of hard snow enabled us to scamper about over the unchancy slabs of the west face of the Dent Blanche. We reminded ourselves that the west face of the Rothorn had remained unclimbed by reason of a similar slope of slab; and we argued that the same aspect and structure should be susceptible of the same snow condition. A few days later, accordingly, we crossed the Trifthorn from Zermatt, ran down the snow dunes to the western base of the Rothorn, and found our prediction triumphantly vindicated; there above us shone a gleaming wall of hard snow, mounting from bergschrund to summit ridge.

Speed was still important to Geoffrey, and the account in his Journal gives the time taken for each stage of the expedition: "August 24, left Zermatt 1.15 a.m.; top of Trift moraine 3 hours; Trifthorn 5¼ hours; round to bergschrund ¾ hour. Thence straight up snow-covered slabs to the Rothorn Gabel 2¼ hours; to summit ½ hour." The only trouble they had was when a party high above them on the ordinary route disturbed some stones which came whizzing down at great speed. Josef Knubel was hit on the head by a small pebble, "no larger than a button", and momentarily stunned.

There was more climbing when Geoffrey returned to Britain – first some new routes on the crags of Northumberland where he visited the Trevelyans, then on the Cuillin Ridge in Skye with

George Trevelyan: "A good time: misty but lovely: good talks with G.M.T. Back in very fit health."

Towards the end of 1910 his office transferred him to inspect schools in the Birmingham area and the Potteries. In December, together with his mother, he was in Preston helping Hilton to reduce the Conservative majority there by 800 votes in the second general election of that turbulent year. He went to Cambridge to attend the first dinner of the Cambridge Alpine Club, then to Oxford to spend a weekend with Arnold Lunn of Balliol, discussing ways of stimulating more mountain enthusiasm among the Oxford students.

Early that year Lunn had sent Geoffrey a fan letter. Half a century later, writing the centenary celebration volume for the Alpine Club, *A Century of Mountaineering: 1857–1957,* he said:

> My friendship with Geoffrey Young began when I was an undergraduate at Oxford. His first book of poems, *Wind and Hill,* was sent for review to the *Isis,* the undergraduates' weekly of which I was then the editor, and I never open that slim grey-covered book without a wave of nostalgic memories. Many poets had sung of mountains without climbing them but here for the first time a member of our own brotherhood had translated into noble poetry the aspirations and ardours of mountaineering.

Lunn was on his sick-bed at that time, still recovering from a serious fall he had had the previous August on the Cyfrwy Arête of Cader Idris. He sent a letter of appreciation to Geoffrey and a lifelong friendship was launched. The two men were of similar interests, though Lunn's later contribution to mountaineering was more to do with skiing than with climbing.

Geoffrey's Oxford connection, confirmed by the meeting at Balliol, was to be a fruitful one.

The Christmas gathering at Pen-y-Pass included several children, in what Geoffrey described as "a bold but successful attempt to leaven the party with youth". Mallory was there too, and many of the veteran regulars, and there was much climbing as well as the usual singing and ragging. On the way home Geoffrey spent "delightful days" with the Slingsby family. As Slingsby's guest, he attended the dinner of the Yorkshire Ramblers' Club and delivered an address. His reputation as an effective and charming speaker on such occasions was growing fast. He had lectured to the Yorkshire Ramblers two years earlier and the secretary's letter of thanks had said, "I hear on all sides how charmed everyone was by your most piquant and realistic lecture, an intellectual feast." He had lectured

Above, Formosa Place, the handsome riverside home near Cookham where Geoffrey and his brothers grew up. Geoffrey wrote: "An Admiral ancestor piled chalk upon a group of Thames eyots, in a great angle of the river. He set upon it lawns and trees and bridges and trailing roses; and an 18th-century house that should give him the feeling of his flag-ship."

Below, the Young family in the early 1880s. Back row, left to right: Georis; Sir George, the 3rd baronet; Alice, Lady Young, his wife; middle row: Dr Kennedy; Mrs Collins; Eacy Kennedy (sisters of Lady Young); front row: Constance Kennedy; Hilton, Geoffrey; Eacy Young.

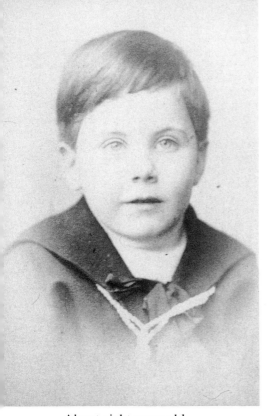

About eight years old

Schoolboy

The youthful Geoffrey

Cambridge student

Soon after leaving Cambridge

The Query Club, December 1898. Club members gathered in Geoffrey's rooms in Great Court, Trinity College, to celebrate their second anniversary. The three men seated on the right and the one standing extreme right were visitors. The Club members were, standing, left to right: J.H. Jeans (astronomer); A.M. ("Sandy") Mackay (lawyer); John Talbot (Headmaster of Haileybury); R.G. Hawtrey (Treasury); G.H. Hardy (mathematics professor); F.W. Dobbs (Eton teacher). Seated, left to right: Hilton Young; C.K. Clague (H.M.I.); J.P. Sclater (clergyman); C.M. Jones (civil servant); F.H. Lucas (author of the India Act); C. Gunterman (I.C.S).

Alpine climbing. *Above left*, Geoffrey perched on the balanced block on the day in August 1906 when he and Josef Knubel traversed the Grand Charmoz, the Grépon and the Blaitière in one glorious long day. *Above right*, Knubel at the Col des Nantillons that same day. *Below*, George Mallory in languid balance on the Moine Ridge of the Aiguille Verte, August 13, 1909. Geoffrey took the photograph while protecting Mallory's descent.

The South Face of the Täschhorn, first climbed by V.J.E. Ryan, Franz and Josef Lochmatter, Geoffrey and Knubel on August 11, 1906. Geoffrey wrote in his Journal: "did not expect for about six hours to get back alive".

Above, some of those who were at Pen-y-Pass, Snowdonia, at Easter 1907 for the first of Geoffrey's annual parties. Standing, left to right: O.K. Williamson; unknown; Marcus Heywood; Geoffrey; Percy Farrar; J.M. Archer Thomson. Seated, middle row: W.R. Reade; Geoffrey Bartrum; George Mallory. Seated, front row: E.B. Harris; F. Don; F. Sparrow; Oscar Eckenstein.

Below, Geoffrey and Charles Trevelyan at Seatoller House, Borrowdale, wearing the red sashes that denote them as "hares" for the day's man-hunting across the fells, just before the outbreak of the First World War.

Above, Geoffrey and the Curé of St Pierre, Charles Del'Aere, in late 1914, before the town was completely destroyed by shell-fire. *Below left*, Soeur Marguerite, whom Geoffrey described as "angelic and quietly witty". Their work together in Ypres was the foundation of a life-long friendship. *Below right*, Geoffrey and G.M. Trevelyan with a group of Italian officers, some time in 1916. Geoffrey is extreme right, Trevelyan next to him.

Italy.

Geoffrey and Herbert Dyne with one of the vehicles of the Friends' Ambulance Unit.

This sketch, drawn by S.B. Meyer for *Bolts from the Blues*, shows Geoffrey at the back of an ambulance on the "Plava night run" which Geoffrey did more than thirty times.

Two pages from Geoffrey's Italian Journal, written on September 1, 1917, the day after his left leg was shattered by an Austrian shell.

to other clubs as well and given after-dinner speeches, developing a distinctive style – measured and unrhetorical in delivery, with touches of quiet humour but always with some serious, carefully thought-out message.

On his way south, he stayed with friends to attend the Worcestershire Hunt Ball, and noted in the Journal: "Much amused to find my appearance caused 'continual inquiries', and hear I have been christened the 'Duc de Richelieu' by this set of young ladies! (me!). Now one is getting bald-looking and older, something of 'distinction' I see in my mother seems to appear to compensate. Well, one has to be agreeable to other folk, and so why be shy about it?"

Geoffrey was not shy about it. He was aware of his good looks and ability to charm. Time and again, when photographs were being taken, he would present his profile to the camera, giving an air of apartness and distinction that grew more pronounced in later years. He never took any particular pride in these personable qualities but felt that, since he had been given them, it would be churlish not to make the most of them.

The death of another friend, Christopher Wordsworth, shook him in the early months of 1911, twenty years after their exchanged vows of friendship on their first terrifying night in the dormitory at Marlborough College. The friendship had survived their schooldays together and then Cambridge. In 1910 Wordsworth had married Alice Stopford, Geoffrey's cousin, and Geoffrey had been best man. Now Wordsworth died in India, the victim of fevers contracted on colonial service in Nigeria. In his Journal Geoffrey wrote:

"Dear fellow: the oldest friend, and the third of my greatest friends to die early. Just another large gap."

The gaps were filled by more new friends and acquaintances. At Cambridge he met Jacques Raverat; Lytton Strachey (who had a passion for Mallory); Duncan Grant (also admired by Strachey); the eccentric pianist Leo Pavia (later the companion of James Agate, the theatre critic); and, as Geoffrey said in the Journal, "other of the peculiar people", meaning homosexuals. Another Journal entry soon after says: "Gradually opened out my own life, through Pavia etc."

On a three-day climbing foray to Ogwen in Snowdonia he met some of the new Oxbridge generation, Claude Elliott and Geoffrey Madan from Cambridge and Hugh Rose Pope of New College, Oxford, and launched the idea of a book of essays on mountaineering, to be written by Oxford students and supervised by himself.

The Pen-y-Pass party at Easter 1911 was the biggest so far, filling the hotel and the shacks outside. In his Journal Geoffrey wrote: "Huge and gay party at Pen-y-Pass . . . Splendid singing; all delighted. Hilton quite converted . . . Climbed much." It was Hilton's first attendance at one of the parties. Another newcomer, who was to play an even more important role in Geoffrey's life, was a fifteen-year-old schoolgirl, Eleanor Slingsby, who was brought by her older brother Laurence. Len, as everyone came to call her, never forgot it. Sixty years later, writing for the *Journal* of the Pinnacle Club, she said:

> Such a galaxy of stars as possibly never met again there, and as I was a very young and rather shy teenager, it was indeed exciting. Professor Farmer, Oscar Eckenstein, Dr Karl Blodig, George Mallory, a talkative son of Professor Gilbert Murray, two high-up civil servants, and the particular and unforgettable Irish group who had sailed over in one of their yachts; led by Geoffrey's cousin, Page Dickinson, they were active in the hills, irrepressibly witty and amusing . . . There was a gallant rescue on the Parson's Nose of a very city-clad gentleman from a Lancashire town – with, I remember, a gold watch – who offered a pound later to his rescuers, of whom I well remember Mallory was one. And I can never forget Dr Karl Blodig's Austrian voice echoing over South Snowdon with '*Die Wacht am Rhein*', three years before the Kaiser's War!

On Good Friday Geoffrey took Len and Laurence Slingsby to Tryfan and Laurence led them up the Gashed Crag route, Len's first rock climb. She described it, with characteristic breathless enthusiasm, in a letter to her father:

> It was a glorious day, not much wind, at least hardly any and it really was a good climb . . . Mr Young is a splendid person to look after you. He bustles us all out of the Hotel every morning off somewhere and tells you all what you are going to do before you have time to think for yourself. Then if he sees some solitary looking person sitting in the smoking room, he takes him off for a walk somewhere at once!

Many years later, in the 1960s, Len told me more about those early days. She recalled her first meeting with Mallory:

> I went into the hotel smoking room and there he was, leaning on the mantelpiece, in a red shirt – I'd never seen anyone in a red shirt before. He had a beautiful voice and he was absolutely beautiful, though not sexually attractive. He was not really a very interesting man, not an original thinker though he liked intellectual discussion and worried a lot about improving the world. One of his great friends was Cottie Sanders [the novelist Ann

Bridge], who was also very beautiful, tall and elegant. They used to get very intense together talking about Shelley, to general amusement.

The people Len admired were the oddballs:

I remember Eckenstein very well at the 1911 party, hammering things in the hall and smoking his awful pipe tobacco. He had a bushy beard at that time and was regarded as something of a prophet figure. Karl Blodig was a wonderful man. He said the two things you needed in the mountains were butter and alcohol, and that amused Geoffrey very much. And Archer Thomson, a very grand man, very dignified.

Her favourites were the Irish: "Page Dickinson was handsome, charming, most entertaining and fascinating. Everyone fell for him. And Conor O'Brien, the great small boat sailor, one of the most lovable characters. He always climbed in bare feet and never stopped talking."

Len said she was a little upset, long afterwards, when Don Whillans spoke of the Pen-y-Pass gatherings as "elegant evenings": "We weren't really elegant at all – fairly scruffy, lots of smoking and some beer drinking. No heavy drinking though, we were too full of spirits without it. There was lots of good talk. Everyone wrote verses. And there was a lot of singing, accompanied by a terrible old piano."

They may not have been elegant, but it was all very different from the way Whillans and his mates spent their evenings after a day's climbing.

The triumphant gaiety of the 1911 party, one year exactly after the death of Donald Robertson, was followed by another bereavement – the death of George Trevelyan's much-loved son Theo, four and a half years old, from appendicitis. They took the body to Langdale to be buried in the churchyard at Chapel Stile, close to their holiday cottage at Robin Ghyll, and Trevelyan wrote to a friend: ". . . now my bravest hopes lie buried here in the fellside graveyard, beneath the bracken and the rocks, and this is the place of my heart." Geoffrey was an immediate support and comfort and hurried to join the Trevelyans at Robin Ghyll: "To see my own philosophy of life really triumphing over such pain; a great effect on one's life to have shared it with them: walked over Pikes to Rosthwaite in snow."

This entry in his Journal is immediately followed by a strange and very different one that suggests that his "philosophy of life" was perhaps not so settled and steady as he thought:

Took flying week in Berlin. Of this I cannot write. To have at last lived in an atmosphere where one could talk, and live and flower *naturally*, a glorious week of self-realisation, understanding. And after it back feeling like 16, with the great oppression of years unloaded. Just to have lived out, and with such fascinating folk as Count Pepi Raschka, Leo, Hugo and all the brilliant right circles. The natural life, the life of natural powers, and refined pleasure, talk, music, theatres and, for me, wholesome love. I have at last found myself and my creed and my own sphere of contributing to the sum of good.

For some time Geoffrey and friends had been busy setting up their Donald Robertson Travel Fund scheme. By now, according to the *Journal*, they had £275 and a guaranteed annual income of more than £50 in subscriptions, so they organised mountain holidays for four boys, and made anonymous donations to others. "A difficult task of selection," Geoffrey noted.

It was a year of continuing and brilliant weather: "Met Sybil Cropper, whom they all resolved I'm to marry: she *is* charming." There were several "jolly dances" and "jolly dinner parties", he did a lot of swimming, and the wonderful weather held when the summer holdays came along: "The summer of our lives, one rush of gorgeous weather from June to October. With an ideal companion, and weather, resolved to finish my 'ambitious' climbing, in my 35th year, with a record season."

The "ideal companion" was Humphrey Owen Jones, a Welshman and a brilliant scientist. He had won a scholarship to the University College of Wales at the age of sixteen, gone on to study chemistry at Clare College, Cambridge, and become a Fellow there in 1902. He was also an accomplished climber and mountaineer, a regular attender of the Pen-y-Pass parties from 1907 onwards and an annual visitor to the Alps. In *On High Hills* Geoffrey wrote:

> There is no comradeship like that of two friends mountaineering together. They can achieve a sympathy of movement greater than that of any machine; and the closer their accord in action, the readier is their appreciation of each other's dissimilar temperament or divergent point of view. H.O. was an ideal comrade. His climbing was a model of agile, accurate and elegant movement. He had the eye and judgement of the trained observer, the detachment of the philosopher, and the humorous enthusiasm of the good Celt.

Ralph Todhunter was also with them for part of the season, which was energetic even by Geoffrey's standards and which saw the making of some impressive new routes. They went first to the Dauphiné region and made a new route up the Dôme de Neige des Écrins by the west ridge. Then they moved to Courmayeur on the south side of Mont Blanc to explore the east ridge of the Grandes Jorasses, and then make the first ascent of the west ridge, with Knubel as their guide. Next, with Dr Blodig in the party, they climbed the Brouillard Ridge of Mont Blanc. Geoffrey's *Journal* recorded:

> Went tremendously hard, crossed Col du Géant alone, crevasses very difficult; and then we climbed Grépon by the Mer de Glace face, my last great ambition, and the hardest rock climb I have ever had. A gorgeous sunset saw me down from my perhaps last great new climb . . . I never climbed better, and outlasted even Josef. Knubel said the last day, "You *can't* get tired." He is greatly proud that in nine years we have never either of us had a slip when climbing together. *Safety*, he declares, is my great quality!

Geoffrey called it "the season of seasons".

He went home by way of Munich and Berlin where he enjoyed "a riotous few days of their perfect theatres, right life and joy of pleasure. A wonderful contrast in sensations; each period forgotten in turn." Presumably he is contrasting his Alpine days of hard, outdoor adventure with the indoor delights of life with his German friends. A few lines later in the *Journal* he exclaims: "What a contrast my life is!"

Geoffrey had many friends in several different areas of life, but some of the old enemies were still evident too. The Journal says cryptically: "The Eton row revived by Calvert of Troy (after all I'd done for his kid!)." The reference is to Frank Calvert, an Englishman by birth who had been American vice-consul in the region where the remains of Priam's city had been found. In 1869 he had helped the German archaeologist Heinrich Schliemann to find the location, and he was still there in 1902 when Geoffrey and his brother Georis visited the site. They stayed one night at Calvert's farm and, in his unpublished diary of the trip, Geoffrey described Calvert as an "odd, black-bearded ex-consul of the 3rd generation, with a turn for spiritualism and Homer". He also mentions a "jolly blond baby boy", who he later succeeded in getting into a school at Holt in Norfolk. In *The Grace of Forgetting*, written half a century later, Geoffrey describes the visit to Troy but makes no mention of the Calverts. I can find no further reference to Calvert in any of Geoffrey's writings.

In the autumn of 1911 Geoffrey wrote a long paragraph of

introspection into the Journal. It is more than usually convoluted in style and imprecise in its allusions, but leaves, nonetheless, a strong impression of a man deeply apprehensive of what would happen to his life if his homosexuality became publicly known. This is what he said:

> The glorious and record summer at last running out. Half way through life, and yet, for all the constant depressions and over-recognition of oldness and aloofness, I can't get old in mind. Feel just as boyish and enthusiastic and keen on young things and the open rush as at 18, perhaps more so! – and immensely strong. We have somehow made ourselves a strange position, we brothers, quite for itself. I am almost *afraid* at the thought of the many friends, in all ages and lines of life, who like me peculiarly and unlike other folk, and what a crash it would mean if my strange nature with its – to it – natural audacities, and complete freedom from old prejudices, principles, religion, convention, and what is called "morality" ever came out – as it may any day – in one of the innumerable corners where I have eddied up and down disregarding the so-called "risk". But for the home tie, Mother especially, I could see it go, with pain no doubt but still ready to start somewhere fresh and naturally – but now, and as it is? – I'm afraid I'm growing too old and if the end comes – well we'll leave it to then to settle!

For all his deep personal conflicts and anxieties, Geoffrey had long been regarded – and had seen himself – as a wise support and mentor to young men, especially those of a wayward or difficult disposition. One such was Bill Slingsby, the most unreliable and troublesome of Cecil Slingsby's children. Two years earlier Geoffrey had helped to fix him up with a job in Nigeria, hoping it might lead to a settled career. Now Will was back in England, creating further havoc. On October 8, 1911, his sister Len wrote to Geoffrey from her school, Queen Margaret's in Scarborough:

> Dear Mr Young,
>   I am writing to tell you about Billy in case you haven't heard, because I know about it first, before any of the others, at least for certain. He is not going to marry Dorothy Hutton now after all. Gwen Hutton, her sister, who is a mistress here, told me last night. I thought you would like to know, because you always like hearing anything about Billy and you are his greatest friend. I am really very glad, not because I don't like her, but because I don't think Billy is a person to settle down and get married. I hope he never will, at least for years . . . What I want to know is, couldn't you stop him ever getting engaged again, at least for years at any rate, because it is such hard luck on her, when it doesn't

come off . . . I am sure you could stop him doing it again, because you are practically the only person who can do anything with him . . .

Geoffrey replied immediately:

Dear Len,

Will's a perfect pig! . . . he's hopeless. No, I can't influence him. It is the one line that a man listens to no advice in, and if a girl, knowing what he is, lets herself get engaged to him, no one can do anything . . . I am myself vexed with him, as he has never written me one word since even before he left. However, one helps folk because they want it, not because one thinks them perfect! . . .

Len's reply to this, which has not survived, must have expressed disappointment, because Geoffrey soon wrote again:

Dear Len,

What a dear little goose you are! Do you think that if I had meant, as you say, to "give up" helping Will, that I should not have done so years ago, when he was much more difficult to help? Just the fact that he does not write could not make any difference. You will find some day that the more you do for people, the more you are anxious to do for them, and it is all quite independent of what they think about it, or say in return! You see, the people who want help most are those who are "across" the ordinary run of the world by nature, and therefore are the least likely to be able, as it were, to make an exchange of friendship, or to say or do nice things in return!

What *is* of use to people is just to be there to help them whenever they come back to you or want it. If once you let them feel you are establishing a *claim* on them, they will resent it, and then you can't be any more use to them.

So don't urge Will to write. I know him very well, and when he feels inclined he will let me hear again. I hate daily letters myself!

But it's nice of you to write to me of him, and to be so loyal . . .

He went on to tell her about his Alpine successes – "the record season of my life" – and concluded by saying, "I liked your letter immensely." Ironically, the continued waywardness of the prodigal brother had helped to set the foundations for a friendship, at first avuncular and largely conducted by correspondence, that was to lead to the most important relationship of the second half of Geoffrey's life.

Before the end of 1911, Geoffrey's office transferred him to London and he was given the job of reorganising the inspectorate there.

The Christmas gathering at Pen-y-Pass was, Geoffrey said, "the most glorious of all parties". All the veterans were there, and Mallory, and the new Oxford friends including Trevenen Huxley and Hugh Pope. Geoffrey summed it up: "Some great climbing, gorgeous music at nights, splendid Christmas on Tryfan etc. We all knew such a time could hardly repeat."

He made another flying visit to Germany, and went to Oxford where there was a grand dinner in his honour. The little book he had suggested, *Oxford Mountaineering Essays*, had just been published.

Its nine student contributors included Arnold Lunn and his brother Hugh Kingsmill, and the Huxley brothers, Julian and Trevenen. The most pertinent of the essays to this story, however, is that by Hugh Rose Pope, *British Hills*, which reveals how close his attitude was to Geoffrey's – or how strong Geoffrey's influence had been upon the younger man:

> But for pleasure unalloyed there is nothing to equal a climb up difficult rock on a fine summer day. Who can describe the exhilaration that comes from the use of muscles responsive to the call, from the sense of mastery and ease in the very face of danger, from the splendid situations and wide outlook? Every faculty is at full stretch. The whole being is stimulated to the intensest appreciation of beauty in all its forms – beauty of life itself and beauty of movement, beauty of height and depth and distance. It must surely have been moments such as these that Stevenson had in mind when he prayed to the Celestial Surgeon:
>
> > "Lord, thy most pointed pleasure take
> > And stab my spirit broad awake."
>
> Such moments are necessarily few. It is one of the limitations of mortal man that he cannot live for long upon the heights. But always and everywhere the climber is most vividly alive. There are continual appeals to so many sides of his nature that he cannot be indifferent to them all. Now one may come home to him, and now another, but at least he never falls a prey to that most deadly of all soul-diseases – apathy.

The Easter 1912 party at Pen-y-Pass was marred only by the absence of Page Dickinson, who had just married. Geoffrey noted what Charles Trevelyan had said of him, that "I need not have children as 'I inform my generation enough, without!' Is this true? It would be a great relief and release. But they are all set on my marrying Sybil Cropper."

He worked hard during the summer term but found time for much travelling – to Berlin, Oxford, Sherborne and Northumberland where he spent a few days with Marcus Heywood, now engaged to marry: "This delightful friendship," he wrote, "only seemed to grow deeper and more affectionate as a result."

The Journal at this time contains a further bout of introspection:

On the whole a great year: defining tastes, and getting far more realisation out of life. Evidently I've a fixed position in our set, a strange one, but then we're all different to others to what we are to ourselves! – Delightful talks with Mother and Hilton. But I must take more time to write, and live less dependent on the continual flux of company and of "it". Without ? , I can be at least useful to individuals in clearing out old cobwebs and leading to *freedom* of thought and action. Just liberty, liberty, liberty, and the room for that great essential *vitality*, the only great quality in living.

The next entry says: "And followed by the most terrible months of my life. Surely, few men living out of the 'adventure' class have had to endure and carry out so much in a few weeks."

He had planned a full Alpine season. He journeyed out with Arnold Lunn. They were to be joined later by Mallory and Pope and H. E. L. Porter, then by H. O. Jones and his new bride. In February Jones had been elected as the youngest Fellow of the Royal Society. On the 1st of August he was married in Bangor Cathedral to Muriel Edwards, another scientist and a keen climber. They would honeymoon in the Alps.

From the start the weather was bad and there was much hanging about in huts, trudging up and down in deep snow. Conditions improved when Jones and his wife arrived. Geoffrey described them as "ideally happy . . . They were ideal companions, equal in intellect and interest." Jones and Geoffrey, with Knubel, made one new route, the Pointe Isolée of the Dames Anglaises on the Peuteret Ridge.

It snowed heavily that night so Geoffrey went down to the valley next morning to collect his mail.

The Joneses remained, with their guide Truffer, planning an attempt on the Mont Rouge de Peuteret. It was a route well within their capabilities. But at some point on the ascent Truffer slipped on comparatively easy but exposed ground and the rope pulled them all to their deaths.

Geoffrey was back in the Gamba Hut by early afternoon, waiting for them. That evening he heard of the fall and he and Knubel raced across the glacier with blankets to find the bodies: "Found them after some search. K most anxious about me but found my nerves iron."

Geoffrey had to organise the retrieval of the bodies, inform relatives, deal with the press and other inquiries, and arrange for the burials in Courmayeur; "Only broke down once when alone with Knubel."

No one was to blame for the accident but Geoffrey always felt that, if circumstances had been different, Jones might have saved the party by quick action to anchor himself with his ice axe. Two years later, writing to George Mallory to dissuade him from the idea of an Alpine honeymoon, he said:

> I saw H.O., one of the coolest and most balanced of minds, distinctly overdoing it. His wife was physically and emotionally overdone those days, *not* by big climbs. He had to take more care of her; both of them were steeped in the double romance of themselves and the mountains. And the accident came of his over-care for her, his distraction from the single eye of the mountaineer, that he *must* have, and that he cannot retain, if he is throwing himself into someone else's being, outlook and performance.

After the funeral Geoffrey and Mallory and Hugh Pope traversed the Tête du Lion and crossed the Col Tournanche to Zermatt, Mallory leading in confident form. Pope thanked Mallory for his "introduction to the Alps", and Mallory lent him an ice axe for his impending trip to the Pyrenees.

Geoffrey went to Berlin, describing the visit in a tortured paragraph in his *Journal*: "Deliberately met sensation with sensation. How heartless it would be called, conventionally, but the other pole of the mere (?) senses the safest and natural remedy for overdone nerves and deeper feelings. Nightly groups of grecian beauty: fun and animalism. Let those judge who alone really know nature and see life squarely and confess it honestly." It is a strange statement, opaque but clearly defiant: he would be true to his "nature" and would not condemn himself for seeking relief from his sorrow in what appears to have been some kind of homosexual orgy. But it seems to me that there is an element of uncertainty here as well. The reiteration, in these passages, of the word "natural" suggests that he was still not entirely sure about his own nature. The next entry in his Journal reinforces the suspicion.

It describes the occasion, already recounted in chapter six, when he thought he was in love with Rachel Lyttelton, proposed to her and sent her a flood of presents and poems and protestations. But the family had serious reservations and before long Geoffrey was completely recovered, convinced that he had only been in love with the idea of being in love.

All round him, though, friends were getting married and starting families. He was frequently a best man. Was he, with his great love of children, to miss out altogether on that side of life?

He was urged to marry by George Trevelyan who wrote to him regretting "that the great majority of men and women whom I value appear never to marry, to condemn themselves to solitude of soul, and – what matters more – to cut off the hopes, otherwise so fair, of future generations of like people". His father, too, writing on the occasion of Geoffrey's thirty-fifth birthday, said: ". . . My last birthday letter contained matter which I will not repeat; but you must consider me as being of the same mind, in advising you, nay in entreating you, to get yourself a wife! You have arrived at an age at which it will not become easier, even though it may not become harder."

Geoffrey went to Cambridge for the memorial service for H. O. Jones, and on his way back to Clare College a friend ran up and handed him a telegram which is now among the Geoffrey Young papers in the archives of the Alpine Club. It read: "Urgent Winthrop Young Trinity Cambridge Hugh Pope missing since Sunday from [indecipherable place name] when he left for Pic dOssau First heard last night Wire this morning saying guides search unsuccessful What do you advise His Mother Tring."

He hurled himself into action, organised a search party that included Arnold Lunn and Claude Elliott, wired three Alpine guides to join them, and rushed to the Pyrenees. He was proud of the hard, logical thinking that led him to the spot where Pope's body lay:

> I concentrated every faculty upon this, and I have never thought harder into another mind, ready to modify my own first impressions by what I knew of his temperament and likings. It had been his first sight of the region, and it was also to be mine: that should help. A study of the map led me to fix first upon the Pic du Midi d'Ossau. The first sight of this peak, from the pass above Gavarni, made me decide, further, that the west face and the north ridge were the two most likely choices.

He organised the search, reserving the north ridge for Knubel and himself. They moved up each side of the ridge, surveying the region below with binoculars. Before long, Knubel spotted the body below them.

Geoffrey told the story in print more than once, but his unpublished Journal account gives a stronger impression of his feelings at that time:

Took line that I felt a mountaineer strange to district would take. I knew he must be there. Found him, with Knubel. Saw him from 200 feet above: he looked like a young god, lying at rest on a rock after bathing. The perfect glory of his unique manhood untouched by time, and only showing a few bruises. I went down alone to cover him and cried like a child, for his beauty, and splendour of character, and his loss. My mountain son.

Geoffrey had been working to get Hugh Pope a job at the Ministry of Education. He saw Pope as the closest and truest reflection of his own spirit in the next generation. Pope had died while climbing alone, and a sentence he had written about the solitary climber shows how Geoffrey-esque he was in his thinking: "He is alone with the hills, and stands like one initiated into a strange and beautiful mystery."

In a short space of time Geoffrey had now lost three friends in the mountains, two of them – Robertson and Pope – young men for whom he felt particularly responsible since it was his example and influence, above all else, that had made them mountaineers.

There had been another death, too, in this period, not so close to him but very shocking. Archer Thomson, the Snowdonia pioneer, deep in nervous depression, had committed suicide in early August 1912 by drinking a bottle of carbolic acid.

10

The Troubled Years: 1912–14

THE TWO YEARS LEADING UP to the outbreak of the First World War were the most disturbed of Geoffrey's long life. He was in his mid-thirties, halfway through the biblical alloted span and always very conscious of the passage of time, the passing of youth. His job as a schools inspector seems to have been going smoothly but it is rarely mentioned in the Journal. He still had a wide circle of friends, in different spheres of life, and spent much time visiting them and enjoying their company. But there is a frenzied air about it now, a sense that he was perplexed and lost, unable to settle long at anything. The violent deaths of so many good friends in so short a space of time set him questioning the point and purpose of all endeavour, even that of mountaineering. The Journal entries take on a manic quality, swinging from self-congratulation to despair, from vigorous, open-air adventure to orgiastic forays into the homosexual haunts of Berlin and Paris and Soho.

On his return home after finding Hugh Pope's body in the Pyrenees, he wrote:

Mentally terribly sore, weary and lightless. My best friends gone. Archer Thomson's suicide, and their loss, closing my great Welsh outlet of happiness. H.O.'s death terminating, with Hugh, my Alpine present and future. The fear of no fresh hopes present in thought. I don't care to see even splendid friends like George and Janet. Bill Slingsby's return, and the relief of eccentric nights round the clubs, boxing rings, ideas quite dissociate, make my one resource. Again let them judge, who know nature and the complex mind. I can't stand sympathy now, which after Don's death I needed. Not even anxious the world should know its loss. It's all so hopeless.

Geoffrey was now spending riotous weekends in Paris and Berlin:

Intrigues, night escapes from jealous competitors, pursuit of beauty, sensation . . . Am I very coarse-grained? I think I am vitally very strong, seriously sensitive but with (now) great control and natural resilience, personally complex to the point of seeming quadruplicity. Not a type made for conventional life or common work; but incapable of escapism, since no one element can drive out any other side or bias . . . So, for the present, and until some great happiness or catastrophe, I swing among my Jekylls and Hydes, each part, however, equally myself, and *not* condemned by any other part.

He must have been unburdening himself to his old friend George Trevelyan. A surviving letter from Trevelyan, dated December 12, 1912, says:

Dear Geoffrey,
   I am unable to tell you by word of mouth how much I admire and love you. You are to me, and as I know to others also, a source of inspiration which we cannot do without. So take care of yourself spiritually, for our sakes, in any event. And perhaps a great good will befall you at last . . .

Another letter from Trevelyan, dated July 19, 1913, said: "My dear, *believe in life*: you have helped many others to do so."

At Christmas 1912 he went to the Alps at the invitation of Arnold Lunn to learn to ski. His boldness and fine sense of balance and athleticism made him a rapid learner. George and Janet Trevelyan were in the party and so was Claude Elliott who got engaged to Gillian Bloxham during the holiday. Geoffrey noted: "I arranged the proposal by Claude, opportunity etc. and brought it off! a delightful pair." Within a few weeks he was committed to be best man for Elliott and Arnold Lunn and Marcus Heywood.

He wrote to Eleanor Slingsby, who was still a schoolgirl.

16.1.'13
17, Cheyne Walk,
Chelsea.

Dear Len,
   I too am sorry: but we can't control fate and dances!
   Let me know in plenty of time the date of *the* Dance!
   We count on your coming to Pen-y-Pass at Easter. Do bring your father and Laurence. Do you think you can manage it?

We shall be a large party of men and their wives, brides and engaged couples!

Best of good wishes for this, I suppose, your last term . . .

Yours ever,

G. Winthrop Young.

Please answer about Wales!

He wrote a series of articles on education for the *Morning Post*. Sometimes, by invitation, he went to inspect public schools like Repton and Harrow. The Admiralty asked him to report on the Royal Naval Colleges at Osborne and Dartmouth, and he was particularly impressed by the atmosphere of these places, when compared to that in the public schools like Harrow and Eton:

The contrast was striking – in vitality, initiative and an early-developed habit of responsibility. This observation brought me at once into correspondence with Herbert Richmond, later Admiral, Master of Downing and leading naval historian. He held that the difference on which I had remarked was due to the qualities released in young cadets by constant practical small-boat sailing, and the responsibility it involved. I had attributed it to the early introduction of a great service tradition and discipline into the young cadets' lives. It was many years later that I came to realise that we had both been right. The adventure of the sea in a small boat, the skill and responsibility of sailing, and, no less, the strong tradition of the naval service introduced in boyhood, had all of them had their share in the only education in the round which then existed in our country.

He increasingly felt that British schools, for the most part, were narrow and blinkered, concerned with only one facet of the human personality, the understanding. Little or no attempt, he thought, was being made to train young men for full, rounded adulthood, with a sense of service to the community.

In the spring of 1913 he noted in the Journal:

Work very satisfactory and complimentable. Inspectors' Committee, my proposal, working well . . . I was asked, a great compliment, to write out my general views on education for the Minister's benefit. Indulged in general prophecy of the half-year schools, camp life etc. Well received. Inspected Repton and wrote all the Modern Language Annual Report. Office seems to accept me as privileged sort of irregular brain; to be indulged – as I've always been! – as a favourite boy!

The manic quality is very apparent now. After that entry in his Journal, Geoffrey wrote:

> Went rather wild in town, Soho etc. "Freddy" turned up again, and had to lodge and support him . . . Wilbert constantly with me, a strange psychological study. Wants to know and see all of life, Soho etc., but not to be of it. Brought his small Westminster friend, Alec Dobbie, a dear little chap, but thoroughly "animal" au fond. Many jolly days and hours together . . . Wonderful artistic "Roman" dances. W is gorgeous in colour and temperament.

Immediately after this, he noted: "Elected President Climbers' Club, unwillingly. Had a great dinner and amusing speeches. Leonard Huxley my guest."

Next he said: "It is jolly to be able to slide from one social stratum to another and be natural to oneself and others in all alike."

"Jolly" was a common word with Geoffrey, but many Journal entries at this period make it clear that his excursions into the homosexual underworld were the cause of much agonising introspection. It was a dangerous game he was playing, mixing freely with boxers and low-life characters. Blackmail was a serious possibility, and public revelation was another, and there can be no doubt that Geoffrey was concerned to keep the truth from his parents, his employers and colleagues, and from the many friends who had no idea that there was this other side to his life.

Just before Easter 1913 he wrote:

> On the whole recovering touch with life, but nerves still very thinly covered, and a great shrinking from people, especially friends. I find they talk of my "spiritual contempt" of general life. I think it more like a discouraged apathy, consequent on having no central interest and a strong vitality and love of all living things. "Nature" in reflection, the one thread left; and the beauty of growth and youth.

Geoffrey was understandably reluctant to resume the Pen-y-Pass party at Easter 1913, but his friends pressed and prevailed: "After much pressure revived the Wales party. Thought it to be small but quite 40–50 came in all. Three to four great weeks at Pen-y-Pass, and afterwards with Mallory and his boys at Quellyn." George Mallory was now teaching at Charterhouse and, following Geoffrey's example, had started taking parties of boys on mountain holidays in North Wales.

The Pen-y-Pass gathering included many of the old faces and some new ones – Claude Elliott and Arnold Lunn and their fiancées, the Oxford contingent, Duncan Grant the painter who came as a guest of Hilton's, and all three Huxley brothers, Trevenen, Julian and Aldous, who was already too short-sighted to take part in any climbing.

Geoffrey summed it up in these words: "A great success. Many delightful letters. Snow at start, and climbing never good: but opened the East Buttress Lliwedd Route II, led the Red Wall twice, made second ascent of Central Gully and of Purple Passage etc. etc. Physically as strong as ever, and nerve as sound. Pleasure and romance less. Too many memories of those five faces of last year, now gone." He was particularly proud of a night search he organised for some climbers lost on Tryfan on Easter Monday: "Gorgeous night and dawn. Picked out five of my 'six-footers', and got them round, and the party up, in 2¼ hours: admirably carried through." One of the "six-footers" was Trevenen Huxley, the eldest of the Huxley boys and thought by many to be the brightest of them. Just over a year later, having fallen in love with a housemaid whom it was socially impossible for him to marry, he hanged himself.

It was about this time that Geoffrey formed a dining club, which he called the "It Club", for congenial mountaineering friends, young and old. One of his motives was to hold the Oxford group together following the death of Hugh Pope and their dispersal from Oxford. Another was to provide a sociable gathering of mountain men that would be free of the inhibitions and feuding and stuffiness that sometimes went with meetings of the official climbing clubs. George Trevelyan and Geoffrey Keynes were among the members, and a new friend George Finch.

After the Pen-y-Pass party he wrote in the Journal: "Back to work hugely in health, stronger than ever. Probably Berlin soon, to let off steam."

This is the last *Journal* entry for over a year. He did not return to it until May 1914, when he tried to summarise and analyse the intervening events. One of these events was of great importance – his resignation from his job as His Majesty's Inspector.

The Journal says:

The inevitable change. I don't think I'll go into it; no point. In the middle of a most successful term officially, the thunderbolt of attack, from the old quarter in a new disguise. However, it must have come shortly. I was tired of the life, and the work, once organised and set going, was growing far duller and not for a man's life. I think I should have stuck to it for another two years, to get "London" really going. But then I should have been older, and it's a time one cannot spare! As it was, let it suffice: in the full flood of successful work, well-recognised, I resigned.

So the resignation was, in a sense, forced upon him. Once again – as at Eton eight years before – his enemies, unnamed, were closing in. There may be some rationalisation in his remarks here, for nowhere else in his Journal is there any hint that he was finding the work dull. He certainly felt it had been worthwhile:

Valuing up my own work during the years, I should say that I was a very valuable public servant, for the *creation* of the new service. Some of my colleagues were better "subject" inspectors. None, I think, had a better or quicker intuition of the *character* of a school, its aims, and how it realised them. I think this was known to all at the office. Certainly I had got to the position of being privately consulted by my chiefs in a very confidential way . . . I know they all liked me, and my love of freedom and unconventional ways of looking at things were not only tolerated but appreciated, because my results were balanced . . . But I was tired of the school and class inspections, which were becoming for us all mechanical. Nor was it the *real* life: though with no means, a hard life to give up. So it came. I left on good terms with all . . . Wrote and said farewells, and felt *free*!

Geoffrey is putting a brave face on it but he must have found it seriously disturbing. Approaching forty, he still had no settled career. Twice, after only a few years' work, he had abruptly lost his job, directly or indirectly through pressure from those mysterious enemies. Geoffrey was not one to let money worries get him down, but he had no capital to draw upon and his style of life – dinners and dances, visiting grand friends, a great deal of travel, the hire of Alpine guides – required money.

The summer of 1913 was a continuous whirl of travelling, companionship and outdoor adventure. First he went to Cornwall again with George Mallory, swimming and sun-bathing and climbing the sea cliffs. Then he crossed over to Dublin, then to Kerry to join Conor O'Brien on his yacht *Kelpie*: "Two lovely weeks! the children incomparably beautiful: the country low, blue, cubistic, strange, haunted and indescribable." Next he went to the Scottish Highlands for a round of dancing, riding and deer-stalking: "Nearly died of wasp stings got while riding." Next came Northumberland, where he stayed with the Heywoods in Newcastle, then with Charles

Trevelyan at Cambo. From here he motored across northern England to spend a few days with the Slingsbys, now living at Whitbarrow Lodge near Grange-over-Sands: ". . . fell more in love with Len!" Then he went to the Lake District to stay with Professor Pigou in his new house at Lower Gatesgarth, Buttermere. Soon after this he was off to the Alps with Len and Laurence Slingsby, conducting them up the Breithorn. And then to Italy – ". . . and at last Monte Fiano! – and there, the end of wandering, and the real peace found!"

Monte Fiano was a house high up in the Apennines, where Geoffrey joined an old friend of his, the painter William Arnold-Forster, who was later to marry George Mallory's widow and become a political adviser to the Labour Party. The house is still there and little changed, though it is now known as Fontebello. Immediately it had a beneficial effect on Geoffrey. He started to write poetry again, and began work on an exhaustive prose analysis of the craft of mountaineering, an attempt to formulate the basic precepts and principles of the sport in all its forms. It was to be published seven years later as *Mountain Craft*.

In his Journal at the time Geoffrey recorded: ". . . the first time of real heart-ease for many years, like a flower re-opening. Six months of peace, re-settlement and the return of youth and the creative fancy . . . One of the great growth-periods of life."

Recalling it all forty years later, for publication in *The Grace of Forgetting*, he slipped easily into his ecstatic vein:

Will Arnold Forster stood at his easel, and I wrote; and we lived in shorts and sunburn and sandals, and the patterned tiles kept the touch of the sun cool. The vines crept thick and green over the balustrade on three sides of us, and the brown-eyed, brown-legged vineyard children used to climb secretly up the vine-stems from below, and watch from between the leaves for any moment when we might break off, and be willing to start an enthralling *Caccia del Tigre* with them . . . At night, the plain two thousand feet below us turned to a warm and velvety dark blue. The lights of Florence and of the scattered villages shone up from this, as if the earth were reflecting the stars shining above it in the misted velvet blue of the sky . . . I have known nothing like the serene beauty of those nights.

For a while he was happy: "I had not believed before that happiness could be conscious, and yet stay happiness; that it could envelop from without like a cloak of sunshine. Celestial fire was my only word for the feeling, the fire that engulfs but does not consume. To be young, to be in love with beauty and with beautiful people, with the joy of movement and with life itself: it was to live each moment in a celestial blaze of light."

Friends came to stay and there was music and good talk. Probably through George Trevelyan, Geoffrey met some of the leading English poets of the "Georgian" school, among them Wilfred Gibson and Lascelles Abercrombie. Once a month they went down to Florence to look at the architecture and paintings and sculptures, and meet some of the remarkable people who gathered there – Eleonora Duse, the great Italian tragic actress; Yvette Guilbert, the cabaret *diseuse* immortalised by Lautrec; the innovative English stage designer and producer, Gordon Craig; and the travel writer and novelist Norman Douglas. Geoffrey saw much to admire in Douglas, describing him in these words: "Olympically free himself of convention and of prejudice, he revelled like a boy in every genuine human impulse and creation. Private morals were for the individual. Condemnation, blistering but modified by a mellow wit, was reserved for pretentiousness and hypocrisy, and for all who offended against good artistry, good manners and human charity."

He returned home for Christmas at Pen-y-Pass. George Mallory was there and a young engineering student from Manchester University, Siegfried Herford, who was an outstanding climber. Geoffrey described Herford as "shapely, powerful, with a wind-blown fair mane and blue thoughtful eyes, scientific in his interests, a poet at heart, coming and going at our meetings with the spontaneousness of the wind, so near to the light and wonder of the hills in spirit that his feats upon their cliffs seemed only natural."

In *Mountains with a Difference* he described the best of their climbs, the double-girdle of the face of Lliwedd's cliff, from east to west, then back again at a higher level:

> . . . as some people remember music, I now recall my view either way across the Lliwedd precipices storming up the sky under ghostly downfalls of ice, forward and back to the agile figures in white sweaters, swinging, turning, belaying in a counterpoint of precision and force, as the occasional sun-gleam glinted from one or other of the rough fair heads white-rimmed with frost from the shadows . . . We serpentined over the snowy buttresses, seeking out the best passages. At the end, we threw in the Slanting Slab, and then turned up the outside Needle Ridge to lunch on a shelf. The white edges of the lake far below looked crisp with wind-rippled ice, and far above on the left the enormous snow-cone of Y Wyddfa was ringed with wisps of snow-cloud in a wind we did not feel. It was all too good to leave. Why make an end? We dropped down a ridge to a promising

level, and then re-crossed the whole face once more, on a higher and even more exacting line, over bastion, wall and chasm. It was the first double Girdle. We travelled on the return even faster, and in a rhythm which I never remember attaining again on stiff rock with a rope of three.

Geoffrey presided over the annual dinner of the Climbers' Club, and attended a dinner of his own "It" Club. Twice in three weeks he paid flying visits to Berlin: "Huge fun: great coffee parties, wrestling, dancing, and a lot of jolly new kiddies." He went to Paris, too, "to explore its underworld", but was disappointed – "very professional and poor fun". According to the Journal, his "real romance" at this period was the Cornish boy, Wilbert Spencer, who had run away from school to be with Geoffrey.

Early 1914 found him back at Monte Fiano:

Like going to a lovely home. All the creative spirit *bubbling*! To have really found at last a place and life where today remains today: no frets or changes or worries: a perfect life, simple, all the day to work, and the sun on one's fingers. A view like the rim of the world, looking inward: part of life and human, but apart, whence one can see people and events in proportion. Just rest and happiness and youth returning: and unspeakably *free*: no longer living by pretences.

On February 19 he wrote to his father: "Here I am, very happily settled in again. The sun has given us a gorgeous week, one of sun-burning and almond blossoms, and roses, and all good things rushing out." He went on to grow confessional and offer an explanation for relinquishing London life:

It's no good thinking I can alter nature – simply must live in natural circumstances – which means good air and objectively cheerful open-air surroundings. If I don't, I simply *can't* be amiable! I have forced myself for years now, and persuaded myself it was fancy and nervousness and so on: but it isn't. I can do it with a sort of nervous suppression of half myself but I can't do it agreeably! This is really meant for an apology. I felt there was so much I should wish to have talked about – and then never could in that absurd sort of life, of noises and silly hurryings and artificial interests. You see, you've always been so much the "ultimate sanction", that one can't change the attitude of mind and talk easily or readily in quick moments, on things about which one cares greatly what your opinion is – or may be.

It is a strange passage, half-revealing and half-concealing, osten-sibly offering an explanation but also holding back from a full explanation, yet giving a clear illustration of Geoffrey's confused state of mind at the time.

The letter also says: "I am getting on with the book; it is a monumental job and will be largely unreadable. It is tiresome to have so much to say about a wholly unimportant corner of interest! But up here I just sit down after breakfast and don't look up till the evening. Then I usually have a short turn at the poems."

The book he refers to was *Mountain Craft*, which Methuen had agreed to publish. At the Pen-y-Pass party that Easter he read passages from it to close climbing friends, seeking their comments and suggestions. Mallory was there of course, and had brought with him one of his brighter sixth-formers, Robert Graves.

Nearly twenty years later Graves gave a brief account of the holiday in his autobiographical book *Goodbye to all That*. He portrays Geoffrey as a man who climbed with "extraordinary care":

It is not merely shown in his preparations for a climb – the careful examination, foot by foot, of the Alpine rope, the attention to his boot-nails and the balanced loading of his knapsack – but also in his cautiousness in the climbing itself. Before making any move he thought it out foot by foot, as though it were a problem in chess. If the next handhold happened to be just a little out of his reach or the next foothold seemed at all unsteady he would stop and think of some way round the difficulty. George used sometimes to get impatient, but Geoffrey refused to be hurried. He was short, which put him at a disadvantage in the matter of reach. He was not as double-jointed and prehensile as Porter or as magnificent as George, but he was the perfect climber.

Geoffrey did not appreciate the tribute. Commenting on Graves' book, he said: ". . . his memory of this time is so inaccurate as to throw doubt on the rest of his Memoirs."

George Mallory was engaged to Ruth Turner by this time, a partnership that had Geoffrey's full approval. He was best man at their wedding in July 1914.

George Trevelyan, who had been faithfully supportive to Geoffrey in his time of need, was now having troubles of his own, though it is not clear what they were. Geoffrey's Journal records:

Helped G.M.T. in his social row; managed to talk him round again and get him hopeful of life. He talks of me as having "a class in living" for all our circle! It is curious how sincerity *is* effective. The friends seem to come to me more and more . . . Success is an odd thing. Few can have "failed" more in a public sense, and yet had it recognised more as "honest" success by friends and acquaintances. Just the effort to be oneself. I used to think myself a fraud and bluffer: keeping step with abler men. I know now that I have learned to live better than most, and that I can help more than most of my contemporaries to bring folk to a clear view of life.

Trevelyan had been impressed by Geoffrey's new poems, and was too successful, perhaps, in convincing Geoffrey of their high merit. Geoffrey noted: "I *can* write lyrics. I can write them more musically than any man now living. I can write more honest stuff than almost any poet since the Greeks . . . I have a better ear and I have, now, learned the craft better than any contemporary." These are very high claims indeed, and the test of time has not vindicated them.

His second slim volume of verse, *Freedom*, was published that summer. It begins with a tribute to G. M. Trevelyan and their Trinity-based friendship, and concludes with a verse tribute to Will Arnold-Forster and Monte Fiano. Between them stand nearly fifty poems, most of them short, proclaiming his faith in life and nature and liberty, his love of childhood and graceful movement and mountains, in the same high-toned, aspirational vein as suffused his first volume. There is no hint here of the personal anguish that he reveals in the Journal – at the deaths of his climbing friends, at the still-raging conflict between his homosexual inclination and the demands of conventional society. The best, and certainly the best-remembered, of the poems are those in praise of the mountains.

One of these is "High Hills":

> There is much comfort in high hills,
> and a great easing of the heart.
> We look upon them, and our nature fills
> with loftier images from their life apart.
> They set our feet on curves of freedom, bent
> to snap the circles of our discontent.
>
> Mountains are moods; of larger rhythm and line,
> moving between the eternal mode and mine.
> Moments in thought, of which I too am part,
> I lose in them my instant of brief ills –
> There is great easing of the heart,
> and cumulance of comfort on high hills.

Another poem that has become an anthologised piece, "The Crags-man", captures the excitement of climbing steep rock more vividly, in my opinion, than any other poem. This is the opening verse:

In this short span
between my finger-tips on the smooth edge
and these tense feet cramped to the crystal ledge
I hold the life of man.
Consciously I embrace
arched from the mountain rock on which I stand
to the firm limit of my lifted hand
the front of time and space:-
> For what is there in all the world for me
> > but what I know and see?
> And what remains of all I see and know
> > if I let go? . . .

One further poem in this collection, not specifically about mountains, proved popular. Entitled "For Any Boy", it is an attempt – along the lines but not in the style of Kipling's *If* – to crystallise what Geoffrey believed were the vital elements in the upbringing of a boy. In a sense, it may be seen as a clear and lapidary statement of Geoffrey's philosophy. It begins:

I wish for him
strength; that he may be strong in every limb,
stubborn and fearless, with no cover to thank,
fighting for men with men in the front rank.

I wish him kind;
that he may have the weak always in mind:
such kindness as first treads the path of fear,
not tendance on the wounded in the rear.

I'd have him grow
deep-breathed, deep-hearted, cherished of wind and snow;
loving delightful laughter, and harsh thrills
in summer rivers and on perilous hills . . .

And it concludes:

Let him be flame,
quenchless and vital, in all winds the same,
fuse soul and body, and refine through years
judgement from passion, joy from his burning tears.

So let him live:
love work, love rest, love all that life can give;
and when he grows too weary to feel joy,
leave life, with laughter, to some other boy.

The Journal does not mention the publication of *Freedom*. It merely says he was planning a summer visit to the Alps to climb with Knubel and the son of his old guide Ruppen. Then there is one final passage of self-contemplation:

So stand clear to life: free of false shams, free of old chains. And the honester I live, and talk, the more I find other folk honest; the more they seem to come to me. I have two understanding friends left, Will Forster and Hilton: two instinctive friends, George and Charles Trevelyan; the former the more affectionate, the latter the less questioning – and a host of friends in general: especially among the young men and boys.

I believe in vitality first of all, and truth.

Myself I *am* vital: I can be strong, if I can have sun; and keep hard at it, to live sincerely to my nature. I have got life in proportion at last. And I can enjoy it, every wriggle of it, every sense, and curve and indulgence and physical and spiritual moment.

That is the last sustained entry in the Journal he had faithfully kept for more than twelve years. Below, under the heading "Summer 1914" there are two lines scribbled in pencil: "The Alps – Return from Monte Fiano via Alps – The War."

His Alpine season was very brief. Together with Siegfried Herford and Knubel and another guide, Brantschen, he climbed the Matterhorn by the Zmutt Ridge: "Up the snow-covered crags of the ridge to the summit we all went separately for the greater speed; and still unroped we raced down the eastern shoulder to Zermatt, beating the return rush of the snow-blizzard up the valley by a few minutes."

Then the international crisis closed in. The outbreak of the First World War came as a surprise and a shock to the peoples of Europe. Suddenly, after decades of peace and growing prosperity, alliances were invoked and great nations were ordering mobilisation. Geoffrey was one tiny part of a continent-wide scurry to get home before the fighting began. In *The Grace of Forgetting* he remembered: "I attended the peace meeting in Trafalgar Square, the last protest of those who had grown up in the age of civilised peace: and then the dogs of war were off in full cry."

The war was to change and influence his life immensely and in many ways. He had always sought adventure and now he was to have more than his share of danger and excitement. He had suffered cruel bereavements but now, like millions of others, he had to endure the loss of friends on an unimaginable scale. Later on he was to lose his leg. But right from the start, the war gave Geoffrey one great and greatly needed blessing – a consuming sense of purpose, the chance to immerse himself in a cause much greater than himself. He did it immediately and completely and with high courage. In return, he was given relief from all the self-doubts and perplexities that had plagued his spirit in recent years. He kept detailed daily diaries, and most of them have survived, but their pages are full of events and actions and decisions. There was no time now to fret about his true nature and identity, his role in life; no time for the endless wanderings, the manic alternations, the troubled self-assessments of his pre-war Journal.

11

War Correspondent: 1914

ALTHOUGH GEOFFREY WAS NEVER A combatant in the First World War, few saw as much of that war, at the closest possible quarters, as he did. He was in Belgium and northern France, as a newspaper correspondent, when the German divisions swept across to threaten Paris in August and early September 1914. He was in or near Ypres from November that year until July 1915, surrounded by ferocious fighting and a daily witness to the destruction of the old town. And he was in the mountains of north-east Italy, managing an ambulance unit, from August 1915 until the night of August 31, 1917, when an Austrian shell shattered his left leg.

Almost continuously throughout this three-year period, often for weeks on end, his life was in danger. Geoffrey was one of those rare people who are able to endure bombardment – the din and danger of it, the endless uncertainty and frequent sleeplessness, the horrors all around – without being broken in mind or nerve or spirit. He could even find it stimulating. In his diary for July 13, 1915, he describes being under very heavy shell-fire in the ruins of Ypres, and adds: "I'm afraid I like the excitement wickedly. I hate being taken by surprise; but when one can calculate the chances closely and just avoid all but the fringes of chance, it has its own pleasure – to feel the complete hold on one's nerves, and study the reactions – without showing them!"

In another diary entry, in April 1915, he remarked: "No one can stand big shells *and* no work." Certainly, it was the work that kept him going and kept him sane. At Ypres and later in Italy, it was vital, life-saving work. All of Geoffrey's humanity responded to the need. He was frequently frustrated and often exhausted, but always sustained by the conviction that he was doing good work and that he was good at it. At no other time of his life, before or after the war, did he display such total, single-minded, intense dedication to the work in hand than he did in his years with the Friends' Ambulance Unit.

It was not through conscious choice that Geoffrey adopted a non-combatant role. He was not a professing pacifist and could not have claimed exemption from carrying arms on any religious grounds. He had attended the peace rally in Trafalgar Square, as many others had done, simply in the hope that something might be brought about at the last moment to halt the plunge into war on which the great European powers seemed intent. He had, after all, a long-standing affection for Germany and many German friends. In *The Grace of Forgetting*, written nearly forty years later, he described the peace rally as "the last protest of those who had grown up in the age of civilised peace". Geoffrey thought of himself as a European, in the liberal tradition of reason and toleration and unprejudiced humanitarianism. He was patriotic but never nationalistic, and had nothing but contempt for the wave of xenophobic violence that disgraced the streets of London and Paris and Berlin in the first weeks of the war.

Some time in the headlong summer weeks of 1914, as the great nations of Europe lurched towards war, Geoffrey proposed marriage to Eleanor Slingsby and was not accepted. A note of his has survived in the family papers, written from 35, Kensington Square, asking her to meet him at Paddington Station at 4.45 next day, Saturday, to catch the train for Cookham and a weekend at Formosa Place. The note says: ". . . Just comfy summer boating things – anything – and a hat that suits your hair! It is the hugest fun: like a dream of adventure! – to me . . ." Len kept the appointment – she was nineteen, only recently out of school – and she kept Geoffrey's note as well. Many years later she scribbled comments on this and on subsequent letters of his, and, although her handwriting grew notoriously hard to decipher, it is clear from these that while they waited for the train, he proposed. One of her scribbles says: "He had proposed to me (still 19!), Paddington Station. I didn't take it in and was otherwise employed." Even so, they went to Formosa Place and had a wonderful weekend. Geoffrey did not abandon hope.

He was then sharing a bachelor flat in London with his journalist brother Hilton. Towards the end of July, a week or so before Britain declared war on Germany, the phone rang. It was from the *Daily News*, the voice of liberalism among Britain's morning papers, asking Hilton to join them as a war correspondent. It so happened, according to Geoffrey's account, that Hilton had volunteered for service with the Navy that very morning. So Geoffrey, never one to miss the chance of an adventure, offered to go instead. "Those among whom I lived," he later said, "would have thought any course at that time impossible, which did not involve personal action to uphold freedom, even for those of us over military age." He was nearly thirty-eight. Two days later he was crossing the Channel, wearing a dark green riding-suit, carrying letters of accreditation to the French armies, and also carrying – strapped round his waist in chamois-leather purses – 200 golden sovereigns.

No diary has survived from his brief spell as a war correspondent. It was a frenzied, disrupted period and he was constantly on the move, and it seems likely that he did not keep one, relying on his reports to the *Daily News* to keep the record. There are two printed sources of information: a collection of his despatches, published in October 1914 under the title *From the Trenches*; and a chapter of his autobiography *The Grace of Forgetting*, written after the Second World War.

For a few weeks, at the very beginning, the First World War was one of rapid movement as the German divisions swept across Belgium and northern France to threaten Paris, then fell back to the line of the River Aisne. Geoffrey was in the thick of it. It helped that he spoke fluent French and German, though the use of German could be dangerous too. The sovereigns came in useful as well. But his greatest assets were those of character: vitality and natural charm, the ability to stay calm in testing circumstances, sharp observation and a fluent pen. Many of the things he saw shocked and horrified him, but there is no doubt that he was also enjoying himself greatly.

He sailed from Newhaven to Calais, on a boat full of young Frenchmen recalled to the colours, and was in Paris by August 1. In *The Grace of Forgetting*, he remembered the strange scene as he emerged from the Gare du Nord: "Outside, mounted dragoons guarded impromptu barriers with drawn swords, demanding passes. The streets were impassable with mobilising troops. Paris was moving in a nightmare: the impossible was happening ; and England was not yet in, in support. Shops with German names were being looted. Spy fever was raging through unruly mobs." In his first despatch to the paper, he spoke out strongly: "The supposed German shops and houses were being wrecked and looted. Every now and then there was a hurried rush of feet through the street, as some suspect was hunted or maltreated . . . It was the first growl of the best that we had let loose, the savage animal in man waking for our purposes of war."

It was soon apparent to Geoffrey that the French authorities had no intention of allowing journalists anywhere near their front lines. He also knew that it was Belgium that was of primary interest to his readers. It was Germany's disregard for Belgian neutrality that had finally persuaded a divided British government that they could no longer hold back from the war. So he hurried to London to get accreditation to the Belgian forces and, armed with new papers, rushed back across the Channel to Brussells. He used friendly contacts in the government there to secure himself a car and a reliable driver, then set off on a series of swift journeys across Belgium in all directions, probing south and east to see how far the Germans had advanced, then to the coast to find someone who would deliver his despatches to the office in London. He sported "a spruce Homburg hat and yellow gloves to emphasise my harmless civilian character".

In the panicky atmosphere that prevailed in towns near the fighting line, the costume was not always convincing. Geoffrey reported:

> I made the experiment, as an obvious stranger, of sitting outside a restaurant. In five minutes a white-whiskered, respectable magistrate sat down opposite and glared dangerously. "You are a renegade!" I made no answer. A crowd began to collect. "You are a German!" It was dangerous to let him go on. Better attract the police than risk the crowd. "You may have the right to question me, sir: you have none to insult me" – and I stood up suddenly, upsetting him behind the little heavy table. A regulation arrest followed; the first. In two hours I was interrogated seven times by different descriptions of uniformed and civilian officialdom; and three times was escorted to various military authorities.

On another occasion, very close to the front line, Geoffrey translated the dying words of a wounded German soldier and was promptly suspected of being a German spy. He was arrested and threatened with summary execution, and was probably only saved by the fact that the Germans were about to over-run the position.

More than once Geoffrey and his driver came very close to parties of marauding German cavalrymen, still carrying their long metal lances:

> In Gastouche the villagers were dragging out babies and bundles and cattle on to the highway. We ran out beyond the village, and turned the corner, and I was gazing square at some dozen mounted German

lancers 200 yards further on. They were busy taking possession of some buildings and fixing up a pole. To make sure of the uniform, and to cover the retreat of the car, I jumped out and walked a few paces down the road towards them, and then looked through my field-glasses. In return, one of the dismounted men raised his to his eyes; and I left him time for a good look, to make certain of my pacific get-up. Then I walked slowly back. Leon [the driver] had backed the car round the corner, and turned it promptly. Once out of sight, I jumped for it, and we ran back through Gastouche, giving the warning.

Geoffrey was, he claims, the only unofficial visitor to gain entry to the fortress at Namur, a few days before it was invested by the Germans. He went north to Louvain, just before it was besieged. He was in Brussels when it became clear that the Belgian army was not going to be able to stop the advance of the overwhelming German forces. The Belgian government, headed by King Albert – "the mountaineer King" as Geoffrey called him in his despatch – left the capital to make a desperate, final stand at the port of Antwerp. Geoffrey followed, pausing only to collect his driver's family and get them to the coast and arrange for their safe delivery to England to find refuge with his parents at Formosa. The roads of Belgium were crowded with refugees, civilian and military.

He quickly realised that Antwerp would not survive a prolonged siege. Somehow he got himself a lift across the Channel. He was thrilled, on arrival in London, to see the *Daily News* placards, proclaiming his reports in bold headline type. For a few hours he was the star of Fleet Street. He was invited to the Foreign Office to give up-to-the-minute information, and when they asked how long Antwerp could hold out, he answered in two words: "Nine days." He was rushed round to the Admiralty and ushered in to speak to the First Lord, Winston Churchill, who asked the same question and received the same reply: ". . . and the next I heard," Geoffrey wrote, "was that our Naval Division was entering Antwerp on its forlorn hope."

Some time in all this travel and confusion Geoffrey received a postcard from Eleanor Slingsby, dated Whitbarrow, August 30, 1914. It said: "We have heard news of you through George Trevelyan – and read your letters daily when they appear. This job will just suit you. Look after yourself however . . . Our railway service, Midland and North-western, was given up to Russians all yesterday, coming southwards to cross to France. Hooray! All good luck to you and best wishes from all of us. Floreat G.W.Y. Yours ever, Len." Wild rumours of all kinds abounded in the over-heated atmosphere of the first days of the war, and this one about train-loads of Russian soldiers being rushed to the western front was among the dottier ones. Even so, for a few days everyone in England seemed to know someone who had seen them, often with the snow still miraculously on their boots.

It was clear by this time that the thrust of the main German forces in the west was against Paris, so Geoffrey hurried there, finding the city strangely quiet. The French government had fled to Bordeaux, leaving General Gallieni to organise the defence of the capital:

> I had known Paris before the war and before the Americans captured even the night clubs and cafés. And now the few of us wandered through streets so deserted as to seem unknown. Even the heights of Montmartre looked as if they had been moved 200 years back in time, to medieval turrets of stone and dark archways of mystery. The garrison soldiery was friendly, and the atmosphere was at once one of tension and of mutual confidence. Every day Jean and I drove out at the first dawn through the fortifications of 1871.

Jean was his driver. Each day they drove north and east to find out how close the Germans were:

> A civilian with no technical knowledge of war, for me it was an adventure worth while. Every dozen miles we ran into some fresh impasse, or some different coloured pass was demanded of us. While my wits were employed in avoiding arrest and circumventing the hindrances from our own armies, every other faculty was on the stretch to discover from signs and movements, or from the sound of the firing, what was happening and how much closer the hammerstroke had approached during the last hours.

He went to Rheims and was horrified to see the destruction German shells had caused to the great cathedral. He expressed his revulsion in the *Daily News*:

> This was, to myself, the second conscious shock in all the two months of warfare – Louvain was the first. The sight of dead and shattered bodies soon passes unrealised. There is nothing of the man who lived, even if we have known him well, left in lifeless remnants. What he meant and what he produced are no longer there. But to see a dead or an injured child, a mutilated work of art or thought, is to see the murder of men's souls: the defacing of the ideal which men live and die to conceive, to embody, and to leave as their contribution to the eternal principles of beauty and continuance.

It is remarkably high-toned stuff for the pages of a popular newspaper but Geoffrey was not one to talk down to his audience and the paper was happy to print his long, colourful and thoughtful despatches in full. They were especially pleased when there was good news to report at last, the retreat of the Germans from the Marne, driven back by Joffre's French armies and the small but highly trained British Expeditionary Force in mid-September. "Our soldiers are in fine fettle," Geoffrey reported, "The men are in great heart." He was close behind the allied armies as they pushed northwards to the River Aisne, and hit the headlines once again when he swam across the river on what he later described as "a personal if mild reconnaissance".

He went out one night with a stretcher party, searching no-man's-land for wounded men, and reported to the *Daily News*:

We stumbled upon five or six bodies, but the enemy had clearly had time to remove their wounded with them. Two, however, left for dead, had been revived by the cold of the night, and were groaning. We found them by the sound. They were some way back from the trench in the wet grass. One had been hit behind the shoulder, presumably while he was retreating. The dark chill of the night, with the little quick flashes of searching lights, and the mutter of occasional orders in the silence, lent additional impressiveness to the steady, business-like courage of the ambulance men. It is a work that requires very practised nerves under modern fighting conditions. None of the excitement of fighting for them, or the stimulus of "hitting back"; yet they get hit themselves often enough. These long days of furious bombardment, raking long lines of hidden positions, trench and village, must inevitably, and without intention, find shells dropping upon man, house or wagon, whose Red Cross is unseen or indistinguishable. The greater credit to the men whose dangerous work and even occasional death can earn them no glory of individual exploit.

Before long, this would be Geoffrey's continuous lot, ambulance work under shell-fire.

Now the soldiers on both sides began to dig in, starting to create the opposing networks of trenches that would soon stretch from the Swiss border to the Channel coast and hold the armies locked in an almost static and murderous stalemate for the next four years. Geoffrey realised, sooner than most, that a new kind of warfare was emerging. He warned his readers:

War, the war of Ilium, of Agincourt, of Waterloo, used to be a brilliant affair. Death harnessed to a glittering car of Juggernaut. Men went under the wheels in a rush and flame of colours, and to the sounds of bands and the applause of multitudes. The car is now hidden in a dull, deadly rolling cloud. We can only hear the rumour of the hidden wheels. Our sons and friends move into the darkness. Of many of them, all we shall ever know is that they have not returned. The greater heroes, that they go as gladly as ever did a chosen knight into crowded lists. The finer men, that they fight as stoutly with no record of their gallantry, no mark even of their death-place.

The big strategic question now was control of the Channel ports. Both armies had been preoccupied with Paris, but as the line there solidified they raced north to try to win the advantage. Geoffrey raced to see the action.

So far he had relied on his own enterprise and guile to get him through, much helped by the fluidity of the situation and the confusion of the authorities, Belgian, French and British. The British, though, were now determined to put an end to his sort of uncontrolled, free-wheeling reporting. At Dunkirk he was arrested by the Royal Navy. Fortunately, the young officer put in charge of him turned out to be one of his former star pupils at Eton, and it was not long before he succeeded in getting away. He headed for Calais and soon came across the remnants of the Belgian army, smashed at the battle of Yser. In *The Grace of Forgetting* he recalled the scene: "Without shelter, in the squalls, all along the stone flags of the wintry quays were scattered the stretchers of the Belgian wounded. Their uniforms and blankets were caked with freezing Flanders mud. Medical provision had been exhausted. A single surgeon and one nurse struggled up and down among the thousand stretchers in the blasting wind and salt sleet."

There was an official of the British Red Cross there, Sir Henry Norman, and it was agreed that Geoffrey should go to London and see what could be done to help. He sought out the President of the Red Cross, Sir Arthur Stanley, who remembered a group of young Quakers, many of them Cambridge men, who had been setting up an ambulance unit. Geoffrey knew them. He had lectured to them about his adventures in Belgium, and two of their leaders, Lawrence Cadbury and Philip Noel-Baker, had been frequent visitors to Formosa. They were contacted by telegram, and a party of forty men and eight ambulance cars was assembled. Geoffrey's old friend Vincent Baddeley, now Financial Secretary at the Admiralty, found them places on the *Invicta*, sailing for Calais.

They found thousands of sick and wounded men – Belgian and

French (mostly from North African regiments), a few British and Germans – with virtually no medical facilities. Immediately, Geoffrey plunged himself into the sort of work that would be the whole of his life for the next three years:

> Our boys and our few doctors were landed on the quays and threw themselves into the work. They worked continuously at first, and then in shifts; in half darkness, in nauseating stench, among always new hundreds of wounded heaped on the floor in delirium, coma and death. It was a grim introduction for young men to the new era of wars. For three days and nights we had no base or lodging for them, and they slept and were fed where they worked, on the open wintry quays. The hopelessly insanitary conditions for operating and bandaging made it improbable that many of the more seriously wounded could survive. I myself, with no experience at all, was called upon several times to give the anaesthetic for emergency operations.

It soon became clear that Geoffrey's real role was that of organiser. Cautiously at first but then with increasing authority, it was he who made the endless decisions, found accommodation, negotiated with army and naval and civil authorities, arranged for transport and supplies. More than 6,000 men were shipped to England, and when the work was completed they were asked if they would go to the area of Ypres to see if they could help there.

The British army now occupied the Ypres sector of the allied line. It was late October when Geoffrey and his group arrived, just in time to see the fine medieval town before its destruction began: "The town was still untouched, in all the quiet beauty of wide streets, picturesque gabled houses, noble public buildings, of its great Cloth Hall and Cathedral, and of a serene burgher life, into which it had retreated after a long historic past."

There was a great bulge in the allied line, the Ypres salient, to the north and the east and the south-east of the old town, which meant that it was wide open to short-range artillery bombardment from many angles.

The arrival of Geoffrey and his party almost coincided with the start of a ferocious German assault which went on for six weeks, to the end of November 1914, a battle which was to become known as the First Ypres. The British held their line but at a fearful cost. In his *History of the First World War* Liddell Hart said: "This defence of Ypres is in a dual sense the supreme memorial to the British Regular Army, for here its officers and men showed the inestimable value of the disciplined morale and unique standard of musketry which were the fruit of long training, and here was their tombstone."

The ambulance unit was not welcomed at first. A stuffy, obstructive colonel of the Royal Army Medical Corps rejected their offers of help, suspecting that his authority was being undermined. It was the first of countless similar difficulties that were to arise in the coming months, and Geoffrey showed from the first that he had the necessary qualities to deal with it – the cool diplomatic manner, patience and persistence.

He moved away and waited a few days. Then, as the battle raged, he moved the unit – fifteen men, three ambulance cars and one lorry – into Ypres to try to set up a hospital. But Ypres was very different now:

> We had left it in medieval beauty. Now, against yellow wreaths of smoke, the sullen glare and red gleam of some 40 columns of fire, from the burning buildings of the deserted city. As we drove in it was to the menacing roar of flames, and to hear the growl rolling in from the vast semi-circle of surrounding trenches where the flower of the Prussian armies was still shattering itself on the unyielding British lines.

The shelling was so insistent they were forced out of the town. They drove north to the village of Woesten, where French regiments had moved in and were delighted to see them. They set to work immediately. It was the end of Geoffrey's career as a war correspondent: "All that I had been seeing these last days had convinced me there were gaps on the front which, say what the authorities might, only our volunteer work could fill for the time being; and that my sort of experience could do better work for the wounded in the war by joining the Unit, than I could ever do by continuing as an amateur correspondent."

They had already named themselves the Friends' Ambulance Unit. They were in business.

12

Ypres: November 1914– August 1915

WHEN THEY ARRIVED IN THE Ypres region their cars still proclaimed their original name, the First Anglo-Belgian Unit. This was clearly no longer appropriate. In *The Grace of Forgetting* Geoffrey said: "At an early conference of Philip Noel-Baker and his brother Joseph, Maxwell our adjutant, Nockolds the principal surgeon, and myself, the question of the renaming of the Unit came up for settlement. Two of our officers were Quakers by birth, while three were not; but we were all personal friends. So I suggested that we should call ourselves the Friends' Ambulance Unit, which should cover the whole case as it stood." The suggestion was adopted and the name stuck.

In later years Geoffrey always felt, with some resentment and some justification too, that his contribution to the formation and secure establishment of the FAU had not been properly recognised in official Quaker accounts. Some time after the Second World War he typed out a couple of large pages, summarising what he had done and expressing his hurt. "The official history of the Unit in the 1914 war", he said, "shows a not uncharacteristic desire on the part of the Quakers to ignore the part taken in the launching and control and placing of the Unit and its work, by those of us who were not 'Friends' in the technical sense. Notably, my own leading part has been suppressed to a startling degree. And since it is one of the best jobs I have done in a somewhat altruistic life, I think I may put on record the facts, in barest outline." He goes on to do so in one sentence: "I brought the FAU out, I named it, I commanded it at the front, I started the civilian work which made its success, and held it through the critical months when all the armies wanted to eject us from the front."

In *The Grace of Forgetting* Geoffrey gives a much fuller description of his work with the Unit, but says nothing about his dissatisfaction with the official Quaker accounts. This is reserved for his unpublished pages – "Friends' Ambulance Unit and G.W.Y." – in which he goes on to say: "I have the greatest admiration for the Quaker spirit and independent attitude. But the convention which compels them to postulate individual inspiration or direction for every personal action or line of conduct I have found to lead to a great deal of intellectual dishonesty. They are, in fact, very difficult folk to deal with collectively, or to have as colleagues." These judgements are reflected again and again in what is by far the most important and immediate source of information for this period of Geoffrey's life – the daily diaries that he kept from November 27, 1914 until July 30, 1915.

In fact he kept the diaries for much longer than that, up to and beyond the end of the war. But from the point of view of this chapter, the vital documents are those which are collectively known as the "Ypres Journal".

It is a monumental and fascinating record, giving a detailed and vivid account of what life, and death, were like in one of the key sectors of the opening year of the war: two great battles; almost continuous shelling; a typhoid epidemic; the first use of poison gas in modern war; the movements and methods of three allied armies, French, British and Canadian; the destruction of an ancient town; and the effects of all this upon the soldiers, on babies and young children and women and old people caught up in the conflict, and on the gallant band of volunteers in the FAU who were doing what they could to help. Naturally, it is a personal statement, one man's uncensored and uninhibited view of what was happening, and it reveals much about Geoffrey's attitudes and principles. But it is also, I believe, a reliable account. Geoffrey was everywhere, endlessly on the move; he was dealing with everyone, from the highest to the lowest levels; he was a mature, intelligent and observant man; and the conditions in which he worked, however punishing, did not upset his mental balance and did much to sharpen his eyes and ears and sympathies. And he wrote it all down, daily, usually at the end of a very long day's labour.

The Ypres Journal covers eight months of intense activity in more than 130,000 words.

He wrote up his diaries in ordinary exercise books: some marbled and some plain; some lined, some unlined; some written on both sides of the paper, others on only one. He wrote in blue ink, usually legibly, though there are signs of exhaustion at times and here and there the ink has faded. Not surprisingly, there are signs of wear-and-tear too, from bombardment and rough travel and candle wax – most of his writing was done at night. Geoffrey said that he kept the diaries for his mother and father. Whenever he managed to get a day or two's break in England, he would leave the last book at Formosa Place and take a new one back with him. There are seven such books dealing with the months in the Ypres region.

In the early 1950s Geoffrey read carefully through the pages of the diaries to refresh his memory and help him in the writing of the two chapters of *The Grace of Forgetting* which deal with the Ypres period. In the result, he produced a fair summary of his experiences, but in this chapter I intend to quote chiefly from the original diaries. They are more immediate and more concrete, and they have not been published. Any quotations from *The Grace of Forgetting* will be acknowledged as such. Unacknowledged quotations are from the Ypres Journal.

The very first entry sets the tone:

> *Nov. 27.* Re-entered Ypres, O.C. and Cadbury. Found it in ruins after the bombardment. A few shells still falling. We met Miss Vanderghote, daughter of Belgian Commissary whose house has been occupied by British staff and who, while acting as guide to them, kept his family of four children during all five weeks of shells; some in garden and fragments in all the rooms. She took us to the Convent St Godalieph and Nazareth Convent opposite, where we found one British RAMC Frederick Harding and one police-soldier "Thomas"; the latter usually drunk and fighting and firing at the looters. Also Albert, a cheery shirker from Blackfriars in uniform and tweed cap, whose regiment had been wiped out, and who was careful therefore not to get back too soon . . . The people all slept in cellars or in the casemates, in appalling smells, getting pleurisy . . . French soldiers looting mildly, bands of apaches at dusk pillaging. No control . . .

The place was physically smashed and abandoned to anarchy. The Belgian civic authorities had fled. The French army, theoretically in control, took no interest in the plight of those civilians who remained. British and French soldiers, who had deserted or simply become separated from their units, searched the ruins for loot and food and pointed their rifles at anyone who threatened to stop them.

His first job, Geoffrey decided, was to get the civilians out of Ypres. He found sixty old people sheltering in a convent, being looked after by ten nursing nuns. He sent for the ambulance cars and had them all transported to Poperinghe, being greatly helped in this work by the Curé of St Pierre, Charles Del'Aere, a man who was to be his loyal friend and support in the months ahead and to become a legendary hero of the Ypres story.

Next day Geoffrey rescued more old folk and began a daily routine of searching through the debris and cellars for wounded people or those who simply did not want to leave. When it became clear that the Belgian authorities in Poperinghe were not going to find hospital places for his civilians, he decided to set up his own hospital ward in Ypres itself. With the Curé's help he found a large room in an abandoned asylum on the western edge of the town, untouched by the shelling so far. In one day, December 1, forty beds were installed and the ward was opened, with one doctor and four nursing sisters. Patients were moved in and next morning the first operation was performed.

In addition to this, ambulance cars of the unit were stationed at aid-posts near the French trenches, ready to rush the wounded back.

The diary entry for December 7 reads:

Desperately busy day. Arrived Ypres to find 70 shells had fallen during night; 14 civilian dead; many wounded; ambulances worked all morning bringing them in; 5 or 6 children, one with foot for amputation; some 3 women; divided up cars to work the town. The roads difficult as impassable shell holes in new places. Shrapnel bombardment nearly all day, and some narrow escapes. Munro arrived with Countess Spahlberg, on behalf of the Queen, to see about rescue of Cathedral relics; turned their attention to the people . . . Seven or eight shells burst in fields near the hospital, aimed at French battery.

In the evening he returned to his headquarters at the village school in Woesten near the French front line trenches, taking with him four young children whose house had been destroyed. But the day's work was not done yet:

. . . One of Munro's cars arrived, in dark search for Ypres children in general – on Miss Fyffe's orders! Advised that it was folly; they returned. Later heard that Queen, on receipt of report, despatched Belgian officers to Ypres to fetch out inhabitants! As they had no cars, they requisitioned Betterham's in passing. Not having enough petrol, he shot some 30–40 into our hospital! where they were put three in a bed! This is a specimen of the sort of problems we deal with. A wet nasty night; constant movement of troops.

Winter was closing in. The roads were crowded and miry and often shell-damaged. But the greatest problem was the absence of any unified control. The French military were preoccupied with their own troubles and only interested in soldier casualties. The British medical officers, so far from being co-operative, seemed to resent the Unit. And now Belgian royals and aristocrats and officials were muscling in and creating further confusion.

Geoffrey's comments are forceful: "*Dec. 29*, 1914 . . . What one *could* write about these muddle-headed Generals and their narrow fussy incompetence." He is referring here to the local French commanders, and turned on them again, a few days later, when it looked as if the Unit was to be moved out:

Jan. 3, 1915 . . . I had hoped that the move when it came might be forward. But the long pause has given too much time to the military busybodies. The immediate need of us has lapsed into habit. The headquarters folk have had time to look behind their killing lines and to meddle; and their care is for uniformity, not for the saving of suffering we represent.

Feb. 1, 1915 . . . Saw offensive little staff officer [a British lieutenant] who said he had orders "to turn us out at 11" – typical this; after three months of work for them . . . Went back to real staff at Chateau and reduced a colonel to some sense of the position and of mine. He would send the captain . . . Returned to Woesten. Captain appeared, at first high-handed, but in ten minutes' talk blown off the earth by "Generals" and "Headquarters" on my part . . . Parted friends – but what imbeciles soldiers are! A whole dramatic talent and some diplomatic gift used to exhaustion to protect work which all of us knew was admirable, and which they couldn't do! A very cheerful lunch in the nuns' kitchen; all quite in heart again. In the middle, in blows our young lieutenant to discharge his corrected orders. I took them stiffly but politely, until he ventured an opinion that neither army wanted us. Then, before the boys, I gave him five minutes' courteous dressing-down that delighted them . . . I enjoyed it hugely.

June 27, 1915 . . . The Brigadier, Stuart Wortley, 46 Division, was the extreme of the old type of soldier, unfortunately left alive – tall, decaying, handsome, infinitely snobbish and boring; "helped the earth enough by living on it" without having to bother to be polite to it. I have so often to explain that these types are not typical – except of their caste – in England.

Geoffrey was a formidable enemy. He was cool and he could be patient and courteous; but he was articulate too and he could be incisive; he did not easily lose his temper but when he did it was to resounding effect. He was physically fit and strong, and drew moral strength from the fact that he was not trying to safeguard or advance his own career, simply fighting for something in which he passionately believed. As the weeks passed and more and more people realised what the Unit was doing, the strength of his position grew. He always believed in using contacts, friends and acquaintances in high places, and made a point of becoming a familiar figure to those who mattered – British, French and Belgian. It was a great help to his standing when, in February 1915, his friend Marcus Heywood turned up in the area, a staff officer to General Plumer, commander of the 5th Corps and later of the 2nd Army. Plumer was soon among his friends as well.

Other factors helped. It was a recurring nuisance to have to fend off interference from at least three different directions – the French, the British and the Belgians – but it meant he could sometimes play them off against each other, use one to confuse the others, refer to directives in different languages. It also helped that he was older and more mature than most of the officers he had to deal with. It certainly helped that his status was nebulous – the officer commanding the Unit and very much in control of it, and yet not, strictly speaking, a British army officer at all, nor an officer of any other army, although he soon took to wearing the uniform of a British major, with a cape and a fine military-type moustache and the pipe clenched between the teeth.

With the men of the Unit he got on, for the most part, very well indeed. He had the highest admiration for the skill and courage of his young drivers, who soon included several old friends – Professor Pigou of Cambridge; Claude Elliott, who had not been accepted by the army because of a knee, damaged in a pre-war fall on Pillar Rock; and Arnold Lunn. Another Cambridge friend, Desmond McCarthy, turned up to work as a cook orderly at Woesten and then as Geoffrey's assistant-adjutant.

Geoffrey had virtually no trouble, too, with the nuns who formed most of his nursing staff. It was the doctors and surgeons who made difficulties. Some resented having to take orders from a lay person, someone totally unqualified in medicine. Things went well enough when they were over-worked, which was much of the time, but in the quieter periods they would all too readily fall to feuding and manoeuvring and trying to undermine his authority. In a Journal entry dated March 23, 1915 he complains that it is lonely work – "managing these men like silly children". And almost at the close of the Ypres period, in June, he was still made angry by the thought of them: ". . . they are ungracious natures. I never worked with a less responsive set of men. Even after seven months I have to make all the efforts myself. This excepts a few more civilised men. I cannot stand the apathetic Quaker greetings. If it is that they won't pretend what they don't feel, they are a singularly ill-natured tribe!"

He lashes out in other directions as well – at the local British Consul who was useless; at obstructive Red Cross officials. He resented the time he had to waste attending to visiting dignitaries. Rudyard Kipling and Somerset Maugham were there in January 1915; the Prince of Wales and King Albert of the Belgians a month later. He gives a full account of one such visit – that of Ramsay MacDonald, the Labour Party leader, on December 22, 1914.

MacDonald had made himself widely hated a few months before by opposing Britain's entry into the war. On his first attempt to visit the front, in early December, he had been arrested and shipped home again. He made a fuss, insisting on his rights as an MP and returned a few weeks later with General Seeley as his escort. They were taken to have lunch at Geoffrey's headquarters in the old school-house at Woesten. In the Ypres Journal Geoffrey dismisses it in one line: "Visit (lunch) from General Seeley, Ramsay MacDonald and Munro. Dull talk." In another of his unpublished papers, about politicians he had encountered, he gives a fuller account:

> . . . They blew in, cordial and dignified . . . but in an atmosphere one felt at once very far removed from our front feeling, with its guns and wounded and over-driven nerves. In the room below at the time two rows of hopelessly wounded men, French Territorials with head wounds, lay dying . . . They [Seeley and MacDonald] talked rather flat politics and generalities while my Quakers looked at first impressed and then bored and drifted off to their cars. At last I too got bored and, being busy and anxious, moved across to stand at my desk and write . . . S and M were left sitting alone by the central stove in our two borrowed chairs, and this is what I heard, as near as may be . . . Seeley: "My dear Ramsay; I have, as you know, opportunities of mixing with many classes of people and very different sets and ranks. And I find, you know Ramsay, they are at the present time divided into two distinct bodies of opinion, singularly opposed. There are those who, weighing up the military position as we now see it, take a thoroughly optimistic view of our future, and feel that all is moving for the best. And there are those, on the other hand, my dear Ramsay, who take the contrary view and regard the future with pessimistic feelings. Now what I want you

to tell me, Ramsay, as a man who has moved much in affairs and sees many worlds, is which of these human divisions do you consider to be right?"

And then Ramsay boomed, in his deep melodious voice and well-cultivated Scottish intonation – and both men, you could hear, were the sort of public speakers who listened to their own voices: "I am, as you say, my dear Seeley, a man who perhaps even more than yourself has mingled with very different sorts of people and is in contact with very wide circles . . . And if, my dear Seeley, you ask me to say as to which of the two very opposite views which you have described I should consider to be the truer description of our situation as it is now and as it may develop later, I should reply, my dear Seeley, that I consider that the trrruth lies somewhere . . . just . . . exactly between the two" – and his hand made a graceful partitioning gesture. As the period rolled to its colossal end I had waited breathlessly, in half-terrified anticipation – and at its melodious final fall I banged my hand down on the desk and gave a hoot of laughter . . . And yet there was something terrifying, in *this* going on here inside, while *that* was going on there outside . . .

What was going on outside was real and terrible. The pages of the Ypres Journal are crammed with horrors:

February 1, 1915 . . . I believe it is true that neither side is using its best troops in the trenches – hence the stories of "bog-prisoners". The stories of madness are frequent. The strain no man seems able to support, under accurate shell-fire. In one British trench all the men were dead when at last relieved after four days. One surviving subaltern had made himself drunk on the men's brandy, to endure it, after having pegged out his senior, who was mad, with bayonets to prevent him shooting himself.

February 12 . . . The pretty child who came in wounded died about 8 p.m. – we shall have to find the family . . . It was just as well we had them alert, as at 12.30 a.m. came a summons to fetch wounded. One of the night shells killed a dozen Life Guards in billet and six civilians, four children. We sent to fetch four more. One more died. The doctors at it all night. Another baby boy died at 5 a.m. . . . Another, of eight, a pretty child is dying of typhoid – meningitis all day in the other ward. The tragedy of these children . . . Some snow today. Summoned in evening to fetch 45 more "frozen feet" soldiers back, for whom no ambulances . . .

This was the disease called "trench feet" which afflicted both sides in the cruel winter of 1914–15 when the trenches were newly dug. Geoffrey described its effects in *The Grace of Forgetting*:

My ambulances picked up a small squad of Kings Royal Rifles literally crawling over the fields. They were brown cold blocks of freezing mud up to their caps; so cold they could not speak, and their rifles and every inch of them inches deep under congealed slimy mud-cake. I had never seen men so utterly done in. They were newly from India, they had ague, they had frozen feet, they had been standing for four days waist-deep in icy mud. Only one of them, the youngest, could use his legs; the rest could only crawl.

Another passage in the same chapter describes what it was like to be working continually in Ypres:

Whenever the bombardment increased, the noise alone could paralyse the will. The nerve-strain and suspense, for anyone working above ground in the town on those days, cannot be reproduced in words; when always to move slower or faster, to turn this way or that, might mean just to escape, or just not to escape, death. There was a throat-catching choking threat in the Ypres atmosphere, under heavy intermittent shell-fall, an unresolved suspense, that wore down in time the nerve of the boldest. I learned to watch every driver, and every one of my group working long under fire, for the signs of strain, suppressed by will and courage, but apt to take revenge in an unexpected breakdown.

On April 22, 1915 a fresh horror was introduced. Geoffrey wrote it up in the Journal during what he described as "an absolute inferno of guns; like the great battles of last November". He had been home for three days on Unit business and returned to the German bombardment that heralded their attempt to straighten out their line in the Second Battle of Ypres. They were using a new weapon:

. . . Two British officers in, badly shaken; had been fishing up on the Yser and came in for the French smash an hour ago – really shattered nerves, poor chaps. This looks like the real German effort, or at least the counter-stroke to Hill 60. And the devils are using gas, as we guessed they would when we saw their notice of the British doing it! Utter poison. Described (by one of the shaken officers) – "I was only near the guns, well back, and began to choke and my eyes to smart – looked across and saw it rolling gently towards us, over the first trenches! – a yellow, bright wall of cloud, 100 feet high, two miles long, creeping up on a light wind. Probably chloride, released from large tubes, as it was quite even in thickness; impossible to live in it." Sounded like H. G. Wells, as he told us; an awful new factor, if it works . . . Is it the big German move? Things near are always magnified, and every soldier back from the trench is always in despair.

It *was* the big German effort, and the weight of the German bombardment forced the Unit to begin next morning to evacuate their Ypres hospital and move all their patients – gassed and wounded soldiers, sick and wounded civilians – first to Poperinghe, then further away from the violent action.

Danger was omnipresent – from German shells and bombs, from allied shells falling short, from fire and falling masonry, and from disease:

March 15, 1915 . . . Little Jeffrey drove – "the angel child" – and Watts came with us. I laughed as we turned by the station square, saying "To go by the Rue d'Elverdinghe is true courage, by the Rue au Beurre – bravado." We heard a shell or two fall, and raced quickly round the corner; were hailed by a pleasant firm-nerved officer to say there were wounded lying beyond the line. As we talked two shells burst close. Watts stayed back inquiring about the wounded. Jeffrey sped the car across the square with self and officer. He told me hurriedly that he had told a squad to hurry, but they dawdled and 3 or 4 were killed, one still alive. It was worth the effort. As we crossed the line another big one burst on the right and the glass shattered round. The street nearly empty; the air full of dust; utter silence; a few figures on the far side of the square behind waiting at the street ends; who all fell flat as the scream went past and the roar followed. As we rushed on I saw a civilian flat on the road; stopped, but the officer called out "He's dead". I ran on with him to a cluster of khaki figures sprawled on the pavement. Jeffrey, with quick head, turned the car rapidly and backed up to us. One was just alive still. As we lifted him, another shell screamed and burst deafeningly just on the left. A brick chip must have grazed my wrist. We crammed him in without waiting to loosen a stretcher. They jumped in and I urged Jeffrey to speed back. As we whirled, another burst behind us. It was curiously menacing and breathless, more like a war picture than anything I've seen – the grim street, dead figures (for the first time in khaki), furious pace. To my utter surprise, as we neared the line, dear old Harold Watts came running to meet us! He had run right across that square alone, falling flat as the shells exploded, and came on. It is the quiet, quaint, humorous men who have the great courage. We stopped on the far side, to see if we could find other men . . . I noticed the faithful pipe had kept in all the time. We just got the soldier into the Field Ambulance here; but he died soon after.

May 5 . . . I patrolled the quarter alone, visiting the cellars. A lonely nervous job, in the utterly deserted rubbled streets, with the continual wheeze and burst of shrapnel overhead; but the fragments showed their usual discretion. Once I walked all down the Rue de Lille, and they hunted me fairly with six shells, straight down the street, overhead – bursting behind and in front, and it was difficult to decide whether to stop or hurry! One gets a sort of deliberate walk in such places, with the uncontrollable check in it at the sound of the passing beast . . . It is haunting to see the poisoned and wounded creeping through the infernal, empty streets; a joy to be able to shove them in and career off, with all the odious necessary slackening in order to crawl over the debris and holes of the Devil's Crossing, the most fatal spot of all . . .

July 13 . . . A scattered party of soldiers waved us to stop, which George did, hesitating. I wanted to make sure it was only *one* corner they were shelling; but couldn't get a clear answer, they were a good deal scared and pale. "There's men been killed here!" "When?" "Two days ago." This was too much, and it was the worst place to stop, on the curve – also to turn would take time. I heard my own voice saying quietly but decidedly, "Go on George – and quickly." He played up finely. But the pause had just spoiled our timing. Fifty yards further a shriek passed exactly over our heads, not ten feet above the car, and the shell thundered white in the field, thirty yards to our left. Not a dropping shell either, for it was on the up-slant. A close shave. We sped on up the hill behind the trees, another exploding further back behind. Shells burst very harmlessly in soft soil!

The Journal, however, is not all horror and danger and dreadfulness. Geoffrey's sharp eye could find beauty in unlikely places. On December 20, 1914 he watched a German plane, high overhead, under attack from French anti-aircraft guns: "Watched Taube shot at as folk returned from Mass along Poperinghe road. Explosion; sudden puff of silver smoke born in dead blue sky; faint report – beautiful but strange." A few days later, on Christmas Day, he returned to his headquarters at Woesten:

. . . Found decorative feast organised by MacCarthy. Holly, lights, colours and spread. Who could have known this from our bare upper room of two months back? Songs and jolly evening; many recitations. Nuns came up and put on coloured caps – picturesque sight – also our refugee children. Dinner excellent . . . Lull on line and little work. Bitter cold and brilliant sunny frost and snow.

When they were forced to leave the hospital in Ypres, Geoffrey took up quarters in an open summer-house in the garden of their new hospital in Poperinghe:

April 30, 1915 . . . The nightingale came back this morning; and there are corners of white blossom in the garden . . .

May 9 . . . They are at it, thunderingly again tonight; and the rifle fire is very clear. It is now sub-conscious, the sound. I only notice silences. The nightingale has given up; only a flirt or two.

May 10. He was at it again early this morning, trial notes; but tonight he has a full song; tentative still, but exquisite on a dark, starry, rather chilly night.

May 20 . . . To finish, a summer-house gossip with Arnold Lunn, and a marvellous turn of my old friend, the nightingale, in the garden dark trees. And the news that Italy has declared war.

The companionship of friends like Arnold Lunn and Marcus Heywood – "a man who walked with sunshine all his days", Geoffrey once said – did much to sustain his spirits. So did the comradeship of his drivers and orderlies, and the nuns who worked as nurses on the wards and ran the orphanage he set up for the children in his care. His greatest admiration, perhaps, was reserved for two Belgians who became legendary heroes of the Ypres story, the Curé and Sœur Marguerite. They had been there longer than he had, and lost much more than he had. Day after day he worked alongside them, and observed them, taking the dangers and the horrors as they came, tireless and selfless and never giving way to despair. On May 3, 1915, when Geoffrey drove into Ypres to help with the gas casualties, he recorded: "Found the Curé active and splendid as ever, and Sœur Marguerite angelic and quietly witty, with the few other sisters of her lot, all there." When there was nothing left of the town except rubble and the carcases of dead horses and dead people, and all civilians had to leave, Geoffrey found her again: ". . . sack ready packed with school books, to tramp with it on shoulder, if she *has* to leave, to England, to resume teaching. She would too! She and the Curé are a pair to have known. Her little laugh, and gentle pointed joke, ready for any dangerous moment."

As well as writing the Journals throughout this period, Geoffrey was writing letters. New of family and friends meant much to him. A few of these leters have survived.

On December 19, 1914, Len Slingsby wrote from Whitbarrow Lodge:

Dear Geoffrey,

If this ever reaches you I shall be surprised – but I want to write and congratulate you on several things you've been doing lately – first your climbing go this summer of which I read and heard – next your present work of which I also read a short account in a Quaker paper this week (on Mother's side we are Quakerish, or were) – and lastly your poems, which I really do like very much . . .

She is referring to his more recent volume *Freedom*, and goes on to talk about her own poetry-writing and her hope that he will help her with advice. She gives news of her brother Laurence, on active service in France, and her own war work – ". . . no end of knitting – looking after dirty babies once a week (while their mothers have a meeting and talking to etc.) . . ."

There are two letters from Geoffrey to Len. The first is merely dated 1915, written at Dunkirk where he was discussing arrangements for the ambulance unit to be sent to Italy and who should take over his duties in Flanders, so it was probably written in late June 1915. He says: ". . . Splendid about your poems, keep them going, and don't forget that I should really care to see them. About my own, it's curious. I like people to like them, but it's only of second importance. I *know* which are good, both as craft and as song: and which are very good. And it only interests me to find people quarrelling with them! . . ."

The other letter was written in July that year to express his concern over Len's sister Alizon, who had married an Italian and was now dangerously ill in Rome. Len and her father were in Rome. Geoffrey says:

My dear Len,
My deep sympathy and anxious thought . . .
Keep me in touch with your plans. And there is always Monte Fiano, above Fiesole – which is empty – if you want a high place for Alizon to rest at.
I won't bother you with a long screed in your anxious time.
But I think of you daily, and share something of your trial, the heat and anxiety, in thought –
as always,
Geoffrey Young.

Geoffrey was home in England for a week at the end of February 1915. A letter from his father says: ". . . Yes, Geoffrey is here. He much needed a spell off. Not that in any particular respect his health was giving way, or his skill or courage failing; but his nerves were suffering from the never-ceasing noise of guns. He says he never minded the explosion of the shells – could keep his pipe alight, when one went off in the garden – but the shriek of the approaching shell . . ."

Most of Geoffrey's time in England was spent in London, lobbying and cajoling for the Unit, explaining their needs to the Quaker committee that controlled their fortunes. He was delighted to find their work was widely known and appreciated. And he took the opportunity to recruit his mother's experienced support, asking her to collect and send him clothing for his staff and patients, toys for the children. The toys were especially important. In his Journal on April 9 he wrote: ". . . Carried the toy box round the wards again; the 'choice' does cheer them all up; pennyworths of pleasure."

On the opening day of that year he had noted: "My hospital is my happiest place: I love the visits to it; my best work – I shouldn't mind being buried there." His greatest pride and pleasure was in the children whose lives he had saved and helped restore. On January 25 he mentions the arrival of a new patient, a fifteen-year-old Belgian boy called Maurice Best who was wounded in the foot. Two operations were needed, but Geoffrey was impressed by the spirit of the boy and his eagerness, as soon as he could, to help. By March 15 he was writing: "Little Maurice Best helped a lot in the ward, looking after the wounded baby. I put the Pathophone in today, and it cheered them greatly. Watched, by chance, another baby die in the women's typhoid ward today; the little, grey, surprised, intent face; besides her a beautiful-featured girl of 15 dying; probably dead tonight."

The first half of 1915 brought news of the deaths of many old friends and acquaintances. The climber Nigel Madan was killed fighting in the Ypres region. In April Rupert Brooke died of septicaemia on his way to the Dardanelles, and Geoffrey wrote: "So Rupert Brooke is dead, at Lemnos. The poetic touch to the last. A fine personality, in a romantic frame. But his value was not the frame the world credited to him; another of the fine all-round humans, mind and body, gone in waste – " A month later Geoffrey suffered a much more personal bereavement, the death of Wilbert Spencer, the boy he had loved and who had become an infantry subaltern: ". . . had letters with all details of Wilbert's death; read in the garden in the only five-minutes rest of the day, with the blossoms evening-sweet, and a red thunder sunset. Well, he died gallantly and suddenly; and they all cared for him – many of his men wept when they heard. Will one ever have time even to be sorry again?" And on May 30, he recorded:

. . . and the usual news – Julian Grenfell, whom Eton called "the fortunate youth" for all his qualities and possessions and who was once really a lot with me, has joined the others – all the leading spirits of those years;

gone. – Well, in case I am grumpy and reacting when I get home, I here record that this is a life of small light quick emotions; that I am interested and cheerful all the day; that the cares are first the unit ones; and the excitements pleasant incidents in summery days; with good companionship, if unexciting. I think the uncertainty is the only real trouble in mind.

But some of the news Geoffrey got was good. His brother Hilton was doing well in the Navy and in February 1915 became MP for Norwich, elected unopposed and in the Liberal cause. It was the start of a long and successful career in politics. Geoffrey, always proud of his brother's achievements, was delighted. He had no political ambitions himself. That same year, as it happens, he was offered the safe Liberal seat that became available when his friend Charles Trevelyan resigned. On June 14 he noted:

I went to the House to hear Arthur Balfour's first utterance as First Lord, and Birrell quipping – all college-debating, infinitely trivial and unreal. Fortunately this came before Charles offered to put me in for his Elland seat; and I know the answer for me. The sight of the Front Bench, with all the *venerable* enemies dithering on each others' shoulders, raked up from celebrated, mediocre pasts; and of the Front Opposition Bench with *no* known face but Henry Chaplin.

There was news, too, of the eldest brother. After many years Georis left the Diplomatic Service, saying he wanted a more active war-time role than he could hope to find in the Lisbon embassy. His resignation was probably a good thing for all concerned. A brilliant man in some ways, a fine linguist and formidable casuist, he was not really cut out for the diplomatic life. He could be a wayward and awkward subordinate, full of his own ideas and quite prepared to go his own way, regardless of instructions from above. He made no secret of his political stance which was on the extreme Left – "the last self-proclaimed Communist to survive in the Diplomatic Service", as someone described him. He soon gained admission to the services, working for a while in the decoding section of Admiralty Intelligence in London, then in the Royal Marines. According to Geoffrey, he ended the war in charge of "a mysterious anti-submarine device, a tower in the Channel".

The approach of mid-summer 1915 found Geoffrey increasingly aware that his work at Ypres was coming to an end. The machinery he had created was running well – the ambulance service, the hospital, his orphanage, the public health campaign to stamp out the typhoid epidemic and ensure a reliable supply of pure water, the distribution of milk. He had proved himself a very able administrator as well as an effective negotiator. Now the recognition was made official. On June 23 an officer friend handed him a copy of *The Times*, opened at the page which listed the names of those who had been "mentioned in despatches for distinguished and gallant service in the field": ". . . and there I saw, in the tiny conspicuous Red Cross group – 'G. W. Young', as usual last and noticeable. It was a delightful surprise."

The town of Ypres had been destroyed. There was nothing left but a few shattered walls and heaps of rubble. Geoffrey spent much of his final weeks there searching in the ruins, often with fires raging and shells falling, helping the Curé to find church valuables (plate and vestments and carvings) and the safes of departed burghers. The gunners were moving in to demolish what was left and set up their batteries. It was time to go.

The Curé and Sœur Marguerite and Geoffrey were the last civilians to leave. In *The Grace of Forgetting* Geoffrey said: ". . . that year had been the most intense experience of our lives". In the Ypres Journal, on July 29, he wrote:

> In many ways the year has renewed youth, physically. It has brought confidence, experience and sure moving. It has brought much of humanity to its true proportions. The real folk have emerged from the flood. I feel that for life they will not be lost again, at least to each other . . . It would have been enough to have lived these six months of work in Ypres – for any man. Enough for a life's work, and enough justification of the years of training for nerve and detachment. A complete work in itself, with a result, in the child life saved and simplicity guarded, that work can rarely bring.

13

Italy: August 1915–
August 1917

ITALY HAD ENTERED THE WAR as an ally, and in the summer of 1915 plans began to be made to send an ambulance unit to the Italian-Austrian front as an earnest of allied goodwill. It was organised by the British Red Cross who asked G. M. Trevelyan, something of a hero in Italy since the publication of his Garibaldi trilogy, to take charge. He went to Rome to pave the way, then returned to England to form the unit. Naturally, he enlisted the help of Philip Noel-Baker, who had created the Friends' Ambulance Unit, and it was equally natural that they should turn to Geoffrey to be their commander at the front. No one had so much experience as he in the problems involved. Trevelyan wrote to Geoffrey on July 19, saying they planned to be in the field by the end of August "because the fighting must be hardest in September and October. After that snow must limit the Italian field of operations . . . we are sure both of work and of *hardship*. There is no fear of its being a 'picnic' under soft Italian skies etc . . ."

Geoffrey was already beginning to suspect that his period of greatest usefulness in Belgium was coming to an end. He left on July 30, noting in his Journal: "By Boulogne to England, and a holiday – All morning a very heavy firing, of big new guns; earth-shaking. So we end, in the fresh yellow dawn outside the ivy, to the old foolish violent thunder – " He took some of his Ypres drivers with him to give stiffening to the new unit, and also Sœur Marguerite and three Belgian boys including Maurice Best.

In some notes he typed out after the war Geoffrey recalled: "I took a long and needed holiday on the Cornish coast, at my old Trevascam haunt – taking down with me the three scouts [the Belgian boys], for their holiday too. Lovely bathing weather, and we camped out, with the Cornish boys and their families all about us and picnicking with us."

Sir George Young had offered his Thames-side meadows at Formosa for the unit's camp. Conscription for military service had not yet been introduced in Britain but it was clearly on the way, so the volunteers they recruited were either below or above the likely age range, under eighteen or well past forty. In his typed notes, Geoffrey said: "We were a happy lot, and free of Quaker swaddlings. Many were mature writers and musicians, civil servants etc. etc. And 12 were the pick of our Friends' lot, who had chosen to go with me. Cousin Cyril Dickinson, witty and athletic, came over from Ireland, to teach any drill they learned! and was made Sergeant Major!"

It was an unusual and high-profile venture and they had a number of distinguished visitors, including the Italian ambassador. Trevelyan was made Commandant; Philip Noel-Baker was his deputy; Geoffrey was in charge of the ambulances. The whole unit comprised doctors and surgeons to run their own forward hospital, and orderlies to help them; mechanics and drivers to keep their twenty-five cars running; a handful of administrative assistants; and Irene Baker, a trained nurse who had just married Philip. The journey out to the Italian front was their honeymoon trip. They all set off on August 20.

There are several sources of first-hand information for the Italian period of Geoffrey's war service. Two of his autobiographical works – *The Grace of Forgetting* and *Mountains with a Difference* – have chapters about it. Trevelyan wrote his own account, *Scenes from Italy's War*. The writer E. V. Lucas, who visited the unit towards the end of 1916, described their work in *Outposts of Mercy*. But the most complete and immediate account, as during the Ypres period, is to be found in Geoffrey's diary, hereafter referred to as the Italian Journal.

It is a larger work than the Ypres Journal because it covers a longer period, from August 20, 1915 until February 1919 when Geoffrey finally returned home. As transcribed many years later by his daughter Marcia, the Italian Journal covers 522 large, closely written pages, well over 310,000 words altogether. Like the Ypres Journal, it has not been published but deserves to be, in an edited form. It is vivid and immediate, often horrific and sometimes lyrical, the forthright presentation of his experiences and feelings and thoughts in another full and very exciting period of his life.

The drive across France and over the Alps to Italy was idyllic, through regions untouched by battle, villages and towns and cities where they were greeted like heroes – Rouen, Chartres, Orléans, Nevers and Lyons – in what Geoffrey described as "a sort of triumphal progress". They averaged about 100 miles a day, the Bakers cruising ahead in a little Ford to find a suitable camping ground for the night. If there was a river nearby, Geoffrey swam. In the evenings they sang around the camp-fire, and there were some fine singers among them. Geoffrey wrote: "As the chorus died I heard a woman murmur 'Céleste!' The end of a perfect evening and of a drive that has been the most romantic in life. Surely all the omens are wonderful, and there is no suggestion of war in the rich, opulent orchard lands, and large comfortable houses, thatched roofs and wooden frames, with black sparkling-eyed children to cheer us past." Later he said: "We needed this week; and it *is* romance . . . And O what fun and rest it is!"

He felt the unit was welding into an easy, companionable whole – with one predictable exception: "The doctors condemned the water of our alternative site today, by a fine waterfall in an alpine field. They are the only folk who have not caught the infection of romance, or trained in as yet. The drivers are tired, but all braced with the adventure and its success. All the cars wound in successfully before dark: to the usual excellent evening meal, and early sleep."

The crossing of the Alps was a nostalgic passage for Geoffrey, then they descended into Italy to a series of tumultuous welcomes. The Italians loaded the whole caravan on to trains for the journey across northern Italy, and with them travelled the British Red Cross Commissioner, Lord Monson, who was to be a recurrent thorn in the unit's side. At first encounter Geoffrey concluded the man was an "ass", and the judgement was confirmed at Vicenza where Monson called the whole unit on parade and lectured them severely about their fate if they took to raping Italian women:

. . . Then back and I found Monson had called another parade – we have had far too many – for "a few words"! I went on parade prepared for the worst. Beyond my fears! Monson lectured us all over again on "Conduct" and claimed to have powers to send anyone home if reported to him! No man would talk to a reformatory as he did to our distinguished middle-aged set of English volunteers and gentlemen. After three minutes, in a whirl of anger, I clapped my cane under my arm, turned my back, and walked off parade. I think it was the one thing to do for the sake of my men. Here I have 12 men, heroes of a year's fine work, insulted; and worse, the little harmony we have established among our difficile new workers destroyed; by a fool who has never been near the front. Oh, I was speechless with anger . . .

At this early stage Geoffrey was worried about his friend, George Trevelyan's ability to cope. He thought he was altogether too tentative and conciliatory in dealing with people like Lord Monson, too readily upset by the delays and frustrations and confusions that attend all military operations. But Trevelyan learned fast, and it was not long before Geoffrey was more than happy under his command.

They were sent to the Isonzo River front, north of the Adriatic, where the coastal plain begins to climb steeply towards the Alps. The Austrians had pulled back to this area when Italy entered the war because it afforded them strong defensive positions on the higher ground above the eastern banks of the river. The main Austrian armies were engaged against Russia, Romania and Serbia. On the Isonzo front the Italians outnumbered them by two-to-one and were expected to mount a major attack before the winter closed in.

The unit set up their field hospital at an old palace in the town of Cormons, and Geoffrey drove into the hills beyond to reconnoitre the region and find a place for his ambulances. They settled in a pleasant villa in the village of Quisca. The local people were Slavs and not particularly welcoming. But the Italian army had moved in and Geoffrey found them charming company: "One can make friends with them," he noted, "quite unlike the French." On September 17 he wrote in his diary:

We are clearly working up for an effort of some sort; tramping troops all night; and a clearing of hospitals. A lot of gastritis; some typhoid; moderating cholera. Attended some of Masspoli's operations at the hospital. He is a first-rate surgeon and now a good friend. They are a queer folk, the layers of humanity unmixed and found in uneven succession in the characters – most kind to children; brutal to animals; too kindly to be good fighters; sparing of lives, democratic in spirit, but autocratic as officers; inconsiderate, inquisitive, sarcastic and inhuman. Their surgery is brilliant, but ferocious; no anaesthetics; exquisite hands; dirty tables . . . They haven't yet conceived of war as we know it.

Most days there was desultory artillery fire in each direction but to Geoffrey's eyes and ears, accustomed to Ypres, it all seemed half-hearted. On both sides everything stopped after lunch, in the afternoon heat, for a two-hour siesta. "It's all like a game," he said.

Beyond Quisca, the road towards the front grew steeper, with hairpin bends and a precipitous unguarded drop on one side. There were stretches where the road was clearly visible from the Austrian gun positions higher up, and their marksmanship was impressive. So Geoffrey made his drivers practise going up and down the road at night, without lights because that attracted enemy fire. It was stressful work, particularly when the road was crowded with soldiers moving up to the front and mules carrying supplies. It was made doubly difficult when heavy rains turned the surface to mud. Geoffrey knew that when the offensive began he would have to take turns at driving to give the others a break, so he practised too:

October 4 . . . Coming up today it was gorgeously, murderously clear. My Red Cross must have been clear as noon. But they shelled me at both salient corners, where one has to slow up to round the cornice-cliff overhanging the precipice. It is the worst sensation I have ever had. To run deliberately towards the enemy – in sight – to have to slow up and drive very carefully – to hear the guns fire, then an unpleasant second and the explosion close. The second shell burst just behind and below the ambulance . . . and all on these appalling roads – ploughed stone fields, dug into quarry holes, and greased with deep slime.

He was proud of his driving skill and quickly became a useful motor mechanic, under the guidance of Gerald Marriage who had been with him at Ypres. He kept busy, too, making their villa more homely and comfortable. He sewed covers for their furniture. On October 9 he recorded: "I made a big divan lounge out of the petrol boxes today, with spare paliasses. We are very cosy; pleasant fresh autumn weather."

Trevelyan often drove up to see them, and he and Geoffrey would spend the day clambering about the slopes, surveying the armies' positions and discussing the unit's problems. It was their kind of country – steep hillsides and panoramic views, fresh mountain air and the dramatic gorge of the Isonzo with sandy banks for sun-bathing and spectacular rock pools where they could dive and swim. But Geoffrey was growing restless. Mid-October came and still there was no attack. The post brought news that Hilton was in the thick of things, with a naval force in Serbia, and Geoffrey wrote: "Well, Hilt and I have often talked of the Adventure of Life, and encouraged each other on its embarkations. He has *his* wish now, and no one has the right to wish him out of it."

At 4 p.m. on October 18 the Italians opened up the bombardment that heralded their long-awaited attack. The Austrian guns replied, and the unit was in action.

The Italian attack was maintained for no more than a few days and came to nothing. It was later discovered that the Austrian engineers had tunnelled into the high ridges of Monte Sabotino, the key objective, to make formidable gun positions. There were heavy Italian casualties and the unit cars were kept frantically busy. Geoffrey reckoned that in one week they carried 1,500 wounded men down to the hospital at Cormons. There was little time for sleep. Geoffrey's chief job was that of making sure all the telephone calls for ambulances were answered as quickly as possible, but he did his share of driving too. On October 23 he noted:

. . . This evening's views incomparable, the whole scene dipped in running gold, with an under rose-glow. And the burning mountains and grey bursts of shells – sparkle of explosions . . . Another hospital asleep at Cormons! and I made hell's own row. Back by a dull moon . . . The wounded as squalid and pathetic as always. Just puzzled hurt animals, only conscious that they no longer exist except as encumbrances to be cleared and bullied out of the way by their late co-equals, the unwounded – The Italian surgery is brilliant, but savage! I saw an arm amputated and a finger taken off and the hand shaped and cut and re-made – all without anaesthetics! They haven't time for anaesthetics here at the front . . . or the chance of real aseptic surgery. I should like to know what proportion of wounds get infected here! The Italians like the French are dirty workers – but brilliant cutters and stitchers. How our careful Flanders domestic surgeons would shudder – And in the dirty rooms, the rows of patient men sitting or lying, in torn stained clothes – What I like least is the abominable fuss made about wounded officers. All the place hums and crowds in on a captain or lieutenant . . . Five hours of sleep – at last.

Another entry, dated October 28, gives a vivid impression of what the night driving was like:

. . . An all-night grim running in pitch dark on worsening slime. This time the roads were not cleared for us – munitions still booming up in careless lorries in the dark. I had 11 in my first load; mudguards down on the wheels. A vile mule-cart came deliberately into me on the wrong side. I had stopped on the very edge to give it room. The pole crashed through, just missed the head of a stretcher case. I got down to extricate but the idiots lost their heads, turned the cart round, and the leverage on the ambulance sent it reeling forward over the edge. One wheel clear over into the air. I just got to the brakes in time to check it. I got all the wounded out in the windy dark, and slowly released the pole, crawling the car backwards up on to the hill. The second run I was charged by an ammunition waggon and again got out without bad damage – but the roads were awful, and the big Grenadiers groaned and called out like children at every bump. The irritation of impotence almost drove me savagely to bump them really! And the Cormons hospitals were as slack and as inconsiderate as usual – fussing for news, wasting precious half hours, losing our blankets. For later runs I put on *full* lights, swore at objecting sentries, and took the offensive in collisions, which gives the car the advantage of impetus and head-on attack . . .

The work called for courage and stamina, patience and self-control, and the ability to assert authority. Geoffrey had all these qualities. His unfamiliar uniform – together with the pipe and monocle and the white scarf he had worn in Ypres – must have helped, as well as his increasingly fluent command of Italian.

Their vehicles were of various makes – Buicks, Renaults, Panhards, Fords. They were badly knocked about but all of them kept running. It was equally punishing work for the drivers but they, too, kept going. Not a single member of the unit was seriously injured. They met their first challenge and won the regard of the Italians – for the speed with which they arrived on the scene, the care with which they treated the wounded. Geoffrey was proud of his men, particularly proud of the Irishmen among them, "the best of them all", he said.

The Italians tried to mount further attacks but they were beaten back, and then the rains began and the front quietened down. By the beginning of December Geoffrey could write: ". . . the weather has broken in hopeless mist and wet, and there is not the faintest chance for the Italians, who are like cats in rain, standing it or advancing."

He was growing disillusioned with the Italians. He described them as "Delightful folk, but amateurs". Their driving was reckless, their traffic control abysmal: ". . . they are the worst organisers in the world." He praised the panache of their initial attacks, but condemned their commanders for failing to exploit the breakthroughs. He made a close study of the strategy, peppering the pages of his Journal with carefully drawn diagrams of the lie of the land and the key positions.

As always, the arrival of the mail meant a great deal: "One lingers over letters here," he wrote. He was glad to hear Hilton had reached safety after a fighting retreat in Serbia, also that the prodigal member of the Slingsby family, Will, had enlisted with the Royal Flying Corps. There are few mentions of Eleanor Slingsby in the Journal at this time, but they were writing to each other and there is no doubt she was much in his thoughts. Some of their letters have survived, and his make it clear that he had neither forgotten nor abandoned the proposal he had made on Paddington Station two years before. The letters also make it apparent that they had managed to spend a week together in London before he set off for Italy.

She wrote to Geoffrey from Whitbarrow Lodge on June 24, 1915, describing her activities which included the entertainment of wounded soldiers. She was organising the presentation of a one-act French play for the Belgians. Her brother Laurence was home on leave: ". . . Laurence is away for a few days. I shall never marry him off, not for years at any rate. He is keen enough to marry but doesn't like 'to face the responsibility'. But it won't hurt him to lose his heart to a really attractive girl all the same, and I shall see that he does." Later she says: ". . . Also I shall not forget I owe you £2. You shall have it someday. I enjoyed our most romantic adventures no end. I shall know in future that I may depend upon you as being thoroughly good company in London." More family news follows – her sister Alizon was about to have an operation for appendicitis in Rome – and she concludes: ". . . Goodbye for the present. I know you now to be an excellent lover, as well as an extremely good companion. I can face the world with a bolder face than ever. You people give me confidence, and now I give you my hand. Good Luck . . ." She signed this letter "Eleanor".

It would, I think, be wrong to assume that Len's words about his being "an excellent lover" imply they had made love during their time together in London. Language changes, and so do moral codes, and it seems likely that she meant no more than that she had been moved and impressed by his protestations of love.

He wrote to her: ". . . We are busy working at the front, in exquisite country with the colours of autumn, on roads that are like Lakeland tracts in January . . . George Trevelyan makes an excellent head, and I have a number of best-tried men from the old Unit with me. Why don't you come up as a VAD?" This was the Voluntary Aid Detachment, a women's nursing organisation. At this stage, Geoffrey's letters were more ardent than hers: ". . . I still rest with joy on the memory of that week in town," he wrote, and concluded: ". . . Remember, it's still your promise to come to Monte Fiano, when we get a breathing space . . . I don't change ideas! All love and a fair end to this – Geoffrey Young."

On November 5 she replied from an address in Edinburgh, where she was undergoing a six-month course in Domestic Economy: ". . . including many useful things which I knew I wanted to learn seriously some day – but I can't say I love doing it and they are all hopelessly Scotch up here." She gave the Slingsby news – sister Alizon was now recovering – and added: "Of course I shall come to Monte Fiano after all this splash is over." This time she signed herself "Len".

Replying on December 8, he said:

> . . . I am still up at the front. We've had it fairly hot and heavy during the offensive, and it has been picturesque fighting. Now the inevitable winter white mists, and pause. I hope to get off about the 14th to see that all is well at Monte Fiano, for next year, though I have doubts that we shall get there even then! But it *must* come, the jolly time you promised to spend there after the war, before we're too old to enjoy the sun and blossom and blue views. I *do* look forward to it. And you've *got* to come, remember. That: and we must have a time in the hills too, and a jolly party and the old friends, if we can re-create that idyllic atmosphere . . . I live in very active incidents, and in the intervals upon pleasant memories, especially that week with you. No; I don't change! . . . It's delightful to sit and chat with you on paper, from up on this hill. And it carries you more thought of you, and love, than you would think – Geoffrey Young.

Geoffrey had long noticed that senior officers were rarely to be seen anywhere near the front. The fact that generals and staff officers settled themselves "miles behind the lines" was a standing joke on the western front, but it was even more noticeable on the Italian front where it was rare to come across anyone above the rank of captain. It was much the same in the medical services:

> There is tremendous indignation among the doctors at the front at the way promotions and places all go to the base men. At the beginning, the professionals bagged all the snug safe jobs; and of course now they are still nearer HQ. It's the old story. The heads don't come to the front and they trust for news to the half-ways up; and they have to pretend to know all about it all the time.

The matter of recognition was important to him – for himself no doubt, but also because he knew it mattered to his men and to the morale of the unit. Time and again in his diaries, at Ypres and in Italy, he gives vent to his feelings about the unfair and arbitrary way in which honours were awarded, more according to who you knew than what you had done. Sometimes he was angry, more often wryly amused. But he was pleased, early in December, to hear that King Albert of the Belgians had determined to honour him for his work at Ypres.

A few days earlier, on November 27, Geoffrey concluded his diary entry with this paragraph: "Yesterday a wounded soldier gave us a puppy from Oslavia. This is our new centre of interest. I have warmed our room up with Turkey red on the walls, to keep off the white wash, and with a tin opener and petrol tins, have carved out some gorgeous silver apses as candle-reflectors."

The puppy was a rough-coated, red-brown terrier bitch who had been born in the trenches on a nearby mountain called Oslavia, so that became her name. She lived all her short life in the sound of gun-fire. Geoffrey later wrote: "I've always determined *not* to get fond of such prematurely mortal creatures as dogs; it's bad enough with humans." But Oslavia gave him no choice in the matter. She adopted the unit immediately, and then attached herself to Geoffrey so doggedly and delightfully that he soon became devoted to her.

The approach to Christmas 1915 brought many parties. There was a farewell party for the Noel-Bakers, bound for Greece, and Geoffrey was sorry to see them go: "I have learned to find in Phil one of the rarest, sweetest natures I have ever met."

He was busy writing lyrics for the unit's Christmas revue. The words have survived and display a talent for chirpy, occasional verse, but they are too topical, too dependent on close acquaintance with unit jokes and personalities, to make quotation worth-while.

On December 18 he escaped for a few days of quiet introspection at Monte Fiano:

No breath of war here. The old atmosphere unchanged, and so bringing back the old trains of thought. Has it all really happened in between? It seems only last week I was here. But it seems 40 years since I came to France that first mad strange day of war. Days just going past – scribbling, seeing the vineyard babies, watching the sky through its old, but always new, changes. I must go back tomorrow, or I'll be too late for the festivities at the villa. Odd, that *that's* all going on – the muddy, bloody line all round the edge of things . . . Shall we really wipe it all out so completely, so quickly, afterwards? Or is it just the mystery of

Monte Fiano and its timeless sort of atmosphere? And if we do, what shall we have gained? What we shall have lost, even here, there is no risk of forgetting. It is more the last, bitter angry insult to one's intelligence, one's sanity, one's humanity, one's heart, viewed in this perspective, than it was when each successive blow came in the old, muddled "incident" life behind the lines. The idea of "idealising" such death – "Patriotism" – "heroism" – the vile misuse by greedy minds of the capacity of finer personalities to live and die in their own imaginations.

After this outburst, he added: "Well-well. Loneliness is the most sociable of occasional companions. I never feel alone when it's with me!"

He was back in Cormons by December 23, and next day the unit had a very distinguished visitor: "Fluster of grey officers in the hall; enter the tiny little wizened man. He made a little inaudible Italian speech to George, who replied rather clumsily in English. Then all over, and out flits the little dignified mannikin, to jam himself into an over-plain car." This was King Victor Emmanuel of Italy, a frequent visitor to the front, presenting G. M. Trevelyan with a Silver Medal for Valour. There was no doubting Trevelyan's courage, as Geoffrey well knew, but he was wryly amused that the particular action mentioned in the citation was a visit to an advanced aid-post under very heavy fire, a trip that Geoffrey had strenuously opposed: "It was not his business, and he took up a 'wounded' seat in a car." He did not begrudge the recognition of his old friend, but felt that it would have been better if the whole unit had been presented with some Order.

On Christmas Day there was a celebratory dinner, followed by the revue: ". . . a glorious success. Every song told, and the men acted and sang inimitably . . . Shouts of laughter. Then a dance; and I sang again my topical parodies. All very appreciative . . . In the intervals I interpreted for the surgeon to a wounded prisoner, who was to have his foot taken off. But he died first."

Just before the New Year 1916 Geoffrey set off on a long leave, not at all sure that he would return to the Italian front. He had confided to his diary: "Four or five could do my job, as well as their own; now that all the machine runs oiled . . . The *actual* work can go on perfectly without me; I'm only again a councillor or sympathiser, marking time in case an emergency comes. And I don't think it will, here."

He went by train to Paris, then to Boulogne and Dunkirk, then to Poperinghe where he met many old colleagues and friends, including

Marcus Heywood and "my countess", Countess Vandersteen, lady-in-waiting to the Belgian Queen and head of the Belgian nursing service.

He was shown round Ypres and Woesten, finding his old homes and offices destroyed by shells. The shelling was still going on. It brought back powerful memories, and he noted: "History is quickly made in war. That all seems to have happened in a twilight of youthful sensation."

On January 3 the Countess told him he had been "commanded to tea at La Panne", the current residence of King Albert and his court. He went that afternoon, took tea with the countess and others:

> . . . Suddenly I was solemnly marched out by the Chamberlain, and left in the low, lighted villa drawing-room. The huge, pink-faced, pince-nezed, blond and fattish khaki giant, Albert, came up and, in infinitely deliberate English, made me a long awkward charming speech – presenting a case with the Croix du Chevalier du Leopold, with swords, the highest order they can give. Then we sat down and had an hour's talk! Most of it the heaviest circle of slow platitudes; heavens, what lives they lead, and minds they get! Like talking in a nightmare to something accidentally in the world! But he clearly enjoyed it, and made an hour of it, in place of the proper 10 minutes.

Leopold was a keen Alpinist but the subject was not raised or their conversation might have gone on much longer.

One book of his Journal ends at this point and the next does not start until the beginning of April 1916, when he was back on the Isonzo front, within the sound of gun-fire. But he began the new diary with a resumé of his three months at home:

> The weeks, months at home were a useful if uneasy change. I could push a little at getting relief out to the Serbians dying in Corfu, of whom Hilton brought reports; share a little in the grief of families of my friends killed; add a little to the fun, rather hectic, of "four-day London" when the young subs and sailors back on leave jollified and rushed round with each other in a small central circle of London gaiety and disappeared, with others succeeding . . .

He stayed at Georis's little house in Holland Street, and saw as many old friends as he could: "Most delightful was Hilt's safe return with the Serbian Mission and the coincidence of his Serbian decoration for valour; resulting in joint notice and portrait in the newspapers . . ." It seems unlikely that he would have failed to organise a meeting with Len Slingsby, but there is no mention of her in these pages. On the whole, he did not care for what he saw of English life: ". . . the English atmosphere intolerable. The little big men all struggling to keep each his own head up, helpless in the big national tide."

He was beginning to fear that the whole generation of bright spirits, whose companionship he had enjoyed in the pre-war years, was facing extinction: "The last weeks were clouded by the deaths of Herford, that genius and spirit of mountain-climbing . . . Also of Nigel Madan, almost the last of the Eton group of mountaineers . . . And of Morris Slingsby, athlete, soldier, explorer . . ." There were some of them still left, however: George Mallory had volunteered for the Royal Artillery; Conor O'Brien was in mine-sweepers; Page Dickinson was in a training camp on Salisbury Plain.

In February Geoffrey received a letter from George Trevelyan saying he must decide for himself whether or not to return to the unit in Italy: ". . . If you come back to carry us on we shall all love it. But I cannot call you back as for necessity, against your will. Choose freely." He chose to go back.

He found things very quiet. "It's a gentlemanly war here," he noted: "This front is utterly inert." He organised a new line of out-stations, reaching as far north as the Caporetto area. There was occasional shelling from both sides and some skirmishing, which gave intermittent work for the ambulances, but Geoffrey's chief problem that spring and into the summer was keeping his men occupied and happy. They enjoyed the sunshine; played badminton tournaments; and Geoffrey made himself familiar with all the roads in the region. Oslavia went with him "for company". Lord Monson reappeared from time to time to earn more of Geoffrey's contumely.

It was not until the beginning of August that the Italians launched a new attack. Things went better for them this time. Monte Sabotino was taken, and the Austrians were forced to evacuate the key town of Gorizia on the eastern bank of the Isonzo. They failed to destroy the road bridge before leaving but it was a prime and easy target for their gunners on the mountainside beyond. It made for hazardous driving, but when the call came for them to pick up wounded cavalrymen from Gorizia itself, four ambulances set off with Geoffrey's in the lead. It was the evening of August 9. He later said it was "the most exciting night of my life".

His Journal picks up the story as they approached the 250-foot long bridge:

> . . . The trenches about us were filled with rifles and broken service litter and the usual terrible smell – The bridge was reported "broken but just possible". Long battery trains, man-handled, were slowly creeping over, one by one. No car had yet crossed. Passing the enormous barricade of tree trunks at the near end, I walked across. The river spread exquisitely under the white moon-light . . . The bridge was torn and holed like a sponge. Every few yards gaped a ragged hole, revealing the river rushing deep below. In three places two-thirds of the whole breadth of the bridge were smashed away, the girders prickling into yawning space like fish-bones. The guns were being man-handled over . . . A couple of soldiers had stepped through the sudden holes and disappeared . . . We are absolutely the first ambulances to attempt the crossing . . . I crossed separately and on foot, piloting each car – we *just* got them all over. During the many crossings I had some close shaves, of dropping through the manholes.

They picked their way through the dark streets, searching for the wounded and loading up, then drove back to the bridge, whose condition had been made even more uncertain by the passage of more guns. Once again he fought his way across the bridge to persuade the Italians to stop crossing while they tried to get the ambulances over: "Then Sessions got my small Ford over, with only inches to spare at the gaps. Every heavy wheel that passed dug away more of the broken edges." Geoffrey walked back to escort the other small ambulance across, but on the way one wheel went through the wreckage and they had to prise the car out with levers. They finally got this car across, and then Geoffrey and Sessions walked back again: "As he and I returned on foot I saw a mule walking ahead on the sideway. The rail and side path suddenly melted away into space like an opening fan. And mule and man disappeared. It was now hopeless to get our bigger cars over. Yet at dawn the Austrians could begin shelling and two of our cars and their wounded were still stuck on the wrong side!"

Geoffrey decided that the only solution was to drive the two small cars down to his headquarters and return with an empty ambulance, then carry the stretchers from the other cars over to it, if the bridge was still there. Unfortunately, the road ahead was now so packed with troops and supplies moving up to Gorizia, that they could get no further than a few yards. So Geoffrey and Sessions set off to walk down.

They arrived at 3.30 a.m., recruited help, packed some sacks with coffee and brandy and food, and set off back again, to reach the area of the bridge as dawn was breaking:

> The Austrians sent a shell or two on to the far end of the bridge. We pushed up on to it on foot, and half-way across I saw one of our big cars from the far side "rushing" one of the worst gaps, over which a few loose logs had been thrown in the interval. I was just in time to guide him across and to stop a nervously racing battery from blocking him on the near side. As the light broke, everyone – and the batteries – were scuttling for cover. Behind this car came our big Buick, Christie's. With a really fine nerve and dash he raced and swerved at top speed – the only chance! – over the narrow remains and jumping logs at the worst gaps. As dangerous a job as I've ever been in; the bridge was literally shaking down in fragments and noise under our feet. I thought it might go any moment.

The road was clearer now the Austrians were shelling, and they got the ambulances moving. As they left, two shells finished the bridge off. They were back home at 7.30 that morning. Geoffrey reckoned he had walked thirty kilometres that night, and crossed the shattered bridge more than twenty times.

He got one hour's sleep and then embarked on another long day's driving and organising. George Trevelyan was with him now. They found that Italian engineers had been working hard to make the bridge driveable, and the Gorizia ambulance service resumed. They reconnoitred the roads beyond Gorizia, now in Italian hands: "Back through Gorizia; with only tyre troubles, from the sudden shell-holes. Some traffic to solve. What a hectoring, hoarse-voiced bully they must think me!" It was 3.30 next morning before he got to bed.

Geoffrey was at his best at times like this – apparently inexhaustible, calm, able to think clearly in desperate situations, decisive and authoritative, concerned only with the job of saving lives. In one week of frenzied activity his ambulances carried 1,100 stretcher cases and 1,300 other wounded down to hospitals, covering 19,000 kilometres.

Then the front grew quiet again, with occasional shelling. They moved their headquarters into Gorizia and set about patching up their vehicles. The news of the death in action of another friend, F. N. Finlay of Eton, prompted gloomy reflections:

> *August 21* . . . Nothing left of our climbing set, of which I hoped everything for the future; all the athletes, all the idealists, all the brains and *hearts* are dead . . . Thankful that life is always the present – that

something must always be there, to do and think. What else remains? Today is the anniversary of our leaving England. A year out here – I shall be old after the war, and too big a gap to bridge to the new generation. Who will there be to call me "Geoffrey", or laugh over the "ribbons"? But for those two at home, or three, what need to care how the shells come, or fall? And yet tomorrow I shall be just as keen, as cautious, as contriving. A grateful thing, the detail of a job!

At the end of August he had another narrow escape:

. . . We had just turned up into the Corso; high narrow houses and stone-tiled street, when "crash", a small high-explosive burst *right* over the car. I've always argued that one does *not hear* the approach, if they're straight at one. I thought the car and everything had gone into space. The head hit the road a few inches in front. A roar of fragments and the roof edge which it had hit en route smashed, I thought, right on to us. But Sessions held on, with a rush, and the whole hail missed us by inches only, behind . . . Metcalfe, beside me, called out "Are you all right?", and as I felt my eyeglass still fixed in, I knew I was. And not one of us was touched; and the car has not a scratch . . . Mine is a curious and constant protection!

Many men in the First World War came to believe they had some special invulnerability, and most of them, sooner or later, learned that they had not.

As the fighting died down, old troubles resurfaced. There was the perennial problem of keeping the men busy and cheerful. An Italian general sent orders that their ambulances should only use one mountain road, one that was literally undriveable. Lord Monson reappeared, pompous and interfering as ever: "Monson is a beast again . . . He really *is* the Gadarene swine." And there was a new anxiety. Conscription was soon to be introduced in Britain, and all the young men who had come out with the unit were now over 18 and would be liable for call-up. Geoffrey urged Trevelyan to fight hard for their retention in the ambulance service, where their work was both dangerous and invaluable.

There were consolations too. Geoffrey drove down to Cormons one day and took a hot bath, his first for three months. Oslavia, now his almost inseparable companion, produced puppies. And Geoffrey discovered another outlet for his urge to philanthropy. On September 14 he wrote in the Journal:

Today I saw a note in a local paper of the Italians having established a refuge for civilian children and orphans. So I hunted it out with Barbour.

We found a big shelled-up Ursuline convent up the steep old shattered streets leading to the castle. Every house is bust up and deserted here. A dry, but I think good little nun, the Superior, Mother Matilda, opened out. They have six small orphans, chiefly Slav, there always; and 56 children who come for the day. It has been there all the war. At one time they had over 200. She left once, last year, but later got leave from the Emperor at Vienna to return. The Italians continue to encourage it . . . After talk with an Italian military priest there, I found they're all right for food, but we could do something for stuff for clothes, shoes of course, and above all *toys*. I'm writing home about it . . .

His mother was an expert at organising collections and soon the parcels were arriving.

On October 25, his fortieth birthday, he noted:

Rain. About 4 the house was shaken by four huge explosions, big shells bursting close by, one just in the garden end . . . I dispersed the cars round the house, rowed my lad for rushing out to find the pieces! and retired to the eternal Patience. They're a young company now, and the place is the better for it, and the work . . . They make me feel old and apart, but it's part of the price of officer-dom!

He was distressed to see signs that he was at last beginning to feel the strain, sudden flarings of rage that he could not control: "My nerves are not so well-covered as they were," he wrote. Though George Trevelyan was a frequent visitor, there were many moments when he felt the need for some older man to whom he could confide his feelings. So he was delighted at the end of November when E. V. Lucas, the essayist, turned up to spend a couple of days with them: ". . . I like E.V.L. with his rather weighty silences, brilliant little thrusts, and evident interest in all *real* things . . . We got on really well. And talked continuously for enough hours to leave me exhausted after so long an abstention." Next morning he drove Lucas to the aid posts and they came under shelling: ". . . E.V.L. took it very quietly, but thoroughly sensibly, like me! and his confidence in me, subsequently, was gratifyingly outspoken for so dry and silent a man. Of the morning he said later, after a good lunch, that he felt there had been *too* much in it; of the kind of thing he wanted a grandchild for, to tell him about it."

The Italians had sited several of their batteries close to the house in Gorizia where the unit's headquarters were, so there was constant danger from the Austrian shells. Miraculously almost, not a member of the unit had been seriously wounded since their arrival on the Italian front some fifteen months before. On December 1 however, Geoffrey's final entry for the day said: "I'm feeling all cross and nervy today. So is Oslavia!"

The next entry began: "December 2. That feeling had a curious premonition." It goes on to describe fierce shelling during the night until some time after 3 a.m. when he was disturbed by shouts from downstairs. The stairway was full of sulphurous fumes, and the ground floor was devastated. They knew that Hamish Allan, electrician and driver, had been sleeping there:

> I raced back for my torch; George for wet towels for our mouths. I followed him in, and, tripping in the dark over debris of furniture and stones, we shouted to Allan to "keep calling", so as to find him. I scorched my bare feet on the red hot dust, and thought I was cutting them on broken glass. The pain blended with the sense of nightmare, and seemed right . . . Then I heard Hamish's coaxing little drawl, only without its usual faint stutter – "It's my right femur; get me out quick."

They got him out, still on his blood-soaked mattress, and down to the basement:

> W. Kennedy at once took charge of the bandaging with stuff from my refugee store. I held Hamish, sitting up, and washed his face. He was perfectly cool, and knew more about it than we did . . . The 10th section sent up their best dresser, who splinted the leg rapidly and well, if rather roughly. Hamish held me close, but never winced. Once I hoped he had fainted. No more painful operation – without anaesthetic – is conceivable.

They finally got him away in an ambulance.

The next day was spent clearing up and making the place habitable again. Back in his room that evening Geoffrey wrote: "I wish my nerve-covers were better. I'm all right, but thin as paper to strain or shock now. Not like two years ago. The sound of guns makes one sickish, but that will pass. Ordinary case of shell-shock, I expect!"

Hamish Allan was successfully operated on, though one leg would always be shorter than the other.

The shelling ceased with the approach of Christmas 1916, and Geoffrey was again kept busy writing lyrics for the unit show. At New Year there was a fancy dress dance: "The dance was charming, spontaneous and most ingeniously dressed . . . I played the fool at my best, and Miss Power [Emily Power, Matron at the Cormons hospital], who is now my ally, said primly she'd have come if only to see me dance, while G.M.T remarked that he'd no idea 'dancing could suggest such potentialities of wickedness!'" Geoffrey later added a footnote to this entry: "This was my *last* dance; I was in long boots, officer's breeks and shirt, and I let myself go, dancing with every inch of me . . ."

In January 1917 he left on another long leave, first to Florence and then back to Flanders to see old friends including the countess and Marcus Heywood. At Calais he went out of his way to find the home of Leon, the man who had been his chauffeur during the retreat across Belgium, and whose family Geoffrey had helped to rescue from the German advance: "He and his wife were just going to bed; but we had a great séance, and his two lovely babies tumbled out in their pyjamas, and sat and laughed, each on one knee, and recalled the famous flight from Brussells . . . What a mad dream it all was then. But O the first touch and hold of children again, after a year!"

He went to Paris and then to England, and everyone he talked to seemed to be convinced that the war must end in 1917, the Germans were sure to cave in before the end of the year.

It was April before he was back in Italy, and then it was to visit Rome on unit business. At Florence he saw much of Norman Douglas: ". . . One of the most able, eccentric and companionable of bohemian ex-diplomatics; with an incomparable knowledge of Italy and Italians . . ." Geoffrey had been growing increasingly disillusioned with the Italian reluctance to prosecute the war with any fervour. Another offensive had been planned towards the end of 1916, then cancelled because it had started to rain. Geoffrey knew that the crumbling of Russian and Romanian resistance to the north meant that the Austrians would soon be in a position to reinforce their armies in Italy, so it was important for the Italians to strike soon. But they showed little enthusiasm: "Douglas explains it as the hereditary weariness of a race that has fought too much in the past – a good analysis; also our difference from them, generally, as that of a race that learns to control its reflexes in youth compared with one that does not – which is even better, it gets at the root of our want of understanding of southern peoples . . ."

Back at last with the ambulance unit on the Isonzo front, he found no signs of a resumed offensive. He also found that prolonged inactivity had led to considerable slackening of discipline and morale in the unit, and promptly set about finding them things to do and tightening up all round.

He was glad to be reunited with Oslavia, who had produced more puppies: "Oslavia is now my shadow. Dogs me everywhere. She hears if I steal out on tip-toe when she's asleep, and I listen instinctively for the pit-pat of her following me up and down stairs, if it's a hundred times a day. A friendly foolish little beast."

He was delighted, too, to visit the Ursuline Convent again and see his orphans: "April 25. Fairly steady shelling on the town edges, and bright weather. Spent most of the afternoon at the Ursulines; a great talk with the Superior and two lay-teacher ladies; in at least three languages. The boys and babies are to me a great rest, like a breath of natural work again. Left them new toys and things."

By this time the unit had twenty-eight ambulance cars altogether, serving three Italian armies. Geoffrey had fifteen cars and twenty-five men under his direct command. One new recruit was Maurice Best, the wounded Belgian boy Geoffrey had half-adopted, who had been trained in vehicle repair and maintenance.

They had a hectic week in mid-May when the Italians launched an attack on Monte San Gabriele by a heavy artillery bombardment. The Austrians replied with a fierce shelling of Gorizia:

> *May 13* . . . I met White spurting up the road and steadied him with the sight of my pipe. I came back and sent up Holmes instead. Then walked down again, horribly afraid in spite of the pipe . . . I clambered with Bill over the rubbish heaps that had been houses, all littered with human remnants and heads. We heard one call and Bill clambered up the broken wall. But the man, hanging there, died as he did so. Arundel showed reckless gallantry; continuing to clamber over the ruins "on the chance", when at any second another shell might have come. I had to stay with him, tho' I *hated* it! . . .

A few moments later Geoffrey was hit on the head by a "cascade of stones and shell fragments", but not badly hurt.

The unit continued very busy until the end of May, and Geoffrey was proud of the way his men conducted themselves, especially a young and irrepressible Irish driver called George Metcalfe. Geoffrey described him as "a miracle of a lad", and writing of him, said: "Queer gift, personality, or rather vitality. Just Ireland!"

The fighting subsided, with little or nothing gained, and early June ushered in a period of what Geoffrey called "summer idleness". During the day they lived in shorts and shirt-sleeves. They spent a lot of time diving and swimming in the river, and Geoffrey explored the region, on foot and by car. He was awarded an Italian medal for valour which he reckoned was equivalent to the British DSO. He and one of his men, the artist S. B. Meyer, worked on a booklet about their work, to be sold in Britain to raise money for the Red Cross. Meyer did the sketches, and Geoffrey wrote a series of lively verses. The little book, called *Bolts from the Blues*, sold out in a few weeks.

Geoffrey's eye for natural beauty had lost none of its sharpness, and he still loved to hear the birds, impressed by the way they would sing on when shells were falling around. There were nightingales here, and a rarer delight: "A triumph! I have spoken before of my bird in the trees about here, with the rare, contralto, reed song. Metcalfe has seen him, big and brown, with a luminous golden throat. He is probably – of all the glorious names for such a voice – the Golden Oriole. The sound of it! and the sound of his song!"

On July 7, 1917 he sat down at his typewriter and wrote a long letter to Len Slingsby, who had now taken an acting job at the famous Liverpool Repertory Theatre:

> . . . You've always too colossal a vitality to be tied anywhere, and why not use it any way that pleases you best? I knew it before – but these years have proved it to most men: there is no such thing as a "career" or "success": the thing is to live life out, and to have the joy of doing it, and to keep the capacity to enjoy. *Vitality* is the only thing that counts! Think of the folk you like in the world! in the end it's only those who are *vital* whom you remember! Who *give*; and aren't parasites, and Ministers and – O God! – successes in the conventional sense. That's why you and I find Will always so ripping, in spite! He's so immensely alive!

Geoffrey cites his younger brother as another example:

> Hilton has gone off to shoot vast guns in France, to "experience" a bit more of the passing hour. He's *The* man! My word, what a mind, and a just sense of the values of things as they are! I'm tied here . . . It's hell at times, as the years don't ease the nerve-wear; but between it's cosy enough. For instance, I've a nice big house and garden. The house has some quite habitable rooms still, and the fact that the corner has been knocked out of my room is an advantage in summer. The garden is chiefly trenches, but that's only a danger if one strolls moon-lighting at night! Which, as you aren't here, there's little temptation to do! I've found *the* bathing place in the green-rushing Isonzo: splendid headers, white-hot sand, and green trees to lie under. The sun is eternal this year.

I, and some others, spend three or four hours a day in the water and sun; and I'm burned dark bronze all over, and fit as a woodsman. My word, you'd enjoy it! The little "boch" [sic] can see us from his sweltering hill-trenches, as we gymnasticise on the sands, and that adds to the pleasure. Once or twice he's tried a shrapnel, which looks pretty and pink on the blue sky. And I lie in the sun, and smoke, and take a plunge when it gets too hot, and think of all the beautiful things, and folk, I've seen in the world – that's where you come in! – a queer pagan life.

He recommends her to read Norman Douglas's *South Wind* – "a real detached world-wanderer's book, unmoral, genially cynical and extraordinarily human and amusing . . . a delight for the intellectual vagrant" – and then goes on:

The thought of the Hills is the one great standby, and promise for the future. When I want a good hour, I retire in thought and re-live old climbs. *They* will be here afterwards, the Hills; and we must manage somehow to rebuild something of the old sort of company to visit them with. I often think of the day with you on Tryfan, and Laurence, and the mass of your hair on the grey old rocks. I remember always in "pictures".

She had sent him a photograph of her and he was critical: "No, I don't think I like that portrait, too espiègle and Irvingish, though of course it's immensely pretty. Only I want the colour, and the eyes, and the direct look – probably it's just because it's not *yourself*, and that's what I want most to see!"

He signed off with the words: "Very good wishes, and more thoughts than you might expect – Geoffrey Young."

In late July the ever-faithful Oslavia began to suffer a form of creeping paralysis: "Oslavia gets worse. It's pathetic; I have to carry her up and down stairs. And she walks restlessly about my room, and comes up to put her head against me, and wag her tail, in protest against the world that's weakening her legs, but without pain." Five days after writing this, he noted:

August 10. I had to have Oslavia shot this morning. I was up all night again with her, clearly in great pain. As I can't get at the means of possible cure here for her, it's the only course . . . Up till the last I could quiet the paroxysms and send her to sleep by keeping my hand on her head, and I mesmerised her into complete coma before that good fellow Palmi took her off; so that she never knew or stirred. Buried in the garden here . . . And I always said I would never get fond of a dog, for just the reasons that hurt me now!

There were further deaths that month to hurt him even more. On August 19 he recalled that it was two years since they drove out from Cookham, bound for the Italian front. He estimated that in that time they had carried more than 100,000 wounded and sick, and lost only one car. Remarkably, not a single member of the unit had been killed.

The next day a recently arrived member of the team, an Irish barrister called Meredith, died of dysentery. The same day brought terrible news from home:

> I've just heard that Laurence Slingsby has been killed, after three years of war and a serious wound. The last of the younger men, whom I knew as boys in the hills, and with whom I hoped to grow old, in them, later. A blue-eyed, soft-voiced, stalwart Yorkshireman, who confided all his child life and school life to me, and who had grown into a fine, resolute man, of curious, gently humorous charm.

Later in the same Journal entry he reflects: "It is singular, but almost natural, that all the finest hopes of those who lived for the vital things of air and beauty and vigour, should have been killed; while the useless and poor-hearted, innumerable and clever, seem to have suffered so little, among one's acquaintance." He recalled taking Laurence Slingsby, when he was nine years old, up a route on Great Gable, and a few years after that leading Laurence and his sister Len up a climb on Tryfan:

> . . . both climbing slowly and with great finish. I can see their rough fair heads, and big china-blue eyes, coming up over the rocks from below, towards me, full of the excitement and effort. But what's the use of memory? – I was greatly touched. Maurice Best, my Belgian lad, was sitting in the room – he is always nervous when heavy shells come near and no wonder after two wounds. I said something thoughtless and bitter about the distaste that comes of living when what one cares for is gone. And in a second there was a furious burst of tears, and a sobbed "You shouldn't say such things". It made me feel so base, for a hasty and unintended outburst at chance. And now I see when I get back he's asleep in his clothes on his bed, exhausted like a child. What a pig one is to rail, when there's so much to do still, and so much to care for.

It is not surprising, though, that Geoffrey should have been distressed to the point of despair by the relentless casualty lists. Not long before, in his Journal, he had made a list of the men he had known who had been killed in the war so far; it amounted to twenty-five friends and twenty-four acquaintances.

Immediately he wrote to the Slingsbys. He knew that his old friend Cecil Slingsby would never entirely recover from this blow. To Len he wrote:

> I did not think anything could hurt me so much still. Except Hilton's going. They are *all* gone: all the men I had seen grow up, all those with heart, courage and vitality; all those I had thought to grow old among, caring for the same things . . . And, Oh Len, hardly one of them old enough to have left a child. And the earth stays full of the worthless, and the parasitic, and the miserable unvital dull fools.
>
> My dear, I can't write to you of your loss. Such a companionship of thought and life as you two shared is too sacred even to express sympathy for. You see life very fully, and you know how little a third person can say about what lay between you two. I think you were everything to him. He had not a thought he did not share with you. You were in a sense just *himself* to him. If this was to be the end, what better could one wish for him in his life. Death is utterly evil, the only evil. The crash and roar and screaming vulgarity of it is round me while I write. Minute by minute it is falling within a few feet. Which of us cares for it, regards it, as it affects ourselves! It is such a small thing, compared with the things we live for, and which we *will* live by, though death may lie across the path any second . . .

The second half of August 1917 brought another period of intense activity for the unit as the Italians launched attacks on the Austrian mountain positions. There was fierce fighting. On some days Geoffrey worked for eighteen hours without rest, organising the service, encouraging his men, driving on occasion. It was more dangerous than ever:

> *August 29* . . . The great steep road, like a section of ploughed field sown with blocks, hampered with old wire barricades, and pockled with fearsome shell holes, zags up to the saddle, perhaps 1,500 feet. It was cumbered by mules, shadowy nervous soldiers, water carts and wounded. At the "rock corner" we found a bad jam. The Hun was shelling the road beyond . . . I had to tramp up a long section of road over which the machine gun bullets whistled uninterruptedly. How I hated the mules, who kept the inside, under the cliff . . . Beyond the corner it was a case of big shells, which were bumped down the hillside to try and catch the road traffic . . . Beyond this the shell holes and wire were really bad. The moonlight was fickle. One shell hit the cliff just above us, and sent a mass of rocks and stuff over the car. A fragment hit my boot heel . . . It was romantic enough, up there in the moonlight, but so absurd a position that I laughed again and

again. Here we were doing with *motors* front-line stretcher-bearer work! A mile or so beyond what *horse*-carts could do – and miles beyond any Italian car. Diplomacy in excelsis! Tho' I doubted any *humanitarian* gain to the wounded, in being bumped in a car down that fearsome dark "road".

The following night was equally hectic and just before he turned in to rest he wrote in the Journal: "What a night-life it is! Moonlight, and gaunt white ruins, and the thunderous echoes and dark gorge, and lapping red flame, and the glaring white-moon-road. And noise! crack and rumble, and the queer dull groan, like boards hit together, shaking the air. And through it the vicious 'swash' of shells passing. They *are* at it! both ways! – Well, to sleep."

He wrote a couple of lines next day before the night's work started: "August 31. Usual day. No news yet of Gabriele. Have tried to get the run up to Dol organised and the wounded to meet us at top. Heavy shelling up there, and in the town." The day's entry breaks off at this point. He started to write his account of what happened to him in the interim the following day "in great pain, with leg prisoned in ice". In the circumstances, it is remarkably considered and literate. After dusk, he says, he drove up with George Trevelyan to their forward aid post, where he set about organising the night's work. A report came down that the road ahead had been smashed by shell-fire, and he arranged for an Italian engineer to go up. The man did not return, and Geoffrey's drivers, Metcalfe especially, grew impatient. Geoffrey decided to take the chance and rode up at the head of the convoy in Metcalfe's ambulance:

From the start the road was one devilish block of scared mules and men. I was jumping ahead of the car practically all the way, cursing and thrashing mule-ends. I smashed my cane. And slowly, surgingly, Metcalfe drove the car through the lane I made, shouting his sort of excited gaiety. I knew it was pretty desperate.

Crump and crash, again and again, big shrapnel and high-explosive crashed over the road before and behind us. The moon was dazzlingly clear. After passing Casa Bianca we must be in full view, with a noise of whacked mules and squeaks, and engines, and abuse.

And at the turn of the bend beyond Casa Bianca the jam got hopeless; all too frightened to round the corner and blocking the whole road. I went at it furiously, back and forwards, shoving, striking, kicking, heaving; Metcalfe surging close to me, and shouldering my gap open with his wings. At last I got hold of a single blocking man and mule, jagged him round the corner, and turned to walk back to meet the car, which M. sent heaving up to me round the cleared bend.

Then all the world went cr-rr-up close beside and behind me. I felt a fearful, stabbing blow on the inside left thigh, simultaneously another harder and duller crash all up the right side.

I knew what had happened. I judged, without thinking, that it was the end for me. Life went out too easily, and oddly, as I'd seen it happen this war, for there to be a chance that something vital had not gone with *two* such smashes. Then (but these are all instantaneous, simultaneous thought flashes) I felt I was smashed partially outside of myself, and half *saw* myself. (I have noticed this effect of nervous shock even more complete, in its severance, in climbing falls.) I was conscious of my cap and face above (no doubt because they so clearly still existed while I continued *conscious*). The rest of me was two huge wire springs, with flat ends, joined at an odd angle – like that (only I can't draw – the type of spring which was like a pulley-spring) . . .

– and here Geoffrey attempted a drawing of the spring he had in mind. The narrative resumed:

Now, these were, of course, the two lines of conscious pain: (the springs suggested by the tremendous force of brace and "give" of the muscles over the two areas struck by fragments and concussion). That is they represented *all* the body part of me that retained *any* consciousness after the shock – the left thigh and right side. The fact that I visualised a *spring* bending, not a rigid line, with a break, is interesting, as it fits in with the character of the wounds and their light penetration. Not improbably I had time, with my very quick reflexes, which I have noted before, to brace instinctively, furiously against the first air concussion; which preceded (and so armed me a little against) the fragments when they came in their turn. Joining up the springs and all through them I saw a sort of "float" of green grass and valley. It was of course the view before me of the Isonzo valley below, and the grass round the road. But to *me* it meant at the instant consciousness, and (the same thing) the life I had to hold on to. If it began to dissolve and float away, I felt it would be all up. I *willed* to see it, against and round the broken springs (especially the higher spring on the left of me). I knew that as long as I could keep it clear in sight, I had top-hand of the situation still.

That all passed before the fragments had stopped or the yellow flare had quite died away out of the corner of my eye.

I saw M.'s car swinging up, hardly advanced an inch from where my last view had stamped it. I walked down towards it. I felt the springs and greenness get afloat, but M. says I walked so steadily that he thought I had not been hit at all! I saw he was going by, so I called out "I'm hit, George." "Good Lord, are you?" – by this time I had hold of the spare wheel outside the car beside him, and felt the car stop. The green curve began to run out at all the edges, and I let it go. Consciously, I fainted; for a few seconds later I felt them cutting at my things and thought, "Well, that was a real faint anyway!" Then I thought I'd better leave things to them, and save up. I knew we had to turn the car on that open narrow road, and get back through the mule press, and past the other cars! It seemed a poor chance.

Then I was lying on the stretcher, in the car, head downwards on the incline, with the heel of my bad leg anchoring me to the upper stretcher end. I felt myself laughing, the situation was so inconceivably beyond any *worse* additions! The arms were all right, so I anchored them round the central uprights, which carry the stretchers, and held myself up. I heard M. shouting, shouting, forcing, swerving to get down through the frightened troops; and again and again, crash, another exploded somewhere about . . . I felt a tourniquet fixed on my leg. G.M.T. was there; a delightful feeling as his arms went round me; dear fellow . . .

It is an amazing account, though one detail is hard to accept as the literal truth. Could Geoffrey, with the appalling injury – his left thigh was broken and smashed, high above the knee – possibly have walked down the road to Metcalfe's car? Many years later, at one of the last annual gatherings of veterans of the Unit, Geoffrey's son Jocelin put his doubts to George Metcalfe, who replied: "Of course, you are right. He just fell and I rushed over to him. But he cannot have been fully conscious what was going on, and I did not attempt to contradict his account later."

Geoffrey always believed the description he wrote in his Journal. In *Mountains with a Difference*, he expanded upon it:

. . . There was a huge cavity in the road behind me. I got round it, and walked on down the moonlit slope. The road was now drifting along under my feet, so that I seemed hardly to keep up with it. I had my eyes fixed upon the dark cliff and the tree-shadow down by the turn, so as to hold all the scenery firmly in its place. I saw the car come surging blackly up into the moonlight to meet me, out of the last edge of the shadow, summoned I think by the sound of that near explosion; and I caught hold of the top of the hard black apron beside the driving seat: "I've been hit, Giorgio" . . .

14

Amputation and After: September 1917– January 1918

THE NEXT MORNING, SEPTEMBER 1, 1917, Trevelyan scribbled a reassuring note to Sir George and Lady Young, saying their son Geoffrey had been slightly wounded by a bursting shell while trying to force a way through for one of his ambulances on a mountain road. "His gallantry," Trevelyan said, "and that of his favourite drivers particularly on that road have for some time so much roused the friendship and admiration of his Italian colleagues that this seems rather a small price to pay for it all, although I confess I did not think so last night when I first found him."

It was understandable wishful thinking on Trevelyan's part, but the account in Geoffrey's Journal, which he began writing that same morning, makes it clear that he had no illusions about the seriousness of his injuries. Immediately after the passage quoted in the preceding chapter, Geoffrey wrote:

Then down at last, on a stretcher, down into the cellar, the light on the faces of all the crowding friendly anxious officers. I felt I still had hold; but nothing to spare. Got hold of Henderson with one hand and whispered what I wanted to him, including the guarding of my eye-glass! Cold sweat and uncontrollable lassitude. But I just noted with satisfaction that they got my long boots off without cutting them. They injected saline. This pulled me round . . . Anti-tet. injection, and another morphine. Then the discussion as to injuries. I took it for granted my left thigh was smashed and didn't attend . . .

They got him down to the unit hospital, still trying to persuade him his leg was going to be all right: "I had sent for my fawn and

blue dressing-gown and cap, so as to look quite decent on arrival!"
X-rays were made and at first things looked hopeful. Geoffrey felt
terrible – "nerves all tearful and wild; impossible to find a position
to rest; no sleep" – but determined to fight with all his strength to
save the leg.

September 4 brought news that Lionel Sessions, one of the drivers,
had been caught in shell-fire at the same point on the mountain road
where Geoffrey was hit. Sessions' leg was amputated the next day.

But the news from the front was good – the Italians had at last
taken Monte Gabriele:

> Trev says today's battle on Gabriele was tremendous, and our work,
> right up to the Col, was the crown of all the preparations we've given
> it for months. Great value and much appreciated. The men doing
> their utmost and running it themselves; the merit of my system of
> "non-interference" comes out in emergencies. They're proud to be *able*
> to keep it all going on their own. Trev sees it all; helps indefatigably at
> the danger points and "relationships" and is really splendid. And I go
> on fighting this dull battle for an effective leg! The physique is helping
> Nature enormously; the doctors are giving Her every chance.

Geofrey always believed that his mountain fitness, maintained by
regular exercise, saved his life in these days. In *Mountains with a
Difference* he wrote: "I ought to have been dead in five minutes,
said the operating surgeons, with great vein and artery both severed,
had not muscle made silk by climbing whipped in round and closed
them."

For all his acute discomfort and anxiety, Geoffrey's brain remained
cool and incisive as the hour of the operation approached:

> *September 6.* 4 p.m. Another bad night, but the leg is doing all that we
> could expect. Today they decided that the time had come to open, and
> tie up the broken artery. As they explained that they *might* find injury of
> a greater character to vein etc., which would in the end ruin the leg and
> involved greater risk by leaving, I have agreed to letting them amputate
> at once, if they are convinced no constructive method is possible. I've
> been ready for it for several days . . . It's just one of the facts, to be dealt
> with by training, and cheerfully. There's no alternatives to worry about.
> It's a little odd, to have to "leave it open", to wake up with one or two
> legs, according to a hidden chance. It should be a lively moment, when
> consciousness comes back, and I find out!

The operation took place on the morning of September 7:

They operated at about 9 o'clock. When I gave the authorisation, I asked the surgeons – taking for basis the calculation that they usually risked leaving the leg *on* if that was compatible with a 60% chance of life – in my case, in view of my estimate of the terms upon which life was worth having, to leave it on if there was only a 40% chance of life. Just before it, I put the two bare feet together for a last confab and look; old tried friends in so many adventures! – for I think I knew I should not see one again . . . The operation was only just in time. It was touch and go afterwards for a week.

One book of the Italian Journal ends at this point, and it was not until some two months later – after the German/Austrian break-through at Caporetto and a desperate headlong retreat – that Geoffrey opened a new volume with a remarkable account of the ferocious internal battle he fought for survival immediately after the operation:

I had not looked to beginning this again. But circumstances have made it just worth while recalling things that happened *after* the operation. *That* was very easy. My first *un*conscious remark to Matron [Emily Power] was "There you stand, with your usual tact! What is it? I'm not afraid to hear." But I came suddenly to consciousness, with Trevvy's great tragic eyes looking enormously at me; and resolved at once to make him laugh. "What magnificent eyes you have, George!"

I guessed at once from the atmosphere of all of them that the leg had been removed after all. But as, in that case, already prepared for, I was expecting them all to be cheerful and helping to make light of it, the faces and air of tragedy for the next few days really frightened me. For they must mean that worse lay behind, and that for some reason I was not expected to recover! I made them laugh and tried to get them to be reciprocally cheerful, as I *felt* my nerves were the great danger. But they were all too fond of me, and concerned, to play the right game. The difficulty was that having "managed" them all for two years, the parts could not suddenly be reversed, and my brain, working furiously half in delirium but extraordinarily acute, saw through them all like paper.

For four days it was touch and go; and I knew it all the time. I had lost unconscionably of blood, at the first wounding, and then for the six days that aneurism was increasing . . . I had only one fixed idea, to keep the leg motionless, as I knew all depended on *that* healing without check. I kept it at times utterly immovable for forty hours at a stretch, through all the tossing of nervous fever and half delirium, night and day, spinning and beating round it like a butterfly on a fixed pin. I simply lived; willing, willing.

Thought raced and raced. Every thought ended in bruised scarlet ends, like the rose-buds suddenly ending the lengths of a creeper; that was the picture I had all the time, as every thought ended in some ghastly

accident, or bandaging, or mutilation; and each time as thought got
there, down came the will-shutter – "I won't think that!" At times the
shutter was clapping down like a wind-fan, so fast thought ran, and so
steadily will pursued it and slammed down on its inevitable close. Time
stopped still. I would look at the watch; will myself to sleep; pass into
half-dreams; and "bang" even in sleep will clapped the shutter on the
close, and woke me. "Surely that was half an hour?", and I would look
at the watch, whose marks looked like red plush, to find 2½ minutes
had passed! I lived through De Quincey's aeons of dark horrors, terrible
gulfs of blackness, endless and unformed. I had no idea my mind could
contain such vastness of space, times, and formless fears.

All the time I was morphia-poisoned. Felt it, tasted it, smelt it, lived
it: feeeling yellow and corrupt with it, through every inch of flesh.

Then he describes the moment when he realised his friends had
given up all hope for him:

. . . I felt they were giving up, and was angry at the little help they'd
given me, in cheering and pretending.

I knew I had to switch off the will-power from the leg, and fight
another battle, as I didn't feel the least like dying . . .

When I was wounded I expected not to live. But after all *this* I was *not*
going to be cheated of living! So I got Perceval in a chair, and told him
what to say to me, and to cheer things up; which he did admirably, so
as almost to take me in. And then I set my teeth, and *willed* the fever to
go, and *willed* sleep to come without morphia. I refused it three times
before midnight – and won! Sleep came; and the fever fell like lightning,
and never came back. Next day I knew I'd won the second round; and
the healing had never checked.

The Journal ends here and does not resume until eight months
later. The story is taken up, though not in such detail, in the pages
of *The Grace of Forgetting*.

A few weeks after the operation Geoffrey was moving about on
crutches, getting himself accustomed to the new kind of balance he
had to master. All prospects, however, for a leisurely rehabilitation
were shattered at the end of October when German and Austrian
divisions, under General Otto von Below, broke through the thinly
held Italian defences at Caporetto, high in the mountains, and
poured down towards the plains. The Italian Second Army was
virtually destroyed. Retreat became rout. Within days the enemy
had regained all the ground conceded in three years of fighting,
and soon he was across the Tagliamento River, and finally across
the Piave and threatening Venice itself.

It was a time of high panic and confusion, and Geoffrey – one leg gone and still struggling to get the hang of movement on crutches – was in the middle of it. Luckily, loyal friends from the unit were around him. "The Italian collapse at Caporetto," he wrote, "and the disastrous retreat which involved us and all our stations and hospital, meant for me the first return to voluntary effort." It was he who had to make the decision: "I myself was just enough recovered to take part in the decision to evacuate our base. On my own authority I ordered this finally about midnight . . . For the second – or third – time in the war I lost all my own clothes, outfit, photographs and records."

So they took to the roads, and the situation there was chaotic. They were clogged almost solid with army lorries and guns and the ox-carts of the peasantry, piled high with families and belongings. No one was trying to impose order or organisation, and every now and then the whole procession would be swept by rumours of the enemy's approach. Herbert Dyne was driving Geoffrey's car, and Emily Power, the Matron, was with them. The car would move forwards a few yards, then be forced to halt for long periods: "We drove out into the dark with the menacing red glare of explosions and fires all round the horizon. For all the first night under moonlight, and during all the following day, we were sitting for many hours together motionless in the block, or crawling a few grudging feet forward."

The cars were running out of petrol and Geoffrey was faced with another decision: "Dyne put to me the dreadful decision, to abandon our cars, for my confirmation. I made it, choking; because our self-respect, as well as our whole war work, was involved in them."

Now he was on his crutches: "So tight was the jam that to get through I had often to shuffle along sideways on them crab-wise. Presently, in the mud and crush I could not squeeze through at all." So they took to the fields, muddier than the roads but less obstructed. The men helped Geoffrey over ditches and other obstacles, and Matron Power carried his fur coat – "all that I saved of uniform or kit". It must have been immensely gruelling for a man who was still far from recovered from the trauma of his dismemberment and the loss of blood and the operation and the week-long struggle to survive. Miraculously, they came across Philip Noel-Baker, who told them his Ford was not far ahead and still able to move:

The small car could still wriggle through and thrust its way forward. By spectacular driving, Philip scraped, skimmed, surged yard by yard through the abandoned lorries and gun carriages. I never exulted in more reckless car steeple-chasing. We rushed at, and over, gaps in the roadside hedges; our aides shoved down walls where the car could climb over their ruins and the ditches, and we bumped on across plough and field drains . . .

Even the little Ford ground at last to a halt, so the young drivers were organised into four-man teams to share turns as Geoffrey's stretcher-bearers. He walked as much as he could, to spare them the hard labour. At one point they got him a lift on a farm-buggy, pulled by a horse. After that, they came across railway tracks and a repair trolley, and the young men pushed and Geoffrey sailed across the Tagliamento in style. Then another of the unit vehicles, Cyril Dickinson's ambulance car, appeared and Geoffrey got another long lift.

The traffic was moving more freely now. A new danger came from retreating Italian soldiers, demanding lifts with menaces:

I had just repelled one more such military raid, when a furious little South Italian captain dashed across the road, stopped the ambulance in front of me, and ordered its driver to take up a full load of men. I shouted my explanations from the car behind. He stormed and gestured, for all reply, and beckoned the crowd to climb in. I ordered the car to drive on; calling his attention, among other things, to my superior rank and the order forbidding us to carry combatants. He drew a revolver and held it to the young driver's head. Quick action seemed to be indicated. I vaulted forward on an arm-swing over the bonnet of my car, caught the captain's wrist, and discharged my most throaty Florentine curses in counterblast to his abusive yelps. He wrestled to bring his arm down to shoot. The position grew unstable. I was holding him with one hand while balancing on one leg, and with my other hand I was steadying myself against the radiator behind. I suppose my next movement would have been to fling both arms round him and overwhelm him with avoirdupois. But at that instant an Italian orderly from our hospital burst through the simmering hostile crowd and passionately arraigned the small fiery lunatic – for assaulting a *mutilato di guerra*.

This did the trick and the captain retired from the field, though Geoffrey felt disappointed "at the real issue being obscured by this *argumentum ad hominem*".

They finally found billets at a place called Castelbelforte on the Lombardy plain, and it was here that Geoffrey wrote the account, already quoted, of his post-operational days of crisis. Now, at last, he could get on with the patient business of recuperation. The only serious interruption was a welcome one. He heard a familiar voice one day, calling across the road to ask the way, and it was his old friend Marcus Heywood, still ADC to General Plumer who had been rushed to the scene to inject some stiffening and order into the Italian defences. Plumer made his headquarters briefly near-by and Geoffrey was vastly impressed by the quiet and very firm way in which he set about his task.

In January 1918 Geoffrey returned home to England to complete his convalescence.

There must have been dozens of letters of condolence on his injury but few have survived. Len Slingsby's mother Alizon wrote to Lady Young: "His life is the great thing one hopes and prays for, but we do grieve to think of one so full of life and athletic power being thus disabled. It means much more for him than it would to a less active man." Will Arnold-Forster, also writing to Lady Young, made a similar point: "It might have been even worse, much worse, but one can't think of that – one only thinks of the *beauty* of the way he walked on the mountains, and the way he leapt on to a bus as he left one in the street, and the way he climbed down into a pool in Italy . . ."

George Mallory, home for treatment for an ankle injury, wrote to Lady Young:

> I never believed in Geoffrey so much as now. He'll be fine in his misfortune – finer than ever. There'll be a gesture to rise above it, still gracefully. He'll be more distinguished, too not by the fact itself but by his beautiful attitude towards it. The greatness of him will be seen more than ever in his spiritual endowment; he'll be wonderful always with that. And won't he – alert, imaginative, and profoundly interested – be happy, too?

Mallory wrote to Geoffrey too, prompting a forward-looking response:

> I am frankly diverted with the prospect of seeing how far I can work up to my old standard of motion with the aid of a sham leg and my trusty old right! I couldn't, at 42, have *bettered* my old hill-going. Now I shall have the immense stimulus of a new start, with every little inch of progress a joy instead of a commonplace. I count on my great-hearts, like you, to share in the fun of that game with me.

15

Marriage and Return to Italy

THERE IS NO JOURNAL FOR the early months of 1918 and it is a pity since it was a very important period in Geoffrey's life. Before the end of April he was a married man.

It is not known exactly when he re-proposed to Eleanor Slingsby and was, this time, accepted. But one letter of his, written from the Italian front against a background of gun-fire, reveals a marked intensification of feeling. The letter is undated but seems to have been written some time after the days they had spent together in London at the beginning of 1917.

Dear Lassie,

I think of you every day, and always in pleasant places and sunlight. It is like the thought of a clean-cut rock or mountain stream. An atmosphere more than a portrait: something essential and elemental: without covering an impression of fresh lines and charming sounds and views: physical, like all sweet impressions, and abstract too. But not etherialised absurdly: thank goodness, no! Above all, natural, true, direct.

What days they were. Not only for the words and sight of you, but the feeling and thought of you. I could just shoot words – talk without thought, sure that you had the feeling that explained them, would not catch on the mere words.

I love to think of you, back on our hills, with the thought of you lying beside some rocky stream, revelling in sun and the thrill of cold water . . . The heavy guns give an odd undercurrent to thought. There has just been heavy shelling round us here: and *that* made me think of you too! It accentuates the thought of life, outlines the living body for one: accentuates the enormousness of its value. And you are just *that*: vitality, the beauty of life, movement in the rush of limbs, in the curve of shape: continuance in the rush of thought, the sympathy of feeling. Goodnight, sweet life,

Geoffrey.

There also survives a scribbled fragment, from Len to Geoffrey. It is undated too, and speaks of passion scarcely under control. She was writing in a great hurry, in the midst of other jobs, and trying to impose the discipline of verse upon her feelings:

> Dear Geoffrey! If I could one moment longer stay
> To write you how I love you - all the way
> I should be happier still but – this you *know*
> My heart is yours, and sings (?) for you alone –
> And every flash of light that meets you on your way
> Is mine as well – and Night, though dreary, brings her fill
> Of thoughts and dreams that whisper round me – low . . .

And the turn-over page dissolves into incoherence and crossings-out and illegibility. She apologises for the "fearful nonsense", and adds: "Forgive the rhyme, but learn the Reason!"

G. M. Trevelyan wrote from Italy to congratulate Geoffrey on the engagement:

> The thought of you *happy* with all your immense powers of spiritual happiness so long denied their full expression is to me a joy that is with me every hour supporting me through this dreadful time. And I know Eleanor and can imagine it all and know she has a soul worthy of yours and able to meet it, simply on your own heights, and yet to tread the daily paths that love makes magical in their so restful surety and blessed commonness.

This note is not dated, but Trevelyan wrote again, on March 24, 1918, with a further demonstration of his loving thoughtfulness:

> I have naturally been thinking about you and Eleanor most of yesterday (I gave your love to the mountains and they smiled, the first time they have done so for more than three years) and I want to give you my first serious thought. It is this. Ought you not to reconsider your gallant and to me most delightful determination to rejoin us? In writing this I am putting my own happiness very much on one side; but that ought not and shall not weigh in these times. That it would also be a loss to the Unit cannot be doubted, but one may weigh the service you could do the country through us out here (considerable as it would be) against the service you could do the country in some well-chosen, important, *paid* job at home. If the two balanced, as regards service to the country in these times, ought not the *pay* to kick the beam now that you are marrying. Also ought you not to set up house at once and live together, and cannot that be done if you get some paid job of public service at home. Your lost leg makes that your right, makes it the natural course that everyone would expect you

to take on marriage, for the remainder of the war. Might it not perchance result in the end in better results for the country, as well as greater happiness for her whose interests are now to be considered *before* those of the Unit, before any other interests *except* those of the country.

Some time in April 1918 Hilton wrote to the betrothed couple: ". . . I hope you both really mean it, because I have taken you at your words and arranged for the ceremony (under instructions from G. W. that I assumed to be seriously intended) at St George's, Hanover Square." He added a special note for Len: "Dear Len – this is a bright affair: and it is happy to think of you; as happy as I think that you are going to be. You are the great benefactors; because it is good to have happy things to think about. I can see Laurence opening his eyes very wide, and hitching his shoulders up with a grin; and I think he would say in a soft undertone 'Some rag!'"

London, when Geoffrey arrived there, was undergoing nightly air raids "in an atmosphere of dignified astonishment", as he described it. One night, he recalled in his autobiography, he had been dining in Westminster with brother Georis and they sat up so late there were no cabs on the streets when the time came to go home:

> So I had to return to my rooms in full evening kit and sitting astride, rather than in, the wayward high-sprung perambulator of my youngest nephew. It was a fragile and a delicate feat of balance. Whitehall and Piccadilly were completely deserted, and as my brother, likewise in evening dress and silk hat, pushed me precariously and powerfully up the long moon-lit inclines, keeping to the road centre to avoid falling tiles, there was not even a policeman left to smile at us.

In the same work Geoffrey makes laconic mention of the wedding: "Eleanor Slingsby and I became engaged, and planned the largest and liveliest of London war weddings, purposely to enliven the black weeks of the break-through on our Western front." The Germans had launched their last, massive and desperate attempts to break through the allied lines north of Paris, hoping to deliver a clinching blow before the imminent Americans arrived in force. They had considerable initial successes.

The last weeks before the wedding are portrayed in a series of short letters Geoffrey wrote to Len on Lansdowne Hotel notepaper:

> My darling. Yours received . . . The folks at home all *very* happy, and Father busy picking pretty things out of cabinets for you. Mother *loved*

your letter to her. Dear heart, yours to me yesterday had more poetry than all my books!

I've just steered Cecil Hanbury through a "Piccadilly lunch": at the end of which he spontaneously offered La Mortola to us, as a brilliant surprise thought! I was *overwhelmed*! – the old dear: with a carriage and two old horses, and servants, and bathing, and flowers! Shall we ever leave it, heart's heart? Now I'm just off to the jewellers, to set some of your stones. I shan't come till Monday, as I *must* buy the ring. This place is in the parish of St George's, Hanover Square, which would save taking any extra lodging, if your Mother approves it? It's an ugly church, but fashionable for such occasions! . . . Such a lot of small jobs! Darling, what stuff to write to you about! – but I just dream and dream of all you are. Just think of it – Mortola, and sea, and flowers in May, and *you*, sunlight and May and sea in one, for me – Geoffrey.

La Mortola was the Hanburys' house on the Italian Riviera.

Geoffrey was planning a quick trip north to see Len and the Slingsby family:

Sunlight! I *couldn't* get off: it's one rush of little things until tomorrow. So it shall be *Monday*, the usual train. Oh my heart, the joy to see you again . . . Hilton is fixing it all, at a *pace*. St George's Hanover Square: at 12 o'clock (provisionally) 25th April: (Mind you're there!) By banns. Will you have yours called thrice at Milnthorpe, and the parson to send us a certificate that they have been called: and no "objections"! I enclose the Bishop of Norwich's answer to my request to marry us: he is a dear: and very dignified. So we'll have all the forms: and a full choir, but not an anthem (?). I'll remember a few of your list of orders! Trust an old best-man not to forget the bridesmaids . . . Dearest you shall give me nothing but what you have already given. Indeed there is nothing else I want. And I've always indulged myself with everything I needed all my life! What spring sunshine; just recalling you. My sweet-heart, Geoffrey.

The next note must have been written immediately after his visit to the Slingsby home at Beetham:

My heart's darling. I must write you a line, to say it's just beastly without you! I had a good journey, with "Patience", the sandwiches, and three bonnie children to beam at me. Hilton met me here: rejoicing. Alas, he has been sent off by the Admiralty on a secret job, tomorrow: so I can't depend on him for all the work, but he'll be here on the 25th. However, my Father has come up and is being very helpful . . .

Hilton's "secret job" was with Admiral Keyes' daring night attack, on April 22, to try to close the submarine exit route from Zeebrugge by sinking block-ships across the approach.

One final note from Geoffrey to Len has survived:

Heart's sunshine!

Yours to greet me this morning, and send me fairly cheerful through the day. The world all beams at us, up here: and a host of jolly letters. Hilton's going *may* hang me up till Monday, but I hope not. Dear heart, how I think and dream of you. Thinking we were going off at once, without pretty things, Mother and Father actually sat down to the Formosa treasures, and made you up a cornelian and garnet necklace etc. with their own hands: too dear of them! Now I'll get them all nicely "set" up here for you: a few beautiful stones they are, as well. Charles and Molly Trevelyan have just been in: just gorgeous! She simply full of true romance, and understanding it all . . . Dear love, dear love, I simply burble away, and was grateful to Molly who listened while I talked of you for 20 minutes: it was next best thing to seeing you: but a long way behind! . . .

Hilton was on board the cruiser *Vindictive* in the fierce action at Zeebrugge. He won the Distinguished Service Cross for gallantry, but lost an arm. He was back in England by April 24, the day before the wedding, but in Chatham Hospital, unable to carry out his duties as best man.

The ceremony went ahead, with Georis's son Gerry, aged eleven, taking Hilton's role. The Slingsbys were there in force, and the Youngs, and many mountaineers including George Mallory. The Bishop of Norwich, an old friend of Geoffrey's, performed the ceremony. There were four bridesmaids – two of Len's nieces and two of Geoffrey's. Cecil Slingsby gave his daughter away.

They made a cheerful occasion of it, but Geoffrey's thoughts must have strayed, more than once, to all those members of his pre-war brotherhood who could not be with them. He later recalled the first evenings of the honeymoon, "pacing the Embankment under the stars, and watching the heaviest air raid of the war flashing fire and tumult over the Thames beside us".

It had been a climactic few months. It must have felt as if his life had entered a manic phase, swinging from horrors and terrors and mutilation to the heights of romance: the loss of the leg, the retreat from Caporetto, his homecoming and engagement, Hilton's amputation, then the wedding and the honeymoon.

Geoffrey was halfway through his life – he was forty-one and a half years old and was to live a further forty – and it is possible to see this as a great turning-point. Certainly, after the First World War he emerged as a considerably changed man – quieter and more reflective in manner, not so preoccupied with his own perplexities and anxieties, more considerate of others, not so self-regarding and flamboyant as he had been formerly. Len was astonished to find, for example, that his wardrobe contained forty-two waistcoats. In this respect, he changed completely. After his marriage he rarely bought new clothes, and when he got them he made them last. He did go on wearing a cloak but this was because it was easier to manage. If it also gave him a dramatic air, he did not mind about that.

It is a matter for conjecture how much of this transformation was due to the normal processes of aging and maturing; how much to his intense experiences of war; how much to the influence of Len and the responsibilities of domestic life.

Their son Jocelin, who was born in October 1919, recalls that someone – he cannot remember who – once said: "It is most important for the Youngs not to marry wives who sit at their feet."

Despite the age difference between them, there was never any danger that this young woman, full of life and spirit and brought up in the direct, robust Yorkshire manner, was going to be a docile worshipper at anyone's feet.

They were a disparate couple in more ways than just the age difference. He was part of the upper-class Liberal establishment, well-educated and widely travelled, not worldly but experienced in the ways of the world. She was a North-country girl and proud of it. He was good at practical things, clever and patient with his hands, while Len was far from that and not particularly interested in domestic chores. He had all the time in the world for children and she did not. He was demonstratively affectionate, fond of touching, and she was not. His ways were gentle, poised and considered and controlled, whereas she was quick in thought and movement, enthusiastic, impatient at times, inclined to exclamation and impetuosity.

It did not make for a serene household. Len had a quick temper that flared up suddenly. It rarely lasted long, and could usually be defused by making her laugh, but it was formidable while it lasted. His temper was short-fused too, so there were many rows and they were audible all over the house. She yelled and threw things at him – the butter-dish on one occasion. He had an infuriating way of growing whiter and quieter in anger. Once he was heard politely asking: "Is there any room in this house in which you are not going to be?" It became a family joke that she had shouted at him: "Don't talk when I'm interrupting!" She explained that her parents had rowed continually and noisily so it seemed to her a natural part of connubial life.

For all this, it was a much happier marriage than most. They loved each other and went on doing so for more than forty years. The qualities they shared were stronger than their differences – relish for life and a relaxed, confident approach to its challenges; the sense of fun and adventure; the sense of drama too, and appreciation of the incongruous; a refusal to worry over much about money and the shortage of it. They were together most of the time, and things were rarely dull. In the mid-1970s, long after Geoffrey's death, when Len was helping me with the book I was writing about the pioneer climbers of Snowdonia, she wrote me a letter about what her marriage had meant to her. She quoted a paragraph from Jessica Mitford's *Hons and Rebels* in which the author pays tribute to her young husband Esmond Romilly who was killed in action in 1941. The words, Len said, exactly described her feelings about Geoffrey: ". . . to me he was my whole world, my rescuer, the translator of all my dreams into reality, the fascinating companion of my whole adult life . . . and the centre of all happiness." And long after that, when Len was a very old woman, she said the thing she missed most was being with Geoffrey, there was no one she could talk to as she had talked to him, no one who listened as he did.

Hilton's son, the writer Wayland Young (now Lord Kennet of the Dene), recalls that Len once said, in apparent puzzlement: "I can't think why Geoffrey married me." In a way, it is harder to understand why she married him. She was young and bright and beautiful, and there can have been no shortage of offers from altogether more conventionally eligible men. She was taking on a formidable task – married life with a man already middle-aged and a distinguished figure in several spheres, and who now had the problem of adjusting himself, physically and mentally, to the loss of a leg.

But Len was tough and independent, quite undaunted by eminence and grand connections, happy to take on and enliven any company. She had a strong personality and a strong voice, and a great deal of Geoffrey's histrionic qualities. She liked dressing up and role-playing and holding centre-stage. Her time as an apprentice actress with the Liverpool Repertory Theatre had been brief, but it made a lasting effect. She loved live theatre, enjoyed the company of theatrical folk, and kept contact with actress friends like Lola Duncan, Sybil Thorndike and Evelyn Laye.

Before they married Geoffrey told Len that he was homosexual. He had no expectation, presumably, that marriage would bring that side of his life to an end. In fact, his Journals from 1914 onwards make no mention of homosexual affairs, or even yearnings, but that is not surprising. The war-time Journals, unlike those of the pre-war years, were to be read by his mother and father, and Geoffrey may well have cherished the hope that they might be published one day.

The news must have been a shock to Len, but she determined to accept it. Geoffrey did go on having homosexual affairs, discreet and occasional, after the marriage, and it was a continuing source of distress to her. Long after Geoffrey's death, when I had made friends with Len, I once summoned up the nerve to ask her if he had been homosexual and her eyes filled with tears before she replied: "Yes, he was." It was years after his death before she told the children about it, and what an anguish it had been to her.

But it did not destroy the marriage. They found an acceptable *modus vivendi*. Len had love affairs as well, and they often took separate holidays. Each knew where the other was going, and with whom. It was what would now be called "an open marriage", and – for all the tensions and tantrums – it worked. The love between them did not diminish. Every year – on her birthday and on their wedding anniversary – he would write a short, celebratory love lyric for her. In one of his more serious *Songs to April* poems, written in the early 1920s, he speaks of his hope "that somehow, somewhere, we should bridge the stream and talk life out together".

That is what they did.

They had a month together in England after the wedding, then Geoffrey returned to the Unit in Italy, resuming his Journal entries the day he set off, May 28, 1918.

He went by train to Southampton, crossed to Le Havre, then by train to Paris where he was forcibly reminded of his stay there in September 1914 because once again the front-line guns were clearly audible from the French capital. The Germans were near the Marne again but there was none of the previous panic. "Somehow," Geoffrey noted, "instinct says it will be all right."

He took the train to Turin and spent a couple of nights with his old friend Sir Walter Becker: "So I slid back into luxury and kindly enthusiasm. This villa is the centre of life for the British army out here. It *is* glorious, in summer, with wonderful gardens, and Alpine views, and full of art treasures and kindly talk: – dear old hard-working hedonist. And *her* music a treat." He was amused to hear of his old enemy: "My visit did Sir W. good, he said, for I could sympathise with him in his last row with Lord Monson and the Red Cross, who have been treating him insultingly about the hospital he equipped and presented through them. Most foolishly too, for he stands as the friend and host of all the Army out here. But oh, the Red Cross muddles."

At Padova he was reunited with his Belgian protégé:

About 9 p.m. in rushed Maurice Best, too excited at seeing me to be able to talk, almost! He says they are all rejoiced at my return. In rain and dark we started. And so it came that we failed to notice two of my precious sacks had been stolen out of the car while it waited for me to pay the bill! Containing about £60 worth of my kit, special boots, leg, camera, glasses, bath etc. Bad luck to lose it all for the second time in eight months. I was really worried and did not get over it for days; a sign that the journey had tired me nervously after all!

He was writing to Len almost daily and very lovingly at this time, and many of the letters have survived. He was welcomed by Trevelyan and the Unit colleagues at their new headquarters, a house called the Villa Trieste near Monselice in the Euganean hills. He told Len: "All really and openly glad to see me. Then came furious rain and cold: so I lay up all day, resting and talking till I was muddled. They treat me like a spoiled and delicate infant!" But as soon as the weather cleared he had himself driven into the Dolomites, touring the new outposts and finding out about the changed situation. He was glad he had decided to return: ". . . Yes, it was right to come. But I *do* miss you all the time, and wake up to think of you: and lie now, resting after tea, in the hot sun, and think such lovely thoughts of you, with just the ache in them, that *you* are not there, only the idea of you, always."

In the Journal on June 3 he wrote:

Two days of rest, and perpetual talk. Then sun! And at once I began bathing in the splendid little lake. The first day I took a nine-foot header; and I can still swim faster than the average lad. The joy of feeling free motion again! Just the glorious seconds of flight in the air, and the rush through the water of the arm stroke. Who but one who has valued it so, and missed it for a year, could know the exquisite delight that free rhythmic movement can bring, in its recovery, if only for seconds.

Ten days later he noted:

Eleanor's letter came, saying she is *in* No. I, Cheniston Studios, so I sang all the way as we drove in the sun up and down through the lovely lanes of the Euganean hills. *Such* jolly children there, all the way! And as the British Army have all their training schools dotted about in the valleys and lanes, there's always sight of the bronzed swinging British troopers in their light khaki, dawdling or washing or playing with the kiddies. *Not* the Western Front certainly!

The British were there in numbers by this time, and Geoffrey thought their example had done much to improve the discipline and training of the Italian troops. Units of the American Red Cross, lavishly equipped, were also much in evidence, and there were persistent rumours that the Friends' Unit was soon to be withdrawn.

In mid-June the enemy launched an attack. George Trevelyan and Philip Noel-Baker were now running the front-line ambulance services, but it was impossible for Geoffrey to keep away for long. Rather to his surprise, he found it exhilarating:

June 17 . . . A soldier by the road shouted "Gas!" and clearly the ambulance had checked for this. I felt sure it was only smoke. I had been laughing aloud all up the lanes with the delight of "getting back" – and yet I'd never known I enjoyed it before! I got out in spite of Phil's warnings, and walked ahead. Out of the ambulance jumped three figures with helmets and the fearful British gas mask. One tore his off, and there was Trevvy, roaring with the absurdity of my turning up then and there, with eyeglass and pipe! It was a relief to them, as they'd all lived in the panic of the breaking regiments, and I could bring them reassurance of the unbroken front and hurrying supports.

June 24 . . . Trev and Phil did a fine geste. They heard of the wounded Austrians in a hole in the great sloping false bank of the river . . . They got down and got out the four still alive, with some Italian soldiers helping kindly but grudgingly. It was full in sight of the other bank, and at one time they began to be shelled. But they got them away. "Why not bayonet them? It's much easier!" – "Ah," said Phil, "you Italians always *say* that, but you never *do* it!"

Geoffrey was convinced all over again of the unique value of the Unit's work, and increasingly incensed at the pressures for their withdrawal. He had no doubt these moves were being engineered by Lord Monson and his cronies: "The Red Cross muddle moves a stage further . . . What a set of worthless shirkers they are, at the top there . . . If only one of them could think of the *work*, and not of their petty credit or fear of a social squabble." On June 27 he went to Vicenza to meet them and try to find out what the plans were:

> . . . I tried in vain to get some *certain* programme, but it was useless. Monson was at his worst, and most irritatingly verbose and patronising. I *just* kept temper. But at last, as I was walking out, he wound up a silly condescending speech about *his* having all the hard work, and it being "easy for you fellows" (!) by adding his assurance that the ambassador – all of them and particularly the ambassador – were still of the "same opinion" as to our going, I could *not* resist! I stopped, and said softly and pointedly, "Which opinion?" That went home! And there was a last ten minutes of white-faced, almost insane talk, justifying the change of view, the absurd blunder of the fixed date; with all the subsequent weather-cocking.

The battle along the Piave still continued, but the allied defences were holding and Geoffrey was confident that the counter-attack would soon come. He did a lot of swimming and sun-bathing, and wrote many letters to Len, full of love and advice about furnishing their studio flat: "We must have a large divan for dressing-gown talks." He invented a nick-name for her – "apple blossom" – and wrote her a lyrical tribute:

> Sunshine and shade: and yet more sun and shadow:
> And still my lady dances in the meadow.
> Sweetheart: just heart of me; and yet more sweet:
> The apple blossom brushes round your feet.
> The petals flush against your cheek: your eyes
> Dance through the blossoms, blue of sun-lit skies.

Soon he would have to go to Bologna where hospital technicians were constructing a new artificial leg for him, so they planned that Len should come to Italy to spend a fortnight or so with him. She made her way across southern Europe, using charm and determination to surmount all obstacles, and they were blissfully reunited in Turin: "I joined her there, and looked so brown and youthful that she almost walked past me on the platform, unrecognising – and she just radiant! Such days there at the good Beckers, with nice little Miss Elliott having her own affair with Captain Riggs."

They had a day or two in Florence and Fiesole, then moved up to Bagnolo on the summit ridge of the Apennines to stay with some friends called the Beggs: "We never went back. Ideal air, appetites, tennis, stream bathing, dancing and perfect company, with adoring troops of kiddies. Begg scouring the hills for food, and Mrs Begg a social marvel of great charm, talent and kindness. With Mrs Begg I got into the semi-final in a tennis tournament! I found I could get across to Bologna by bus, and that fixed it."

He was back again with the Unit by the end of August: "An attack was to be made on Maio. I crawled up the gorge in a car, banged and crammed in the old way and pitch dark, by the lorries and troops. Pouring rain and black. I sang with joy to be near action again . . ."

September brought news of his brothers. Georis was now a gunner with the Marines, and Hilton, three months after losing his arm, was off to Archangel to take command of an armoured train, trying to ensure that the collapse of Russia into revolution and civil strife did not enable the Germans to seize the port.

On the western front the allies were advancing powerfully. The final break-through seemed imminent. "I expect the Curé and Sœur Marguerite are cheering now!" Geoffrey wrote to his mother. He grew very impatient with the Italian generals who were still holding back from the long-awaited attack that would put further pressure, perhaps the clinching pressure, on the enemy.

On September 10 he wrote to Len: "I have just heard that Will Forster *is* to marry Ka Cox, quietly and shortly. They ought to have cleverer babes than ours but I think we shall pull it off on looks and physique!! We'll have to look to this seriously now." Kathleen ("Ka") Cox, who did marry Forster, had been a student at Cambridge before the war, a keen Socialist and member of the Bloomsbury set, involved in confused emotional entanglements with Henry Lamb and Rupert Brooke.

When he returned to the Unit Geoffrey found himself in charge because George Trevelyan had been summoned to London for top-level discussions about their future. "It's rather fun commanding, and recalls old times," he wrote to Len who was still in Italy. Soon after she moved into the war zone. Geoffrey wrote to Cecil Slingsby, her father:

Len is up in the hills, not a day from me. She has first-rate company and good all-but-Swiss air. She is working at Italian and French . . . I

am sure you will agree that it is better to take some real share of front
work, so long as it is possible, than stick in an office at home. She seems
delighted to be out; and it is a good and rather romantic start of our
companionship. I have some stations in the Alps, and when I go up there
now and feel the unmistakable August-in-the-Alps feeling, I get a pang
or two. Well, we will see whether they are still *my* hills or not, when the
time comes! Meanwhile I am swimming and playing tennis, when down
with Len, and trying to get back as much mobility as Fate will allow.
I hope for some help from the Bologna workmen, who are artists, and
interested in my suggestion for a "mountaineering leg". You can't think
of the joy to have her out here. It is just making this sort of life possible
and pleasant, in prospect of seeing her again, and in retrospect. She is a
joy. You know, down here they call her "Madame la Jeunesse" . . .

His idea was to have two artificial legs made, one for everyday
social life and one that would enable him to resume his mountaineering. In mid-August he and Len were at the Orthopaedic Hospital
in Bologna "to start my new leg", and then they went on to enjoy
"another perfect week" with their friends at Bagnolo.

He was working hard, probably driving, himself too hard. On
September 26 he conducted two senior British Army surgeons on a
tour of the Unit's outposts, then took them on a mountain expedition
to take a close look at the front-line dispositions. They rode some
3,000 feet up on the backs of mules, then dismounted to scramble
up steep and rocky ground: "First up rough, rock tracks, over a pass
and into a trench overhanging the Austrians. Then bang *into* the rock,
and winding up a low, wet, curlycue rock tunnel, up sheer ladders
and wet slides; all in half electric-lit darkness. So out on to a scree
slide under the final peak."

Their Italian guide took the opportunity of throwing a few "hand
bombs" down towards the Austrian positions, and provoked some
desultory return fire.

Geoffrey enjoyed the adventure and was delighted at the way he
had managed: "I had to use Phil's arm, for balance, up and down.
But Jones said my walking was an 'inspiration', and he wrote a long
account of it next day to Medical Headquarters, so as to let other
legless folk know what he had seen done."

But he was over-doing it. Soon after he recorded:

. . . Two days of quiet fun and tennis at Bagnolo, then my leg went all
wrong, suddenly. We agreed I must get down to Bologna, where I was
going anyway for my new "legs" . . . For six days we tried bandaging,
then decided on operating, as the pain and inflammation continued severe

. . . Most happily, one of my wires at last reached Len, by post, and she forced her way through the night before the operation. The Italian brutes refused to make room for her in the autobus, so she *drove* to Florence, donkey-cart and horse-cart, some 40 miles, and, as the Consul failed her, made her own entry into the war zone by the conquest of Carabinieri and R.T.O.s – a fine feat!

It was another crisis period:

There we were for five weeks, in a room with a good view out over Veneto, and cosy teas and talk. All went well for three weeks; then they advised starting exercises etc. too soon, and I relapsed for a fortnight. Finally, as I was fretting myself into bad nerve storms, Putti, most sportingly, let me get out of bed and come up to the front on crutches . . . I was radiographed by Professor Corti, my Alpine friend; this showed small fragments of bone left at the amputation – shavings which had set up several centres of irritation under the use I gave the leg this year. Happily, its good condition made the crisis come only with a single rush at the end. The shell fragment, never found before, appeared in *front* of the bone, and is still there.

At the end of October the Italians, with strong British support, finally launched the attack, and within a few days the Austrians were surrendering in large numbers. For the last time the Unit ambulances were fully engaged. Len was with Geoffrey, close to the front lines, when a ceasefire was agreed on November 5. They were at Treviso six days later when they heard that Germany had signed the armistice:

It brought no conscious pleasure. It was only like the relief to one's head of the stopping of some great roaring engine, to which one was so accustomed that one missed it, oddly, through the relief of the silence. I felt the only sensation of *surprise* later, in the dusk as we drove down slowly making out the bad print of the Gazzettino in the dark, and reading that Bavaria had declared a republic, and that all the little kings were falling.

The Italians now rushed ahead to take Trieste. The Unit ambulances were hard on their heels, and it was in Trieste that Geoffrey performed his last major humanitarian act of the war. The sudden collapse of the Austrians had turned loose tens of thousands of Italian prisoners-of-war, and most of them made for the Trieste docks:

In a few days these increased to 60,000! The Italians were helpless; the hoarded food soon ran out . . . All the Italians could do was was to run a boat with 3,000 a day to Venice; the influx was faster. There were some

100,000 on the docks; with no shelter, fires got from burning the sheds; no food. An epidemic, and a revolt all round threatened. Rain would precipitate it – the bitter hill winds in any case made their life a misery. Nothing was being done. The Italian authorities never even visited.

With help from British Red Cross officials, Geoffrey acted fast. First he got the British Army to deliver convoys of food to the docks; then he set about shaming the Italian authorities into action. "It has been our last and almost our best job," he noted. "Then we drove down to the villa and Len. It had been a six days' round of very moving 'winding up' at the heels, and then ahead of, the armies. And not unfatiguing for a man on crutches. But it had served to close the wound finally, and only muscle fatigue had to be rested off."

The War Office offered Geoffrey a job helping to prepare British soldiers for demobilisation: "I felt I had not the reserve of strength for new exacting work. Also I wished to finish the war as I had fought through it, in front-line work and not at a base, and with the atmosphere of personal freedom and of direct effort to relieve suffering. So I shall not go home in a military Captain's uniform, nor with Captain's pay! The old absurd coat and its hybrid colours must serve to the end."

The final weeks in north-east Italy were heavy with nostalgia. He showed Len all the places where he had stayed and worked and played – the bathing pools, Gorizia, the Isonzo bridge, the mountain road where the shell had severed his thigh: "Of course, I saluted every familiar hair-pin and 'shelly' corner." On December 22 he wrote: "We rushed on, for the Villa. We crossed the Piave by the Salgareda pontoon, through those grim fighting zones of ruins etc., on through Treviso and Padova to VT. May time never dim those wonderful clear days of summary and review, into which the memories of the 2½ years of work and sensation were condensed and made alive again."

On December 23 he wrote to Trevelyan from the Villa Trieste:

We are all together here tonight for the first time. I am tired, though with no reason . . . I took a last great drive on the front, with unique views of the old battle line. The roads were only changed with ox-carts and staring peasants. The trenches and all the land of hills silent and back in their loneliness of line, with nature working underground at the repair. And just the crumbling crosses in their thousands to remember the years of noise and frightened thousands of humans. Monte Nero a white sheeted ghost watching all the plains.

217

He also said: "A few days ago we had a triumphant and beautiful tree for all the local babes, who devoured Francesco's cake on the steps while their mothers scraped the residue off their clothes."

There were many parties and farewells as the Unit closed itself down. Geoffrey wrote new songs and Len danced. In another letter to Trevelyan, written on December 29, Geoffrey said: "Christmas was one of our successes. The talent and programme lasted out for two evenings, without a pause . . . 'Daddy' and I sat side by side for it the last night – the eve before he left – and almost sobbed. I had my first break-down in speaking, when I tried to propose his health, with him in front of me in tears, and the rest of the table really in sobs. I have never worked with a more perfect character, the dear man." This was "Daddy" Dyne who had been Geoffrey's driver at Ypres and worked alongside him ever since, "with never a cloud or disagreement".

He and Len drove across to spend New Year with the Beggs, then down to Florence where he was offered the directorship of the newly formed British Institute. He turned it down: "First, because I don't want to settle here; second, because I don't care for Italians enough to give the necessary study to them and their language."

They spent several weeks in Florence and one incident led him to modify his view of the Italians. He described it in a letter to his mother:

There was a delightfully spontaneous meal at a small restaurant here the other day, which left me with a different impression of Florence and the real inner feeling of these folk. We went there by chance, and found a small collection of lawyers and businessmen at lunch. One of them we knew. Presently the atmosphere got very cordial. We found we were in a nest of patriots and anglophils. Wine and biscuits were presented to us; then flowers were sent for, for Len. Then a sudden outburst of cordial speeches to me, even handshakings and kissings, very touching. I was quite moved. We sat until 4! – and all the time an old "Garibaldino" of 82 slept and blinked over his lunch in the corner, draped in the Italian flag: while the server-boy, the spirit of the whole, rushed and joked about . . . One felt suddenly to have got *through*, and found a real emotion moving behind so much that is hard, selfish and over-brilliant in these natures.

He was very proud of Len and described her in another letter to his mother: "Len looks her best, which means the rest of the world gets into the background: she really is adding an elegance and manner to her radiant directness, so that the world turns round and makes remarks!" Later in the same letter, dated January 14, 1919, he looks to the future: "I feel full of hope that I shall have a lot to write when I settle to it. I don't like idleness as much as I used to think I did, but I still confess to a terror of 'offices' and town life! It will be exciting seeing what comes of it all. Len, I can see, has great plans for exploiting my genius."

In February they were back at the hospital in Bologna, where Geoffrey was inciting the workshops to what he called "revolutionary *mechanical* experiments" in the fashioning of two artificial legs. He was determined to recover, as far as possible, the old mountaineering prowess.

It was during this period that Len suggested reviving the Easter Pen-y-Pass parties. Geoffrey was reluctant to consider it at first – too many of his pre-war "brotherhood" had been killed. But Len drew up a list of those who had survived, and argued that a new generation of young climbers would soon be emerging, and she prevailed.

Geoffrey wrote to George Mallory, who had resumed his teaching at Charterhouse: "I am keen to revive all the hill activities at once and count on you, as almost the only survivor, to do the work of bringing in the young folk. We will do the social side, if you will set the climbing standard."

16

Family Man: 1919–24

THE SPRING OF 1919 brought Geoffrey back to England and launched him into domestic life.

One of the qualities he and Len had in common was a natural disregard for the conventional, "bourgeois" view of success. He did not want to be tied down in a routine office job, and she understood this and sympathised. They both preferred freedom and uncertainty to the lures of security; adventure and discovery to vegetation. Neither of them measured people by the wealth they had accumulated or the office they had attained or their social standing. Neither worried about the need to "keep up appearances". They knew how to live simply. The houses they had were always rented and usually small. They ran a small car because they did a lot of travelling, with Len at the controls, exclaiming at the passing prospects and often waving her arms about in broad gestures of enthusiasm. They rested happily in the faith that "something would always turn up".

They both knew there was no point, and felt that there was nothing honourable either, in expecting to rely on subsidies from their parents. Sir George Young was struggling to maintain the old buildings at Formosa Place in a reasonable state of repair. Cecil Slingsby, no businessman and frequently away from home, was effectively edged out of the family business and almost totally dependent on his wife's money. Much of that was dissipated over the years by the prodigal son Will.

Geoffrey had been promised a pension in recognition of his war service and his disability. It came from the highest source, the Prime Minister, Lloyd George. But the pension did not come. Geoffrey took the disappointment on the chin, quoting a popular line of satirical verse: "He meant it. *How* he meant it at the time!" It confirmed him in his cynical view of politicians, with the exception of Hilton, and their promises.

So the newly-marrieds had to get along as best they could on what Geoffrey might earn as a freelance writer. He wrote dozens of articles for the magazines and newspapers; contributed a chapter on Pen-y-Pass to a book called *The Mountains of Snowdonia* (1925); and produced three books of his own: *Mountain Craft* (1920); *April and Rain*, a collection of new poems (1923); and *On High Hills*, an account of his pre-war climbs (1927). All were reasonably well-received but there was never any chance of any of them becoming a bestseller. As a result, it seems unlikely that Geoffrey earned more than £800 in any of the immediate post-war years. Despite this, they contrived for themselves a full and rich family life and various adventures.

Geoffrey's daily Journals come to an end with the winding up of the Ambulance Unit in Italy. Thereafter, except for a few brief autobiographical notes of his, the chief primary source of information lies in those letters that have survived. Fortunately, there are many of them, within the family and with their friends.

At Easter 1919, after a four-year interval, the tradition of the Pen-y-Pass parties was triumphantly revived, to continue for the next twenty years. "We filled the hotel and shacks and three cottages, to the Owens' delight," Len wrote. The weather was magnificent and many old friends turned up – the Mallorys, the Reades, Conor O'Brien and his sister Kitty, Claude Elliott, Harold Porter and others. On Easter Monday Mallory created an impressive new route on the East Buttress of Lliwedd, the Garter Traverse. But the really remarkable thing about that holiday was Geoffrey's return to rock climbing. True to tradition, they all spent Easter Day on the buttresses of Tryfan and it was there that Geoffrey made his first one-legged climb. He described it in *Mountains with a Difference*:

> The Gashed Crag on Tryfan was my first rock climb, on the same cliffs where as a boy I had seen the first roped party in Wales. After the long months of foot-drag and zigzag up hillsides, it came as a lightening of the spirit to be able to swing lightly upward on arms and hands, and feel again in balance. The final chimney, which is largely for the left foothold, tried its best to be discouraging at the close. But Percy Farrar, most generous of great mountaineers, met me on the slab at its top: "I envy you your nerve" was his characteristic comment. I was so entirely preoccupied, myself, with its mechanical strains and hindrances, that I remember still my surprise.

Geoffrey was, of course, protected by a rope from above. His achievement was due, primarily, to two factors: the strength of his upper body, arms and hands and shoulders, maintained by daily exercises; and the trouble he had gone to in devising a climbing leg for himself.

With the help of the technicians of Bologna, he had contrived what he called his "peg-leg", that enabled him to enjoy rock climbing again. Already he was experimenting with various detachable feet which he could fit on according to the terrain – a leather shoe device, a rubber pad, a ski-ring fitment to stop the leg plunging into snow, and for rock climbing a steel spike, studded with nails, that he could ram into nicks and crannies.

In September he was on the crags once again, this time in the Lake District and with a party that included G. M. Trevelyan, Philip Noel-Baker, Raymond Bicknell, and his father-in-law Cecil Slingsby, who was celebrating his seventieth birthday.

A young engineer from Barrow, George Bower, led them up a steep route on Gimmer Crag, and Slingsby enthused about Geoffrey's performance in a letter:

> . . . I never saw such a magnificent mountaineering feat in my life . . . GWY had to do practically the whole of his climbing with his hands and one foot, the right. Where nature had provided a little foot-hold for the *left* foot, GWY held tight with his hands – often only very minute holds – and hopped up and across with his *right* foot to the foot-hold designed for the *left*. This feat had to be done frequently . . . He never grumbled, but really enjoyed himself.

A few days later they were climbing in Birkness Combe, Buttermere, then – on Slingsby's birthday – they made the long hike to Pillar Rock to tackle the classic North Climb. Bicknell led, with Geoffrey second, and Slingsby third.

> Really it was astounding [Slingsby wrote], to see Geoffrey Young, just above me, climb those very difficult rocks with an artificial leg. Awfully hard work it was for his hands, arms and right leg. He went most brilliantly over that fearsome NOSE . . . We were out for 11½ hours. Geoffrey found the descent from Scarf Gap in the dark to be very tiring but he was helped by willing friends.

Len was pregnant by this time, and in October she and Geoffrey moved north to her parents' new home at Heversham, overlooking Morecambe Bay, in what was then Westmorland. It was from here, on October 25, that Geoffrey wrote to his mother:

A very splendid young athlete arrived at midnight. A beautifully modelled and proportioned boy, with heavy muscular shoulders, a rose-leaf
skin, a great depth (our family!) of headroom, a shock of hair, eyelashes,
broad jolly brick-red cheeks, rolls of fat and muscle, *and* the deep indig-
nant voice of a Chinese gong driven by 40-horse-power lungs! the angry
storm-roar of pure temper that leaves you no doubt as to health! and ends
with an alderman's chuckle of fat content as he gets his comfortable way.

Len was determined he should be a gift on 'our' birthday, and he was,
by about two minutes. Dearest, in the 23 hours of that gallant fight I saw
further into the mystery of pain and the power of the human spirit than
ever for myself or in the years of battle sufferings. The half was not told
me, before.

He ended the letter with this sentence: "The bells are ringing [it
was Sunday evening] and the sturdy scrap with his fine legs (almost
as good as mine!) is already a part of the beautiful world; with his
own personality, will, and freedom to run on the mountains or kick
against his generation, as time and his own soul shall lead him."

It was a particular delight to Geoffrey that his son had contrived,
by the narrowest of margins, to be born on October 25, which was
Geoffrey's birthday and that of his brother Georis too. It is also Balaclava Day and Agincourt Day and in later years Geoffrey's household
traditionally celebrated the multiple anniversaries by listening to Len
reading the "St Crispin's Day" speech from *Henry V*.

Geoffrey chose an unusual but characteristically romantic name for
his son – Jocelin. In an ebullient letter to George Trevelyan he claimed
that it meant "the joyous young sportsman". Jocelin himself says that
he disliked the name as a boy and a young man, but then found it
useful. It is certainly distinctive.

Geoffrey was working at this time on a final revision of his book
about mountaineering. The greater part of it had been written before
the war, with help from experts in special areas – men like Captain
Farrar, Oscar Eckenstein and Professor Norman Collie. He did
much of the writing at Monte Fiano and would take chapters to
the Pen-y-Pass gatherings, reading them aloud in the smoking room
after dinner and getting the comments of his friends. On his return
from Italy, the long interruption of the war over, he got the old
manuscript out and worked over it again.

The result was *Mountain Craft*, a 300-page volume that was published by Methuen in 1920 and subsequently reprinted four times.
The book is unique in the vast library of mountaineering books and
quite unlike everything else that Geoffrey published. His aim, as he

put it, was to offer a statement "of the principles which underlie all correct climbing motions". So he held the romantic, high-flown side of his nature under very tight rein. There are no jokes or anecdotes or illustrative stories, and none of his characteristic rhapsodical flights either. The tone throughout is dry and impersonal, almost academic. It is a book of theory, immensely detailed and comprehensive and thoughtful, a testimony to Geoffrey's climbing experience and the deep thought he had given to every aspect of the sport. It is elegantly written too, but not easy to read.

He allows himself, in the preface, one declaration of what mountaineering meant to him:

> . . . it is a genuine craft, as well as a genuine enthusiasm; an education alike in self-development and in self-subordination; a discipline of character, of infinite variety in its demands and in its reactions upon strength, endurance, nerve, will, and temper, upon powers of organisation as upon powers of dealing with men; a test of personality for which no preparation may be considered excessive, and a science for whose mastery the study of all our active years is barely sufficient. Of its rewards, in health, self-knowledge, aesthetic pleasure and incomparable adventure, it is not the place to speak in a book of practical counsel.

The book was generally welcomed. George Mallory, reviewing it in the *Climbers' Club Journal*, said it was "the most important work on mountaineering which has appeared in this generation". He particularly praised the psychological attention which Geoffrey had shown: "He cares supremely for personal relations in a party of climbers. No previous writer has so emphasised their importance." Others reviewers made the same point. George Trevelyan loved the book. Tom Longstaff, a pioneer of Himalayan exploration and one of the dozen or so who had contributed to the book, wrote to him: "I take off my hat . . . I have, of course, read first my 'own' chapters and am immensely grateful to you for licking it into shape. I hardly recognised my laboured efforts." Another man who had helped, Percy Farrar, was ecstatic: "*The book is magnificent*," he wrote to Geoffrey. "*It will be standard so long as mankind is interested in mountaineering.* The profound amount of work put into it staggers me."

No one, as far as I have found, resorted to the most obvious line – that mountaineering is not a game that can be learned by sitting in a chair and reading, only by going out and doing. But Geoffrey had pre-empted this line of criticism with the second sentence of the book: "I do not myself attach much value to mountaineering handbooks: an open-air pursuit can only be learned by practical attempt and from good example."

He sent a copy, with a grateful inscription, to another man who had helped in the writing, Oscar Eckenstein. Eckenstein wrote back with his thanks, said he was looking forward to reading it, and added sadly: "I wonder whether I shall ever see you again. It would give me very much pleasure to do so. Perhaps some day the spirit will lead you to pay us a visit. I am very much of an invalid now, and you will always find me at home." He had consumption and was living at Oving, near Aylesbury. He died in 1921.

In the spring of 1921 Len and Geoffrey moved to a new home, Birkby Hall at Cark-in-Cartmel, North Lancashire. It was a large, rented farm-house, not far from the Slingsby home and close to one of the grand houses of the region, Holker Hall, residence of the Cavendish family since the sixteenth century.

Geoffrey described their lives there in letters to his mother, who was becoming frail and had to use a wheelchair to get around. He always addressed her as "Dearest". He described their train journey north: ". . . Jocelin made friends all the way as usual. He never rested, but remained agreeable and interested, in spite of it. We found the house just spick and span, with fires everywhere, and bluebells, and so clean you couldn't put down the luggage! We slept tremendous."

The letters are full of rapturous accounts of Jocelin's development, his "radiant activity": "He's like a little dancing sun, of vitality and independence." Geoffrey set about knocking the garden into shape, the beginning of what was to become a regular pastime and delight. He liked the exercise and the fresh air, and the opportunity to use his practical skills and plan the seasonal colour schemes. He became an accomplished axe-man. Len did a lot of knitting, and starred in the local production of *Iolanthe*. They hired a small piano which she played while the others sang along. They saw much of the Slingsbys and made friends with the Cavendishes.

Geoffrey earned small amounts as a jobbing journalist. He wrote articles for *The Times* and for various magazines, especially the *Cornhill*. He did a piece for *The Nation and the Athenaeum* on "The Comfort of the Garden". An ecstatic account of his Mont Blanc climb with H. O. Jones in the glorious summer of 1911 made one of the chapters in a compendium called *Great Hours in Sport*, edited by John Buchan. On a more serious level, he was starting to contemplate a book about his pre-war climbing. He told his mother: "I am at work trying to make a book of my mountain memories. The difficulty is I have too much material, of diverse kinds! But it will be fun to make it into a pie for printers." It was to be published several years later as *On High Hills*.

They did their shopping in Ulverston. They had many visitors, including George Trevelyan and Marcus Heywood and his lively family. They returned these visits, staying with the Trevelyans at Cambo and then with the Heywoods at Longframlington in Northumberland. Geoffrey had to do much travelling, lecturing in Oxford, attending climbing club dinners, but he grew very fond of their home in the north. At the beginning of November he wrote to his mother:

> The hills are lovely in autumn colour, and clean cut against the steely blue autumn sky. I can see every branch across the valley, even the rocks on the Coniston Old Man, 20 miles off. The sun sets marvellously every evening now, over the estuary waves, in indescribable colours and audacious pranks of cloud. And the stars flicker in the nightly wind that sings round our bedroom corner of the house. We are reading aloud Charles James Fox, and having a do at the Victorian politicians, Len reading Bryce's *Essays* on them . . . I have got the garden nearly straight and waged war with the antique ivy, and we are putting in a lot more cupboards and shelves and utilities.

Geoffrey and Len visited George and Ruth Mallory and their two young children at the Holt, their house in Godalming. On one visit Geoffrey raised an idea his brother Georis had put to him – that there were blatant flaws in the English public school system and that it should be possible to devise something more enlightened and broadening. Mallory agreed and the two men discussed the matter at length: "We outlined together the scheme for a new type of school," Geoffrey wrote many years later, "to be half a year at classwork, probably in towns; and all the summer months in permanent camp, engaged on practical open-air activities and crafts. David Pye, afterwards Provost of University College, London, joined in our plan-making; which we completed in considerable detail." In their "ideal school of the future", there would be more active co-operation between teachers and parents – the recurring and total split between school life and home life was too disruptive and damaging; the boys would be taught about the lives of ordinary working people around them – the school would include a working farm; and there would be less emphasis on team games, less adulation of the heroes of the playing fields. The school of the future would offer "an atmosphere friendly to intellectual effort". Nothing came of the scheme, but it indicates the lines along which Geoffrey's fertile mind was moving. Later, when he found out what the educational reformer Kurt Hahn was doing in Germany, it would be with recognition as well as delight.

Geoffrey had long been George Mallory's mentor, and he was now to exert a climactic influence on the younger man. Plans were being made for a full-scale reconnaissance of the northern approaches to Mount Everest. In early January 1921 Geoffrey wrote to his old friend General Bruce suggesting that Josef Knubel should be a member of the climbing party, but Bruce replied that they wanted to keep it "British all through". Almost inevitably, this meant the inclusion of George Mallory, thirty-five-year-old and an all-round mountaineer of great experience. Mallory was reluctant though. He was happily married, with three young children by this time, and wondering whether to leave the classroom and try to make a living as a writer. It was Geoffrey who changed his mind about Everest. In a marginal note, written in ink on the appropriate page of David Pye's 1927 biography of Mallory, Geoffrey repudiated Pye's claim that Mallory had simply found the Everest idea "irresistible". Geoffrey commented: "What happened was – he 'left it to Ruth'. She was *against* it. *He was going to refuse.* I saw them both together, and in 20 minutes' talk, Ruth saw what I meant: how much the label of Everest would mean to his career, and educational plans. She told him to *go*. Pye has it all *wrong*."

On February 10, 1921, Mallory wrote to Geoffrey: "I am just fixed for Everest . . . I expect I shall have no cause to regret your persuasions in the cause of Everest; at present I am highly elated at the prospect and so is Ruth: thank you for that."

In the event Mallory did not enjoy the long and arduous expedition that summer. There was little understanding then of the weather patterns of the region so they carried on throughout the monsoon, and there was no appreciation at all of the debilitating effects of high altitude over a prolonged period. They used no oxygen; the food was awful and their equipment not much better; the leadership was often inept and confused. Mallory described his feelings about all this, very forcefully, in letters to Geoffrey. For all the suffering however, he became obsessed with Everest and the prospect of its conquest. He wrote, almost in panic: "Geoffrey, at what point am I going to stop? . . . I almost hope I shall be the first to give out!"

Geoffrey was disturbed by this and wrote back, advising caution: "The result is nothing compared to the rightness of the attempt. Keep it 'right', then; and let no desire for result spoil the effort by overstretching the safe limits within which it must move . . . Good fortune! and the 'resolution to return', even against ambition!"

On September 24 Mallory led two other British climbers and three Sherpas to the North Col, which was to prove the key to the ascent of the mountain from the north. His companions could not go on, so they descended again. Mallory was disappointed, but Geoffrey's prediction proved true – he returned home a national hero, famous and fêted, the man the people indentified with the highest mountain on earth. He wrote of his disappointment to Geoffrey, who replied:

> You write, in the natural reaction after a touch with superhuman circumstance, of "failure". You will find this end of the world is only using the word *success* – success unexpected, tremendously deserved, and beyond what we hoped . . . I can assure you that the colossal effort of lifting an entirely unsuitable party, at the first attempt, on a single pair of shoulders, not only onto the right line but well up it, against hopeless conditions, forms an episode by itself in the history of mountain exploration, and will only be the more appreciated the more time goes on.

Geoffrey had been back among the mountains in September 1921. He sailed from Harwich to Antwerp, and there spent a couple of days with his protégé from the first days at Ypres, Maurice Best, who was now married and beginning to build up a brilliant career in a shipping firm in the Antwerp docks. He went on by train to the Alps, to a hero's welcome: ". . . and from Brig stumped up to Bel Alp in five hours, to spend a week with Mrs Tyndale at the chalet, and I bathed in the little lake, and sun-basket as if in August. Knubel joined me there, and we gossiped endlessly. The peaks produced no tragic thrill; all just familiar and friendly. Like going up a home avenue, every crest and line showing up unexpectedly like an old friend."

He travelled on: "At San Niklaus I gossiped infinitely with the guides, seeing all the old friends, and having to drink infinitely of their wine cellars. Franz Lochmatter remains the greatest of them."

He went on to Venice, then returned home by way of Ypres and more reunions – with the Curé who was now the Dean, and Gustave the porter, and with Sœur Marguerite who had been seriously ill and was not expected, erroneously as it turned out, to live much longer. He had a long chat with the Curé and Sœur Marguerite:

So we three sat in her little office, and talked of the present work . . . and if their thoughts were like mine, it was a ghostly company. So we had sat so often, in the Convent St Marie, while the shells screamed and burst outside, and we waited for the message that meant those two hurrying first to the tending of some remainder of a cellar family. And even now there came across the fields the dull thudding of explosions, where the British firm was exploding old dumps of shells; and she looked across and smiled the same half-mocking, half-spiritual smile of complicity.

Geoffrey was deeply moved by this meeting: "I felt as if I had had a glimpse of spirit world, and felt for a moment how angels feel, and what a love – almost adoration that has nothing of the body in it – must mean. An angel would not give it; it could only come to me through something so intensely human, sympathetic, vivacious." He described Ypres as "the home of the best work of my life".

Len was in Norway that summer, escorting her father on one of his last trips to the scene of his great mountaineering feats of forty years before. They went to Oslo where Cecil Slingsby was received by King Haakon, then into the mountains where, according to Len's report to Geoffrey, they were given "an almost royal welcome in every district through which he passed". Geoffrey wrote to her from the Heywood home in Northumberland, where he was staying with Jocelin (now nicknamed "Jock"): "I'm longing to hear how the mountains have gone . . . Jock sleeps perfectly, and eats well; and babbles long incoherent sentences. The morning tea always suggests 'Mamma' to him. But I'm not sure quite of the context. I see it all with your eyes all the time, dear heart, and I don't think you are ever out of my thought for two seconds!"

Some time that year, 1921, Len was in London, theatre-going with friends, and Geoffrey sent her a letter in jokey doggerel, commenting on the fact that she was going to all the Grand Guignol horror plays being presented by Sybil and Russell Thorndike. The letter ends with characteristic words: "I've £200 (!!!!!!!) at the Bank !!! – so you can blow it all you like – my beautiful incomparable April." Increasingly, at this time, he was seeing her as the personification of spring.

The next year, 1922, saw two major events in the Young family – the marriage of Hilton and the death of Lady Young.

Geoffrey's diaries and letters up to this moment give ample and continuous evidence of his affection and admiration for his younger brother. He had long recognised that Hilton was not only better-educated than he but also that he was cleverer and more ambitious, much more at home in the worlds of finance and public affairs. But Hilton was also a witty and articulate man, and an accomplished poet, moving easily on the fringes of the élitist Bloomsbury Group, the close friend of E. M. Forster and Lytton Strachey. The war had revealed him as an able and courageous officer, and his book about his experiences in action *By Sea and Land* (1920) showed that he shared something of Geoffrey's romantic approach to adventure. Throughout the war, when many of his friends were in danger, it was Hilton's fate that was always uppermost in Geoffrey's concern.

Now Hilton was forty-three and set, it seemed, for high office. The year before he had been appointed Financial Secretary to the Treasury in Lloyd George's coalition government. In 1922 he was made Chief Whip to the Liberal Party in the House of Commons, and a Privy Councillor.

His bride was Kathleen Scott, the widow of the Antarctic explorer Robert Falcon Scott and mother of Peter Scott, who was to become a leading protagonist of wild-life conservation. She was also in the Bloomsbury set, a sculptress, and a woman of striking looks and strong personality.

Her arrival in the family presaged the end of the close relationship with his brother that had meant so much to Geoffrey. At first things went on as before. There were occasional family get-togethers, and Geoffrey's letters show no diminution in his interest in Hilton's fortunes. But after a few years it became clear to Geoffrey that he and his family were being kept at arm's length. A coolness descended, and turned icy. It caused him great distress. In one of his private papers, he later described the attractions of the younger Hilton and went on to say: "In later middle life he left me, abandoned our heart-intimate fraternity, and has left a wound that will only heal with my death."

Estrangements like this often occur after a marriage, one partner draws the other away from those who were once close. This estrangement was predicted. When Hilton and Kathleen married, Helen Young (Georis's wife) said to Len: "Now we shall all lose Hilton – Kathleen will never want to be part of the family."

Kathleen's diaries advance another reason though. She and Hilton had a son, Wayland Young, who grew up to be a successful political journalist, member of the House of Lords, and, briefly, a member of the European Parliament. He remembers his uncle Geoffrey with warmth, as a distinguished and avuncular figure, kind and usually jolly and invariably charming with children. He remembers the estrangement too: "I think my mother reacted very strongly against the homosexual element in Geoffrey. She was not in favour of that at all. She didn't want me to grow up that way. In my mother's diaries there are one or two passages in which she makes it quite clear that that was her thinking."

In the event the brothers grew closer again in later life, after Kathleen's death in 1947. But for many years Geoffrey felt that his devotion to Hilton had been betrayed. He was even – though he kept it to himself – rather resentful of the fact that Hilton was so successful, making money, becoming a minister in Mr Baldwin's government in the 1930s, and being created the first Baron Kennet of the Dene in 1935.

Kathleen made no secret of the fact that she was much more interested in men and their careers than in women. When she met Len she would always say: "And how's Jocelin?" Len always replied: "Marcia's very well."

Lady Young died in the late summer. The first warning came in a letter to Geoffrey from his father, dated June 20: ". . . Alice is not quite so strong, has felt it better to stay upstairs the last two days. I am afraid I am partly to blame, for she has been most tenderly solicitous about my health, I having had an upset of my usual sort, stomachic, the result of a pipe. Yes, I *won't* go on smoking . . ." It did not seem serious at this stage, and Sir George ended the letter chirpily: ". . . My kind regards to Mr Jocelin. He is still four months short of the age whence I date my first recollection – Willy's christening (October 1840) and the clerk kicking a hassock under the gallery. But I expect he's a precocious one, he!"

But Lady Young was now eighty-two years old and she died a few weeks later. Geoffrey had been devoted to her all his life. He would not hear a word of criticism against her, but she was far from universally liked. Her "grande dame" manner was more likely to offend than to impress people who had grown up in the post-Victorian period. Len, though she concealed her feelings from Geoffrey, actively disliked her. Years later she scribbled a marginal note on a letter Geoffrey had received from Sir George: "I could always talk to him and him to me – unlike Geoffrey's mother!"

Sir George was eighty-five years old when his wife died but still vigorous, both physically and intellectually. He swam regularly in the river and took long walks. He was a governor of several schools, active in the management of London University and in the nurturing of Reading University. He kept in touch with the family, invited them to Formosa and kept up a steady flow of bright, cheerful letters. And he launched himself into the massive labour of writing a learned volume on *English Prosody* for the Cambridge University Press. As the chapters were completed he sent them to Geoffrey for comment.

Geoffrey kept busy with his journalism, writing many articles for the *Cornhill*. Lord Baden-Powell commissioned a 2,000-word piece on "climbing as an educative activity for Boy Scouts". He returned to poetry too, writing a series of short love lyrics, celebrating his life with Len. In a letter he wrote to his mother shortly before her death, he talked about poetry-writing and said: "Words are such a delight to play with! The best toys!"

On July 8, Len's birthday, he presented her with his poetic tribute:

> When
> the 8th comes in
> for you,
> Len! –
> then
> comes in for me,
> for Jocelin,
> for all three,
> always
> the best of days! –
> for on the 8th uncloses,
> ever anew,
> the loveliest of summer roses –
> YOU!

There was another major British expedition to Everest in 1922, this time an attempt to gain the summit. Geoffrey was not directly involved but he knew many of those who were and took a close interest. The expedition leader this time was Charles Bruce, the extrovert Gurkha general whom Geoffrey had first met in the hills of Arran in 1903. Two Lake District friends were among the climbers, Dr Howard Somervell and Dr A. W. Wakefield. And George Mallory was once again a key figure.

The expedition came close to success. George Finch and Geoffrey Bruce, a nephew of the general's, reached an altitude of 27,235 feet, using oxygen. Mallory himself, disdaining oxygen on ethical grounds, climbed to 26,800 feet, and on the descent it was his quick reaction with rope and ice-axe that saved the lives of four climbers when one of his companions slipped. But there was a tragic accident on the steep slopes approaching the North Col, when seven Sherpas were killed by an avalanche. Mallory had led the way up and blamed himself for the disaster, for failing to realise that the snow was likely to give. Geoffrey wrote to Mallory to dissuade him from self-condemnation:

> Put *entirely* out of your mind that anyone has ever thought of placing any responsibility for the accident on you . . . You made all the allowance for the safety of your party that your experience suggested . . . The immense percentage of "chance", or we may call it of the "unknown", present still in this hitherto unattempted region of mountaineering, turned for once against you. Well? What then? You took your full share, a leading share, in the risk. In the war we had to do worse: we had to *order* men into danger at times when we could not share it. And surely we learned then that to take on ourselves afterwards the responsibility for their deaths, to debate with ourselves the "might-have-beens", was the road to madness . . . It has been a great and very gallant attempt, and has accomplished far more than I for one ever expected.

In the late summer of 1922 Geoffrey got a letter from a young mountaineer called Youard who had lost one leg, below the knee. He responded immediately with sympathy, encouragement and advice:

> You may be confident of this, that with such an amputation there is practically no active sport – except football – which you will not, with time and gradual practice, be able to resume successfully. You have, first, to work out a type of artificial leg, especially the bucket, that allows you light and easy movement, and that does not hurt you with long use. Secondly, to remember that you have had, muscularly and nervously, a great shock; and that it must take time and steady practice before you can tune your muscular system up to doing all you did before. Therefore, you must *go slow*, and not attempt at once heroic feats! Thirdly, the muscles of the leg, and probably of one side of the body, will have "gone back" a lot during invalidism, and can only be brought back *gradually* to taking their fair share of work; and can only be kept equally fit afterwards by voluntary daily exercises. (I do a few minutes of special exercises every day, before the cold bath.) Fourthly, the body and legs have to learn a new set of balances or adjustments altogether; and you must not *hurry* them unduly, in the process.

He went on to point out that he had lost almost the whole of his leg and was over forty when it happened, and yet – after five years of effort and exercise – he was now able to tramp the hills for eight to ten hours and manage "all but the most difficult rock climbs without help". He concluded: "Don't be in a hurry! – and go on steadily practising! Above all, *never lose confidence that you are going to be able to do everything again.* A stout heart is more than three-quarters of the road to complete recovery of activity."

In another letter a few weeks later he gave a detailed account of his morning exercises, which he did before a looking-glass, "as that keeps one from doing them slackly". The fit of the new leg was the vital first move: "Go on going back till it is really right. The leg is to fit you, not you to fit yourself to the leg! – which is what the leg-maker is always trying to persuade us!"

In 1923 Geoffrey's third and last volume of new verse was published, *April and Rain*. His style is unchanged from that of his pre-war verse. The publication in the meantime of the poems of G. M. Hopkins and Wilfred Owen and the break-through early verse of T. S. Eliot had no effect whatsoever on him. He remained an unregenerate Georgian. He never cared for Eliot's poetry, finding it arid and academic. His voice was still serious, controlled, high-toned and unashamedly romantic. Many of his themes are the same as before, mountains and landscape, water and weather. But the new volume also included poems of love and affection, mostly addressed to Len, one or two to Jocelin, and this was a new departure. He always thought of Len in terms of April and apple-blossom, flowers and freedom. In one lyric he recalled their first meeting:

> I saw you first, a golden child of seven,
> > wild roses dancing on a mountain wind,
> > > and laughing with the hours.
> The tangled sunshine, fretting through your curls,
> > escaped across hill flowers.
> Straight-limbed, with mischief eyes half-filled with heaven,
> you swung your days of youth on ropes of pearls
> > to trip love's feet behind.
> I wonder when he ceased his shy pretence
> that passing years could make no difference?

One of the mountain poems, affirming his old Alpine faith, has become an anthology piece:

> I have not lost the magic of long days:
> > I live them, dream them still.

Still am I master of the starry ways,
   and freeman of the hill.
Shattered my glass, ere half the sands had run, –
I hold the heights, I hold the heights I won.

Mine still the hope that hailed me from each height,
   mine the unresting flame.
With dreams I charmed each doing to delight;
   I charm my rest the same.
Severed my skein, ere half the strands were spun, –
I keep the dreams, I keep the dreams I won.

What if I live no more those kingly days?
   their night sleeps with me still.
I dream my feet upon the starry ways;
   my heart rests in the hill.
I may not grudge the little left undone;
I hold the heights, I keep the dreams I won.

It reads like a noble farewell to his long days of Alpine adventure, but he was still pondering the problems of one-legged mountaineering and the sort of artificial leg that would make it possible. In *Mountains with a Difference* he reflected: ". . . a man who loses the whole of one leg loses more than half his activity, because he has lost also the power to balance, the power to run or accelerate, the power to anticipate rightly the next movement – and, with that, all rhythm in his movement." He made enquiries across Europe and got no help. There was no lack of mutilated men, but everywhere he went he found them being treated in a heartless and perfunctory fashion: "like defaulters, herding them for hours and even days in squalid discomfort while they wait for their 'fittings'."

The making of artificial limbs was still a crude business. Geoffrey knew that by thought and ingenuity and experimenting he could come up with something that would make hard mountaineering, on mixed terrain, not just possible but even pleasurable again. He studied the basic principles of leg movement and devised a mechanical peg that enabled him to adjust the length of the "peg-leg", to make it shorter for steep ground, shorter or longer for contouring. He reckoned this reduced by as much as forty per cent the fatigue that came from using the stiff, production-line "legs". In the hills of the Lake District and Snowdonia, helped by many friends, he experimented with ways of using their heads, shoulders, elbows or rucksacks to maintain balance over rough ground:

The exhaustion, the rasps and jars, even the loss of conscious pleasure in movement, mattered less and less, as gradually the words "physically impossible" could be wiped off another corner and another steep contour of the map, and as – however clumsily and achingly – it became practicable once more to climb to a windy summit, to feel the nature of hard rock and to forget all the troubled effort in the views over serene distance.

It was a long, hard struggle but he was not a man to give up or to give way to self-pity.

On June 8, 1924 he showed how far he had progressed. The Fell and Rock Climbing Club of the English Lake District had acquired a vast tract of mountain country which included Great Gable. In the rock on Gable's summit they set a bronze tablet inscribed with the names of the twenty club members who had been killed in the war. Geoffrey was asked to read a tribute at the unveiling ceremony.

Since the loss of his leg he had not tackled any climb so long and rough as this, and the weather did not help. He left Professor Pigou's house at Lower Gatesgarth, Buttermere, in cold driving rain, the hills all round swirling in cloud. They made their way up Wharnscale and along the flanks of Grey Knotts and Brandreth, into the teeth of a gale. Great Gable was invisible, blanketed in cloud.

Geoffrey was exhausted but hot coffee revived him, and they pushed on to Windy Gap. As they scrambled up the final steep section to the summit, the rain ceased and the wind subsided. In the mist more than 500 people had assembled for the ceremony. Dr A. W. Wakefied, the Club President, unveiled the memorial, and Geoffrey spoke his words of tribute, consciously modelled on President Lincoln's speech at Gettysburg:

> Upon this mountain we are met today to dedicate this space of hills to freedom.
>
> Upon this rock are set the names of men – our brothers, and our comrades upon these cliffs – who held, with us, that there is no freedom of the soil where the spirit of man is in bondage; and who surrendered their part in the fellowship of hill and wind and sunshine, that the freedom of this land, the freedom of our spirit, should endure . . .
>
> By this symbol we affirm a two-fold trust: That which hills only can give to their children, the disciplining of strength in freedom, the freeing of the spirit through generous service, these free hills shall give again, and for all time. The memory of all that these children of hills have given, service, and inspiration, fulfilled, and perpetual, this free heart of our hills shall guard.

Describing the ceremony in *Mountains with a Difference* Geoffrey said: "As I spoke the words, well as I knew them, the emotion of their meaning welled up through them, and it held me like an inspiration; for once I felt that I was speaking to mountains, in the terms in which they had spoken all my mountaineering life to me."

17

Return to Alpine Heights: 1924–8

THE MALLORYS MOVED TO Cambridge in 1923 and soon were close neighbours. George Mallory had finally succeeded in escaping from classroom duties and got himself a job with the Board of Extra-Mural Studies at Cambridge, as assistant secretary and lecturer. Geoffrey's influence had helped to bring this about but he claimed that the clinching factor had been Mallory's new-found fame as "the man of Everest" – exactly as Geoffrey had predicted two years before.

Another attempt on Everest was being prepared, with high hopes. They knew more by this time about the mountain's defences, and two years before Finch and Bruce, using oxygen, had climbed to within a few hundred feet of the summit.

George Mallory was closely involved with the planning for the 1924 attempt, but not at all sure that he would go himself. There were three young children now and he was just starting a promising new job. He had developed a love-hate relationship with Mount Everest, fascinated by it and at the same time repelled. Towards the end of the 1922 expedition he had written to David Pye: "David, it's an infernal mountain, cold and treacherous. Frankly, the game is not good enough: the risks of getting caught are too great; the margin of strength when men are at great heights is too small."

Even though he was told he would be the climbing leader this time, Mallory held back, reluctant to commit himself. Geoffrey advised him not to go. After months of debate and hesitation, Mallory let others make the decision for him. He applied for the requisite leave to the Board of Extra-Mural Studies, more than half hoping they would say no. They did not however, and so he wrote to Geoffrey: "A line to let you know I am going once more. Not the slightest opposition from the Board here. But a big tug for me with the ends of a new job gathering in my hands; and Ruth will feel it more this time too." To another friend, Geoffrey Keynes, Mallory wrote prophetically: "This is going to be more like war than mountaineering. I don't expect to come back."

Mallory and his companion Andrew Irvine were last seen "going strong for the top" in the early afternoon of June 8, 1924. The witness was Noel Odell, a Cambridge geologist and an experienced mountaineer, who was on his way up to the top camp when the clouds above him cleared for a few minutes and he was able to make out two tiny figures advancing steadily towards the summit slopes along the north-east ridge. They had just surmounted a rock step when the clouds closed in again and Odell could see no more.

Nobody knows what happened next, and it is unlikely that they ever will. The modern consensus, widely but not universally held, is that they did not gain the summit. They were already well behind their schedule, and the weather turned quickly worse after their last sighting. The likelihood seems to be that they decided to retreat and that on the descent one of them slipped and both fell to their deaths. The bodies have not been discovered. But nine years later an ice axe that must have belonged to Mallory or Irvine was found on smooth slabs a few hundred yards from the place where they were last seen.

At the time there was a natural tendency, in Britain at any rate, to suppose that the two men had attained the summit. Geoffrey, equally naturally, was of that persuasion. Others were more doubtful. Colonel E. F. Norton, for example, who had gained a record height on Everest without using oxygen, commented: "It remains a case of 'not proven', and that is all that can be said about it." He was certainly wrong in the second part of his statement. Geoffrey was angered by Norton's judgement and wrote:

> . . . after nearly 20 years knowledge of Mallory as a mountaineer, I can say that difficult as it would have been for any mountaineer to turn back with the only difficulty past – to Mallory it would have been an impossibility . . . Of course there must always be an inclination in such an open question for those who hope to return to the attack to care to think the summit still unclimbed. It is an emotion which above all things these fine fellows should avoid giving to the public unless there is more evidence to contradict the probable interpretation of the facts . . .

Geoffrey never abandoned his faith that his famous protégé and friend had attained the highest point of land on earth. In *On*

High Hills (1927) he gives a long account of his Alpine climbs with Mallory in 1909, and recalls that they reached the foot of the formidable south-east ridge of the Nesthorn at 12.30 p.m. to be confronted with a similar decision to that which Mallory had to make on Everest. In a footnote Geoffrey says:

> Upon the ridge of Mount Everest Mallory and Irvine were last seen at this hour and in just about the same relation to the summit. At this point Mallory must have had to make the same choice, whether to push on to the summit or to retreat. The risk of failure upon Everest was greater but the difficulties still remaining were less, and the inducements to advance infinitely stronger. I have no doubt Mallory made the same decision which we had made together in not very dissimilar circumstances upon the Nesthorn. This being so, I think they probably reached the summit.

It is intriguing, though pointless from any practical point of view, to speculate what might have happened if Geoffrey had not lost a leg and if, as seems likely, he had been a member of the Everest parties of the 1920s. He was forty-seven and a half years old in the early summer of 1924, which seems elderly for very high mountaineering, though in recent years Everest has been climbed by more than one man past the age of fifty. He was immensely experienced, and he was also extremely strong and fit, as he was to prove in the Alps in the next few years. It is impossible to say with absolute certainty how he would have reacted to life at very high altitude, but he had certainly proved himself a fast and formidable goer at Alpine altitudes. One thing can be said with confidence: had he got to the North Col on Everest, he would have made a far better summit companion for George Mallory than the young but inexperienced Irvine. With Geoffrey there, Mallory might well have not only gained the summit but he would also have stood a much greater chance of getting down intact to the high camp.

In a tribute to Mallory, published in *The Nation and the Athenaeum*, Geoffrey described him as "the magical and adventurous spirit of youth personified" and went on: "Neither time nor his own disregard could age or alter the impression the presence of his flame-like vitality produced. Mallory could make no movement that was not in itself beautiful. Inevitably he was a mountaineer, since climbing is the supreme opportunity for perfect motion . . ."

He wrote to Ruth Mallory on June 30: "I was in France, and until we knew more I *could* not write. And I can't really now: it's a long numbness of pain, and yet but a shadow of yours, for indeed one cannot think of you separately. An unspeakable pride in that magnificent courage and endurance, that joyous and supreme triumph of a human spirit over all circumstances, all mortal resistance; and the loss unutterable . . ."

Geoffrey always took a long time to recover from serious bereavements. In July he wrote to G. M. Trevelyan:

And so, here I am in middle life, with not one left of my alpine companions and pupils . . . Just memories. I am thinking of George Mallory and the last venture, day and night. So fatally unnecessary – but a fate has dogged the leadership on Everest. In every year the leadership has lapsed to him, without the responsibility that *might* have steadied his judgement into a cooler detachment. In weighing the balance, I attach no glamour or importance to the circumstance of his death: it was as accidental a consequence of his choice of life, and of his temperament, as my losing my leg. It was his *life* was important . . . Yes, I often think of that sentence on that day: "The memory of all that these children of hills *have* given, sacrifice and inspiration, fulfilled and perpetual, the great *heart* of our hills shall guard."

And he added, in a postscript: "You know, for what it is worth, I agree with Odell that they reached the top. Nothing else fits the facts, and the men so far as we know, and knew, them. What a miracle was his one sight of them – in the 'Chariot of cloud'!"

Geoffrey kept himself busy, in the early 1920s, in a variety of ways. He did a lot of writing and some public speaking, lectures and club dinners. He enjoyed gardening and took continual delight in Jocelin's development. There were family holidays to Cornwall and the Isle of Wight. He continued to experiment with the artificial leg, looking for ways to extend his mobility and improve his stamina on rough ground. His regular letters to his father show that he made several visits to Europe. At one time he was at the League of Nations in Geneva; at others he was in Germany. It is not clear precisely what he was doing on these journeys, but it seems that he was being commissioned by various philanthropic groups to investigate and report back on the cultural and educational climate in European countries shattered by the war. By far the biggest of these bodies was the Rockefeller Foundation, founded in 1913 by the American oil millionaire to find ways of using his vast wealth for the general benefit of mankind, through medical research and educational reform. It was to prove a valuable association for Geoffrey.

At the end of 1924 the Youngs moved from North Lancashire to Cambridge. On January 17, 1925 Geoffrey wrote to his father from a small house near the Cam which they had rented, 215, Chesterton Road:

> Term has begun again. So we must expect the beginning of social calls etc. It was well thought to come here and get a start before outside duties began. Jocelin starts going to a small school tomorrow. Two nice women, highly qualified in all the latest methods but, so far as I can judge, sensible, have a school for small girls and boys, chiefly boys. He is really quite ready for it and keen to go. It will rest us a little! His energy is inexhaustible, and a few hours absence in the morning will give the household a chance of getting its head up again!

In his next letter, dated February 28, Geoffrey said: "Miss Collingwood has just come to stay. She is a daughter of Ruskin's artist and archaeological secretary [W. G. Collingwood], and trained for 'these things'; and will be looking after Eleanor in our expected event."

Their second and final child was born on March 11, a girl they called Marcia – possibly in tribute to her godfather Marcus Heywood.

Geoffrey had scores of friends and acquaintances in Cambridge, some of them of considerable eminence by this time. John Maynard Keynes was Bursar of King's as well as an international adviser in economics. In 1927 G. M. Trevelyan, famous for his books on Italian and English history, returned to Cambridge to be Professor of Modern History. There were many more, and Geoffrey's friendly charm and high reputation – as mountaineer, writer, war hero and educationalist – soon made him the centre of a circle of bright undergraduates.

By the start of 1926 the Youngs had moved into a grander house at 5, Benet Place, where there was scope for more generous hospitality. Here, during term-time in the years that followed, they held regular Sunday evening "at-homes" for their friends. They were not particularly lavish or extravagant parties – the food was simple and there was no excessive drinking – but they are universally remembered, sixty years on, with warmth and gratitude.

One of the outstanding students was Jack Longland, who developed into an all-round mountaineer, became Director of Education for Derbyshire, and made himself nationally known as a radio broadcaster. Longland was a notable athlete at Cambridge and the moving figure in the restoration of the university's Mountaineering Club, and years later he wrote:

It was no accident that the revival of the CUMC in the 1920s coincided with the years during which Geoffrey and Len Young lived in Cambridge. Their house at Benet Place was the centre for all the most active, ambitious and no doubt insufferable among young Cambridge climbers. Looking back, I marvel at the patience with which G. W. Y. instructed, inspired and cautioned us all, and still more at his generosity in making us free of the traditions and the company at Pen-y-Pass.

There were other distinguished names in the circle: Gino Watkins the Arctic explorer; "Freddy" Spencer Chapman who went on to become an explorer, mountaineer, Second World War hero and pioneer of the Outward Bound movement; Robert Chew who became headmaster of Gordonstoun; and two sons of Raymond Bicknell, who had climbed with Geoffrey before the First World War.

The eldest son, Peter Bicknell, studied architecture at Cambridge and went on to be a professional architect and also a great book-man and bibliographical scholar, especially concerned with books about mountains. I went to talk to him at his Cambridge home in October 1992, to find that his memories of Geoffrey went back eighty years. "I first met Geoffrey," he told me, "when I was five or six, changing trains at Peterborough. He was changing trains too and Father recognised him and they chatted. I remember how splendid he looked, even at that age I was impressed. He was friendly too, and gallant – he gave my sister Ellen a bunch of red roses."

Peter Bicknell went up to Cambridge in 1925:

> I used to go to the Sunday evening at-homes as often as I could, to sit at Geoffrey's feet and meet interesting people. We would have dinner in hall, then go on to Benet Place. They had a tremendous range of friends. Len was lovely. But Geoffrey was in charge, the centre of things. He did not dominate – he would let people talk – but he was a strong presence. One felt that it was almost a part he was playing, that he knew how impressive his personality was. There were some women, I recall, who thought him altogether too charming, so gracious and polished that it must be something of an act. It was a dated atmosphere in a way, Edwardian, pre-1914 – very civilised and decorous – but at that age I felt deeply flattered to be accepted. It was fascinating. There would be a little drink offered, but it was mainly just meeting and talking – a wonderful experience that played an important part in my life, bringing in new interests. Geoffrey was a catalyst. He liked to bring other people out.

The younger brother, Claud Bicknell, turned up in Cambridge in the early 1930s to read law. He, too, recalls the "at-homes":

It was a wonderful link with the past for young mountaineers. The pioneer explorers would be there. And there was tremendous hero-worship for Geoffrey, as the creator of the great pre-war Alpine routes. He seemed almost a God-figure to us. He had presence, and very careful intonation. You always felt he was working out the words he was using very precisely. It seemed contrived at times and there were some climbers, like Tom Longstaff, who could be irritated by it. They never seemed to worry about money, and there was a strong sense of the old liberal tradition of the need to perform public service.

Others confirm these impressions. Ivan Waller, one of the moving spirits behind the revival of Snowdonian climbing in the late 1920s, stresses Geoffrey's skill at bringing people together: "He worked to get on with people, and to get them to get on with each other." And Tony Dummett remembers Geoffrey as "a sort of elder statesman. People would open up with him in a way they wouldn't with other older men."

These young men were all invited to the Easter gatherings at Pen-y-Pass, which now blossomed into something approaching their pre-war glory. On April 10, 1926 Geoffrey wrote to his father:

We have had a wonderful Easter: a week of sunny weather and glorious views, and the best party since the war – 48 of us! – and good talks and songs. Everyone, of course, in happy mood. I went up Snowdon again by myself; and Eleanor led my rope up a buttress on Tryfan – which gave me good climbing once more, and fun! It was an incomparable Easter Day; and we basked on the top, on hot rocks, and watched the dragons of thin white cloud creeping down over the Glyders . . . I have just seen off Claude Elliott, up Lliwedd, with our latest recruit, a young Austrian prince, Andrew of Lichtenstein – a most charming enthusiast. These parties retain a singular quality of sociability, and have recovered much of their naturalness and freshness. They are worth a little trouble.

Jack Longland wrote:

I hardly missed a Pen-y-Pass Easter between 1927 and 1936. It was at P-y-P that we began to learn something of Welsh crags and their traditions. It was from P-y-P that we began to venture with slightly bolder steps, and bring back small offerings like Purgatory and the Red Wall Continuation on Lliwedd . . . The West Buttress Route on Du'r Arddu was partly worked out during the Pen-y-Pass Easter of 1928 . . .

The days were outdoor and vigorous. There would be hot baths and then dinner, and after that various forms of entertainment,

A publicity portrait of Len, taken when she was an actress with the Liverpool Repertory Theatre. Geoffrey acknowledged it was pretty, but said he did not care for it because it was not her – "I want the colour, and the eyes, and the direct look."

Len and Geoffrey leaving St George's Hanover Square, London, after their wedding on April 25, 1918.

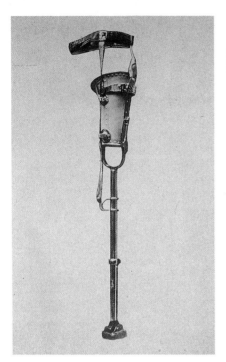

Above left, the climbing leg that Geoffrey designed and had made for himself; *above right*, with Len in North Wales, testing out the new leg; *below*, Jack Longland brings Geoffrey safely to the top of the Teryn Slabs.

Left, on the Weisshorn Ridge, 1929; *below*, resting on the Grépon Ridge, August, 1929.

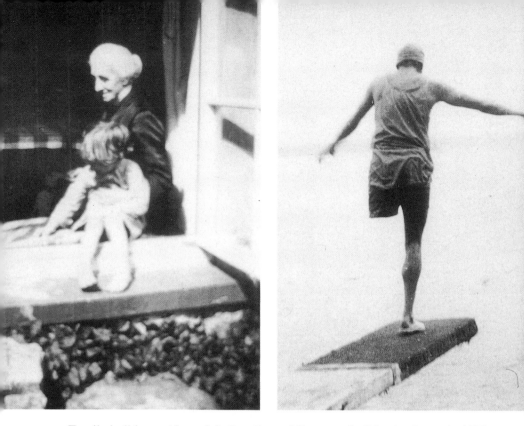

Family holidays. *Above left*, Jocelin and Frau, on holiday in the early 1920s; *above right*, taking a one-legged header, St Ives, September 1928; *below*, Geoffrey and Jocelin on the Thames, 1930.

The immediate family. *Above left*, Marcia, shortly before her marriage; *above right*, Jocelin, an officer in the RNVR, in Bombay, 1945; *left*, Geoffrey and Len at the Temple of Apollo, Delphi. When Jocelin's son Mark was shown the photograph, he called it "Waiting for the bus".

Geoffrey's greatest friends. *Above left*, the historian, G.M. Trevelyan, a close and loyal friend for sixty years. This picture was taken in the Langdale valley where Trevelyan had a holiday cottage, Robin Ghyll. *Above right*, Kurt Hahn, the German educational reformer who, with Geoffrey's active help, founded Gordonstoun School in Scotland and launched the Outward Bound movement. *Below*, three elderly climbers recalling their great Alpine days of long ago: Geoffrey, his favourite guide Josef Knubel, and Marcus Heywood who had been a pupil of Geoffrey's at Eton and whom Geoffrey once described as "a man who walked in sunshine all his life".

Above, Grovehurst, Kent, the last of Geoffrey's many homes and the only one he owned; *below left*, Geoffrey taking the sun and surveying his garden at Grovehurst, 1957; *below right*, the proud grandfather, with Jocelin's first child, Mark.

The Grand Old Man, a distinguished and distinctive figure in old age; what he self-mockingly described in his Journal as "an elderly celebrity, second-class".

sociable and sometimes vigorous too. Writing for *Mountain Magazine*, sixty years later, Longland recalled:

> Pen-y-Pass evenings were quite something special. It will shock today's tigers, but I can't remember that we drank much at any time – a pint and a half at most was all seemed to be needed. There were other things to do – especially the singing! There were always songs after dinner, some of them led by musicians with really trained voices, and Geoffrey had a repertoire of his own mountain songs. In sober truth, some of us younger ones got a bit fed up with the singing . . . So we engineered indoor gymnastics as a substitute, for some evenings at least; jumping on to a highish mantelpiece without falling over backwards: balancing a half-full glass on your forehead, removing it on to the floor between your knees, drinking it without touch of hands, using knees again to put it back on your forehead, and then standing up again with the empty glass back on your forehead – my special trick: oh and of course, climbing round a kitchen chair, and back on the seat without the chair tilting over! Much climbing talk as well, those Easter evenings.

Peter Bicknell remembers his brother Claud and their father climbing out of a window to escape the singing.

Among the company in the late 1920s were two men who were to make names for themselves in the Himalayas in the next decade – Lawrence Wager who climbed to 28,126 feet on Everest in 1933 and found the Mallory/Irvine ice axe; and Frank Smythe, who was a member of all three Everest expeditions of the 1930s and the author of many successful mountaineering books.

A more unlikely member of the Pen-y-Pass community was a young American engineering student from Cambridge, Coleman S. Williams. His technical expertise was to prove a great help to Geoffrey in constructing the peg-leg that would make Alpine routes possible again. The basic design was Geoffrey's, but Williams modified it and improved it, and then built it in light duralium, an alloy much lighter and every bit as strong as the steel which had been used until then. Geoffrey reckoned that the resulting leg reduced the fatigue from long trudges across rough, mixed ground by at least forty per cent. In *Mountains with a Difference*, written after the Second World War, he had this praise for Williams: "His workmanship has lasted for 25 years of the rudest climbing strains, jars and wrenches, and only two nuts and bolts, which I cracked in mountain falls, have had to be renewed."

Geoffrey had a more-or-less conventional artifical limb for everyday urban wear on level surfaces, which was known as "the polite leg". The climbing leg was more complicated. It was necessary to devise something that would stand up to continuous hard pounding, and yet be flexible and versatile enough to enable him to move on all kinds of ground – turf and rock and loose scree; snow and ice; uphill and downhill and contouring – with reasonable comfort and speed and without exhausting himself totally.

He noticed a strange, psychological result of his disability, that he described in *Mountains with a Difference*:

> One subtle enemy of the legless stayed long unsuspected even by myself. I write of it now because a second war has made my' experience of service again. The enemy is inertia, suggested and encouraged by the false registration of fatigues that follows amputation. The severed nerves short-circuit the recurring jars of every other step in exaggerated messages to the brain. As a result, the mind, long accustomed to record fatigue by one register of sensation, may become just as convinced of fatigue after ten minutes of trudging over a hard, jarring surface, as it would have been after a fast game of hockey, or a last round in the ring, on two legs. The one-legged man feels "tired" at once, decides it is hopeless ever to regain normal activity, and gives up trying.

Geoffrey would not give up. By willpower, he forced himself to ignore the inertia barrier in his mind. Soon he realised that the feeling of exhaustion passed after a brief period of rest. He pushed himself harder and harder, on the hills of Britain, and found that he could manage as much as eleven hours of rough, mixed going, with occasional brief rests. Gradually, his hopes of a return to the big Alpine routes began to seem realisable.

He improved his chances by introducing what he called a "pogo" spring, which fitted inside the duralium tube to give vertical flexibility and cushion the constant jarring:

> Finally, by steadily disregarding what I "felt" by all former fatigue registers, and steadily increasing the length of the mountain days, I discovered that I was actually very little more "tired" by expeditions of 12, 15, and in the end 24 hours of continuous climbing, than I had been in earlier years. That is, I could still start off fresh the following morning, irrespective of the amount of "exhaustion" experienced.

There were further difficulties. He would inevitably be a lot slower than before and this called for acceptance on his part and made it important that he should find companions and guides who were prepared to be patient. However clever the peg-leg, he could not hope to retrieve anything approaching his original, natural balance, so on difficult or dangerous ground it would always be necessary to have someone within reach, for the balancing touch. A key made it possible for him to lengthen or shorten the leg to suit the conditions, but the problem of sinking into deep snow or soggy turf was not completely soluble.

In his rucksack he carried alternative feet: a leather shoe or a rubber pad for firm, reasonably level going; a metal spike, with tricouni nails in the base, to grip into steep rock or hard ice; and a wide base, with a ski-ring, to try to prevent him sinking into soft surfaces. None of them was entirely satisfactory, and the sheer slog of plunging thigh-deep into soft ground and then having to haul the leg out again for the next plunge made many of his Alpine excursions very tough indeed. It is an impressive measure of Geoffrey's hunger for the high places that he should have been prepared to submit himself to such long and laborious and sometimes painful preparations.

The golden days of his pre-war Alpine seasons were at the forefront of his mind at this time because he was writing *On High Hills*, the story of his apprenticeship on British hills and its wonderful fulfilment in the Alps. It is a long book and many have considered it Geoffrey's best. In his review in the *Times Literary Supplement*, published in January 1927, G. M. Trevelyan ranked it with the masterpieces of mountain literature, Leslie Stephen and Whymper, but also remarked, perceptively, that Geoffrey's tone and tenor are quite different from theirs, entirely his own, highly individual and highly charged.

It is an adventure story, rooted in Geoffrey's regard for high mountaineering. He describes his failures and errors of judgement and near-disasters as fully as the triumphs. The narrative style is rich and vivid and colourful, sometimes almost unbearably immediate, as in his terrifying account of the long epic on the South Face of the Täschhorn, quoted at length in chapter 7. But the narrative is interspersed with lyrical passages and also with deeply reflective comments on all aspects of the sport, especially the psychological.

In the last chapter Geoffrey describes his summer season with Siegfried Herford in 1914, clouded by apprehensions of approaching war, and considers the nature of the distinction between the thrills of battle and those of climbing. He concludes:

. . . how could anyone who had lived through even a week of destruction in Ypres and a day of action and sight upon the Matterhorn continue to compare their jangling monochord of death with the deep resonant chords of life with which our every sense responded to "the chief things of the ancient mountains and the precious things of the lasting hills". The breath of the mountains is life-giving and humane. Their very perils are incitements to hardihood, to sincerity and to self-discovery. Even to those of us to whom they have brought death the mountains have first given a just appreciation of life, and the knowledge of a right way of living in which the probability of death could count for but little among many higher values.

In February 1927 Geoffrey wrote to his father: "*On High Hills* has a very good press; and I hear other pleasant appreciations. Bumpus spoke of it as 'probably the book of the year'. I expect he meant among travel books! Some day you must give me your own views on the writing. Which gave me a deal of thought and revision."

On the domestic front things were going well. Len was busy editing the *Journal* of the Pinnacle Club, the women's climbing club. The children were a continuing delight: "Jocelin grows steadily in grace and in partnership in our life," Geoffrey told his father: "Marcia and he now tumble all over the floor, evenings, and dance charmingly together. She develops fast, and progresses in looks, activity – and character!" Relations with Hilton and his family were still cordial, despite the fact that Hilton had forsaken the divided Liberal Party and joined the Conservatives. Geoffrey was spending much time in Europe, at the League of Nations in Geneva and also in Germany, preparing a report for the Rockefeller Foundation on the current state of Germany's cultural and university life. He was hoping for a permanent appointment from the Foundation.

Geoffrey was often in Geneva, an internationalists' gathering-place at this time, and there met the Spanish historian and philosopher Salvador de Madariaga, who made a remark that Geoffrey always treasured: "Ah yes, the Young brothers. The youngest lost his arm and went Conservative. The middle one lost his leg and stayed Liberal. And the eldest lost his head and went Labour."

Hilton had switched to the Conservatives in 1926. He was in Geneva the next year, on business at the League of Nations, and his wife Kathleen and her son Peter Scott were there too. In a letter to Len from Switzerland, Geoffrey gave the first hint that Hilton's new family were beginning to distance themselves: "Dear old H. of course is busy up to the edge of his now 'conserved vitality'. But K. and Peter are really too self-absorbed to be possible! Haven't seen them for four days, and my pub is across the way from them! Such a nuisance, marriage! you cease to be able to nudge up even a brother about his social ties and home atmospheres!"

On a happier note the Swiss climber Charles Gos called on Geoffrey while he was in Geneva and took him to the studio of his famous painter father, Albert Gos. In the letter to Len he described the visit and the old artist:

> . . . the most wonderful type! Must have been handsome, a complete wandering artist, half genius. Great fiddler – was a professional and gave it up for painting. Complete Bohemian . . . Then he picked up the fiddle – he is like a small Don Quixote – and wandered round the pictures, playing to each of them – really quite marvellously still, at 75! He has composed some wild melody for each mountain, reproducing its "lines" and "forms"! He always takes the fiddle up when he's painting on the heights, and plays to the hills and himself, as a rest. Then he illustrated some folk dance steps, beautifully, like a young man! Quite unique, and a child of nature.

Geoffrey's father, Sir George, took a lively interest in everything – the family, current affairs, questions educational and literary. He was ninety years old but still vigorous both physically and intellectually. His big work on *Prosody* completed, he turned his attention to his own family history, reading through the letters that had been preserved. On April 9, 1927 Geoffrey wrote to him, detailing his negotiations with the Rockefeller Foundation and looking forward to the Pen-y-Pass party: ". . . Ourselves drive off to Wales on Tuesday. This year we shall fill the whole place once again – as before the war! . . . And I finished my new 'walking' leg at Roehampton: and made certain that Mr Slingsby was comfortable and content at a 'home' near Shepperton."

Two distinguished French climbers, Paul Chevalier and Henri de Segogue, were at Pen-y-Pass that Easter, and Geoffrey gave the finished leg a thorough work-out. He had grown increasingly restless for a trial summer season in the Alps, and increasingly confident that he could make a go of it.

He took Len and the two children with him to Europe, and reported to his father from Grindelwald on August 25:

> We had bad weather for the last week at Annecy; and drove the family over to Geneva for a night. Thence to Berne and Interlaken by train, on a sunny day, and a drive up here. Happily our first day was bright. So

Jocelin had a good first sight of the big summits. He has a real interest for mountains and scenery: not only "talk", I think. We got half a day on the upper glacier, and he went well. Len led the party like an expert.

When Len and the children returned home, Geoffrey went to join Claude and Gillian Elliott in the Lötschenthal region, north of the Rhone. Franz Lochmatter and Hans Brantschen had been hired as guides, and they were in close attendance when Geoffrey put his leg to the Alpine test. The results were reassuring, so they took the railway up the Visp gorges for an attempt on the Riffelhorn, Geoffrey's return to Alpine rock after thirteen eventful years. Lochmatter accompanied him, not bothering to rope up, and they worked out a new, necessary system: "The easy rock skyline of the little peak went amusingly, because I could use my hands up most of the way; and Franz climbing immediately behind me, sinuous and swift, quickly corrected any mis-step of the loose clanging peg." The quotation is from *Mountains with a Difference*, published in 1951, which recounts Geoffrey's mountaineering career, its interruption by the war and the loss of his leg, and his long struggle to return to the Alpine heights.

The party moved to Zermatt and settled on Monte Rosa for Geoffrey's first serious one-legged ascent. His companions were Claude Elliott, Hans Brantschen and Franz Lochmatter, a powerful support team, but the whole expedition proved tougher and longer than any of them had expected. They set off at midnight and struggled through the dark up steepening walls of hard-frozen snow. Geoffrey was close to despair when the dull dawn broke, and angry with himself for feeling so weary. When they finally gained the narrow, ice-glazed summit ridge, he was ashamed that he could only manage it by crawling along, with Brantschen stepping close behind and gripping his waist-loop. The summit, in a bitter wind, brought no sense of achievement or euphoria: "There were too many doubts and aches and shocks at my revealed incompetence clamouring inside me to leave room for self-gratulation."

The descent was even worse. The sun was out full and heavy by this time, turning the frosty slopes to a deep mush so that the peg-leg plunged in deep at every step. In the end Lochmatter produced from his rucksack "some ten inches of the toe of a ski". A rope was tied to its tip and Geoffrey sat astride the ski, hoisting his feet into the air, and the three of them set about hauling him down through the slushy swamp. He fell off often and was frequently banged against outcrops of rock or ice. It was painful and uncomfortable, but faster than the alternative.

Altogether that day they were on the go for eighteen hours, with one pause for rest. Geoffrey was shocked at how long it had taken, and how exhausted he had felt. But he had done it, the highest top in the Swiss Alps. He would be back again next year.

He returned to Cambridge to find very good news waiting. Up to this point the Rockefeller Foundation had been employing him on an annual contract, September to September. Now they said they would pay him 10,000 dollars a year for the next three years. For Geoffrey and his family it ushered in the period of their greatest financial security. It meant the children could be sent to good schools. It meant they could offer grander hospitality to their friends. It was during this time that they had a marquee in the garden and a dance, to celebrate the twenty-first birthdays of Robert Chew and his twin sister. Apart from these things, though, there was no great change in the family life-style. It meant that they did not have to worry about money, but they did not do that anyway.

It was good news to Geoffrey for more than financial reasons. It was work for which he was well-suited and it was a task that greatly appealed to him.

The Foundation's idealistic managers in New York, shocked by the devastation of much of Europe in the war and disturbed by the subsequent disruption in many countries, felt they should do all they could to encourage a revival of interest in the humanities in Europe. They were already spending large sums of money to stimulate scientific and medical research. Now, they argued, attention should also be paid to those branches of learning that had, after all, formed the basis of European culture – the classics, literature, philosophy and political thought.

Geoffrey was their adviser and he had begun by looking chiefly at Germany, partly because that was the country he knew best but also because that was where the need was greatest. There had been many moments, a decade before, when he had hated the Germans. More than once the Italian Journal records his revulsion at hearing the language spoken among prisoners-of-war. But the hatred quickly passed. Germany was smashed by the war and humiliated by the peace terms that followed, and Geoffrey realised, with greater prescience than most at that time, that the future of Europe and the world would be safer if the forces of German moderation and reason and liberalism could be encouraged. Already there were ominous signs of extremism, Left and Right. Geoffrey threw himself into the work.

There was another enjoyable Pen-y-Pass gathering at Easter 1928, and Geoffrey was back there at Whitsun. He described it in a letter to his father, dated May 30:

> When I reached Pen-y-Pass, I had the delightful surprise of finding Hilton and Kathleen already there, on a raid of their own! And to hear his voice calling down to me from the stairs as I came into the hall! So we had great moments together, in the intervals of our days on the mountains. My young men took me up a great climb on Lliwedd, which went well, in spite of my years! – but left me stiff for the next day, when we tramped up the western side of Snowdon, to a high cwm and lake called Arddu, where we had designs upon the last great unclimbed buttress in the islands perhaps. I bathed in the lake, and lay out all the afternoon in the sun beside it, watching the great climb done – a magnificent performance! – and led by one of my Cambridge young men, Longland.

This was the Western Buttress of Clogwyn Du'r Arddu, the great black crag that climbers call "Cloggy". Its Eastern Buttress had been first climbed the previous year by a party led by Fred Pigott of the Rucksack Club, and since that there had been much scrutiny of the other buttress. It was finally conquered by what is now known as Longland's Route in tribute to the leader, Jack Longland. Pigott and Frank Smythe were in close support. It is a long and serious route, on steep, overlapping slabs, and Geoffrey felt privileged to have seen it accomplished. Longland recalled later: "Geoffrey Young came with us, striding across the moor with his peg leg; I remember envying him his dive into Lyn du'r Arddu several hundred feet below me, as I wrestled with the intricacies of Faith and Friction's slab!" These two routes on "Cloggy" are generally seen as the launching-pad for the great revival of Welsh climbing that followed.

Geoffrey was back in the high European mountains that summer. He travelled by way of Belgium to see old friends, and described it all in a letter to Len:

> Maurice and Louise [Best] met me at Ostend. A lovely plum-coloured car, and Louise looked really pretty in clever white linen frock and hat. Drove to Bruges. Found the Curé: a big place he's bought and built for girl orphans. Lovely garden and well-equipped school. Nine Sisters to help. He is older, and looks delicate. But delightful as ever. We supped with him, like in old Ypres days. And then went out to see his children in the play-ground. The most unforgettable sight. They clamoured round

him, clearly adoring him, and asking for his goodnight blessing. And he joked, and petted them. In the beautiful evening garden it was the most moving picture of a happy old age. And with an indescribable spirit in it. Then a starry, quiet night drive to Ypres; and to sleep in the tremendous silence outside the Menin Gate. Next morning very hot. Ypres noisy and car-full. A long visit to Sœur Marguerite, delightful as ever, but looking tired, and older. Full of inquiries. Her grey-hazel eyes lighting up with the same fun as ever . . . Then the Ypres Sisters – all alive still, and *exactly* the same! Like a dream world reviving, for them all, and for me . . .

Then he headed south to join Claude and Gillian Elliott.

They tried the Dolomites first but Geoffrey found that the steep rock walls put too high a premium on neat footwork, the hand-holds were rounded and weathered, so they were soon heading north for the Alps. A successful and enjoyable ascent of the Wellenkuppe emboldened him to attempt a return to his favourite summit, "the incomparable Weisshorn". He and Claude Elliott hired three younger members of the Lochmatter family as their guides, with Geoffrey roped between two of them, one several yards in front, the other close behind.

It began with another apparently interminable slog through deep snow in the pre-dawn darkness. By the time they gained the east ridge Geoffrey was worried about his slow progress, all the more worried because he could sense Elliott's anxiety about their timing. In the end they decided to forego the final summit, partly because of getting down before darkness and partly because the slopes above them looked avalanche-prone: "I knew, and in every inch of me, that we must turn back. I knew that the snow was unsound, and that in any case I had no business to lose more time in threshing foot by foot up the last reluctant spire." Their decision was vindicated a few moments later when a powerful avalanche swept across their projected route above. Much lower down Geoffrey gazed across to the South Face of the Täschhorn and the memories flooded into his mind. It was 8.30 p.m. when they regained the hut, after twenty-one hours of almost continuous climbing.

The summer of 1928 was hot and dry in the Alps. For some time Geoffrey had been thinking of the Matterhorn. The weather meant that it would be chiefly rock; there would be little snow and ice to contend with. He knew the spell that the Matterhorn cast over the public's imagination and felt that its conquest by him would be a great encouragement to all the people who had lost a limb in the war, "a practical demonstration that the fatigue or inertia from which all who have lost legs suffer is a nervous fiction". He put it to Hans Brantschen, who thought they could do it. A second guide was hired, a young man called Schenton, and a mule to carry Geoffrey from the outskirts of Zermatt to the Belvedere, the start of the real climbing, to help conserve his strength.

There is a full account in *Mountains with a Difference*, but Geoffrey gave a more immediate description in the letter he wrote to Len on July 26. At the Belvedere, he says, he chatted with some guides, and had dinner at 7.30 p.m.:

> Then I lay down and got some sleep, in spite of an amorous German couple through the paper-like wall. At 9.45, by plan, Hans waked me. I had kept even my leg and coat on, and after some coffee we set off at 10 p.m. The climb starts almost at once. The bitter north wind blew out the lantern, so, as we roped, I suggested doing without. It was a brilliant night of stars, with a hidden moon, low down behind the Matterhorn, giving some diffused light. The black mountain was utterly still, and to ourselves: and the great peaks round all exquisitely filmed in silver and black. A marvellous quiet world with only the roar of the wind behind the ridge, catching us when we had to come out on to the edge. And an occasional thunder of rock or ice fall, far off. A wonderful night. And we pushed ahead, and aloft, all through it. Awkward climbing when one couldn't see the holds, especially for my left foot. But Schenton secured us ahead with the rope, and Hans, gorgeously strong, skilful and understanding, close behind, outside, or ahead of me, and gave me a hand, knee or shoulder everywhere, generally, for all the hours, placing my left foot with his hand on the holds, as neatly as moving a pawn at chess. This saved me the tiresome "pendulum" grope, and swing, of that stupid foot.

At the Solvay hut, which was new then, they rested briefly:

> Soon after this, looking down into space, we saw the lanterns, four or five, of the parties starting the climb at the more usual hour . . . Nearing the "Shoulder", the leading parties, and the dawn, began to catch us up. I had all the sense of moving at the old tremendous pace! But as soon as there was some relative standard, I realised again how slow I have now actually to move! Up near the Shoulder the parties began passing us. And the sun came up on a red-gold morning; very cold, but glitteringly clear.

The rest of this letter, unfortunately, has not survived. But the rest of the story is known. They were on the summit by 7.30 a.m., the eighth time Geoffrey had been there. They found a ledge out of the wind and he rested for an hour, "drifting at once into the true Matterhorn-summit dream, an enchanted drowsy state between half-thought and half-sleep, between realised achievement and uncontrolled imagining". Once again he was filled with memories.

Then came the long, careful, equally slow descent. It was 4 p.m. by the time they reached the Belvedere, and there the mule was waiting to carry Geoffrey down to Zermatt in time for dinner. The whole excursion had lasted twenty-four hours.

Geoffrey had been right about the publicity value of his climb. To the British public in particular the Matterhorn had long been *the* Alpine peak, so the newspapers were full of it, and much of his time, over the next few months, was spent in responding to a flood of letters from people who had lost a leg.

Long after the event, Len loved to tell the story of how she was visiting her father, at his nursing home, one morning in late July. Cecil Slingsby was physically very frail by that time and his memory was almost entirely gone. They were sitting together in the garden, in the sunlight, when an old gentleman at a nearby table, reading his morning paper, called across: "Slingsby, there's something in the *Telegraph* just up your street. A fellow with one leg has been up the Matterhorn." She told her father it must be Geoffrey. There was a long pause and she was not sure he had taken it in. He gazed straight ahead, and then said – the last words she heard from him: "Magnificent! Magnificent! Of course, he shouldn't have done it, you know." He died a few months later.

18

The German Connection

THE MATTERHORN WAS THE CLIMAX of Geoffrey's 1928 season but not the end of it. A few days later he gained the summit of Monte Rosa, describing the ascent in a letter to Len:

> Such an epic! In short, the ascent from the Betemps Hut took 9½ hours: the descent some 4½: and the glacier walk back here another 4: in all 18 hours, with only an hour's halt at the hut. And I'm not so tired today as after Snowdon! Only my right foot a little achey with all the jarring. So you see what that training we did together has done! And my face is dark beetroot colour with the hours of snow-glare through mist . . . And the whole world here all agog with it [the Matterhorn climb] – if only you were here to enjoy all the fun of the fuss they are making! Everybody rushes up to congratulate. How we *do* miss you! . . .

His letters to Len are as full of love and longing as they ever were. But the separation was prolonged this time. From the Alps he went on to Geneva on Rockefeller Foundation business, lengthy meetings and negotiations with Americans and Canadians and the representatives of many European countries. He found much of it tedious, but there was also plenty of time for swimming and "headers" and sun-bathing. Hilton was there part of the time, and Geoffrey's old artist friend Will Arnold-Forster, whose son Mark had been Jocelin's best friend since 1924 when he made his first visit to the Arnold-Forster home in Cornwall, Eagle's Nest.

Geoffrey kept his father fully informed about his work with the Rockefeller Foundation. There was an important meeting in Paris in October 1928 and Geoffrey reported: "It was a good time. I had nothing but success, and satisfactory meetings and news in Germany; all confirming the early effects of the Foundation . . . The Presidential Committee did all they ought, and didn't do what they oughtn't. And we go ahead." What Geoffrey had been doing was looking for influential and liberal-minded people, whose work would help to keep Germany on the right lines and qualify them for Foundation subsidies. In an unpublished account of his career in education, he wrote:

> I began at the top, with introductions to the notabilities in every department. That led me nowhere, because its celebrities are no longer the activating forces in a country. I began again at the bottom, with the small clubs and organisations, and gradually worked upwards, pursuing their recommendations to their particular deities. At a medium social level, I came suddenly upon a plane where I found that all the active leaders – artists, officials, academics, scientists – all knew something, if only by hearsay, of each other's work and its scope. I had reached the plane where, for about ten years in each man's life, and in the life of the country, the real leaders of the community are at work . . . In the first two years we found a hundred, and as many more each year of the six we were in operation, of remarkable personalities in need of relief, release or guidance.

In early 1929 there was a meeting at the Foundation headquarters in New York and Geoffrey and Len crossed the Atlantic in the *Mauretania*. On their return to Cambridge, he wrote to Sir George:

> I must tell you at length, later, about the campaign over there. It was a *personal* success. I have been given a definite footing, with the proud title of "Consultant in the Humanities, for Europe" . . . The whole centre of activity is to be transferred from New York to Paris, for European work – which is good. And in September an American "Director" in the Humanities is to be appointed to Paris; with whom I shall work . . . It will mean more, and longer, absences abroad, I foresee.

Geoffrey's office was at 20, Rue de la Baume. The European operation was given its separate name, the Abraham Lincoln Foundation. Geoffrey suggested this: "No better way of indicating the character of our work could be found than that name," he wrote.

There was another successful Pen-y-Pass gathering that Easter, and Geoffrey was back in the Alps in the summer for what was perhaps the most remarkable of all his Alpine seasons. He summed it up in a letter to his father, written at the end of July:

> My dear Father,
> Len and I got back here from the Alps early this morning. She joined me for a quick week out there at the end; and we had one long expedition

up the Aletsch Glacier together, sleeping at the Concordia. But bad weather beat us for any peaks. Before that I managed to climb the little Charmoz, then the Requin, and lastly the Grépon; the two last bigger than anything I've managed since the war. In fact, the "machine" shows no signs of age – or none, at least, that I can't put down cheerfully to the leg! And I'm in vast health and fitness, as the result. Somehow I enjoy the considerable "discipline" of the sustained effort almost as much as I did the rushing exultation of former days. The Elliotts, J. Montagu Butler, the present Sir T. Fowell Buxton and others looked after me. And we all wound up in cloud at the Eggishorn, in the Oberland . . .

Sir George was ninety-two years old, but his reply shows that his mind was still sharp. It also makes it apparent that he had shed his former reluctance to talk about mountaineering:

Your letter is of the kind it is a pleasure to receive . . . I know what the Requin and the Aiguille are like, and have read your climb of the Grépon . . . As for the long walk on the Aletsch Glacier, which I took with Llewellyn Davies one year, indeed I remember it all, and I remember sleeping two nights at the Concordia hut in the rain, waiting to do – I think – the Finsteraarhorn – till I gave up in disgust, left my party, and walked round, by Brig and the Grimsel, straight to Grindelwald in time for morning church on Sunday.

In *Mountains with a Difference* Geoffrey gave a full account of his climbs that season, and full vent to his feelings about the competitive and nationalistic spirit that was beginning to infect the sport he loved. On the Nantillons Glacier he was astonished to see big groups of young people charging about, quite regardless of the stone avalanches they were creating:

. . . the disregard of every mountain rule was shocking. I should have been happy to think that these were all super-boys and girls, or that Alpine climbing had grown into its second and harmless childhood, had I not seen during ten days at the Montenvers three separate and fatal accidents. A young German, one of those engaged upon, and engaged for, the siege of the Grandes Jorasses north face, told me that it was needless to pay any attention to the weather in climbing; but that the worse the weather, the greater of course the réclame if one survived. Secondly, that he had been unemployed and all but starving, but now trusted by getting his name into the papers to be given a State job. Thirdly, in a burst of confidence, that nobody's nerves could last out three years in climbing of this order, and he doubted whether his own would last another season, if he failed this year on the north climb. I recall it as a woeful epitome of what this stunt and State climbing, in international rivalry and for its réclame, became between the wars.

Geoffrey's guides on the Requin climb were the ever-reliable Hans Brantschen and a new man, Johann Perren. Geoffrey disliked the over-crowded state of the Requin hut – "a noisy picnicky sort of blotch on the glacier landscape" – but he enjoyed the almost continuous rock climbing that came with the dawn. After a rest on the summit block, they abseiled down the long chimney, at the foot of which they began to ascend some steep slabs:

> I had just put all my weight on the peg, for a step upward in balance, when I felt it give under me, sickeningly. I could feel the metallic gritting, and knew that one fork of the Y-joint which hinges the peg on to the bucket had come adrift, and that the other fork was threatening to snap off. The nut had worked loose and the screw jumped out. Luckily I found both of them caught in the cloth lower down; and after elaborate manoeuvres on the ledge I re-fixed it, re-dressed and started again. After five minutes of the slab climbing, I felt the fork was again loose . . .

The next part of the descent was nightmarish. Every few minutes he had to halt and carefully re-fix the leg. At every step he was afraid the whole leg would collapse under him. Finally, he lost patience: "I sat firmly down on the steep slabs, took the leg right off, grasped a large granite chunk, and beat it heavily and with animosity upon the culpable, unfixable nut." To his astonishment, it worked and they were back at Montenvers by nightfall.

There they met Geoffrey's old guide Josef Knubel, who went down to Chamonix with Brantschen to get the recalcitrant joint repaired. Very quickly, the legend spread among mountaineers that Knubel had asked for help because a "Herr" had broken his leg on the Requin, and when someone directed him to a surgeon he had cried: "It's not a surgeon I want, it's a mechanic!"

The peg-leg was soon operational again and Geoffrey determined to have a go at the Grépon, an old friend and technically the most challenging peak he had attempted since losing his leg. The weather was stormy and unpromising, but he forecast a change: "This, after all, was going to be the supreme test," he wrote. "It was the last day of my best season as a revenant, and the opportunity was most unlikely to recur."

Hans Brantschen was his guide once more, and they were accompanied by two accomplished young mountaineers from the

Cambridge group, Jack Longland and George Lowthian Trevelyan, a nephew of the historian. It was dark when they trudged up the glacier and the weather was still in threatening mood. They had set off later than intended because of worries about the weather. Now Geoffrey was determined to make up for lost time. Longland remarked later that they maintained a speed "that would have been creditable to a party with the usual number of legs".

First light brought clear promise of a fine day after all, so they set about the steepening rock in high spirits. When they came to the formidable "Mummery Crack", Geoffrey's ascent was protected by two ropes, one guide above him, the other below: "There could be no question," Geoffrey later wrote, "of my really climbing the historic crack, which requires before all a left leg with which to jam. The foothold had to come from upward springs with the right foot, while handhold and the two ropes did the rest."

Trevelyan was watching, and vastly impressed. Speaking to me sixty-four years after the event, he remembered it clearly: "It was a tremendous thing to do, with just one leg and his arms. It was a lovely occasion."

At the top Geoffrey rested in the sunshine and surveyed the crest of the long, broken and intricate ridge of sharp rock that lay ahead. It is an airy and dramatic route, and he found it delightful.

How can I suggest [he wrote in *Mountains with a Difference*], the length and depth of pleasure, once again to sway in balance, to press up and to swing on hands and foot over and along those bronze-tinted and golden-hearted rock ribs and rents and upright rejoicing corners? Even if the clatter of the clumsy peg drowned any poetry out of motion, the wealth of rugged holding made it possible for the rest of me to move in balance, with once again some sense of rhythm and pace.

When they came to the final steep chimney, Geoffrey was determined to do it in style, without relying on the two ropes that held him from above:

I started with deliberation. The very entry upon the crack has a catch in it. So I repeated the movements for this three times before I was satisfied with the style. Then I took hold and struggled upward, using every trick and wriggle of attachment to compensate for the missing left foot. Higher up, where the angle steepened and the holds diminished, I used clenched fist-holds and clothes-friction to cover the clinging seconds while the right foot found a higher stance. But again, who shall say how much the rope above me really made it possible? Hans leaned over, and locked his fingers in mine for the last difficult movement upward in balance, as I came up out of the crack, and stepped on to the summit. I was breathless and I was muscle-tired: and I dropped at once on to the huge projecting rock, with my back propped against the iron figure of Our Lady of the Rocks, which had been carried up and erected on the summit since my last visit.

The Grépon climb and traverse was the high point of Geoffrey's one-legged mountaineering. Although he had greatly enjoyed it, there was no more serious mountaineering for several years. He was too busy.

There was a full and happy home life in Cambridge as the children developed and went off to school. He knew many of the senior dignitaries of the university, and the circle of his student disciples expanded. His work for the Rockefeller Foundation kept him continually on the move between Paris and Berlin and Geneva.

His father, Sir George, was beginning to feel his age at last. In a letter to Geoffrey dated March 12, 1930, still firmly legible and full of spirit, he said: "I am in sight of the end of official work, through increasing want of hearing. I resign this week my most important function, the chairmanship of the Higher Education Sub-committee. I had hoped – in vain – to keep it, with an ear-trumpet; but nobody ever seems to remember that distinctness, not bawling, is what deaf people (those at least whose deafness comes of old age) require, to hear what they say."

Sir George had long been maintaining a chirpy correspondence with Jocelin, and took a close interest in Marcia's progress too. His great work on Prosody was published by the Cambridge University Press when he was ninety years old, and he then wrote *Homer and the Greek Accents* which was published in 1930, the year he died. He was in his ninety-second year.

So Georis succeeded at last to the baronetcy and took over at Formosa Place, extending the scope for his eccentric energies. The previous year he had won the Yale Review Award for the best article on international affairs. He had also campaigned, unsuccessfully, in the general election – as Labour Party candidate in the South Norfolk constituency.

At the election in the summer of 1930 the Labour Party won most seats but not an overall majority; the Conservatives were not far behind, and the Liberals held the balance between them. Hilton, now under the Conservative banner, had defied the national trend and increased his majority. Geoffrey noted the fact with his customary family pride.

But his great political concern was now with Europe, particularly Germany where there was mounting cause for anxiety. The government's grasp on affairs was weakening in the wake of the 1929 financial crash and the slump that followed. They could do little to discourage the increasingly open and violent clashes between Fascists and Communists. The prospects began to look bleak for the Rockefeller Foundation's schemes to promote the influence of Germany's moderate and humane elements.

Geoffrey's work with the Foundation had introduced him to scores of such liberal-minded people, and his special interest in education had already brought him into contact with the leading reformer, Kurt Hahn.

Hahn was ten years younger than Geoffrey, born in 1886 in Berlin of wealthy Jewish parents. At the age of eighteen he went to Christ Church, Oxford, to study classical philology. Two years later he returned to Germany to work at various universities, Berlin, Heidelberg, Freiburg and Göttingen, then he went back to Oxford for further studies and to confirm his earlier admiration for the British way of life and the English public school system, especially as practised at Eton. He liked the concept of training to produce a whole, well-balanced adult – physically fit, alert in mind, independent and generous in spirit. He was struck by the contrast with the rigid, narrow, authoritarian ethos of German education, and began to think about establishing his own school in Germany. He made friends and contacts in Britain and became particularly fond of the Findhorn valley in Morayshire.

The imminence of war in 1914 forced Hahn to hurry home. He worked at the German Foreign Office, interpreting the British press. He became Private Secretary to Prince Max of Baden, a man with an international reputation for moderation and honour. In September 1918, when it was clear that Germany's defeat was inevitable, Prince Max was made the last imperial Chancellor of Germany, with the unenviable task of negotiating terms with the victors. Hahn stayed with him and was a member of the German delegation at Versailles in early 1919.

In the summer of 1919 Prince Max returned to Salem and Hahn, a close friend by this time, went with him. The prince offered him space for his school in various wings of a medieval Cistercian monastery, secularised in 1803 and presented by Napoleon to the

Grand Dukes of Baden in part-restitution for territories of theirs he had seized west of the Rhine. It stands in quiet, rolling country, with hills and woods all round, and not far from Lake Constance. It seemed ideal. One of the things that had impressed Hahn about Eton was its "sense" of history. Respect for tradition, he believed, was inculcated by time-honoured surroundings.

The school was opened in 1920. Prince Max's son was the first pupil. It was a boarding school, unusual in Germany, so most of the early pupils were the children of upper-class German families with liberal inclinations and often with English connections. But Hahn did not want an élitist reputation, so he soon introduced a system of fees graded to suit the resources of parents. The school was also co-educational, something else that was uncommon in Germany at that time.

Geoffrey knew about the work being done at Salem. His brother Georis's two daughters, Joan and Virginia, had been there in the early 1920s, and several members of the Trevelyan family were interested too. He went to see for himself in 1926 and was impressed. In his account of his educational development, he said:

> While operating the Lincoln Foundation in Germany, I had had reason to visit the Palace of Salem, in order to consult Kurt Hahn, director of the school. By chance almost, because I had been seeing too many experimental schools in too many lands, I waited to dine in hall with the boys, and I saw something in their expression and bearing which I had only seen once before, among cadets under British naval training . . . Kurt Hahn, a reforming idealist, but also – I soon saw – a practical educator of resource and intuition without his like in my experience, was combining the more liberal of Plato's educational methods with the better of our public school traditional practices; and he was readjusting the emphasis they placed on brainwork, handiwork, games, the arts and so on, in accordance with our clearer modern knowledge of how our young grow. The results were conspicuously successful, especially in the higher percentage of boys of average mentality to whom justice was being done. Salem boys, I found, were no more like angels than any ordinary boys; but they were realising their natural endowment to the full, whatever it might be. They were growing up healthy, interested and responsible . . . They were to a considerable degree self-governing; but the governors were selected by the community on character, not on position in class or prominence in games.

Geoffrey was delighted to find that Salem's conception of sport was wider than just team games and athletics; it embraced climbing and hill walking, canoeing and small boat sailing: "The mountains and the sea, Hahn demonstrated, could and ought to be used to supply the element of adventure, of self-discipline and of comradeship needed in every boy's normal training for life."

Geoffrey and Hahn took to each other immediately. For once it was Geoffrey's turn to be the disciple. Their ideas about education were similar but it was Hahn who was putting them into practice.

In the summer of 1932 both Geoffrey and Len spent a few months teaching at Salem. He wrote to Marcia: ". . . Mother and I are very busy teaching, and she has a rather stupid and naughty class of boys and girls!" A week later he wrote again: ". . . Mother keeps tremendous order in her class! I think she must look like this . . .", followed by a pencil caricature of Len looking fierce.

Hahn was rarely at ease with women, but Len's directness and openness, her ebullient sense of humour, won him over completely. He wrote to her in 1930: The meeting with you all this summer is one of the best things which happened to me for a long time. I like to talk things over with Geoffrey more than any other man I know. I find that he stimulates all that is creative in the man he talks to. And I agree with him on all the essentials. Any unexpected or expected visit of both of you would be a real joy . . ."

Jocelin was at the King's Choir School in Cambridge by this time, and hating it. So at Christmas 1930 Len wrote to Hahn asking if Salem would admit Jocelin. The reply was a prompt and delighted yes, and in March 1931 Jocelin, eleven years old, joined Salem junior school which was accommodated in Hohenfels, an old castle of the Teutonic knights. He was homesick for a while and had to struggle to learn German quickly, but in a surprisingly short time found himself very happy.

One story from this period illustrates Geoffrey's cavalier attitude towards money. He had found himself with some spare capital, possibly the inheritance from his father, and, after taking professional advice, invested it all in a Swedish firm of match-manufacturers that had been doing spectacularly well. Almost immediately the company went bust. The Young family were visiting Salem when the news reached them, and Jocelin recalls: "We were staying at an hotel in Uberlingen on Lake Constance, and I remember my father walking up and down the bank, roaring with laughter."

In the spring of 1931 Len and Geoffrey and Jocelin went to Salem together, and Peter Bicknell, who had already done a little work at the school, went with them as driver and companion. Bicknell recalls the journey with pleasure: "They were delightful company. It was particularly fascinating because we went by way of Antwerp and stayed there with Maurice Best. He and his wife entertained us and I heard the whole story of how Geoffrey had rescued him from the ruins of Ypres and befriended him."

By this time Maurice Best was a highly successful businessman, the manager and assistant director of one of the firms that was reconstructing the Antwerp docks. Geoffrey described the visit:

> . . . a large private house with luxurious rooms for reception. Oh, Maurice's delight, to produce his new acquisitions, and wines, and decorations, and show them to us! And always with that current of laughing at his own pride, and of repeated and never-forgotten gratitude – "You know, it's all due to you, Geoffrey!" I never knew such an unchanged, boyish freshness of nature and of gratitude.

They drove out one day to the Ypres region, and Bicknell says: "I remember one place where Maurice stopped his car and said to Geoffrey, 'Do you remember seeing the Germans behind those trees over there?' It was the exact place."

The war was still fresh in adult minds, and the prospects for future European peace were already beginning to look dubious. In some countries – Italy and Russia – control had been seized by autocratic, extremist forces. In others – like Britain and France – the keynotes were apprehension and prevarication. And Germany was sliding towards either anarchy or autarchy. In September 1930 Hitler's National Socialist Party had increased its representation in the Reichstag from 12 to 107 seats. Within two years, in new general elections, they more than doubled that number to become the largest single party. In four years the Nazis had gained 13 million votes, most of them at the expense of the middle-class moderates. The struggle between the two extremes, Fascist and Communist, intensified. In August 1932 President von Hindenburg found it necessary to rebuke Hitler about the open street brutality of his Storm troopers.

There had been a spate of ugly incidents, especially in Silesia and East Prussia. On August 9, at a place called Beuthen in Silesia, a young Communist had been kicked to death by five Nazi storm-troopers before the eyes of his mother. The government announced that all convicted of political murder would face the death penalty. On August 22 the five men were convicted and sentenced. Hitler sent them a telegram: "My comrades: In the face of this most monstrous and bloody sentence I feel myself bound to you in limitless loyalty.

From this moment, your liberation is a question of our honour. To fight against a government which could allow this is our duty."

When he heard of this, Kurt Hahn sent a letter to all Salem's former pupils: "By the telegram of Hitler to the 'comrades' of Beuthen a fight has been initiated which goes far beyond politics. Germany is at stake, its Christian way of life, its reputation, the honour of its soldiers; Salem cannot remain neutral. I call upon the members of the Salem association who are engaged on SA or SS work to break their allegiance either to Hitler or to Salem." It was a bold thing to do. Some of Hahn's friends thought it foolhardy. But he went on to expound his opposition to the Nazi ideology in two public speeches.

On January 30, 1933, as a desperate last-ditch measure, Hindenburg appointed Hitler Chancellor of Germany, charged with forming a national government on a constitutional basis. A month later the destruction of the Reichstag by fire gave Hitler the opportunity he needed. He took draconian powers and his men arrested thousands of Communists and Socialists and liberals across Germany.

At 2 a.m. on March 11 storm-troopers surrounded Salem School. At 11 a.m. they arrested Hahn and took him to Überlingen gaol.

Geoffrey heard the news the next day in a telegram from Ka Arnold-Forster, who was in Salem because her son Mark had joined Jocelin at the junior school there. The children, she said, were well.

On the day of the arrest the Margrave of Baden, now Prince Berthold (Prince Max had died in 1929), sent a telegram to President von Hindenburg. It argued Hahn's services to Germany, the high reputation of his school across Europe, and protested that his arrest and imprisonment was a slander on the Margrave and his family.

Geoffrey soon got more information, in a long, disjointed letter from Ka Arnold-Forster, giving more details and urging immediate protests to the German government. The Nazis, she said, had control of the Baden police. She had driven to Switzerland to post the letter because she was sure the mail was being intercepted and read. "O my dear", she concluded, "it is a beastly world. Some of the mountains looked so heavenly as we came by today. But how vile is man."

Geoffrey was now living in Huntley Street in Bloomsbury, close to the new buildings of London University. In 1932, as his contract with the Rockefeller Foundation came to an end, he had secured a new job, as Reader in Comparative Education at the university. The post was endowed by Thomas Wall, the successful sausage manufacturer, and Geoffrey conveyed the good news to Len with a characteristic telegram: "Elected unanimously sausages".

From his home in London he was able to get things moving quickly.

He wired Neville Butler, the Foreign Office adviser to the Prime Minister, Ramsay MacDonald. Butler, who was at the League of Nations in Geneva, had special reasons to be concerned. In 1914, at the outbreak of the war, he had been trapped in Germany and interned. It was through the influence of Kurt Hahn that he was released and returned to England. So he now quickly drafted a letter of protest for MacDonald to send to the German Foreign Minister, Baron von Neurath. Butler's accompanying note to MacDonald read: "P. M. Would you be disposed to sign this. In 1914–15 I owed Hahn almost everything – except money . . ."

On March 17 MacDonald sent a private letter to von Neurath. He spoke of his anxiety about what was happening to Hahn and its possible repercussions on Anglo-German relations. Hahn, he said, "has worked hard to create friendships between our two countries". And he added a personal touch: "I have another cause for interest in him with which I think you will sympathise. He has spent many summers in a certain neighbourhood in my native Morayshire, which is particularly dear to me, and he too is an ardent lover of it."

In fact, Hahn had been released the day before this letter was sent. In his reply von Neurath claimed that the release was "on account of my intervention", and added: "Unfortunately I am unable to say now whether it will be possible for him to resume his former duties at the school at Salem." Hahn was, in the event, exiled from the state of Baden.

In the meantime Geoffrey had been busy drafting a letter for publication in *The Times* and getting eminent signatories for it, and alerting many other newspapers to get maximum publicity. He was successful in that, though his *Times* letter did not appear before Hahn was released.

Len hurried out to Salem to take some of the pressure off Ka Arnold-Forster. There she was asked to help get some of Hahn's secret papers back to England. Nazi searchers had failed to find them, hidden at the back of an ancient cupboard. Len cabled Geoffrey with her news, using agreed code words, then enlisted the aid of a young American called Warriner, who had been teaching at Salem junior school. He had an open sports car. They hid the papers under the passenger seat. There were some moments of anxiety when they ran over a hen at the frontier village and two German policemen bore down on them. Len sat tight, doing her impression of a grand Englishwoman, dumb and sulky and about to lose her temper. They got through.

On Len's return Geoffrey went to Germany to see Hahn who, unable to go to Salem, had headed north to Berlin. He found him deep in conspiracies with others, mostly army officers who hated Hitler and the Nazis. These were high-level dissidents. They included General Frieherr von Hammerstein, former Commander-in-Chief of the German army; Major-General Kurt von Schleicher, who had been Chancellor of Germany briefly until Hilter took over in January 1933 and who was regarded as the political brains of the army; and a younger man, Herr von Haeften whom Geoffrey regarded as "the finest young statesman in Germany". Geoffrey met this group some time in April, and Hahn later said: "They all were deeply impressed with Geoffrey's attitude towards Germany." According to Geoffrey they were even more impressed with Hahn. One of his favourite anecdotes was about one of these meetings when Hahn was more than usually brilliant, directing and dominating the talk by sheer force of intelligence, so much so that when it was breaking up Schleicher went up to him and said: "Herr Hahn, when this is all over I want to come to Salem and work as a house master and learn from you." Schleicher was murdered soon after, in the "night of the long knives", June 29–30, 1934.

From Berlin Hahn moved further north, to Heringsdorf on the Baltic coast, where he stayed with an old Scottish friend, Lady Cumming. He felt it was only a matter of time before they arrested him again. On June 19 Prince Berthold wrote to Geoffrey with the news that a state commissioner had been appointed to run Salem School, and adding: "I think the time has come for your friend Kurt – his waiting is of no use. For his own sake I think it is essential that he should be persuaded to have a complete change. It would be very kind of you if you could induce him to settle for a bit in your country as I fear a breakdown if he stays on where he is."

Hahn decided to leave Germany. He got to Berlin by car, then by train to France. On July 11 he cabled Geoffrey from Utrecht: "Arriving tomorrow Wednesday morning via Hook".

On September 13 he wrote to the Home Office, explaining why he needed permission for a lengthy stay in Britain: "It is now evident that at least up to March 1934 I cannot anticipate any resumption of my work in Germany. I have been asked by friends to remain here as

their guest during the winter. I have also had the offer of giving three lectures at the London Institute of Education, on the Salem system."
He appended a list of referees, which included Neville Butler; R. M. Barrington-Ward, the *Times'* Foreign Editor; and Geoffrey. Geoffrey had kept close contact with Barrington-Ward throughout the crisis. Others who had rallied to his support were the historian J. W. Wheeler-Bennett, and the Shakespearian scholar, Professor John Dover Wilson of London University, who had become a friend.

Geoffrey did all he could in the months that followed to establish Hahn in Britain and help him set up his educational system here. He introduced him to a circle of friends and sympathisers and influential contacts of all kinds. The school was opened at Gordonstoun on the shores of the Moray Firth in April 1934. Geoffrey was chairman of the Board of Governors, and the membership of the board reflects the extent of his influence. It included G. M. Trevelyan, Wheeler-Bennett, Barrington-Ward and Ka Arnold-Forster.

Salem itself survived as a school. For a year or two Hahn allowed himself to hope he might return there, expecting "a wave of reasonableness" to sweep over Germany. Prince Berthold did what he could to keep some of the Hahn traditions alive, and the school was not completely taken into Nazi control until 1944.

Right up until the outbreak of war in 1939 Geoffrey continued to work closely with the anti-Nazi forces inside Germany.

In the summer of 1933 his old friend Will Arnold-Forster, now acting as an adviser to the Labour Party on European affairs, contrived to get himself shown round the concentration camp at Dachau, near Munich. He was with a small group of British and North Americans. In his report, dated August 2, he said: "We were not allowed to see the prison part, but the camp itself was appalling enough. I don't understand why they were so ready to take us there . . ."

The camp held more than 2,000 men, mostly Socialists, Communists and other critics of the Nazi regime. There were not many Jews. There were teenage boys and old men, intellectuals and labourers:

> . . . a great mass of men of all ages, naked save for bathing slips (the best thing for them in that lovely weather), and all the younger ones hungry. They have to eat in the week only a ration of black bread, some sausage, and some potato wash: this last they all spoke bitterly of. One man beckoned me aside and gave me some taste in the tin bowl. It looked like grey Stickphast – paste with some lumps in it. I took one mouthful, retched three times, covered my mouth quickly with a handkerchief; my

eyes filled with tears but I avoided being visibly sick. For an hour later I was suffering from that indescribably awful taste; I suppose there was some rancid material in the cooking.

They inspected the over-crowded sleeping quarters, and asked about brutalities. But camp officers were in attendance and the prisoners could not reply, though one managed to say to Arnold-Forster in English: "There have been 14 killed in this camp, in horrible ways. There is much maltreatment. It is like the Middle Ages."

He left wondering what it would be like in the huts when the bad weather came, and how long young men could survive on such rations. Towards the end of the report he said:

> If I could convey that sight – that mass of naked men trying to speak to one with their eyes; the Commandant in his black uniform and the mark on his mouth of one compelling himself to suppress his humanity, under orders; the young bloods in the SA uniform; the feeling that they were there without hope, indefinitely, and without trial, puzzled many of them as to why they were there at all – then the feeling that all hope of German unity was being destroyed by this insensate wrong . . . It is a cruelty done with a certain German cleanliness and efficiency; but it is deadly to those who inflict it and to all those who can tolerate it . . .

Arnold-Forster's findings were not entirely new. Some British newspapers had carried stories about the camps, and Archbishop William Temple of York had been so disturbed by the reports he had engaged an eminent lawyer to sift the evidence. The lawyer reported that he had found "a large body of testimony" to show the existence in Germany of "a pitiless tyranny". His report said: "The statements are made at first hand by competent witnesses who describe atrocious ill-usage which they and others had undergone because of their political associations or activities, actual or suspected; and make it clear that extreme cruelty was employed in numerous instances to bring about suicide, and that many died of ill-usage and many were shot."

A powerful group came together, including the Archbishop and Kurt Hahn and Geoffrey, who felt that the time had come to send an appeal to Hitler, asking him to use his influence to end the "systematic brutality practised in the concentration camps".

An appeal letter was drafted, quoting the lawyer's report but couched in measured, almost conciliatory terms. It expressed concern for Germany's honour, and the wish for "the co-operation of the

German nation with our own and with others in the common enterprise of civilisation". It also expressed the hope that "barbarous methods" might already have been abandoned in the camps.

A formidable list of signatories was assembled, headed by the Archbishop himself. The others were the Bishop of Chichester; Lord Buckmaster, a former Lord Chancellor; two eminent historians, G. M. Trevelyan and G. P. Gooch; Maynard Keynes; two heads of Oxford colleges, A. D. Lindsay of Balliol and Sir Michael Sadler of University College; Dame Sybil Thorndike the actress; and Douglas Lowe, an athlete of international repute.

It was Archbishop Temple's belief that the best hope of ending these horrors was not by publication in Britain, which would anger Hitler and intensify his paranoia, but by a polite and personal approach. It was possible that Hitler did not know about conditions in the camps.

Two emissaries were asked to take the appeal letter to Berlin and try to make sure that it reached Hitler. They were Geoffrey and a retired British general, Sir Wyndham Deedes. The aim was to get access to Hitler himself, present him with the appeal and a covering letter from the Archbishop, and to hear his response. They were in Berlin for five days, from May 24 to 29, 1934, and, despite repeated efforts, failed to present the appeal to the German Chancellor.

In his report Geoffrey said they tried three avenues of approach.

The first was through the German Foreign Office, and met with an immediate rebuff. The Secretary of State sent them a message that it was hopeless, the Chancellor had "forbidden any further communications being transmitted to him on anything touching upon the matter of concentration camps".

So they tried the more direct line, through the Kanzlei, the Chancellor's office. They were told that Hitler was away, but assured that if they left the Archbishop's covering letter it would be handed to him on his return. They knew Hitler was back in Berlin the next day, a Saturday, because they saw him in their hotel. The Sunday papers said he had now gone to Dresden. On Monday they were told, by telephone, that his return was not to be expected until Wednesday or Thursday, and he had not seen the Archbishop's letter because of other pressing business. They went again to the Kanzlei but could only see a junior official, who asked them to leave the appeal with him. They refused to do this. In his report Geoffrey explained: "It had appeared probable to us before this that under no circumstances would our personal communication of the appeal to the Chancellor be permitted. And that, if we transmitted it through official channels, it would very improbably ever reach his hands."

This was the virtual end of their mission, but they went ahead with their third option and spent the last day at Hitler's press office, dropping heavy hints about the gravity of the contents of the appeal.

In the autobiographical notes that he wrote after the Second World War Geoffrey recorded his impressions of some of the leading figures he met or saw at this period. He summed up their failed mission with these words: "A nervous time, and the secret interviews were as many as the open. It was only two days before the horrible Blood Purge of the Party when Schleicher and Roehm were murdered." (Geoffrey's chronology is slightly out here. The great purge took place at the end of June, more than a month later.)

The notes go on to recall the afternoon when Hitler came into their hotel restaurant for coffee:

Hitler came in looking short, erect but flabby, in his plain uniform – with the famous curl down over his forehead – face already lined and dirty-looking. General look that of a rather seedy actor, and I said "Harry Tate" first to myself, and then as the time went on, qualified it with "and even more of Charles Hawtrey". It was a wholly actor's makeup. The dark, beady eyes were alone remarkable. From the first they suggested to me the fanatic and self-intoxicated visionary. I watched them a long time; but never saw a flash of humour or of "soul" in them. He was conscious of himself the whole time, and, while silent and seemingly oblivious of all the company, was (to me) desperately aware of them and his effects. There were several of the gang with him, and some three infatuated women including Frau Goebbels. They all sat round the table and talked in lively fashion. Hitler sat in the middle, under the wall, looking straight across at our small table. He looked sometimes at a paper, but hardly spoke. Twice, I think, great fat older Germans got up from tables where they sat with their wives, and, marching across, stood at the Hitler salute, some three strides from his table. He made a point of not noticing them for quite a time. Then, and almost without looking at them, Hitler made a slight return of the salute, and they beamed like jellies all over, and slumped off back to their tables . . . After his coffee, he began to talk across to one of the men, but never to the females at the tables. His voice was resonant and well-managed. Clearly again he was listening to himself . . .

A year or so before the 1933 mission to Berlin Geoffrey had had a long interview with Franz von Papen, the former Chancellor. He had marvelled at the man's smooth charm – "the entirely perfect and quiet manners of the best class of Englishman". But he was not fooled by this, dismissing von Papen as "the silken villain".

He had had an interview, too, with Joachim von Ribbentrop, the German ambassador in London. This was when Geoffrey was campaigning to save Salem School:

> I put all my case, and he sympathised and made promises and reservations and so on. He obviously enjoyed the talk, for he could have ended it sooner. When I got up to go, he followed me across the room to the door, with a faintly tragic expression on his rather handsome and greyish face; and at the door he put his hand on my arm and detained me, saying, almost under his breath and with great intensity – "My *dear* Mr Young, you have no idea how *fortunate* you are – to have been born in England!" I was rather moved; and, though I now believe the man to be capable of any falsity and any brutality, I have sometimes wondered whether, just for the once, he had not had the flash of a wish that things had been otherwise with him?

During the 1930s Geoffrey came to know many of the leading anti-Nazis well, and many of them he liked personally and admired their courage. But he had doubts about their effectiveness and their discretion. They knew they were surrounded by Nazi spies and informers, that their letters were sometimes opened, their telephones tapped. Yet they disdained elementary precautions. He recalled a late session with Generals Schleicher and Hammerstein and others:

> After supper, which was served by some half dozen footmen with white gloves, we talked with the greatest freedom of the political situation. I was amazed, even at that time, at the way in which the whole group spoke in open condemnation of the Hitler gang and the Nazis. Germans have often puzzled me by this. They seemed to have the belief that that which was not meant to be carried further, never would be. I've no doubt now that half those footmen were in the Nazi Party.

One of the leading conspirators in the later 1930s was Carl Goerdeler, a former mayor of Leipzig, a man of noble ideals but dangerously talkative and naive about the thoroughness and the ruthlessness of the Nazi organisation. Geoffrey was his contact man in Britain, and when Goerdeler came to London in 1937 for secret talks with Neville Chamberlain, the Prime Minister, Geoffrey made the arrangements. Knowing that Goerdeler would be followed, he arranged for him to enter the Senate House buildings of London University, where his office was, by the main entrance, then whisked him out through a back door to a waiting car. It appeared to work, but within a couple of days the British press knew the interview had taken place. Goerdeler was one of those who was seized and executed after the 1944 bomb plot.

The conspirators' last pre-war chance to stop Hitler was in 1938. Many of Germany's military commanders, especially in the army, were desperately concerned at the accelerating rush towards war – the *Anschluss* with Austria, the dismemberment of Czechoslovakia, the mounting hysteria in Hitler's public speeches. Plans were discussed at length to seize power, depose Hitler and replace him by some form of constitutional monarchy. They came to nothing. They waited too long for "the right moment to strike". They were pre-empted by the pace of events.

Geoffrey's views are summarised in letters he sent to Jocelin. On November 5, 1938 he wrote:

. . . It's been a full week. I got news of what was happening in Hun-land, and was the first to get it to the Foreign Office – who knew nothing of course! (But this is a dark secret, so tell no one!) Meanwhile, the enemy have struck first and won the first trick. It's wearying, the way the nicer folk over there are simply incapable of *acting*. They talk too much, and wait, and plan – and t'other chap at last looks up and says "By George, why shouldn't *I* act first?" And then down go the good chaps.

Two weeks later he wrote: ". . . I had the echoes of the German plot to deal with, which fizzled out because they talked too much, and went for a monarchy – which was idiotic as a first step. Result – Hitler for the time stronger than ever."

19

The 1930s

GEOFFREY'S LIFE IN THE 1930s was full and varied and involved much travel and separation. He believed in maintaining strong family links, and achieved this with a steady flow of lively and affectionate letters. Marcia was away at various boarding schools. Jocelin, given the choice in 1933 of staying with Kurt Hahn or going to his father's old school at Marlborough, opted to join Hahn in Scotland, together with Mark Arnold-Forster, in the enterprise that led to the foundation of Gordonstoun six months later.

Geoffrey's letters to the children are mostly bright and chirpy, often enlivened with comic drawings, sometimes giving serious counsel. A high proportion of them have survived.

On October 21, 1932, when Jocelin was still at Salem, they sent him a parcel with their birthday greetings, a book, and loving messages. Geoffrey wrote: ". . . and I sit after supper, in the brown velvet coat, and shake my silvery locks off a lofty brow, and think as I write 'This goes to Jocelin. Our Jocelin. I wonder if he means half as much to himself as he means to us? – Bless him! . . ." Then comes a drawing of Geoffrey and Len attacking a huge birthday cake with knives. He continued: ". . . Meanwhile I am beginning to get hold of my job, and not to be so moiled and dithery about it. And Len is having hosts of answers to her offer to teach folk to elocute. Which is not the same as electrocute, mark you! . . ." Then he did a drawing of Len teaching.

October 25 was his as well as Jocelin's birthday, so four days later Geoffrey was writing: ". . . I was really moved by your birthday card, and letter. The simple taste is *perfect* (how beautiful those classical lines are! But I don't think I found that out as early as you have). And I just loved your letter: and sat long over it, with Len . . ." He was also moved by the fact that Frau, his nurse more than half a century before, had remembered both of them: "Dear Frau remembered! As she did yours too! It is sad to think she won't be able to 'remember' yours for 56 years too – and never miss arriving on the right day!"

Further letters describe the redecoration of the new flat in Bloomsbury, with the help of a man-servant whom Geoffrey refers to as "Jeeves". Geoffrey is fixing a bicycle for Jocelin's holidays and making a sledge. He sends messages to his Cambridge protégé Robert Chew, who is now teaching at Salem, and gives the family news. "London is beastly," he says, "and I suspect I shall never, if I can help it, go out while we live here; except to escape and see a green view."

There are similar cheery letters to Marcia, addressed to "Dearest Marcianess" and "Cara Marchesa", lavishly illustrated with poems and drawings, ending "Yours hugfully" and "Hugs and hurrahs".

In return, he wanted their news. To Jocelin he said: "Write me (and Mummy!) about your daily doings. They interest us: just like keeping up a *talk*. Even the small things. And what you're *at* . . ."

Many of the letters to Jocelin at Gordonstoun give fatherly encouragement and advice. In October 1934 he wrote: "Stick it out, as I know you do – And keep on trying; as I know you are. It's the 'game of life', to carry on as best one can, for the sake of the good carrying-on; and better than doing so for the sake of one's own 'success', or the opinion of other people . . . Lord! I *know* how hard it is, and how much one minds all the same! My heart is with you."

He warns Jocelin against over-competitiveness, and being a poor loser. That way, he says, he will make himself unpopular and miserable. He must change his attitudes, think more of other people and their feelings. Later, when Jocelin was being pressed to be confirmed as a member of the Church of England, Geoffrey told him not to do so unless he believed: "Ceremonies are meaningless, unless they are symbols of a belief or attitude of mind which you *feel* to be true or to be your *own*."

Another piece of advice was about music: "Flute. I should greatly wish that you could *make* time, as the position clears and things settle. Music is very important in your life, and, in things that mean much to us, it is essential to be *creative*, as well as receptive."

Geoffrey wrote no books in the 1930s and no serious poetry either, just the traditional occasional verses to mark birthdays and anniversaries. He continued to write articles for magazines and climbing club journals though, and used his lectures at London

University in the 1932–3 session as the basis of a chapter in a book called *Edwardian England,* which was published in 1933. He deals, in an original and thoughtful way, with the changes that took place in English education in the opening decade of the century, drawing on his experiences as a teacher at Eton and then as one of His Majesty's inspectors. The Edwardian period, he said, saw the dawning of English educational consciousness: ". . . it is the moment in time at which our national educational process reached its own stage of maturity, and began responsibly to set its house in order." And he concluded with a statement of educational faith:

> There is no contradiction between the conception of education as the release of individual personality, and that of education as the training for national citizenship. By releasing the individual personality we release also his portion in the national personality, that is, in the longer continuity of a people's life and purpose, of which he and his contemporaries are the only present expression and the only trustees for the future . . . Education is for the wholeness of living.

Geoffrey said my little in his letters about his work at London University, but one letter he received gives some indication of his teaching. It was sent in June 1941 by Lieutenant H. J. Rousseau from military college in South Africa, and it said:

> Ever since Munich, when the evidence became too strong for any sane person to doubt, I have felt I ought to apologise to you. Perhaps you remember in 1934 a young South African at the Institute challenging your views about the German national character and education. The young fool was me, and I just want to say how sorry I am that, with such want of experience of Germans as against your long and wide experience, I questioned your views. Had I been right, we should not now have been engaged in the most barbarous war even civilised people have been able to devise.

Although he was approaching sixty and a busy man in a variety of ways, mountaineering was still important to Geoffrey. In the early 1930s the whole family managed to snatch brief holidays together in the Alps. Marcia was walking on the glacier at the age of six, and Jocelin was taken by Hans Brantschen to the summit of the Riffelhorn. In 1933 Jocelin and his parents, and two attendant guides, traversed the Hohstock Ridge above Bel Alp in the Oberland.

In the summer of that year Geoffrey had been shattered to hear of the death on the Weisshorn of Franz Lochmatter, his old friend and guide, the man who led the party out of extreme danger on the South Face of the Täschhorn in 1906. The news of the death of friends always hit Geoffrey unusually hard. Most people feel devastated for a day or two, then begin to recover. With Geoffrey it could be several days before he could start to return to normal life.

He went to St Niklaus to speak at the dedication of a memorial rock. He wrote a long and heart-felt and beautiful obituary for the *Alpine Journal*, paying tribute to the man's character and his climbing:

> . . . Of all the great climbers whom I have been privileged to watch in action, or whose methods and achievements I have been able to study, Franz seemed to me the most perfectly constituted, physically and temperamentally, for the mastery of difficulty. A tall man, with high shoulders, a short trunk and long arms and legs, every joint in him seemed to possess its own independent vitality, superb strength and a separate prehensile capacity. His reserves of energy were never once in his life exhausted, and his mechanism was perfectly controlled. His walk, as he seemed to lounge down a glacier or track, was a model of economy: each leg-swing had only just enough impetus to carry it through; but, at the end, his small feet – which he used as most people do their hands – would settle, adjusting themselves to any inequality, at any angle, with absolute precision. In climbing, as the difficulty increased, the appropriate energy came out to meet it in the same easy progression. Until, without any perceptible change beyond a greater liveliness and a more swinging grace in the rhythm, he would gradually be discovered to be mastering the very outside of the humanly feasible. I never saw him "struggle". Every movement upon rock, ice or snow came of the same perfect co-ordination of eye and limb: it appeared effortless. For the same reason he could increase the pace, when he considered suitable, until he was moving faster on a mountain, and over every nature of surface, than any man I have ever seen.

In 1935 Geoffrey's old friend Marcus Heywood persuaded him to return to high Alpine mountaineering. He hired the services of Josef Knubel for two weeks in July. The plan was an ambitious one, an attempt on the Rothorn. It was an offer Geoffrey could not resist. It was twenty-one years since he had climbed with Knubel. And he had the highest regard for Heywood, whom he had first encountered as a schoolboy when he was a teacher at Eton. In *Mountains with a Difference* he wrote: "Marcus Heywood had the gift of making every prospect please . . . All his life the sunlight came in with him; and, as an old Irishwoman said of him: 'The Lord threw gold-dust over him!' His appearance, his voice and manner shone with it, and it was real gold . . ."

They did some preliminary excursions and Geoffrey found that "somehow fitness seemed slow in coming". They hired a second guide, Lagger, and set off from the Trift hostel at about 11 p.m. In a letter to Len, written at the Riffelalp on July 26, Geoffrey told the story of his last big Alpine ascent:

We did the Rothorn on Wednesday; Marcus, Josef, Lagger and I. Perfect conditions. But it took me from 11 p.m. (from the Trift) to between 12 and 1 the next night. I recognised en route that this scale is beyond me – lovely as it was. We had glorious views and a joyous party. On the way down I fell, and, thanks to little J [Knubel], had an escape of such a miraculous kind as perhaps few have had, and none can better measure than myself. Result – only a few scrapes and a cut, and great fatigue. Walked down from the Trift yesterday, and am being *exquisitely* patched and cared for by Margery [Heywood's wife] – a *genius* as a nurse – and dear Marcus. Josef trotting in and out . . . *No one* knows of the fall, but ourselves. But – it's to be my last big climb. And the mountains have been kind to me, to the end. I said goodbye to them – up there – as I came down, happily enough. They're still the same at levels safe for me!

Fifteen years later Geoffrey wrote a much fuller, more vivid and more detailed account of the Rothorn experience, which formed the final chapter of *Mountains with a Difference*. It is a brilliant, compelling description, one of his great bravura pieces, and it makes it clear that in his letter to Len, out of concern for her feelings, he was being what is now called "economical with the truth". It was far from being "a joyous party".

The initial, interminable pull up loose moraines proved arduous, and it was followed by a struggle up icy slopes and then a period of wading through deep snowy sludge. Almost from the start Geoffrey was aware that he was struggling, and soon he was painfully aware of his comrades' anxieties about his progress. It took them more than thirteen hours to gain the summit; before the war he had done it in under five. They ate on the summit, surveying the prospect all around, but Geoffrey felt none of the old elation. "Something had gone out of my Alpine mountaineering," he wrote. "There and then, as I lay and rested and looked out, I determined that this should be my last great ascent."

He did not convey his decision to the others. They set off down; Heywood and Lagger going ahead, roped together; Geoffrey following, protected by a rope to the vigilant Knubel. The first rocky section went easily. Then Knubel paid the rope out cautiously as Geoffrey floundered down snow-plastered slabs. They moved on towards the exposed traverse of the west face that they had to cross to gain the main ridge. Geoffrey found a stance just before the start of the traverse and called Josef to join him there. He saw him set off, then – reaching up to adjust his snow-glasses – simply lost balance and toppled off:

A desolating irony – of those dearest to me living on – of myself incredibly ending. A revulsion – at the squalor attending death in the mountains. Always the bitter grey ironic mist . . . is this falling? . . . is this dreaming? . . . am I dead? . . . *I?* . . . irrevocably? – *I?* There was a straining through all the haze, to know, to be certain; as one struggles to come awake from intolerable nightmare. There was absolutely no consciousness of hurt, or shock, or of any contact. And this, although Marcus, who from the crest of the ridge lower down looked back and upward at the sound, saw me falling from the traverse on the wall, and describes the fall as "spinning over and over down the slabs in a clatter of stones and metal". No doubt as I revolved the metal peg thrashed round loosely against the rock.

Suddenly out of the mist I had a blurred impression downwards, over appalling depth of glaciers . . . I *am* falling . . . it *is* death . . . This must have been the instant when the rope first tautened, checking me in mid-spin as I shot out over the overhang. Because the enveloping haze of grey irony closed in again . . . Ending in a violent rend-back into consciousness as the rope caught me finally and I twirled dangling over space. All my life I have wakened instantly after sleep into full awareness. And now, even before physical feeling returned to the body, I knew I had fallen a great height, and that such a fall should have meant serious or fatal injury. Instantaneously I had moved head, arms, thighs – nothing broken! Then back rushed physical sensation – an ache and a scorch, in right elbow and right side. Simultaneously I looked upward. Far above my head the rope disappeared, straining thinly over a jagged edge – it must be bruised – injured – might part at any moment.

Altogether he had fallen about eighty feet, the last part of it clear. Knubel saw him start to topple, fixed his right hand on to a good hold, braced himself on tenuous footholds, and clenched his left hand round the rope. The strain when it came severely cut the palm of his left hand, but Knubel was a strong man – he worked as a stonemason and quarryman out of season – and he held tight, and then found the strength to twitch the rope behind a convenient spike of rock and tie it on. He untied himself from the rope and made his way down towards the other two to get their rope and begin to engineer the rescue. He climbed as close as he could to a point above the overhang and to the left of Geoffrey, tied a loop in the end of the rope, and lowered it down, swinging it across the face.

Geoffrey, meanwhile, held by the rope to his waist, had planted himself on tiny wrinkle holds on the wall, and jammed his right hand firmly into a two-finger crack. He saw the second rope being lowered and at the third attempt managed to grab it and pass it rapidly behind his left shoulder. He knew it was vital to get the loop right round his upper body, but found that his right hand refused to quit the reassurance of its little crack. He brought all his willpower to bear and used his left hand to prise the two fingers free and pass the loop under his right shoulder:

> Even now I felt a reluctance to start again, and to trust to the painful wrench of the ropes alone. Then I gave the hail. Marcus had come across to join Knubel long before this, and the second guide had joined him. There were now three powerful men pulling on the two ropes in the same line, and I was not allowed to pause again. With a swirl like the fling of wave-spray up a cliff, they tore me up the precipitous rock scoop. Twenty feet higher, I began to find a skin-flint hold here or there on the slabs, enough to ease the rope-drag on my side. Thirty feet above me, I could see them now, crouching and intent, on ledges against the brown upright slabs. At the same instant I came on a new-looking white wool glove, black-patterned with reindeer, wind-blown from the ridge and preserved in a crack; and the sight of this did what the ropes had not done: it suddenly seemed to join me on to the living once more, as two lenses click into the same focus. Then, but only when I saw the glove, I let myself realise that I should survive.

He did survive. He was hauled back to comparative safety. His right elbow bone had been exposed by his wounds, but they made an ice-pack and strapped it on to his arm and it was there for the next thirty hours. Then they roped up again, in the original order, and resumed the descent.

At some point on the long downward struggle Geoffrey overheard Knubel firmly instructing the other guide, who was shaken, that no word about the fall was to be spoken in the valley: "It was like Josef Knubel not to think anything could be worth recording of his own phenomenal feat, which concentrated a lifetime of experience and training into a single instant of decision and power, and to be concerned only with the unseemliness of its intrusion, in common talk, upon the venerable saga of our long, happy and always safe partnership." The world did not hear of the fall until *Mountains with a Difference* was published twenty-two years later.

The descent must have seemed endless to all of them. They were out of food and drink. The last of the daylight drained away as they struggled through deep slushy snow. It was pitch dark by the time they reached the moraine debris. Geoffrey slept briefly, then they started the long, punishing slog, with Knubel protecting Geoffrey all the way on the rope and Heywood giving a shoulder whenever possible. By the time they gained the Trift hostel they had been on the go, almost continuously, for twenty-six hours. It was Geoffrey's last great Alpine excursion.

But he did not lose his interest in the high hills.

He wrote to the French Alpine Club, protesting against a plan to build a téléphérique to the summit of the Meije. Such a noble and difficult summit, he said, should not be vulgarised but kept "as a trust upon which Frenchmen of the future can still learn some of the lessons of courage, endurance, comradeship and the right service of beauty".

The 1930s saw renewed British attempts on Mount Everest and Geoffrey knew most of the men involved. In January 1933 Hugh Ruttledge, the leader of that year's expedition, wrote to him from the ship on which they were sailing out to India: "As for the troops, they *are* good. Shipton, I feel, hides under a quiet manner the most desperate resolution, quite untainted by personal ambition." It was a perceptive appreciation of Eric Shipton, then aged twenty-five and at the start of his climbing career, who was to become a good friend of Geoffrey's. Other friends who took part in the luckless attempts of the 1930s included Noel Odell, Frank Smythe, and two of his Cambridge protégés, Lawrence Wager and Jack Longland. Another disciple was the New Zealander Scott Russell, who wrote to Geoffrey in November 1938 with the news that he had been chosen to accompany the Tilman/Shipton reconnaissance of the Everest region. He said: "That I am likely to realise one of my great ambitions is due – to a far greater extent than you would believe – to you. Your influence, both on the appreciation of hills and the techniques of the game, counted for far more than any other stimulus when I had first come to know hills and was determined – not knowing quite how

– to become a mountaineer." Russell sent long, cheerful letters to Geoffrey, recounting their adventures. On June 27, 1939 he wrote: "It is too early to say how this party will go but I'm optimistic. One wonders whether Eric's previous successes were due to, or in spite of, his extreme casualness. He believes the former! He is amazingly vague about such things as meals! But there is no doubt about it he is a grand man to be with."

Geoffrey was still in demand as a speaker at climbing club dinners where he got to know the new generation of climbers. Some became friends, men like Menlove Edwards and Wilfrid Noyce, David Cox and Robin Hodgkin of Oxford, and a tough, direct-mannered little Lancashireman called A. B. (Alan) Hargreaves, who later married one of Len's nieces. Geoffrey helped Menlove Edwards with his revision of the climbers' guide to Lliwedd and got a letter of thanks that included a revealing sentence: "Your continued cheerfulness really is the *best* lesson for morbid young people like self."

The fortunes of Gordonstoun were a continuing preoccupation throughout the 1930s and long after.

At the launching of the school Geoffrey was chairman of the governors. He took the job seriously and remained a governor for many years, paying regular visits and always enjoying them. He recruited many excellent governors to join him.

The school opened in April 1934 with some two dozen boys, half of them Germans from Salem and several of the others there as a result of Geoffrey's enthusiasm and powers of persuasion. Jocelin and Mark Arnold-Forster were founder-pupils. They were soon joined by Francis Noel-Baker and Laurence Slingsby, a son of Len's prodigal brother Will who had abandoned his family, leaving Laurence to be brought up by Len and Geoffrey. Another early recruit was Bill Richmond, son of Admiral Sir Herbert Richmond. Yet another was a member of the deposed Greek royal family, Prince Philip.

Unlike Salem, Gordonstoun was not (until thirty years later) co-educational. Apparently, Kurt Hahn wanted to avoid being labelled "progressive". Despite perennial money problems, the number of pupils – German, Spanish and British – grew year by year. The school's activities expanded and its fame spread.

Kurt Hahn, a big man of high ideals and abounding vitality, put his unique imprint on the place from the start. "There are two methods of governing the young," he said. "You can tether them by distrust or bind them by trust. I would back a spirited boy to defeat the first method. I believe in the second method, which was

Thomas Arnold's, but only on the condition you fortify it by a daily incentive to self-supervision." The keynotes were honesty, effort and self-discipline. Health and fitness and learning were important, but the central purpose was the forming of character, the building of good, alert, humane and caring citizens.

Unlike most idealists, Hahn had few illusions about human frailty. His favourite quotation was from *Tom Jones*: "Human nature is very prevalent." And he often said: "You cannot overestimate the power of self-deception." He believed in treating each boy as an individual. When Jocelin failed a Latin exam and his teacher complained that he was too lazy, Hahn replied: "Yes, but you see, you pour and pour but you never look to see if the lid is off."

He ruled the school by a sort of creative turbulence. He was full of ideas and experiments, and liked to surprise everyone now and then with a sudden, arbitrary switch in schedules or procedures. He liked staff who would stand up to him and argue their corner. He wanted men of spirit and independence around him. It could be upsetting but it was never dull.

Gordonstoun has become famous as the school for Britain's princes. Prince Philip made sure his sons went to his old school, though one of them at least, Prince Charles, did not take to it so whole-heartedly as his father had. It has also acquired a general reputation as a hearty, outdoor, boy-against-the-elements sort of place, all cold-water plunges and cross-country runs and endeavour against waves and tempests and steep mountainsides. The reasons are obvious. Kurt Hahn did believe in the character-strengthening power of small boat sailing and mountain climbing. "No boy," he said, "should be compelled into opinions but it is criminal negligence not to compel him into experience." If the boy hated the experience, however, he would not be made to repeat it. And there was much more to Gordonstoun than this.

Great emphasis was laid on cultural activities, music and drama especially. And a key factor, for Hahn, was the idea that the school should give service to the local area and community. In 1935 they began a Coastguard Watch, and this was later extended to a fire service and a mountain-rescue team. In this way, Hahn believed, the school could help the community that had welcomed them, and the boys could learn practical skills and social responsibility.

Hahn wanted the boys to experience and enjoy adventure, but he was rigorous in insisting that their expeditions, by sea or land, should be made as safe as possible.

Geoffrey spent several days at Gordonstoun in the summer of 1937, when preparations were being made to sail a newly acquired ketch across the North Sea to Norway. Hahn showed Geoffrey round and introduced him to the skipper, the former master of a windjammer. Geoffrey was impressed by ship and skipper, adding: "Though I am not really in a position to judge either. But as a climber I do know about ropes, and some of the rigging is, in my opinion, rotten." Hahn summoned professional sailmakers and the rigging was renewed, and ever after that, when some dangerous trip was being planned, Hahn would cry: "Ropes, my boy, don't forget the ropes!"

Geoffrey had long talks with Jocelin, still nicknamed "Jock", on this visit and reported to Len: "Jock looks well, set up, healthy, hard. Delighted with flute, which is pronounced a gem. Frau Lachmann tells me he is *really* musical. And rejoices in him. He gave me two hours talk last night; critical, pessimistic, but *it does not go deep*. The boy is *sound* throughout. I find I can smile at his woes, and end them with a joke: at which he skips away on to something else quite cheerfully." Later the letter speaks of "Crowds of ushers and oddments, whom I haven't yet identified. Salemish crowd. All on the boil as usual." And it ends: "I have my old central room, and a comfy bed: flowers and a fire. How blessed we are in our children – my dear love . . ."

The sailing of the ketch moved Geoffrey to the depths of his romantic soul. Jocelin – a very senior boy by this time and a very able seaman – was in the crew and so was Mark Arnold-Forster, whose mother was also visiting the school. In a letter to Len, dated July 28, 1936, Geoffrey described the scene the evening before they set sail:

> . . . Ka drove me down. The boys were in the fo'c'sle below, but soon up on deck, busy battening down, and Jocelin lighting the ship's lamps. A golden half-moon, and the dark little port with the sea beyond, and the busy intent figures in blue jerseys and slacks, oh so earnest over their jobs! Jocelin slim, active, the most seamanlike of all, and jokes in low voices, and the adventure ahead . . . Curiously impressive. I said to Ka as we watched, near midnight, "To be 16, and lighting the lamp on the night of your first adventure voyage!" Just the top of life, if they knew it! J swinging up the rigging to send you his love, and a few stars, and lights in the grey port cottages: and stillness.

He did not intend to get up early next morning to see them setting off, but awoke at 4.30 a.m. "to a heavenly dawn", and got up. He got a lift to the harbour where a small crowd had gathered, including Ka and Kurt Hahn:

The crew too busy to give us a glance in the cold sunny breeze of the sunrise. Ruffled seas: far blue coastline of hills. We watched them warp her out with the engine. Then all climbed out along the high sea wall, saw her fan out close below us, moving with the first waves. J – still busy, very intent – waved up. Then as we scaled the highest pier (Hahn's hat blew off as he struggled up – the pledge to fortune!) and watched the heavy sails creak up, and the ketch drive quickly away northward, with just the wide sea (no other boat) and the dim blue coast, and distance, away to the north.

I think we *all* felt that sunrise start strangely poetical, and a symbol. "The greatest sight we've seen at Gordonstoun, sir," said one boy to me. Hahn came back across the harbour with me, silent too. I think it must have meant *much* to him.

And I thought of that *other* voyage, now near its ending, down there with you. And they *fitted* – it was as it should be.

Dear love, as I waved at the disappearing sails, I only wished for *you* to be there. Small in its way, this sea trip; but it was the soul of our boy going out into the sunlight, with a favouring wind and a whitened sea – on his own adventure, for the first time.

Geoffrey and Len had just moved from Bloomsbury to a more countrified setting at Gomshall in Surrey, a few miles east of Guildford. There they rented a small, two-storey house with enough garden to keep Geoffrey happily pottering and planting. The house did not have room enough to hold all Geoffrey's books and papers so, with the help of a part-time handyman called Ireland, he constructed what he called the Garden Room, a timber shed, capacious enough to hold hundreds of his mountaineering books, many of the children's toys, a ping-pong table and much else.

The house was called "Birches" and Geoffrey used it in his traditional birthday tribute to Len:

> In this new home of ours
> – fruit of such stern researches! –
> where lighter cleaner hours,
> bird-song and trees,
> bluebell and ferns
> blossom with a new ease,
> let it be said with flowers –
>   "Many the happy returns
>   of this Birthday . . . at Birches!"

They had not been long installed when a fire in the flue ignited the roof of the Garden Room and the whole structure went up in flames. Writing about the fire to Marcia, Geoffrey was concerned that she be stout-hearted at the loss of her favourite toys. But the real tragedy was the loss of his Alpine library and records. It is an indication of the affection and respect in which Geoffrey was held that when news of this got round, the mountaineering fraternity conspired to replace as much as they could of it, as a gift. At the beginning of March 1938 he received a note from Douglas Busk: "God willing and weather permitting Carter Patterson will deliver to you one of these days some books which your friends have presented to replace in some small part your loss . . ." There were almost fifty contributors: many of Geoffrey's younger friends, several Trevelyans, and some old friends like Vincent Baddeley, Professor Pigou and Claude Elliott who was now headmaster of Eton.

Geoffrey was very moved, even more a short time later when Peter Bicknell sent him the copy of Cecil Slingsby's book *Norway: the Northern Playground* that Slingsby had presented, with an inscription, to Edward Whymper. Geoffrey wrote to Bicknell:

> . . . I am extraordinarily touched by your "sending" and letter. Len is the same. It came at a time when one had been ill long enough to begin to feel rather useless, and when most of the bigger interests in the world, human and liberal, were going all wrong. So it was *doubly* delightful and cheering. I've pasted the letter in it. So now it includes you, Whymper, Slingsby and self – enshrined . . .

Geoffrey wrote to Jocelin when he heard his friends were collecting books to present to him: "It has moved me much," he said. "So many young folk now suffer from a sense of despair. No wonder! But the answer is – one's own *dynamic* principle. It's a worthy and tremendous game, this living, and it has to be lived and all one's force put into it. Otherwise, the 'little things' and worries get one under, seriatim."

Jocelin was in his final months at Gordonstoun, Vice-Guardian (deputy head boy) of the school as well as "Helper of Seamanship" and captain of the hockey team. Geoffrey was anxious that he should use his position to contribute to the school life: "You have the will," he wrote, "much of the knowledge needed, and (I know it now, this holidays) the POWER. A forceful personality need not assert itself.

The force is felt . . ." In a later letter he said: "I don't suppose anyone was ever happier, in a serene way, about his infants, than I am – and not because I'm blinded about them either!"

Towards the close of 1937 Geoffrey had a bad attack of flu that took a long time to clear up. A few months later he was more seriously ill, a weakness in the wall of the stomach, and had an operation. His medical adviser, Egon Plesch, used the opportunity to persuade Geoffrey to give up pipe-smoking. Plesch, a Hungarian Jew, was a brilliant man, an art expert as well as an able doctor, who never charged the Youngs for his professional services. He had been recommended to Geoffrey by Kurt Hahn, who took health matters seriously and knew all the best specialists. In his letters Geoffrey often refers to Plesch as "the Devil" or "satanic" but he meant it jokingly – he had the highest regard for him and from this time onwards he and Len went to him for regular check-ups.

In July 1938, when Geoffrey was recovering, Jack Longland wrote to him:

> . . . it's a miracle that things haven't caught you out before, after more than 20 years of doing what practically nobody else on two legs could have attempted. I used to get worried when I was climbing with you, and wonder how the tremendous strain *could* be kept up with; but I remember how astonishingly quickly you were on top again after the Grépon day, and simply concluded that none of the usual rules applied to GWY!

In that same year Geoffrey made his only speech in the House of Commons, to the committee which was considering the creation of national parks in Britain to give protection to regions of special and vulnerable natural beauty. He spoke quietly and with feeling. His old friend Philip Noel-Baker, a Labour MP, wrote to him: "I hear from all the members who were there that you made a frightfully good speech."

The deteriorating international situation of the later 1930s, as Hitler increased his demands and the western leaders tried desperately to conciliate him and avoid war, filled Geoffrey with dismay and apprehension. He knew Germany far better than most; he was still in close contact with the anti-Nazis there. And he knew a lot of history. He had no doubt where it was all leading.

Shortly after the Munich agreement of September 1938, Geoffrey was at Eton as a guest of Claude Elliott. Another guest was the editor of *The Times*, Geoffrey Dawson, an arch-appeaser, who held forth at length in praise of Prime Minister Neville Chamberlain and his work for "peace in our time". Geoffrey held his tongue while this went on, but as soon as Dawson left the room, stumped angrily across and said: "Terrible! Terrible! To think that man has condemned millions of young European men to die in the next war!"

Britain was bitterly divided over appeasement and Munich, and Geoffrey's side was the minority. His old friend G. M. Trevelyan was strongly pro-Chamberlain, but anxious that disagreement should not damage their friendship: "And never come mischance between us twain," he wrote.

Geoffrey's letters to Jocelin often refer to politics and make it clear that he had scant regard for Britain's leaders. In November 1937 he commented:

> Neville Chamberlain's Guildhall speech was flat as flat. I fear he's no more than a second-rater, and any successor is far to seek. We're weak in statesmen. The three separated parts of the triangle, Italy, Germany and Japan, declare an "ideal past" as a gesture, and we reply by sending nice religious blokes like Halifax to one or t'other to ask, "Now, dears, what is it you *really* want?"

He had little respect for Anthony Eden too: "Eden only gets real when he feels angry about something. Better for his career if life had been a bit harder and made his temper thinner. He's all muffled in heredity and prosperity and even his voice has a curls-and-silk-collar stifle in it."

He wrote to Duff-Cooper after Munich congratulating him on resigning from Chamberlain's government. In September 1939 – after Germany had invaded Poland but before Britain declared war – he wrote to congratulate the Conservative Leo Amery on his famous shout across the floor of the House when the acting leader of the Labour Party, Arthur Greenwood, rose to speak: "Speak for England, Arthur!"

The only statesman who commanded Geoffrey's total admiration in the 1930s was the South African Jan Christiaan Smuts. In 1934 Geoffrey told Jocelin: "Smuts is the only man talking with sense or courage on public affairs." Later he praised him as "Certainly the greatest man of this century".

For all his ill health and forebodings, he contrived to get much pleasure and amusement out of life. They visited Marcia's school, Downe House, for concerts, and wrote conscientiously to both children.

In June 1939 he reported from Gomshall, where he had been gardening and sun-bathing: "A thunderstorm has driven me in, from wiring up the garden against the birds and planting seedlings out. A willow-wren and a tit deliberately came up to the wire and walked through the meshes while I was actually patching up the holes I supposed they were using." Soon after he told Marcia: "At work on the garden . . . Not a rabbit has penetrated the Vauban defence system yet I am ever on the alert, and walk the walls at eve."

He was a pioneer performer on British television: "The television practice went off well," he wrote, "and we have a rehearsal next Wednesday afternoon, the performance in the evening. I am asked to appear in my brown velvet coat! and to wind it all up with dignity. There are five other explorers talking before me."

He went to Oxford and told Marcia: "I had a good time at All Souls', which contains only *very* clever men, who all talk *so* cleverly that they are usually too afraid to be anything but silent if another one of them is there."

"Mother is in joyous form." And again to Marcia: "Glad you can dance outside now. I *did* love dancing! and miss it still!"

Jocelin was in Geneva from January to August 1939, studying French and Music. He took every opportunity to get into the mountains, to his father's delight: "Like to think of you off with a sack, in my old haunts of the Oberland." He was further pleased to hear that Jocelin had climbed the Rothorn: "That was very charming of you – the Rothorn. To take it up, where I left off three years ago, nearly to a day. And one of your 'surprises' that have several times given me thrills of pleasure."

When the war came and Jocelin was called up, his Gordonstoun training left no room for doubt as to which service he would go for. He became a Midshipman in the Royal Navy Volunteer reserve. Geoffrey saw great significance in the date when Jocelin joined the service, October 21:

Trafalgar Day, 1939.
Dear Man,
    Having started life on Agincourt and Balaclava day, you have the satisfaction of correcting the military preponderance, and launching

again on a naval career on the greatest of all naval days. Good omen . . .

War is entirely futile, from our modern view. But it can still act as the friction which produces fine actions and motives. And sea-service is real enough to produce some of the finest . . .

20

The Second World War

FOR THE SECOND WORLD WAR Geoffrey went back to keeping a detailed private diary, the habit he had abandoned at the end of the First World War. It became a massive work, amounting to well over 300,000 words, in single-spaced typing on large sheets. He is frank and honest, and the result is a fascinating portrait of the period and the man. For the first time in his life Geoffrey came close to despair at times. There are outbursts of rage and bitterness and uncharacteristic rancour.

He was in his mid-sixties when the war started. His health was beginning to fail – severe stomach troubles, bronchitis, shooting pains in the non-existent leg and arthritis in the other one. He no longer did his morning ritual of exercises. For a long time he found it hard to walk any distance. Worse than all this, he was a prey to continual anxiety – about the war and his friends, about his immediate family, and especially about Jocelin who was at sea and in danger much of the time. He suffered from sleeplessness, lying awake and going over things in his mind. When he finally slept, there were often bad dreams.

Geoffrey had long been a man of unusual empathy, sensitive to the feelings of others. During the Second World War, however, he raised this quality to an intensity that was remarkable even for him, so much so that it is almost true to say that he experienced the war through Jocelin's experiences of it. In February 1940 he wrote to him: "I suppose I am more in this job with you in imagination than I ever was in another man's doing. The result, I take it, of having for 20 years renounced, or seen I must do without, the *delight* in movement and action . . ." That explanation is only a small part of it. Geoffrey loved his son, as he loved all his immediate family, and was angry that fate had denied Jocelin the chance that had meant so much to him, three years of blossoming and discovery in the relaxed university atmosphere. He did not think Jocelin would survive the war and neither did Len, though it was not until hostilities were over that they confessed this to each other. Jocelin himself did not expect to survive and deliberately, for that reason, kept clear of love affairs. So Geoffrey wrote to his son, every other day and sometimes daily, giving all the news and occasionally advice, putting up a confident, cheerful front. He grew impatient and anxious if the replies did not arrive regularly. And when Jocelin was home on leave he wanted to know everything that had happened, in full detail. He was enormously proud, as well as continuously worried. In September 1940, when Jocelin's sloop *Scarborough* was on convoy duty in the Atlantic, Geoffrey wrote: "I need not tell you of my pride – in your work, and that you have fitted yourself so well for its responsibilities – in your ship, and the steady, dangerous, unnoticed service she is fulfilling . . ."

The Second World War lasted longer than the First and imposed greater dangers and austerities on the people at home. There was much more bombing. There was more civil upheaval, with the movement of refugees and the arrival of foreign servicemen in large numbers. Travel was difficult and uncomfortable. Rationing was severe, embracing food, clothes and petrol. It grew ever harder to get things done. For a long time the news was very disheartening.

In fact, Geoffrey never faltered in his belief that Britain would ultimately prevail, and never doubted that the fight was honourable and worthwhile. His war-time depression sprang partly from his own poor health and constant anxieties, exacerbated by an acute sense that he could do little or nothing to help. In the previous war he had abandoned himself to action, regardless of self and regardless of danger. Now he felt useless, no more than a burden on an over-burdened country. Jocelin was fighting hard throughout. Marcia was eventually to join the WRNS, the women's auxiliary to the Navy. Len hurled herself into the First Aid Nursing Yeomanry and drove ambulances all over England; she worked in a communal kitchen and an American hostel and raised money for many causes. When she was at home she managed the house and knitted relentlessly. In contrast to all this, Geoffrey had to confine himself to growing vegetables and soft fruits, chopping wood, mending clothes, doing the washing and ironing. There were moments when even his exuberant vitality and optimism failed him, and he felt weary. For a long time, except for letters and his diary, he found himself unable to write. On May 23, 1944 he noted: "Georis writes urging me to take up better education of Hitler Youth prisoners with the War Office and the authorities . . .

I believe it is pretty hopeless, with this generation. And I don't really feel I can take up that kind of strenuosity now . . . I have no heart at present."

Fortunately, such moments were rare. He kept his mind active and his ever-widening circle of friendships in good repair. Whenever he could, he sought refreshment of spirit in the hills of Wales and the Lake District and Derbyshire. He held his family together. And he made two characteristic and seminal contributions during the war years. As President of the Alpine Club he took that venerable institution by the scruff of its neck, shook it into reforming activity, and engineered the creation of the British Mountaineering Council, fulfilling an ambition he had conceived some forty years before. And he supported Kurt Hahn in the setting up of a sea school at Aberdovey in North Wales, a venture that was to lead, after the war, to the Outward Bound movement.

When the war broke out Geoffrey and Len were still in the house at Gomshall, near Guildford.

Geoffrey disliked the months of the "phoney war" when the only fighting was at sea, and the Chamberlain government looked as if it would still like to wriggle free of all-out conflict. It came as a relief almost when the German army took Denmark and Norway, Holland and Belgium, and knocked France out of the reckoning in a few astonishing weeks of April and May 1940. Chamberlain was replaced by Churchill, and Geoffrey immediately sensed a transformation in the British spirit. He wrote to Jocelin on May 25:

> There's a great atmosphere of resolution and pulling together every-where. At last we've waked our rulers up, and we're beginning. The truth emerges more and more; this is not the irritating disturbance of a life we felt entitled to pursue on civilised lines (as one was inclined to see it all at first) – but a great upheaval in the world's history . . . At such times the values of life become more clearly defined than ever – freedom or serfdom, of mind and body – and Good or Evil . . .

Time and again, throughout the war, Geoffrey's intelligence combined with his knowledge of human nature and his grasp of the broad lines of European history to enable him to appreciate the true import of events, not unerringly but far more accurately than most. He admired Churchill for his dynamism, his determination, and for the blunt, brave, considered rhetoric of his speeches to Parliament and to the nation.

After the evacuation of the Dunkirk beaches, he wrote in his diary:

"We heard and saw the long lines of trains passing along through here and to the West, one every eight minutes some nights, carrying the rescued soldiers and French . . . Len went down to Guildford and helped give them tea and things all the night . . . Thousands on thousands." A few lines further down, he unburdened his heart:

> The last war one lived through and worked through, and the end came, and one could look back and count the perils and pains, knowing the end of the story. But – to do it all again. And this time not to be able to do anything by work, but to have to wait only . . . And not face danger in one's own person, but now with a thousandfold greater pain, in one's child, and children . . . If I could only know that J would be all well, as I begin to be sure that the country will be all well, I could face it not without serenity. After all, pain and pleasure are much the same to oneself in age. One does not live in oneself any more. But I cannot forgive, I know, any German – ever – the bringing back on me in age the uncertain end not to myself, as before, but now to that which I care for a million times more in life . . .

Later, when London was being bombed nightly, he wrote again about the Germans:

> It is intolerable pain, that one's own short generation should have had twice to go through this shadow of hell, deeper and darker each time – owing to these slave-souled Germans . . . I recollect on the Italian front in the last war being shocked one evening at hearing Irene Noel-Baker sing a German song. The sounds had a bad taste. I got over all that and did 20 years work for their betterment. But never again forgiveness in my lifetime, for those I have known or not known, there. I know them now . . .

For the Italians, who entered the war against us after the fall of France, his contempt was total. In his diary he said: "Somehow the Italian treachery is so doubly revolting, after our historic help to them, and our individual work for them in the last war, that I enjoy their defeats even more than the Hun crushing." When the Italian fleet was smashed at Taranto in November 1940 he wrote to Jocelin: "It's great that the Wops have got this all-round banging. And in port too, and not even in action. I cheered. I have detested their treachery in coming in . . ."

But his fiercest contumely was reserved for the French leaders, who caved in completely and collaborated whole-heartedly with the Germans. In May 1941 he noted: "The dastardly Vichy French intriguing further with Laval and Darlan to betray Syria etc. France will not recover this moral collapse, worse than any Balkan small country, for centuries. And does not deserve to. Their people have put up less after-resistance than even Belgium. Much less than Norway and Holland."

From the start Jocelin had been in the thick of things, on convoy duties to the Mediterranean and across the Atlantic. It was hard, relentless and dangerous work, and Geoffrey was shocked by his son's strained condition when he came home on leave:

October 28, 1940 . . . Turned up taller, thin, and tried by the tinned foods and work. They've had a terrible time. The Hun, Italian and French submarines are all out on that one approach by N. Ireland, and have it all mapped out. They have a new technique too, which is defeating the Asdic and the slower boats like J's *Scarborough*. They lost half their convoy going out, and more coming back . . . Appalling nerve trial. These losses are more than we can meet, and threaten us seriously. I can only trust our emergency genius to find the way once again . . . If it weren't for these few days torn from the shadows, I could wish to fall asleep and not wake again. Not that I have doubts of the issue. But I dread the long agonies to come first.

November 2. The second evening we had the story of the terrible convoy losses, and the effects on the nerves . . . I got him to have his hair "scrimbled" in our family way of soothing, which my mother began. And he at once went quiet. But I think the steam had been blown off first. It had to come out. And how can one reassure in these circumstances?

Sitting on the floor by his father's chair and having his head "scrimbled", or massaged, while they listened to classical music together on the radio or the gramophone, did much to help Jocelin overcome the effects of intensive work and stress.

Another young RNVR officer often visited them on leave, Mark Arnold-Forster, Jocelin's childhood friend whom Geoffrey described as "a second son since Ka died".

When not ambulance driving all over England Len kept herself fully occupied, revising her father's book *Norway: the Northern Playground* for republication. It came out in 1941, prefaced by a brief biography of Cecil Slingsby, written by Geoffrey. He had always loved and admired his father-in-law, both as a man and as an outstanding all-round mountaineer, and now paid tribute to him as "a traditional English Tory with an active interest in politics and education, with a love of mankind and of human society as an unbroken continuity which kept him the most democratic of men in personal intercourse, and with an unfailing power of drawing the best out of the people of all races whom he met, out of children, and out of animals, which perpetually renewed his happy confidence in the world order."

Slingsby had climbed creatively in the Alps and in the British hills but his chief claim to fame was as "the Father of Norwegian mountaineering". It seems strange that Geoffrey never climbed in Norway, but he always said it was a deliberate decision, out of respect for Len – Norway was her territory. So Geoffrey never even visited Scandinavia, and it was left to Len, and later to Jocelin, to keep the Norwegian connection alive and flourishing. Jocelin was there with Len and some of her grandsons, in 1976, for the centenary ascent of Slingsby's peak, Skagastolstind.

Geoffrey was very upset, in March 1941, when vital Slingsby family possessions – papers, letters, photographs, portraits, medals and much else – were lost when a London depository was destroyed by fire in an air raid. He was distressed particularly for Len's sake, because the collection included many mementoes of her beloved brother Laurence, killed in the First World War. Geoffrey had already made sure this could not happen to his valuables, burying them in a deep hole in the garden at Birches. Stray bombs occasionally fell in the Gomshall region and he was taking no chances.

By coincidence, the closing weeks of 1940 brought positions of distinction to Geoffrey and to his dearest old friend. G. M. Trevelyan was installed as Master of Trinity College, Cambridge, and Geoffrey attended the ceremony: "Lunch in hall. I had a seat of honour opposite the new Master . . . George gave me one of his strange, eagle looks of affection across the table." And Geoffrey was elected, at last, to be President of the Alpine Club. The honour was overdue, but also well-timed. The Club was in one of its semi-moribund phases. Geoffrey, in his diary, summed up most of the attending members as "old, stuffy, undistinguished, jealous mostly, factious . . ." There was much he wanted to do with his presidential years and he knew there would be strong opposition, but he also knew he could count on the loyal support of men like Leo Amery, Geoffrey Bartrum, Jack Longland and Claude Elliott. He looked forward to the battle.

Despite the difficulties of transport – petrol was severely rationed and the trains were over-crowded – Len and Geoffrey did a lot of travelling during the war. He was still in demand as a speaker or distinguished guest at climbing club dinners, and he particularly enjoyed visits to the Rucksack Club in Manchester, when he stayed with his old friend Eustace Thomas, a retired engineer. The circle of their acquaintance grew even wider. Freya Stark called when she was in England, and Geoffrey made friends with A. A. Milne. He and Len went regularly to Gordonstoun, which had transferred to Llandinam in Montgomeryshire, soon after the war started. They usually stayed several days and benefited greatly from the physical rest and the mental and spiritual stimulus. Kurt Hahn was as dynamic as ever, and Geoffrey was more than a governor of the school by this time – a revered adviser and father-figure.

They saw a great deal of Geoffrey's elder brother Georis and Helen his wife, whose health was now frail. They were having a struggle to maintain Formosa and finally had to turn part of it into a guest-house. But Georis' maverick mind was still hyper-active and his flow of ideas and theories never failed to entertain and impress Geoffrey. They occasionally saw Hilton too, but relations grew no better between them and this was a source of sorrow to Geoffrey every time he thought about it. In December 1941 Hilton visited them at Gomshall, and Geoffrey wrote in his diary: "Hilton turned up last night . . . He was amusing and gentle, and looked distinguished and well. Of course nothing can now recover the old intimacy, which he destroyed in those painful years; but his affection remains." There are other, more vituperative references to Hilton in the diary. Hilton was a peer in his own right, with a distinguished government job and several directorships in the City. Geoffrey, by contrast, was a poor man, and some of the diary entries make it clear that he sometimes resented the scant rewards he had gained from a life of hard work. But the bitterness sprang from the gulf that Hilton had allowed to grow between them, a gulf made even wider by Hilton's material success. Geoffrey's job at London University came to an end, after ten years, in the summer of 1941. He had known this blow was coming. On April 22 he noted:

> I have just been with Carson Roberts and learned that we shall now have to live on between £550 and £750, with luck, a year, after taxation and end of my job. Means no servant and other stiff changes. Fate has been hard – after 45 years of work for public ends in various forms I had looked for a rest time at least when I retired. And we shall be much where I was when I started, with the family now still to carry, and no chance of employment . . . Len taking the situation as one would expect. Full of plans and counsel.

For all his regrets, he knew that his course of life had been of his own choosing: "Life not only starts unevenly, it plays itself out very unevenly, as between brothers, in the degrees of pain to be endured and profit to be enjoyed. And yet I have had a quality of happiness given to few, and have never been misled as to real values."

In June 1941 he had to go into hospital for another operation. The weaknesses in his stomach wall were still causing problems, probably aggravated by over-exertion in the garden. Plesch told him to take things more carefully in future.

One of the hospital's findings amused him: "Cassidy diverted me by asking what was that 'metal' I had under my right shoulder . . . Then I remembered that besides the shell fragment that is still buried in my left thigh, there had been another which had penetrated my right side at the back. This must now have wandered up, high under the right clavicle! They may give bother, if I am cremated!"

When the Germans attacked Russia, he had no doubts about its military significance: "I'm amused at our characteristic British insistence that Russia makes no difference at all! Whatever happens there, it means immense consumption of men and materials for Hitler, and less to meet our growing strength." He also saw that it was only a matter of time before the Americans joined in: "The USA is in effect in the war now. It makes the future certain. It has been slow once again; but then so were we at the start." He admired President Roosevelt's statesmanship and his skilful management of American public opinion.

At the beginning of 1942 they left Gomshall. The lease was up and they could not afford to renew it. Len found them rooms at 5B, Chaucer Road, Cambridge. There was less space for them there and much less scope for Geoffrey's gardening, and the damp Cambridge climate did not suit them, but they were closer to Marcia's boarding school and had scores of old friends in the university. George Trevelyan welcomed them and within weeks had arranged for the Council of Trinity to offer Geoffrey dining rights in the college and "the use of the Parlour". Geoffrey took full advantage of these privileges, enjoying the conversation of such eminences as the philosophers Bertrand Russell and G. E. Moore, scientists like Sir Arthur Eddington, and many old friends including Professor Pigou, Maynard Keynes and Lord Adrian.

He continued to keep a close eye on the Donald Robertson Fund that he had set up before the First World War: "A relief to read the reports from the Donald Robertson boys, on their holidays. That was one of the things that were worth-while having started, that

Fund. The surprised joy of these young folk in their first discovery
of big nature and open air living . . ."

By this time Jocelin had a command of his own, a small, fast,
heavily armed motor gunboat that was chiefly used to stop German
ships passing through the Channel. He loved being in charge and
exercising his skills in seamanship and navigation, and learning the
skills of man-management. He described it as "the picked job of the
war, because it is the only one in which you are always on the attack".
But it was very testing. They were at sea for hours on end, six nights
out of seven some weeks, in danger and darkness and all weathers.
Living conditions were cramped and the food was often poor, so
that when Jocelin came home on leave he was suffering acutely from
boils as well as the accumulated tension. Geoffrey was proud of his
son but increasingly anxious for him, and – when he thought about
it – furious that so many of Jocelin's contemporaries had been found
safe berths. In October 1942 he wrote in the diary: "The majority
of my kinsmen's and friends' sons are now safely pocketed in the
Ministry of Information and other survival holes." He fulminated
against "such upper-class escapers, of whom the government offices
are full", and remarked: "Those of us who hang on year after year
for the agony of that 'phone call that shall end real life for us, may be
forgiven for a little grudge of the inequality with which the danger
is being shared even among our kin and friends."

Geoffrey was happiest on the rare occasions when the whole
family was reunited. Once when Jocelin was on leave they went
to see Marcia dance in a school performance of a Greek play –
"looking extraordinarily lovely and with an entirely unusual beauty
and rhythm of movement. It caught me in the throat to see, and
then to know that by a miracle Jocelin was there too . . . Len and
I need never exchange words, a look is enough in matters of art."
On another occasion, having watched Marcia dancing, he noted: "I
think movement and in rhythm the loveliest thing in the world and
the nearest to the heart of life."

The family were together again in May 1943, at Weymouth where
Jocelin was based. Geoffrey and Len and Marcia spent several sunny
days looking over his ship, ML 24, and getting to know his crew and
his friends. They saw them sail out one evening for night exercises,
and Geoffrey was deeply impressed:

> . . . a grey-silver camouflaged ML with J of course invisible up on the
> bridge and a small army of men lining the sides . . . They moved out

quietly, a lovely sight, and gathering pace, and making always a deeper roar of engines . . . So amazing to think it was our small picturesque Jocelin who was in control of it all, and that it was war . . . I shall never forget the gleam of evening light on the slim lines and grey-silver ship . . . Quite late, we saw them return, all dark then on darker waters, and the moon almost full above. And seeing the ship disappear behind the mole and move down to its berth, I could sleep easy once again, with Marcia with us under a roof, and J known safe just over there . . .

The experience moved him to write a short poem "Small Craft" in praise of these ships and their work. It is not, to my mind, one of his better works, but it had a considerable success at the time, probably because it reflected the spirit of the nation.

Next month Geoffrey and Len were in Wales for another nautical occasion. Geoffrey prepared for it with care: "Measured for grey cord trousers; my first purchase of clothes in four years, I think." They went to attend the ceremonial christening of a ketch that Kurt Hahn had acquired to start an Outward Bound sea-school at Aberdovey. Its name was to be *Garibaldi*, so G. M. Trevelyan was invited to perform the ceremony.

It was Trevelyan's first encounter with Hahn and he was highly impressed. Taking Geoffrey to one side on the first evening there, he pronounded his verdict: "A *very* big mind. If it ever gets carried away, it won't be on personal grounds."

The ketch was a present from the shipping line Alfred Holt and Co. Hahn had been casting round for some way of resuming the Gordonstoun tradition of sea training. He came across Lawrence Holt, a director of the company, who had been concerned since the start of the war by the terrible losses suffered by merchant seamen, forced to take to small boats after being torpedoed. He believed that small boat training would reduce such losses considerably. Both were men of action, and before long trials were conducted that led to the creation of the Aberdovey Sea-School and the beginning of the Outward Bound movement.

The ceremony took place on June 26, 1943. Mr Holt presided; Trevelyan made the christening speech; and Geoffrey brought the proceedings to an end with a short, more-or-less impromptu statement of faith, which went down so well he had to write it out, as best he could recall it, for publication later. It included this paragraph:

To realise his better self everyone must pass in youth through some test of adventure and hardship and the adventure must be real; a conflict with the natural environment and yet it must be adjustable, so as not to overtax adolescence. The forces of nature alone provide these natural adventures and tests of personality: the winds, the roughened surface of the sea, and the rough hill surface of the land.

Although he was no longer able to do much in the way of active mountaineering Geoffrey's interest in the sport, and his concern for its well-being, remained undiminished. He kept contact with old climbing friends and disciples, and was still making new ones. He was a pioneer protagonist of the idea that training in the mountains would do much to improve the fitness and endurance and alertness of Britain's soldiers, and that the training should begin before conscription. He wrote a letter to *The Times* about this, presaging the Commando idea. He introduced a young army officer with similar notions, Major John Hunt, to Kurt Hahn. In January 1942 Hahn wrote to Geoffrey: "I regard the meeting which you brought about between Major Hunt and myself as possibly fraught with important consequences. I have never met anybody inside or outside the Services with whom I am in such complete agreement on the basic soldierly virtues and the methods of training them." This led to the organising of a "Toughening Course" for the 20th Armoured Brigade, held over two weeks in May at Helyg in North Wales. John Hunt wrote to Geoffrey from there:

> I wish you could come up and see me at work (or play) here. Wilfrid [Noyce] tells me that you know of the course and its ideas and that you approve. It is the thing I have dreamt of doing for ages. There are 20 students, of all ranks from private to major, and four permanent instructors – Wilf and Alf Bridge are helpers . . . They are finding out their own capabilities, winning battles over their own fears and prejudices, and gaining immense self-confidence . . .

Shortly before he was made President of the Alpine Club, Geoffrey read a paper there which he called *Should the Mountain be brought to Mahomet?* It was published in the 1940 *Alpine Journal*. It outlined his views on what had happened to mountaineering in the inter-war years.

He began by acknowledging that there had always been an element of competition, even of what he called "stunting", in the sport, especially in rock climbing. Unfortunately, he went on to argue, that element was now threatening to take over completely, especially in the Alps. Climbers were being encouraged to risk their lives for all the wrong reasons – for national or ideological aggrandizement, for publicity, public acclaim, medals and money. To Geoffrey's way of thinking, this approach denied everything that was precious about the sport – respect for the mountain, love of adventure and exploration, the fostering of skills and self-control and comradeship, mountaineering as a spiritual as well as a physical experience, a way of escaping, not promoting, the self. "There is a way of pursuing an activity," he said:

> in which our aim is to assert ourselves, our own superiority, to subdue, to smash anything that opposes us into submission. And there is another way of activity in which, whether it be our object or not, we find that we ourselves become submerged. We lose ourselves in our interest, in our pursuit. We earn our reward in this very absorption: it is the transfiguration which attends the practice of all the creative arts.

For Geoffrey, mountaineering was about pleasure, not profit of some sort. Climbing was not a question of crude conquest. What mattered above all else was the spirit in which it was done, and the style. For the same reasons, he disliked the growing emphasis on equipment and techniques and categorisation. He derided in verse the

> . . . Long grey valleys of technique
> Where the dry bones of dead sport await us,
> Graphs, formulae and apparatus.

It would be wrong to deduce from all this that Geoffrey was on the side of the Alpine Club reactionaries, the élitist and blinkered old men who automatically opposed all change. Geoffrey's reformist instincts remained strong, and, with the Club presidency his for four years, he set himself two main targets. The first was to liven the Club up, to make it generally more friendly and interesting and cheerful, and this he achieved by sheer force of his personality. His second aim was more complex, calling on all his powers of persuasion and diplomacy.

More than forty years earlier he had felt that there should be a single central body to speak for the interests of the whole of British mountaineering. He still believed that, and now he was in a position where it might be achieved. He liked the regional climbing clubs and was a long-term member of some of them – the Climbers' Club, the Rucksack Club of Manchester, the Yorkshire Ramblers'. But he thought that some national body, with representatives from all these clubs and able to speak for all of them, would give them a far stronger voice on such issues as safety, training, environmental threats, the National Parks idea and so on, than they could ever hope to exert in their disparate and sometimes divided state.

His first, urgent job as President was to get the Club's valuables – pictures and books – to safety, for the Alpine Club then was in South Audley Street and it was obvious to all that London would soon be heavily bombed. He supervised distribution to various safer venues. He also inaugurated a system of lunch-time meetings, sociable occasions with women guests and brief speeches, followed by the committee meetings. The first of these took place on February 25, 1941 and, according to Geoffrey's diary, was a success: "Great fun! I made an elegant speech . . . Got the whole room going sociably, and with some uplift about the future. Lots of old friends, all very congratulatory. Then got through some complications at committee meeting. Ran it rather well . . . On the whole a great success, and justified my policy in pre-arrangements." Geoffrey had faith in the careful planning of such occasions.

On July 1 he recorded: "Kept the AC folk bright and sociable. The committee is now pleasantly informal and we get things done. They all pressed me much to undertake to write the History of the AC, equivalent to a history of mountaineering. But I shan't. I know myself well enough to know I should never now carry it through, with all its research and boil-down."

This was shrewd self-assessment on Geoffrey's part. His gifts as a writer were for personal, impressionistic and psychological narrative, not for history with its demands for facts and dates and strict accuracy. The job was entrusted to Arnold Lunn and the result – *A Century of Mountaineering: 1857–1957* – justified the choice.

Now began the long process of preparing the ground for his revolutionary proposals. It is hard now to envisage the enormity of the task Geoffrey set himself, but in the years between the wars the Alpine Club, the oldest climbing club in the world and the largest in Britain, had declined into a stuffy, snobbish, backward-looking institution. Its dominant figure was Colonel E. L. Strutt, a member of the 1922 Everest expedition, later President of the Club and for many years the autocratic and powerfully outspoken editor of the *Alpine Journal*. His views were rigid and intolerant. The only decent and honourable way to climb was the way in which he had climbed as a young man. Crampons were inadmissible; pitons anathema. He had no regard for rock climbing on the hills of Britain. It was the Alpine Club and its chief interest had to be the Alps, although he was prepared to take account of Alpine-type mountaineering in even higher ranges, so long as it was properly conducted. There were many members who agreed with the Strutt attitudes, especially among the Scots – men like W. N. Ling and Graham Brown, notable for his cantankerous ways and his unforgiving feud against Frank Smythe about some dispute that had arisen in the 1920s when they were opening up the Brenva Face of Mont Blanc.

Geoffrey had the measure of the opposition forces though, and he also knew he had many loyal supporters. He liked politicking, exercising his powers of persuasion and manoeuvre. He got John Clapham, a good friend and President of the Royal Academy, made a Vice-President of the Club. In September 1943 he succeeded in getting another old friend Leo Amery, now Secretary of State for India in Mr Churchill's government, nominated to be the next President. By November he could note in his diary: "All my schemes working up well." His triumph came soon after.

He recorded his success in his diary for December 7, 1943:

Tuesday was, I think, in some ways one of the great days of my life. I had the sense, late in the evening, that everything had worked together for the last days and hours, to weave into a sudden bright pattern the two main lines, education and mountaineering, which I had been following separately for some 45 and 55 years respectively. So complete was the control I felt of the difficult committee management at my last sitting, the ability to stop men saying what I didn't want, and get what I wanted said, and later so perfect was my confidence when I got on my feet to speak more or less impromptu at the dinner, of being able to say what I wanted and throw the laugh or the voice about at command, that for a moment or two late at night, I wondered whether I might not, had I been on the regular lines of life to perfect these arts earlier, have filled a far more prominent position. Clearly the gifts and the ability to use them, to think constructively and to speak and write, might have been more fruitfully used . . . But then again I never had the memory or the exam faculty to secure the openings and the regular runs-up; and I might well have failed in the subordinate middle years of careers, though I had the gifts to manage things well once at the top. It is probably best that I should have followed the irregular lines, and have had these moments of realisation at the close . . . Anyway, for some hours I enjoyed what is called the "intoxication of success and power" . . .

The old guard did not go down without a fight. Obscure points of procedure were raised. "So I offered", Geoffrey says, "to make a statement to quiet the old fussers. I never felt so completely in control, and swung them as I liked."

The committee meeting was followed by a general meeting, attended by more than 100 members, and Geoffrey, riding high and confident, outlined his hopes for the future and the formation of a new body that would be able to speak and work for the whole British climbing community. When he concluded, there were a few seconds of silence, then a roar of applause.

Later, Geoffrey and his closest supporters – Bartrum, Marcus Heywood, Eustace Thomas – went to Browns to share their jubilation with Len and Kurt Hahn, "whose ideas", Geoffrey said, "have contributed so much to my putting these lines together late in life, and arriving at such a moment of fulfilment".

His great aim had been realised. The Alpine Club had finally "accepted the principle that it had a responsibility to mountaineering in general". And he had brought this about, he claimed, "without any sacrifice of the friendly and social atmosphere, which has historically distinguished our company". This was being generous in victory, for it was his own genial spirit, more than anything else, that had restored the "friendly and social atmosphere". Eric Shipton, now the British Consul in Kashgar, wrote to him: "It is good to know that in spite of the war the AC is being rejuvenated." Another of Geoffrey's ambitions – that of "bringing mountain climbing into the education and training of our future generations" – was also coming good. Before long many of his friends were running mountain courses in Scotland and Wales for army cadets and boys from public schools.

A few days after his triumphant day, Geoffrey sent a full account to Jocelin, concluding: "I have a queer feeling of in some sort having reached a culmination – rather pleasantly."

In other aspects of his life, things were looking up for him at this time. He received £100 advance to revise *Mountain Craft* for a fifth edition, which came out in 1946 and Eyre and Spottiswood offered an advance of £400 for a mountain autobiography, which was finally published in 1951 as *Mountains with a Difference*.

In April 1944 he and Len enjoyed a nine-day holiday in North Wales. They went back to Pen-y-Pass, where they were rapturously welcomed after a three-year absence. Geoffrey resumed hill walking: ". . . first walk more than half a mile for several years! but it went well." He wrote in the diary:

I had not expected to be able to walk, after these years of semi-invalidism. But all went splendidly, in that fine air. The last day we went up to Lake, and scrambled up the slabs and bluffs to the high Pyg Track, and so home over the little tops, seeing the last cloud clear off the summit, for luck, just before we were out of sight . . . My peg-leg worked all right, but needs a new sole to the disk foot. No such work is now doable anywhere . . . Len looked herself and gay up there, for the first time for long . . . She swung along, Slingsby-fashion, over the slopes and rocks, in slim, elegant, blue-cord breeks, that made her look like a graceful boy.

Close by, a mountain training course was in full swing, primarily for army cadets but also including some public school boys. Geoffrey was impressed how well they got on together, and delighted to find many of his former protégés working as instructors – Geoffrey Bartrum, Claude Elliott, Jack Longland and Peter Bicknell, Alan Hargreaves and Alf Bridge.

By this time Marcia had left school and joined the WRNS. Len's nephew, Laurence Slingsby, was with the British army in Italy. Jocelin, still commanding His Majesty's Motor Launch 245, was training hard for a vanguard role in the coming invasion of the European mainland. It would be his job to lead in the first wave of assault troops of the 50th Northumbrian Division on to the Gold beaches east of Arromanches, at H Hour on D Day, and then to remain off the French coast, supporting the invasion in every way possible, for more than three weeks.

Throughout this period Geoffrey and Len lived in fearful apprehension. "I have spasms of terror", he noted, "of the invasion and J. It would mean the end of life, and yet I should have to go on living, and not escape quickly because of L and M. It's so close, and the fear grows, as it becomes more and more evident that it will have to be an open invasion."

A few days after this entry, he wrote: "Len much over-done again. Indeed, it is very hard work for us, these weeks of waiting anxiety."

When the day came, June 6, there was a continuous roar of allied planes in the sky over Cambridge, heading for France. For days there was no word from Jocelin. When a letter arrived, it was dated June 2. Finally came a postcard, dated the 10th, to say that Jocelin was exhausted but otherwise all right: "June 13 . . . Well, he's been on one of the great doings of history, and he fitted himself for it as few men have the chance or the will to do . . . Our son . . ."

Geoffrey relished the sense of living through great historical moments. When Jocelin was next home on leave he wanted to hear everything that had occurred, during and before the invasion. Everyone had predicted high casualties, especially among the vanguard ships, but they were surprisingly light. Geoffrey was relieved at this, but he was soon enraged by the consistent overlooking of all Jocelin's claims to recognition or promotion. He put it down, perhaps rightly, to the traditional prejudices and jealousies of Royal Navy men when dealing with the RNVR.

He continued to follow the progress of the war closely, and comment perceptively. When Singapore fell to the Japanese, for example, seen by many as the nadir of our fortunes, he remarked in a letter to Jocelin: "However, in the troughs one must stand on one's toes and see over the next crest. And what we are suffering from is the lesser evil, the non-development to the full of the powers which we possess. The enemy has a worse ill to face, the consumption of his maximum forces proceeding. And in the end it is the will power in the man which decides, and not the machines."

His chief pastime was reading. In the evenings at home he and Len would listen to concerts on the radio, and sometimes to variety programmes; Geoffrey's favourite was the popular child impersonator, Harry Hemsley. But reading was the great thing, sometimes for entertainment – P. G. Wodehouse, Arthur Ransome, Sassoon's *The Weald of Youth* – but more often to extend his knowledge of English history. He loved Pepys' diaries – "he's a joy all through," he commented. He liked Keats' letters enormously as well, and read extensively in memoirs and biographies. A life of Nelson prompted the remark: "The man was a human hero because he was nobly lovable, in his love for others and for the splendour of the spirit allowed to man." He was enthralled by Richard Hillary's *The Last Enemy*, published in 1942 and read through his own Ypres Diary, exclaiming in his current diary: "What a dashed effective fellow one *was*!" He also read Churchill's monumental *Life of Marlborough*.

Winston Churchill fascinated him. He deplored the way he retained stodgy old colleagues in his government, and in the latter part of the war he regretted that Churchill seemed so little interested in planning for post-war reconstruction. But he had nothing but admiration for the old man's tireless dynamism and drive, and for his mastery of language. After the call to America in February 1941 – "Give us the tools and we will finish the job" – Geoffrey said in his diary: "It was like hearing the voice of history detonating from the clouds."

He knew several men who were close to the centre of power. Marcus Heywood was back in the army, in charge of the Prime

Minister's security on journeys. Leo Amery was in the government. So Geoffrey soon heard all the Churchill stories circulating, and delightedly recorded the bons mots in his diary and passed them on to Jocelin.

Early in the war, commenting on the calibre of his European allies' leaders, Churchill said. "There must be some quantity of awful bitches in Europe, to have produced such a progeny."

When France was collapsing and Churchill flew to Tours with four companions to try to persuade the French leaders to fight on, after enduring hours of prevarication and defeatist pessimism, he broke through with his famously un-French accent, "*Eh bien, nous voulons manger et nous allons manger.*" And on the plane home: "Finish of Act One! And I must say I look forward, with considerable zest, to Act Two!"

Later, briefing General Catroux for a mission to Algiers to settle a row between Giraud and De Gaulle, and satisfied that Catroux had got the point, he said: "*Je vois, mon General, que vous avez les racines de la matière dans vous*", while a bewildered Catroux looked down at his plate to see what he was eating.

There were many De Gaulle quips, in various versions. One close to home for Churchill was: "Son Randolf is only a lesser cross to bear than the Cross of Lorraine." And to De Gaulle, in exasperation: "*Si vous continuez m'obstructer, je vous liquidaterai!*"

On his return from the Casablanca conference with Roosevelt in January 1943, Churchill clambered off the plane, contemplating the coming session in the House of Commons: "And now for a bloody old row!"

Geoffrey had scant respect for Anthony Eden, usually dismissing him as "a second-rater" and once as "a weeping waistband". He was amused to hear Churchill's description of a long Eden memorandum: "It contains all the clichés I know except 'God will provide' and 'Please adjust your dress before leaving'."

Leo Amery told Geoffrey that he asked to be allowed to accompany Stafford Cripps on his mission to India in 1942, but was refused with the words: "No, Leo, you'd be climbing the Himalaya and falling off."

The Polish general, Sikorski, asked Churchill what he really thought of the Russians. The reply was, "A baboon is all right in its wilds or in a cage; but I can see one would hate having it among one's family and children." Field-Marshal Montgomery did not fare much better: "In battle indomitable: in the after-success, insufferable."

By mid-1944 the war news, on all fronts, was good, but Geoffrey was shattered by the news from inside Germany. The bomb plot against Hitler failed, and was followed by the rapid rounding-up and brutal slaughter of thousands known to be critical of Hitler's leadership. These included Geoffrey's friends and fellow-conspirators of the 1930s – von Haeften and Karl Goerdeler.

In October that year Len and Geoffrey left Cambridge and went to live at 12, Holland Street, Kensington, the little Georgian town house that his parents had acquired in the First World War. London was still under attack, now by unmanned rocket bombs, but the move raised both their spirits. Neither had been particularly well in the damp air of Cambridge. Immediately, they felt altogether better. Their neighbours were friendly and helpful, and it was much easier to get to theatres and cinemas and concerts, restaurants and club meetings. Len resumed her old theatrical friendships with Evelyn Laye and Lola Duncan. She and Geoffrey made the most of the fact that they had caught the London theatre in one of its glittering periods. They saw Gielgud's Hamlet, the young Olivier as Richard III and Hotspur, Richardson as Falstaff and Peer Gynt.

Geoffrey's chief energies went into the setting up of what was to become the British Mountaineering Council. It was a complex and lengthy process, and he was greatly helped by John Barford, an accomplished rock climber who became the first Secretary of the BMC. There was still resistance from the old Alpine Club diehards, and some Scottish clubs preferred to go their own way. But Geoffrey's will prevailed.

The crunch came at the Alpine Club in April 1945. Leo Amery was now President but Geoffrey was still on the committee:

> *April 11.* Yesterday, at a special meeting of the AC, my creation of the BMC and our whole policy, which had been challenged desperately and rudely by a small body of old AC high officers – Strutt, Meade, Spencer, Unna, Eaton, and their dead-head and diehard gang – was affirmed by a colossal majority. In a meeting of 100, the largest for many years, men coming from Cornwall and the North and sacrificing days of their short holidays to vote for us. We trounced them by 84 votes to a variously estimated 12 or 14.

Geoffrey had orchestrated the presentation of his case, allotting different points and angles to his more articulate supporters. For once, he did not speak himself. When it was all over he went off quietly with Marcus Heywood to join Len and dine in peaceful luxury at the Coq D'Or in Stratton Street.

The British Mountaineering Council is still going strong, half a century on. When it started there were some thirty affiliated clubs. Today there are more than 200. It has full-time officials and a country-wide network of Area Committees. It tests new equipment, supervises training for mountain leadership, represents the British point of view on international bodies, and fights for the interests of climbing and climbers wherever they seem threatened.

One of its very earliest initiatives was the production of a paperback handbook, designed to assist and encourage all who wanted to take up hill walking or rock climbing in the British hills. It was written by John Barford, with a great deal of editorial help and support from Geoffrey. Its publication by Penguin Books in 1946 under the title *Climbing in Britain* did more than any other single factor to stimulate the sport in the immediate post-war years.

Geoffrey kept assiduously in touch, throughout the war, with mountaineering friends. Shipton wrote regularly from Kashgar and when he returned to England often called for a talk. After one such visit, Geoffrey noted: "He is 35, quiet and remote, but I feel somehow more akin to him, in the great mountaineering sense, than to any other 'modern'." Later, in January 1945, Geoffrey wrote: "Eric Shipton coming to tea. He is, to me, the next to lead in the highest mountain succession." Later still, after a meeting with Tilman, he said: "I find I feel the intuitive sympathy for him that I have otherwise for Shipton alone: he belongs to my order of mountaineer." He kept in regular contact with Menlove Edwards too, but on February 2, 1945 had to record: "The sad news that Menlove Edwards has broken down mentally, completely. The most brilliant of all our rock climbers, a young psychiatrist of great promise, and a writer whose verse was so striking as to persuade me that a new formula was still possible."

The Japanese conquest of South-east Asia caused great concern. Two friends, Spencer Chapman and Scott Russell, disappeared and nothing was heard of them for years. Then, in January 1944, stories about Chapman reached England, and Geoffrey noted: "An amazing bit of news just now. We hear, as a dead secret . . . how Freddie is alive, and at some fierce hush-hush job, probably behind the Jap armies . . . He will have one of the greatest stories of the war to tell afterwards. Just like Freddie!" Chapman told the story, after the war, in his book *The Jungle is Neutral*.

It was not until the end of June 1945 that Geoffrey heard that Scott Russell had survived terrible years in the Japanese prisoner-of-war camp at Changi. Russell was a biologist and had gone to Malaya as a plant physiologist, working on a rubber plantation, then joined the Indian army when the Japanese invaded. He had three and a half years in Changi, surviving because his work on the market garden did much to supplement and improve the meagre rations and proved a great help to the camp hospital.

After the Japanese surrender he led a convoy of trucks to Singapore to get food for the camp, and while there heard that HMS *Sussex*, in the harbour, had declared open-house for British ex-prisoner officers. He availed himself of the chance, then went up to the quarter-deck to thank the captain, and while there was delighted to see Jocelin arriving with a message. There was a joyful reunion, all the more joyful because Jocelin had reserved a case of whisky for Russell on the off-chance that they would bump into each other.

Jocelin, still in command of his motor launch, had been sent to the Far East by way of India, where he played a lot of hockey, and was soon busy impounding ships of the Japanese Navy, then taking Dutch settlers back to the Indonesian islands, then – very soon afterwards – rescuing the Dutch from islanders who felt it was about time they were freed from alien rule.

Geoffrey's war-time diaries are full of reminiscences. He had high respect for anniversaries, each year remembering his mother with love on the day of her birthday, and Frau his old nurse, and his sister Eacy who had died nearly sixty years before. On April 23, 1943 he wrote: "I find time crowding in with memories. This was Zeebrugge day, and the agony about Hilton, the closest thing in the world to me – as he then was!" Perhaps he was already beginning to think about the proposed autobiography, because now and then he composed his memories into passages that are very similar in style and spirit to the pages of *The Grace of Forgetting*.

In the late summer of 1942 he wrote:

Some soft remarks of Marcia's, about the beauty of living in a lovely house like the Curwen Round House on Belle Isle [Windermere], recalled to me how fortunate we were in our generation; and how little we appreciated it as exceptional. In London, the big town house, like Cadogan Square; very early Sutton Croft, the delightful small house at Cookham that Father and Mother designed and built, and enlarged; then the heavenly holidays at Belgard, the Castle of the Pale, with its vast views to the mountains, falling orchards, great lush fruit gardens, lawns, shrubberies, rookeries, and over-luxuriant masses of tumbling roses and creepers, with the background of horses and carriages and donkeys . . .

And then Formosa itself, with great lawns and woods, and the picturesque river and decorative punts and society folk in the great era of the
Thames; and the bathing places and rushing winter weirs and the sound of
them all the night long; and the large weekend parties, and smart clothes
on the high days! I wish we could have given J and M only a year or
two of this. But one must live with one's times, and those are past.

At the beginning of 1945 news had reached Geoffrey "that my
dear Maurice Best, the protégé of 1914, the lifelong friend, of a
gay, devoted loyalty to me, and then to mine, died last June, a few
days before the landings – which he had so passionately desired. Of
meningitis. And their home destroyed by the Hun . . . The lovely,
sensitive small boy, picked up in the Ypres streets wounded, and
one of the first in my wounded ward at the Sacré Cœur . . ."

Later that year he had a happier reminder of that period: "In reply
to a tentative letter, Sœur Marguerite of Ypres, the heroine of the
last war and my dear friend and colleague, has written from Ypres.
Says she had a good war, and seems in great heart. Speaks of being
63. Wonderful and lovely person."

There was bitter tragedy closer to home. In May 1945 John Amery,
son of Leo, was arrested and charged with treason. From childhood
he had been strange and wayward, hard to manage and impossible to
guide. When he went to Spain to fight for Franco, he came to believe
that the only hope for the world was an alliance between Britain and
Germany to smash Russia. He was in France when the Germans took
over, and in 1943 they employed him to go round the prison camps
trying to induce British internees to join an anti-Russian corps. When
he was captured by the allied forces at the end of the war, he wrote
out a full, unashamed account of it all, and when he was charged with
treason at the Central Criminal Court in London he pleaded guilty
to all counts. There was no alternative. He was sentenced to death.

On December 20, 1945 Geoffrey noted: "The last days have been
miserable, with the thought of the Amerys. And now, incredibly,
they have hanged John Amery."

Geoffrey was incensed at the Attlee government that had been
voted into power in that summer's landslide election:

G. M. Trevelyan writes me that he sent a reasoned petition to the Home
Secretary at Leo's request. And I burst out in moral indignation, as
comment in reply. One knows that a Conservative or Liberal Minister
would not have done it, and that it is the moral weakness of the new
men makes them fear criticism of "favouring". As though it turned on

the life, longer or shorter, of the wretched young man, and not on the condemnation for life of one of the country's and Crown's greatest servants – the man who cried "Speak for England!" to Greenwood in the final debate that downed Chamberlain.

In the summer of 1945 Gordonstoun moved back north to the shores of the Moray Firth. Kurt Hahn supervised this and settled them in, then returned to Germany, to see what he could do for those old friends who had survived and to visit Salem. On October 21 Geoffrey wrote to Jocelin: "We lunched with K. H. yesterday, down from north. He has the whole story of the Resistance Movement in Germany, and the July massacre when the Haeftens, Goerdeler etc. were killed . . . There was great heroism, enough to make a corpus of stories round which to build up the new pride . . . He drove through to Salem. All the neighbourhood wept to meet him! Most moving." Geoffrey was also moved to hear that Prince Berthold's first question to Hahn was: "Is Geoffrey still alive?"

Long before he heard all this though, Geoffrey had relaxed his war-time determination never again to forgive the Germans. He was, characteristically, among the very first in Britain to argue that there were good and decent Germans, that the nation was redeemable. On August 2,1945 a letter of his was printed in *The Times*, pointing out that there had been active German resistance to Hitler before and during the war, and insisting that their heroism was "such as could give us assurance of the possibility of a moral regeneration". He outlined the resistance movement, told the story of Kurt Hahn's stand against Hitler in 1932–3 and Prince Berthold's fight to maintain the Hahn spirit even as the war raged. He concluded: "It is only one instance, but there is significance in this struggle for Salem. It demonstrated that a power for moral resistance could be developed under right training, and it suggests how the re-education of Germany should be begun."

21

The Later Years: 1946–55

GEOFFREY STRUCK A FURTHER BLOW for a return to saner attitudes towards Germany by translating several of the poems of Pastor Dietrich Bonhoeffer and getting them published in *Time and Tide*, the *Fortnightly* and the *New English Review*. Bonhoeffer had seen Hitler from the beginning as "anti-Christ". He worked for his downfall and, as a result, spent years in prisons and concentration camps. Through torture and intense privations he kept his faith and sanity and sense of purpose, writing many poems to expound his ideas and encourage his fellow-prisoners. The war was only four weeks from its end when he was murdered by SS men on direct orders from Himmler.

Geoffrey was nearly seventy when the war came to a close, a tired man and not in the best of health, yet the final years of his life saw a remarkable resurgence in his powers of writing. In this period he produced two full-length books, *Mountains with a Difference* which was published in 1951 and *The Grace of Forgetting*, published in 1953. He also wrote a long account of the origins and pioneer days of climbing in Snowdonia, *From Genesis to Numbers*, which formed part of the book *Snowdon Biography* that came out in 1957. In addition, he wrote articles and lectures, and occasional verses, most of them light-hearted. He kept a diary until May 1957 and wrote innumerable letters. One of the diary entries said: "Most of the day goes in correspondence."

His mind was as lively and powerful as ever, and the words poured from him, in writing and in speech, with an increased fluency. In these years he formed the habit, about the time of his birthday, of surveying his condition. On October 24, 1946 he wrote in the diary:

Tomorrow J is 27, and I pass the human limit of 70. Well! Father said, introducing me to speak at Cookham when I was in the late forties, that

I had kept the "heart of a child". Put it that I still have the mind and ways of a young man, early thirties and forties. How does it balance out? On the one hand, my one-legged exploits and wear have left me with a ruptured midriff that reacts upon heart and digestion and will probably shorten life. Again the over-use of the right leg has set up arthritis of the hip, and some evils in the leg muscles . . . I can still get up hills, even if it hurts after . . . On the other side: My eyes are as good as ever, since I was 15. I can read and sew and thread fine needles without glasses, by artificial light. In hills I can still see the long distances I need to catch movement. My hearing also stays as it was. No sign of failure. I still use my own teeth . . . But fancy – 70! And I felt far older when I passed 21!

His appearance was more distinctive and impressive than ever – the strong, leonine head with flowing white hair and bushy white moustache, the sturdy, erect figure in cloak and bow tie, stumping firmly about on the two walking sticks he now needed. He looked what he was, a figure from the distant past. Almost everywhere he went, he was respected as "The Grand Old Man of the Mountains". He was sometimes surprised by the extent of the lionising, but he enjoyed it and did not let it go to his head. In the diary he could, as we have seen, laugh at himself as "an elderly celebrity, second-class". When he heard the word "legendary" used about himself, he passed the news on to Jocelin and added: "Fun, rather, being a Museum Piece."

The children were quickly demobilised. Marcia – a beautiful young woman, surrounded by admirers – went to study at Goldsmiths' College School of Art in London. Jocelin's future was under discussion. He took the Foreign Office examination but failed. There was talk of a job at UNESCO. Finally, towards the end of 1946, he opted for a "business training course" with ICI.

For Len and Geoffrey the great thing was that the family was intact. They had all survived the war and for a brief spell could enjoy each other's company. Geoffrey noted:

We had a great three weeks in August, at the fine house on Belle Island on Windermere. The marvellous Phyllis Edwards, who always turns up better trumps than even she promises(!), took it and asked us to share. And we had a riot of peace, and on the whole good weather in a bad year, and lovely views. And all the northern friends and relations came to call in boats . . . Lovely drive to picnic at Tarn Hows, and again to Seatoller where they have now hung my picture with the two Trevs.

In November they went to Manchester for the dinner of the Rucksack Club, and stayed with Geoffrey's old mountain friend

Eustace Thomas at his home in Cheshire, Brooklands. This trip was to be a regular annual treat for Len and Geoffrey. They both loved Eustace, in his late seventies, and his older brother Bertram, for their courtesy, consideration, North Country wit and sheer *joie de vivre*. The brothers had made a great success of their electrical engineering business in Manchester, Eustace as inventor and designer, Bertram continuing to run the company although he was over eighty and crippled with arthritis. Laurence Slingsby, who had decided to stay in the army, was with them on this trip, and they were all taken out for walks on Kinder Scout:

> We drove out – cars once again now, after the years! – and I scaled Kinder Low once again, up the steep side, Eustace giving me good talk and company . . . In the evening some 40 climbers and wives in. Fine recall of the past . . . Eustace did an amazing pre-war dinner for 12 of us, and every detail savoured of old days. How long can that continue? The delight of getting up a steep hillside again was tremendous, and the views and air re-creating.

It was some time in 1946 that Robert Chew, Geoffrey's Cambridge protégé who had become a housemaster at Gordonstoun and then spent the war years in Scotland, training officer cadets in mountaincraft and fieldcraft, called on Len and Geoffrey at their Holland Street home and introduced them to Eva Mohr, a young Norwegian war widow. At the end of the war Chew had been sent to Bergen to take over from the defeated Germans. There he had met and fallen in love with Eva, just returned from Britain where she had been a WAAF with the Norwegian Air Force. More than forty-six years later, Eva Chew recalled the fateful afternoon in Holland Street: "I was being vetted for marrying Bobby. I had a strong feeling that it was a very important interview. Bobby thought of them as parents – he owed so much to Geoffrey and regarded him as a man of great wisdom. I must have passed the test. It was a very happy interview, and I loved them ever after." She did better than merely pass the test. Jocelin was there and remembers that, when Len took Eva out to the kitchen, Geoffrey stumped across to Robert Chew and said: "If you don't marry that girl, I'll never speak to you again!"

In the early summer of 1947 Len and Geoffrey spent a few days in Cambridge. He presided over the decision-making about who was to get that year's Donald Robertson Trust grants. They saw friends

– G. M. Trevelyan, Professor Pigou, the Adrians – and on June 3 attended a very grand occasion, the Fourth Centenary celebrations of Trinity College, which were also attended by King George VI and Queen Elizabeth. He was impressed by the bearing and the words of the Master, Trevelyan. After the ceremonial formalities, during a tea party on the lawns, Trevelyan asked Geoffrey if he would like to meet the King and he modestly declined on the grounds that he was "no Trinity celebrity". The party was drawing to a close when Trevelyan's wife Janet came over and told Geoffrey that the Queen ·had asked that he should be presented to her:

> It was entirely unexpected. I had turned down the King. But this I could not, of course, and with all the dignified little assembly listening. So up the green glade left free I walked with my two sticks, and white locks a bit disarranged, I fear, by the breeze. The Queen, erect in bluish pearl grey, and the singularly graceful and personal smile, came a pace to meet me; so that we stood alone. I bent over her hand, really – for me – all a shade confused. "You are a great mountaineer", in the pretty soft Scottish tones.

Geoffrey murmured something about organising climbing for the young and they agreed on the beauty of the Queen's native Lanarkshire hills. Afterwards he admits "Yes, I was gravely pleased", and goes on to reflect:

> I remember often, when a young man, thinking that our father and mother knew everyone of interest in the country, and how insignificant we were in comparison. Now – old too, I suppose – I find that with few claims of intellect or position gained, the "great" are extraordinarily nice to me, and make a fuss of my rare appearances. If anyone in the next generation ever reads this, let them note this: it will be the same with them in their turn! And wherever I have got, it has not been by brains or character. It has been because I loved human beings, and was consistently kind and good-mannered to them – because they all interested me. A good manner wins the world!

Geoffrey was at Gordonstoun in July 1947 when it was announced that the heir to the throne Princess Elizabeth had become engaged to Prince Philip. The school was immediately inundated with reporters, and Kurt Hahn said jubilantly that this would put them on the social map as nothing else could have done. In his diary – though nowhere else – Geoffrey recalled that it was he who had advised Philip's family that Gordonstoun was the place if he wanted to be prepared for a naval career, and he, too, who had put the boy on the plane for England and Gordonstoun: "I recall him as the rough, blond-haired, handsome small boy who dashed into my bedroom at Constance, already dressed at 6 a.m. in sheer excitement at his coming first air-flight. And leaving his passport on the breakfast table in the flurry to get off."

One of the things old people have to accustom themselves to is hearing of the death of friends. More than most folk, for most of his adult life, Geoffrey had suffered bereavement, though he never learned to take it coolly. At the age of seventy and beyond, it was to be expected that a man with such a vast circle of friends and acquaintances should receive sad news frequently. At the end of 1946 Georis's wife Helen died after a long sickness. Six months later Hilton's wife Kathleen died, and was given a generous obituary notice in Geoffrey's diary: "She was a remarkable and fascinating woman and artist, a notable personality in her era. And she did not know what she did when she stole Hilton out of my life, and he ceased not only to be my twin soul but even my brother . . ."

Another, unexpected death was a great shock to Geoffrey, that of John Barford, killed by an avalanche in the Dauphiné Alps in August 1947. They had worked closely together for ten years, creating and organising the British Mountaineering Council. Geoffrey had been looking to Barford, with confidence, to guide the Council through its formative years. He was devastated. But worse was to follow.

Len and Geoffrey were in the North again for the Rucksack Club dinner and staying with Eustace Thomas, where Jocelin joined them. On Len's insistence, Jocelin waited until the festivities were over and then, getting his father alone, broke the news that Marcus Heywood had collapsed and died in London.

They had been friends for almost half a century, ever since Heywood appeared as one of Geoffrey's brighter pupils at Eton. They had climbed together in Wales and the Alps, encountered each other at Ypres and on the Italian front in the First World War, been together on Geoffrey's last Alpine climb on the Rothorn, and enjoyed each other's company and companionship as often as possible. It was an unclouded friendship, almost Geoffrey's oldest and probably his deepest. He wrote a moving obituary for the *Alpine Journal*, but kept his warmest feeling to the pages of his diary. At first he could not believe Marcus was dead:

Incredible. He was more radiantly alive, even with whitening hair, than any man I've ever known . . . Indeed, I think there are very few of

the breed. Great gentleman, fine soldier, sportsman, combined with
desperately hard worker, with a high conscience and an innate purity
and open-airness. His superb vitality drove through all life with a gay
chuckle, but with immense vigour and effectiveness, and an almost royal
ease and unconcern . . . No, I have never known a greater "gentleman"
of the disappearing type. Of such dignity that it is never displayed. It is
incredible that he should not be there, at the edge of the purple moorland
of Simonside, or following a hundred active country pursuits with a
steely arm and fine taste, and a curious nobility of look and talk and
conduct.

For weeks and months afterwards, as the diary reveals, he found
himself thinking of Marcus and mourning his death.

It helped that both Len and Geoffrey kept themselves fully
occupied. She ran the household, did some lecturing on the Brontë
sisters, and assembled a little anthology called *In Praise of Mountains*
for the publishers, Frederick Muller. Geoffrey, while continuing to
work on his new book, revised *Mountain Craft* and *On High Hills* for
new editions, wrote regular diary pieces for *Time and Tide*, travelled
the country to give talks and lectures, presided over management
meetings for Gordonstoun and the Outward Bound, and kept up
his vast correspondence. In February 1948 he was a platform speaker
– along with Chuter Ede, the Home Secretary, Lord Samuel of the
Liberal Party and the spokesman for England's hill walkers, Tom
Stephenson – at a public meeting in the Kingsway Hall to promote
the idea of national parks in England and Wales.

Among his favourite and most enduring forms of relaxation were
the dinners of the Omar Khayyam Club, of which he had been a
member since the early 1930s. It was a light-hearted gathering of
accomplished writers and artists and friends, and Geoffrey sometimes
composed verses, in the style of FitzGerald's translation of the *Rubaiyat*,
to decorate the menu alongside illustrations by the cartoonist
David Low. Writing to Jocelin in November 1949, Geoffrey
said: "Omar Khayyam Dinner, with All-Star Cast – my poem
and David Low's drawing. I had Claude Elliott and Siegfried
Sassoon at dinner, with Herbert Samuel, Sir James Grigg, Walter
Hamilton, Fougasse, Clement Davies etc. as relief. Sassoon quite
charming and we had good talk."

Good talk – serious but not solemn, spiced with wit – was always
a delight. He could talk openly and frankly to the family, to Len and
both the children, and he vastly enjoyed the occasions, not frequent
enough, when he could settle down to an evening of friendly,

wide-ranging, ruminative conversation with friends. In April 1948 he wrote to Jocelin:

> Last night at the Amerys the four of us got into real conversation again, about books and Homer and Europe and such, and I realised that I practically never get that now, which used to be the regular part of life. Conversation being the kind of talk that *grows*, out of itself and between a company, and is a product, like a picture or music. It takes equal wits and training to produce it, and must be treated as one of the arts.

In the spring of 1948 Jocelin resigned from ICI, which had proved a great disappointment, and soon after – at the prompting of Kurt Hahn – went to Greece to work as tutor to the Crown Prince and to found a sister-school to Gordonstoun. Once again, as in the war, the letters began to flow between father and son on an almost daily basis. Geoffrey's were full of advice and interest in this new venture. He urged Jocelin to learn modern Greek, warned him about the Greek love of intrigue, and worried about the possibility of a Communist take-over in Athens.

It was at this time, too, that Marcia became engaged to a young man who had been in the Rifle Brigade and was now beginning a career in publishing, Peter Newbolt, a grandson of the poet Sir Henry Newbolt of *Drake's Drum* fame. Peter Newbolt vividly remembers his first meetings with Marcia's parents:

> Her mother took me to the Café Royal for lunch. She was in her usual form, asking questions and not giving you a chance to answer. But it went off quite well, I thought, and then I had to go to Holland Street to meet her father. I knew something of him, his mountaineering and writing. I went in expecting a sort of interview but it wasn't like that at all. He just casually said "Well, when are you going to get married?", and I suppose I said we'd no house and little money – I was earning £6 a week – and he said "I don't think there need be any difficulty. I don't believe in long engagements. We're going to move out of this house anyway." Which is what happened. They moved out and left a lot of furniture and paid most of the rent for us for the first year or two. He was a wonderful father-in-law. My own father was conservative and conventional, very concerned with what was done and what was not done. It was enormously refreshing and exciting to find someone who was much older than my father but much younger in his attitudes, more open, with no conventional fixed attitudes.

Peter Newbolt was, as many others had been, bowled over by Geoffrey: "He had a wonderful presence, this great charm – there's no English word that describes it fully – something that very few people have that makes you feel there's something very special about them. He was always the most easy person to be with."

And Geoffrey liked Newbolt from the start, feeling sure he would make a good, capable and caring husband for Marcia. Just before the wedding he noted: "What a change now: to feel *happy*, about the children and ourselves, as we look ahead."

The wedding took place in the garden of Lord Adrian's house in Cambridge in July. Jocelin was there from Greece, and Laurence Slingsby, on leave from a Staff College course. Geoffrey gave the bride away, and wrote a romantic description of the day in his diary, ending: "I have never known such a lovely wedding, or one that had the same natural and charming gravity, with its gaiety."

Len and Geoffrey went on to Pen-y-Pass: "Five full and happy days, gossiping with Owen and Miss Jones, and finding the company pleasant, with the usual 'fans'. Walked gently, neither very fit or fresh."

Then Geoffrey went to Gordonstoun, staying with Robert and Eva Chew and meeting, after ten years of separation, Prince Berthold of Baden, whose son was now at the school. He was astonished how smoothly he and Berthold resumed their war-interrupted talk as if there had been no break at all.

Then he headed south to rejoin Len at Carlisle. Her old friend Phyllis Edwards had prepared a place for them to live, for as long as they wanted, at her home, Wooden Walls, in nearby Brisco. Geoffrey was ecstatic about it: "Ideal. A garden in chaos after the war. But views three ways to hills. And quiet. And sleep. And no worry or haste for Len. And friendly, if placid folk. And no queues! And no ill manners such as are now universal in south towns, after war-nerve wear. I literally *fell* back into country garb and open shirt. Began laying out the garden at once."

It was the beginning of a long period when they lived in the far north of England, near Carlisle and then on the other side of the country, at Cambo in Northumberland. The north was Len's homeland and they both liked the direct North-Country manner. But there were serious drawbacks. The heavy rainfall and the cold winters were not good for their ailments – her lumbago, his bronchitis and arthritis – and not good, either, for their spirits. They needed help about the house and it was hard to find. And they were a long way from their family and most of their friends. Even so, Geoffrey was full of optimism at first. "I've clipped a hedge," he told Jocelin, "and feel countrified again." He also wrote: "I find I have a good balance at the Bank, owing to our really great economy in living these last years. Len has been amazing. We have been saving, on our few hundreds a year, by sheer doing without."

Before they settled down to life in the north, however, there was a marvellous break for both of them – a return trip to the Alps, all expenses paid. Geoffrey wrote in his diary:

> The Fairy-Story. It may happen in youth; not so often in age. Shut up for some 10 years in the island, on short rations, during a revolution which took away all comfort and much freedom of movement from our class – one has to know all this to understand the amazing skylight that opened for us. I'd given up all idea of travel abroad, or moving there as we had once hoped, in age. Then, through that excellent Charles Gos, a a man entirely unknown even by name to us, and who had only taken up climbing himself late in life, long after I had stopped, wrote an offer.

This was Count Alain de Suzannet of Lausanne, who offered to pay all their travelling and hotel expenses for a month-long trip and sent them 1,000 Swiss francs to cover incidentals. Geoffrey, who had not been to the Alps since 1935, was not too proud to accept.

They flew out to Geneva at the beginning of September, and the Swiss Alpine Club gave a dinner in Geoffrey's honour, with many speeches. Then they progressed triumphantly through Visp and St Niklaus to Zermatt, greeted all the way by old friends. They had been booked into a suite at the Cervin Hotel, with a fine terrace:

> On to it I walked out, and had my first sight of the Matterhorn, high in the evening. Then, alone, I found the reaction almost overpowering; and for a few hours that night I had the storm I had feared, the being among them again after 13 years, and for the first time knowing I might not climb them. After this first evening, it passed completely. I was readjusted, and even to Zermatt where I rarely went to stay . . . We held court. And met many friends, and made many new . . .

Josef Knubel was there, sixty-eight years old but still taking clients along the great ridges, and many photographs had to be taken. They went up to the Gornergrat, where Geoffrey had to be helped because there was hard snow on the path:

> And that view! Never have I seen it so exquisite! The new snow had somehow modelled the slopes and glaciers, in silver and blue, and peak beyond peak stood up in incomparable brilliance and clarity. No, I had no regrets at all. I knew them all. Indeed I had forgotten how well I

knew them all! And last to rise over the lower shoulders, and first to disappear as we came down, was the unrivalled Weisshorn – queen of my heart, now as then.

Then they went to Lausanne, still the guests of the Count, for more parties and receptions. Len added a characteristic footnote to one of Geoffrey's letters: "Darling Jocelin, How often I wish you were here to laugh with us. So much of this life is just too *unreal* and comic for me! Over-fed, over-automobiled, under-exercised. *But so kind!* our friends are!"

Before returning home, they went to southern Germany. They were shocked by what they saw: "Rags and drawn faces, and poverty and depression. Especially the women." But a visit to Salem brought hope: "The charm of these beautiful buildings, these new beginnings, and with these beautiful young folk and their children in charge, was unspeakable . . . It is strange to think that I have seldom spent a happier week, and none certainly since the war, than in that occupied zone and palace. With its lovely season, and young life, and promise for the future – if uncertain, yet radiant."

They were back at Wooden Walls, near Carlisle, before the end of October, but Geoffrey was soon on his travels again. He was in London for a public meeting where Field-Marshal Montgomery launched what he called a National Trust for Youth, a training scheme on Outward Bound lines. G. M. Trevelyan also spoke and astonished Geoffrey by paying tribute to his work to bring education and mountaineering together: "And to my surprise, the whole room clapped and murmured applause. It was so fantastic – to find in age that, without any public recognition or apparent fame for any particular feat, one is a familiar and not unloved name to so many one does not know. I was quite moved."

He went to North Wales for the Climbers' Club dinner and a reunion of climber friends – Longland, Waller, Peter Bicknell, Alf Bridge – at Pen-y-Pass. There was the Rucksack Club dinner in Manchester, then he went back to London to chair a Gordonstoun meeting, and home by way of Eton where he stayed with the Elliotts, and then Cambridge where he stayed with the Adrians and chatted with E. M. Forster.

In the spring of 1949 he was at Wallington, the Trevelyan family home in Northumberland, and Sir Charles offered him an old dower house in the village of Cambo at a reduced rent: "Luckily Len was as much taken with the roomy and manageable old house as I was, with its southern views over the moors and its 600-feet-upness." The house was called The Two Queens. It had been a pub, and Geoffrey was delighted that the old sign, with portraits of Queen Elizabeth and Mary Queen of Scots, was still there.

They moved there in May. Geoffrey was determined that they should have help with the house-keeping, but it proved hard to find. He wrote in his diary:

> Len must be relieved from fetching coals in snow-storms from outside sheds and always cooking! What a strange revolution our life has seen! In youth we did not count as well off. But there were never less than three to six servants in our houses, and shelves of new clothes as a matter of course. And the structure of life firm under us, and all unseen. Now it seems quite as natural to help in wiping up and making beds and such. I was a kind and considerate boy, I know, but it would have seemed wrong to me to pick up clothes and things off the floor, or arrange bedclothes or such – that would have been trespassing on the servants' province and "not done". They would have thought so too.

In Greece at this time Jocelin was working on the establishment of a Gordonstoun-type school, with the encouragement of the royal family. There was opposition to the scheme and Jocelin's power was resented in some quarters, but the work went ahead. It was exactly the sort of venture to appeal to Geoffrey, whose letters to Jocelin were crammed with advice and bubbling with excitement. "You have one of the most difficult and enticing jobs I've ever heard of," he wrote. The school – Anavryta School at Kifissia, outside Athens – was opened, under Jocelin's headmastership, in October 1949.

The *Alpine Journal* for that year included an article that incensed Geoffrey. Written by T. Graham Brown, who was editor of the *Journal*, it gave a long and detailed account of pioneer climbing on the Innominata Face of Mont Blanc.

Geoffrey had long disliked Graham Brown, as indeed had many others. He was a crusty, cantankerous little Scotsman, a fine mountaineer in his day but hard to get on with, touchy and disputatious. His feud with Frank Smythe had been going on since the 1920s. He was one of the group who tried to obstruct Geoffrey's reforms of the early 1940s. He now published a superficially learned article, full of footnotes and references, that treated the brilliant season of 1911 as if it had been almost entirely the inspiration and work of H. O. Jones, and owed little or nothing to Geoffrey and Josef Knubel.

When he read this, Geoffrey lost no time in composing a lengthy protest and refutation which he sent to Claude Elliott, now President of the Alpine Club, in February 1950. Its concluding paragraphs sum up his complaint:

> I find it deplorable that, some 40 years after the events, and after the deaths of my friends, to the establishing of whose reputations I have devoted, both in my book and in articles and contributions to the *Journal* of the Club, more thought and more space than to any other theme, that an article should appear over the editorial name which by exaggerations, suppressions and innuendo aims at showing that proper justice has not been done to H. O. Jones; with the inference that I, as the survivor and chronicler of the 1911 season, am responsible for this injustice to my friend.
>
> I feel that the new editor would have been better advised to have reflected longer upon the care, scholarship and courtesy shown by his predecessors in producing our *Journal*, and in securing its high reputation, before he launched out to lecture and set right an elder generation, of whose standards of loyalty, both in their mountaineering and their recording, he appears to understand little or nothing.

Geoffrey was not the only member to complain. In his reply, Elliott said the article had given offence "violently and widely". He wrote:

> From what I have learnt, it looks as if people were getting sick of G.B., and as if his out-and-out attacks on those of whom he is jealous are cutting less and less ice. This makes me agree with you that you are not called upon to answer the Innominata article and that the most dignified course is to ignore it. What matters is the future, and I am accordingly writing to G.B. today to tell him that it is our tradition that before any article is printed in the *AJ* which can be constructed as criticism of a member or questions anything he has written, it should first be shown to that member.

He ended with the comment: "The sooner he ceases to be Editor the better." It was, in the event, more than four years before Graham Brown was finally sacked. Geoffrey stayed away from the club during that period. He kept the relevant papers together in a folded paper, on the outside of which he wrote: "The vicious lunatic, Professor Gr. Brown attacked me in *AJ*! C. A. Elliott was President, but could not cope with the man, or his own committee."

Though he avoided the Alpine Club, Geoffrey did not lose his interest in mountaineering. He was very impressed by W. H. Murray's *Mountaineering in Scotland*, which had been written, with amazing recall, in a German prisoner-of-war camp and which was published in 1947. Geoffrey admired Murray's approach to the sport, and the vivid clarity of his writing. Murray prefaced his book with some lines of Geoffrey's verse, and, thanking him for his permission to quote, said: "I think I might now tell you that during the worst days of imprisonment, when I thought for a while that I would never be able to climb again, I was saved again and again from the worst excesses of self-pity by the recollection of what happened to you in the last war and how you faced up to it."

The mountaineers Geoffrey most admired – for their explorations and their writings and their attitudes – were still the veteran companions, Eric Shipton and Bill Tilman. He liked their toughness and spirit of adventure, and particularly relished Tilman's wit. Tilman wrote to him in November 1948, reporting on that summer's expedition in the Himalayas: "We had an amusing season but quite unsuccessful. I think neither of us are the men we were ten years ago – another glimpse of the obvious. I must have travelled God knows how many thousands of miles for the sake of attempting two mountains. Which shows enormous devotion to mountains without a proportionate amount of skill in climbing them." A few months later, preparing for another Himalayan exploration, he wrote: "Peter Lloyd and I have burdened ourselves with a photo-theodolite; the British Museum want bird-skins as well as botany; and R. W. Lloyd wants bugs; it doesn't seem to have occurred to anyone that there are some mountains in Nepal."

There was much that Geoffrey disliked about recent trends in mountaineering. He noted in the diary: "My type of mountaineer, I feel, grows more and more out of date, as technique and mechanism take the place of our romantic pioneering." Shortly after, he wrote: "In fact, and philosophically, I am dropping out of the mountain social world. I don't like modern climbing ways, and technical stunting. And the old romance and distinction are no longer there. Bill Murray I except, and the few Cambridge men out of the past. There is no longer friendship among them, and they don't see hills any more as we did." He was not impressed by the manner of the French conquest of Annapurna in 1950, denouncing the climbers' behaviour as irresponsible and dangerous. And he was incensed when the French complained that their achievement had not been adequately acclaimed:

Some insane offence which the French, in their inferiority complex, have taken about the English not applauding their ascent this summer in the Himalayas – when two of four climbers were permanently injured through bad and ignorant mountaineering – has resulted in none of them answering letters, even my mild requests as to publication etc. They are an impossible people, with their decadence and hyper-sensitivity.

At the beginning of June 1950 Geoffrey received high academic recognition. His old friend G. M. Trevelyan, retiring from the Mastership of Trinity College, Cambridge, had become Chancellor of Durham University. Trevelyan was by this time the outstanding British historian, famous as the author of *English Social History* and loaded with honours, but he never forgot his debts to Geoffrey as his mountain leader and companion fifty years before. He maintained his regard for Geoffrey's writing, the poetry especially, and in his *Autobiography*, published in 1949, had spoken of Geoffrey as "my greatest friend through life". Almost his first decision as Chancellor was to make Geoffrey a Doctor of Letters.

Len and Geoffrey drove down from Cambo for two days of ceremonial and celebration. They were in Durham Cathedral to see Trevelyan's installation, together with many other old friends – Vincent Baddeley, Leo Amery, Claude Elliott who was now Provost of Eton, Lord Adrian who was soon to become Master of Trinity, and Professor Dover-Wilson.

The next day Geoffrey and others received their honorary doctorates from the Chancellor in the Civic Hall, Newcastle. Geoffrey walked at the head of the procession, alongside Vita Sackville-West, who was also to be honoured. Inside the hall, he was the last to go up and be presented:

I stood opposite George – led forward by the Beadle and mace – and we looked into each other's eyes until the hall quieted down. Somehow, even then, I felt that the long friendship, that belonged to the open air and hills and wars, came full circle and clicked its ends together, in the long hand-clasp that ended his little speech. I could feel he was deeply moved; and afterwards, Len says he was near tears, with the emotion of it.

Two weeks later Len drove him across the Pennines for the official opening of the Outward Bound Mountaineering School at Eskdale. It was a big occasion. The press were there in force and many dignitaries, including the Minister of Education and Lord Rowallan, the Chief Scout. But Geoffrey was the star. He was given, he says, "a royal welcome". He spoke impromptu but from the heart and, by all accounts, movingly: "As usual now, I had thought out the line and gone over it in mind twice, but made no notes and left it to the moment to phrase. A good system, once one can trust oneself not to black-out!" He commented wryly in his journal on "the queer apotheosis I now enjoy – as if one could acquire merit for length of life, for the things one did and said better in one's youth, with no one much minding".

In an article he wrote later that year he summed up his hopes for Outward Bound in these words:

> Our Mountain School is *not* there to make climbers. Our Sea Schools are *not* there to make sailors by profession; though they may encourage the right boys to adventure upon that great life. The schools are there to bring the craft of sailing, the craft of mountains, their adventures, their discipline, their traditions of service and of mutual help, to bear upon the characters of boys. They will find there also incitements to the appreciation of beauty, and make acquaintance – willy-nilly – with unfamiliar sensations of reverence, of awe, of fear, of healthy fatigue; and with the glorious realisation that, when endurance is at its limit, will can still win through.

The winter of 1950–51 was unusually bitter, and Len and Geoffrey lived for a while in one room at The Two Queens, to keep warm and economise on fuel. Their spirits were sustained by the prospect of an impending trip to Greece. The news from Athens was good. Jocelin's school had started well, and Jocelin himself had become engaged to a young Swedish countess, Ghislaine de la Gardie. On Trafalgar Day 1950 Geoffrey composed a poem to mark the event:

> Seven years of stormy Quest, and wild sea-faring: –
> The sunlit Isles of Greece
> Saw Jason homeward bound: his Argo bearing
> The Golden Fleece.
>
> Seven years of warfare, and of lone sea-faring: –
> The Isles of Greece – again –
> See Jocelin harbour-bound: his vessel bearing
> Golden Ghislaine.

Len and Geoffrey flew out for the wedding in mid-February 1951. They were delighted to be under sunshine and clear skies again, charmed by Ghislaine, and impressed by Jocelin's school: "The Gordonstoun system simplified and clarified and centralised, with the experience of seven years as a responsible naval officer." They went to many parties; made friends with the King and Queen; and were taken sight-seeing by Jocelin.

One particular drive, to Corinth, inspired Geoffrey with an idea that was to become important to him. He wrote in the diary:

> Indescribable! – the sun on blue bays and seas, and lilac islands, and hills with snow summits beyond. We lunched at Corinth, on polypods and halva. The view through the columns of the Temple of Apollo, over the glittering blue gulf, to the snows of Parnassus – the loveliest, perhaps, I've ever seen. But indeed the proportions of Grecian views are the foundation of proportion in all man's art and thought. To think that in the 150 years, this atmosphere and environment produced the beginnings and *chef d'oeuvres* of art and drama and philosophy. Those three peaks, Parnes, Hymettus and Pentelikon, round our view from our windows, were the framing-work of civilisation and culture. Never too much sea in sight, never too high hills – one passing into the other, and in human grasp. This has never been enough accentuated – the part that these hills took in the beginnings of man's emergence.

The wedding took place on March 11, 1951, with the Greek royal family and most of the Athens diplomatic corps in attendance. Geoffrey noted:

> A most brilliant affair, as a show and occasion. And, so as to make no mistakes, I pencilled the notices for *Times* and *Daily Telegraph*, and showed them to Levides [the Court Chamberlain] on the spot – he entirely approving. Len looked lovely all the day, erect and tall, in black and white and veil. I believe we passed muster as parents, and carried the flag adequately.

After more sight-seeing, they went on to Spain where they had arranged to stay with Georis at his house on the south coast. They flew to Madrid, and while there Geoffrey collapsed, running a high temperature. He was rushed to the Colonial Hospital in Gibraltar, treated with penicillin and allowed to leave after five days. They were driven to Georis's "old monastic house" near Torremolinos, and luxuriated in comfort and sunshine: "We sat in the sunny garden, under palms and paradise trees and pergolas of roses and orange-blossom, and I convalesced in that astounding air. And Len rested." Georis was there, laying a pebble inlaid pavement on the garden paths. Geoffrey wondered at his brother: "Georis, in 79th year, is still slim and agile, and sees without glasses; his mind as amazing as ever, if more inclined than ever to make everything fit into elaborate patterns, every event and action . . . But his human noticing is keener than ever, how one looks, and his response is infinitely kind and even tender."

The trip ended with a visit to Granada and the Alhambra: "A wonder! As we came out on the plain below the Nevadas, the evening sun was roselit on the high snows, and in front was the terrace of lights and shadows of the castellated rocks and city. We lodged in a small, excellent Pension Americana, inside the walls, and were ideally happy . . . An idyll, that did us worlds of good."

By comparison with all this, Northumberland seemed bleak and cheerless when they reached home. For weeks on end, the north-east wind brought cold and rain and fogs. Britain was beset by strikes. Robert Trevelyan had died. On June 5, 1951 Geoffrey wrote in the diary: "I am depressed about the state of things. Sometimes I feel that I have lived too long, into too sad an age. And that I am all too much on the shelf. But, unluckily perhaps, nature leaves my mind and make-up as youthful as ever. So I have the present always about me, happy or sad, and can't, like a respectable veteran, retire on to memories."

August brought better news. On the 24th Marcia gave birth to a baby boy, Thomas, Len and Geoffrey's first grandchild. And next day Geoffrey received a letter from G. M. Trevelyan, praising *Mountains with a Difference* as his best prose work – "a great work and a great memorial". The book was well-reviewed everywhere, especially by Freya Stark in the *Observer*. A few months later it was awarded the Heinemann Prize, worth £100, as "the best literary work of 1951", and Geoffrey was made a Fellow of the Royal Society of Literature.

Soon after *Mountains with a Difference* was completed, Geoffrey set to work on another, and his last, autobiographical book, dealing with the non-mountaineering aspects of his early life – the idyllic childhood by the Thames, his Mediterranean adventures with Georis in the first years of the century, his First World War experiences in Belgium and northern Italy. It was to be published in 1953 under the title *The Grace of Forgetting*.

This period, the early 1950s, brought many reminders of mortality. Will Arnold-Forster died at the end of 1951; the next year brought the deaths of Norman Douglas, Conor O'Brien and Page Dickinson, then Desmond MacCarthy, then – the hardest blow of all – of Georis.

And there were mounting worries about the stability of Kurt Hahn. Geoffrey was still an active member of Gordonstoun's governing body, and a regular visitor. As early as June 1950 he was noting in the diary that Hahn was "impossible some days". Hahn had been driving himself as hard as ever, running the school in Scotland, travelling the world to stimulate interest and raise money, setting up close links between the many schools based on his ideas. He could be his old forceful self one day, virtually hopeless the next. Fears were beginning to grow about the fate of Gordonstoun under his powerful but now erratic guidance.

In September 1952 Geoffrey sent a sealed envelope to Jocelin, together with instructions that it should be opened if he were to die suddenly. It is not apparent what prompted him to this action, but the note inside made his wishes clear enough. Jocelin was to hurry to Len's side as fast as possible. He had set £1,000 aside for Len "for immediate arrangements". He had made a will leaving what was left of his money, after taxation, half to Len and a quarter each to Marcia and Jocelin. He asked Jocelin to look after the family things – documents, letters, pictures, books, collections of coins, autographs and arms. Geoffrey's great concern was for Len's well-being: "Len is not to be left alone," he commanded, "except near one of you, or with a friend she chooses. She is My Little Len, always, and the small girl of seven who recited her poems, and came down to dance with me reluctantly – and was a more radiant girl than any I ever saw . . . Len will be very lonely. See that she takes up her writing again, hard. She could do some good books."

Len and Geoffrey had another long escape holiday to the sun in the winter of 1952–3, this time in New Zealand. They sailed from the Albert Dock, London, on November 28 in a tourist class ship of the New Zealand Line, RMS *Ruahine*. Geoffrey opened a special diary with the words: "So the adventures start, at 76, again."

Arriving at Wellington they were welcomed by the Alpine Club veteran A. P. Harper. Old friends in Britain, especially Scott Russell, had arranged an elaborate programme of journeys and introductions for them, and they travelled extensively, enjoying generous hospitality and admiring the landscape, staying on sheep farms and in mountain huts, greeted everywhere by local branches of the New Zealand Alpine Club, with many dinners and speeches, and much lionising. Geoffrey was astonished that so many, young as well as elderly, knew about him.

He was impressed by the Southern Alps: ". . . plenty of fun, for centuries, for local climbers". But he did not approve of everything he saw: "New Zealand is the least aesthetic country, in architecture, the arts, in dress or music: the taste, in all things, lacking."

They were back in England in April 1953 and Geoffrey recorded: "We returned up an England looking its loveliest, in bursting green hedges and white sudden blossom, to bitter northern and easterly blasts. So we cowered beside fires, while the chimney smoked and the hot water boiler went out, and L. wrestled grimly with cold and isolation. Indeed she feels it more than I do, and it is once again clear that 'this must end'." A few weeks later it was still bleak: "Nothing to be done in the garden. I sit by the fire, and L. moans our fate. I suggest we should have a wailing wall in the house to localise our complaining."

They spent a night at the Eskdale school, where Eric Shipton had taken over: "As usual," Geoffrey noted, "he was charming, distinguished, diffident and quite decided." After leading the first post-war reconnaissance expedition to Everest in Britain's renewed campaign to climb the mountain, he had, amid much mountaineering world furore, been dropped from the 1953 expedition. Shipton had been appointed leader, and was then replaced – possibly on account of an excess of "diffidence" over "decision". Instead John Hunt was marshalling the siege being laid to the newly opened Nepalese side of the mountain.

June 2 was Coronation Day, and they listened to the ceremonies and speeches and celebrations on the radio, "sharing the hysteria and glorifications", as Geoffrey put it. It was also the day when the country heard that Everest had at last been climbed. Geoffrey was less than overjoyed: "Today the Queen knights John Hunt and the New Zealander Hillary. Finally sticking this publicity mountain stunt into vulgarised 'result' shows of modern soulless sport. However, they are good chaps, all the team. And it won't be long before the Variety Show and Music Hall cheering are forgotten, and – now it's done – we shall get back to real mountaineering once more. The really great peaks remain to be climbed."

What did delight Geoffrey was the story he heard some time later – that the telephone in the Alpine Club had rung early that morning. The Club steward was still in bed. His wife who was preparing breakfast, answered and was astonished to hear Prince Philip's voice. She explained that her husband was not yet up, so Philip said: "Tell him to ring up the Press Secretary, and everyone else, and say Colonel Hunt's party has climbed Everest." She said she would. "And now," the prince added, "go on getting breakfast ready. I'm going to get mine. I've rather a full day ahead."

These years were important in Geoffrey's family life. Two more grandchildren arrived: to Jocelin and Ghislaine in Greece, a son they called Mark; to Marcia and Peter, a second son, Harry. Geoffrey settled very happily into the role of fond grandfather.

He was surprised, after the death of Georis, to find himself frequently remembering his elder brother, with affection and gratitude and some wonder. And now, a gradual *rapprochement* with Hilton took place. In December 1953, on a house-hunting tour in the south, he noted: "A night with Hilton, alone as his younger generations had just flown off to Rome. For the first time in many years, we felt at ease together, and chatted easily over the fire. He tries a bit now to come out of his close wall." Four months later, when Geoffrey went into University College Hospital in London for an operation to remove a stomach ulcer, he wrote: "Hilton, when I rang him up that night and told him, asking him to look after Len, played up in our one-time fraternal unity and understanding without words. Indeed L. stayed with him all the time, and we came back to a pleasant intimate footing once again – after all the years of his marriage and painful withdrawal from me."

At Gordonstoun it was a time of crisis. In 1952 Kurt Hahn was committed to a mental hospital in Oxford to be treated for manic depression. He was there for several months. When released, he returned to take charge at Gordonstoun, but there was no discernible improvement in his conduct. He was imperious but often quite irrational, suffering from persecution fantasies.

Something, clearly, had to be done, but there was no one on the spot with the strength of character and resolution to tackle the problem. The only person Hahn would listen to was Geoffrey. He was sent for, immediately saw the seriousness of the situation, and set about resolving it with all his old diplomatic guile.

It was a tough job but he kept at it relentlessly, in private discussions and in the chair at many meetings, remaining cool and clear-headed and articulate. He drafted a letter asking Hahn to resign and got most of the school governors and senior staff to approve it.

All this happened in June/July 1953. Hahn agreed to go, and the governors agreed that the school would be run by joint headmasters, H. L. Brereton and Robert Chew.

In his diary Geoffrey recorded:

Never had a more difficult job in life than the settling of Gordonstoun after Hahn's break-up . . . I found my younger colleagues in great straits, and the senior staff. I took complete charge . . . I need not repeat details of the talks of the settlement. Time will test them. But I am conscious that, had I not been there, I believe the school would have smashed, following upon general resignation by governors and staff.

He also said in his diary: "It was personally deeply painful. I owe so much to Hahn. And I was forced not only to form objective judgements of him as he now is, but to lead colleagues and Hahn's loyal staff to do the same. There was no room for sentiment, with a great school and some 400 folk at stake."

It is a tribute to the bigness of both men that their friendship not only survived, but was even strengthened by these events. At the time Hahn told Geoffrey: "I have known no one who possessed such powers of concentration, together with such vivid awareness of all that was going on round." And a few months later, when Geoffrey was very ill, Hahn wrote to Len:

All my thoughts are with you in these terrible days and all my hopes accompany you. For you this suspense must be hardest to bear. You know I have such faith in the soundness of his physique that I somehow believe he can shake off affliction which would destroy the ordinary man. Doctors should realise that Geoffrey has nerves on which they can rely, in making their decision . . . I regard Geoffrey's friendship as one of the blessings of my life – what does it matter if we read the events of June differently!

The Grace of Forgetting came out at the end of 1953. It was Geoffrey's last book. His son-in-law Peter Newbolt had arranged for Country Life, with whom he was production manager, to publish it. Newbolt took Geoffrey to meet the editorial director, with some trepidation because he knew the firm was not over-generous in its dealings with authors. The normal deal was a 10% royalty on sales. He was amazed and impressed and delighted when Geoffrey came out with a contract for 25% on the entire edition.

Newbolt designed the book and supervised its production. He spent two days closeted with Geoffrey at The Two Queens, going through hundreds of photographs. There was uncertainty about the book's title. Geoffrey suggested *Then and Now*, but no one was enthusiastic. At one stage, Newbolt says, he was in the upstairs room where the books were kept, leafing through Geoffrey's early verse, and came across the lines:

'Tis only the setting
of sorrow that lets us live on;
The grace of forgetting
all else but the joy that is gone . . .

They seemed appropriate. He went downstairs and suggested the third line for the elusive title, and the idea was accepted straightaway.

The sickness that took Geoffrey into University College Hospital, London, in early 1954 was serious. At the time it was said to be for the removal of a stomach ulcer, but it may have marked the first stage of the stomach cancer that was to kill him four and a half years later.

Kurt Hahn was deeply concerned. He wrote to Geoffrey from Salem on February 7:

> Len wrote that you are in hospital for investigation. I know that only necessity would have made you go. So I am naturally in suspense. But I also remember the numerous occasions on which you defeated illness, thanks to a unique resilience in adversity . . . I know no nobler will than yours. In saying this I am thinking less of your achievements on high hills. I have in mind your labours of love in the first world war. They went beyond human strength. My memory goes back to your intervention in my own life. I owe it to you that I survived the wrench from Salem undamaged in my strength. You have powers of friendship which never fail. Your recovery is at this moment my greatest concern.

Hahn's faith in his friend's will and constitution proved justified on this occasion. Geoffrey recovered quickly from the operation and resumed life at the old pace.

He and Len spent months house-hunting in southern England, staying with friends all over the area. They had a new car – a Ford Prefect that cost £185 – and petrol was no longer rationed, so they made the most of their opportunity to explore not only in the south but in the Scottish Border hills, Northumberland, the Yorkshire Dales, North Wales and the Lake District.

One such trip became a favourite family story. Len was driving them along Borrowdale's narrow and twisting road, enthusing about Hugh Walpole and his *Herries Chronicle* stories and the Herries landscape all around, her arms waving about and the car weaving violently between the stone walls. Geoffrey, in the back seat, had long become accustomed to her erratic driving and had learned to bear it with steely calm, but even he, on this occasion, was moved to say at last, very firmly: "Damn Hugh Walpole!"

The Old Dungeon Ghyll Hotel in Langdale was a regular calling-place, chiefly because they liked the company and warm hospitality of the proprietors, Sid and "Jammy" Cross. Sid Cross, one of the first working-class boys to take to rock climbing, had turned the hotel into a popular rendezvous for climbers and mountain walkers. In his diary Geoffrey called him "the wise climbing host".

Sid Cross, who now lives in retirement on the outskirts of Ambleside, remembers Len and Geoffrey with deep affection:

> She was very lively, always. He was quiet, a gentle man, not dominating in manner but a very impressive presence, striking-looking, like Lloyd George. I never saw him lose his temper. I never heard him laying down the law. He would spend hours propped up against the wall near the bridge, gazing up at the circle of crags, and I used to think, "There he is, enjoying his days on the fells." He never moaned about it, that he could no longer go fell walking or climbing.

Cross had converted an old shippon into a rough bar for climbers camping in the valley. It was packed out every evening. He was surprised, after dinner one night, when Geoffrey asked to be taken there:

> I thought, "My God, it's a seething mass in there." But I couldn't get out of it, so I led him in and it stank of wet clothes, drying out, and there was a great din of loud talk – no one drunk, just all exultant climbers. And he said, "It's rather wonderful, isn't it? The company in here." I'd half expected him to be a bit snooty about them, scruffy rag-tag types. But he liked the vivacity of them.

They finally, and with few regrets, took their leave of The Two Queens, Cambo, at the end of July 1954. They left some of their things at the Newbolts' house in Wheathampstead, and put the rest into store. Geoffrey was jubilant to hear from Greece that he now had a granddaughter, Sophie: "After three grandsons, a granddaughter is very welcome."

In October, still without a home in England, they set off on the last of their long winter holidays abroad, to Greece and Italy by way of North Africa.

They sailed from Liverpool on MT *Livorno*, the only passengers on a cargo ship bound for the Mediterranean. "It is much like our large private yacht," Geoffrey wrote. He got along well with the captain, enjoyed the good food and attentive service, and made friends with a greenfinch that had come along for the ride. He lost sight of the bird while they were docked at Algiers, and noted: "He had an effortless migration! and I hope will remember the ports and a ship next time, and tell his family!" Next day the greenfinch reappeared and Geoffrey added: "Clearly, he's booked for the Far East."

They had time ashore at Tripoli and inspected the ruins of Carthage, but it was something else that caught Geoffrey's eye and imagination:

> Then, an indescribable pleasure. A white Arab township, Savia, in the full crowd and flow of its cattle market. The road in, we saw crowded with white moving figures, stately ghosts under the dusty sunshine: scores and scores of them: all white; all in the heavy graceful folds; all absorbed in talk and movement . . . I have never seen anything more classically beautiful than the white buildings under trees, and the moving rhythm of all-white figures, standing, sitting, white-bearded along under walls; slowly changing patterns of altering shades and shapes of whiteness; only broken by the gold and brown faces or grey beards framed in the white folds.

Jocelin and Ghislaine were there to welcome them ashore at Piraeus on the evening of October 23: "Warm night, lights, gentle airs. Thrilling moments of meeting again – and off in the great car, up always vaster roads and thicker buildings to Anavryta." Geoffrey had been anxious that the bitterness between Greece and Britain over the future of Cyprus might be making life difficult for Jocelin. It was, but Jocelin was determined to make this a magical and memorable holiday for his parents and he did.

On his birthday, a few days after arrival, Geoffrey did his usual stock-taking in his diary: "The 79th year. A little stiffer in the surviving leg, and slower at balance and recovery. Otherwise? Hearing as good, sight even better, it seems! – teeth and senses all (I think) as sound: capacity to appreciate, take in, enjoy – as ever. Time is being very kind."

In the next weeks there was much to take in and enjoy. Greek food and wine suited him, and he was delighted to find he could eat and drink heartily without any fear of the old stomach upsets. They went to many parties, dances, lunches and dinners, and spent long days sight-seeing in the sunshine and clear air. He portrayed it in glowing details in the pages of his diary. Once again he was vividly reminded of his journeys with Georis fifty years ago. He was deeply moved by Mycenae and enchanted by Corinth. Best of all, on November 18, was a mystery trip arranged by Jocelin which took them to Delphi for a brief stay.

Jocelin reconnoitred and found a way of getting the car high up the hillside, so Geoffrey might walk, with a little help, down through the sanctuary to the Temple of Apollo:

> Immediately, as I stood on the great pavement looking out through the remaining yellow towering columns at the great precipices and chasms across the amphitheatre, I exclaimed aloud. For here again, though the Temple from below had looked too long for its breadth, I saw that the unfailing sense of proportion had got the scale absolutely right: the columns and the Treasure were large enough to fit the scale of cliffs, mountains and valley, but not *too* large: at once settling into it, and enhancing its natural features. Once again it was overwhelming that the scenery was not there as a setting for the sacred and artistic monuments, but that the monuments were stacked up on the bases of the cliffs as acknowledgment of the over-powering atmosphere of the place; the awe, religiosity or what-you-will expressed by its proportion, grandeur and perfect balance of colour, form, lighting, distances and height.

At the end of the short visit, he noted: "I was never before tipsy to the point of fatigue, with changing beauty, beauty that came as a new *surprise* every few minutes, and for all an evening and day."

These powerful impressions led immediately to what he called "a Delphic ode", and later to a lecture on *The Influence of Mountains upon the Development of Human Intelligence*.

Back in Athens, Geoffrey was pleased to meet and chat with a writer he had long admired, the former war correspondent Alan Moorhead who was now working on a book about the Gallipoli campaign. There were further parties and excursions. Geoffrey was most impressed by the way Jocelin ran the school, and grew very fond of his grandson Mark: "A delightful and observant companion," he noted. "I shall miss him."

They left by ship on December 4, had a brief stay on Corfu, then sailed on to Venice, where they were met by their old friend Freya Stark who whisked them off to her grand villa in the hills at Asolo. Due to leave for more travels, she handed the place over to them for the next four months.

It was a big, comfortable house, full of books and treasures from its owner's travels, with a charming garden and fine views, run by an excellent staff. Geoffrey wrote in the diary: "Strange, this throw-back of a life, after harsh years. Service, meals, comfort, consideration, leisure; and they had all gone since '39. We shall profit by it, even when it ceases on our return." He also said: "I have ambled in the garden for over an hour every day; and am robust as not for years."

They were not entirely idle. Len set about learning Italian, and drove Geoffrey north to look at the places he had known so well when he ran the ambulance unit in the First World War. He began to work on his Grecian thoughts: "Writing a paper on the influence of Mountain Proportion."

Ghislaine and Mark came for a visit in January 1955: "Mark comes on a lot," Geoffrey noted. "Vastly vigorous, gay, boyish, and yet amenable. With a sense of humour that always plays up. When he flushes, and his eyes flash, he has looks as well as charm. Always trying new words, and imitating intonations."

The Newbolts telegraphed to say another grandchild had arrived, their third son, Barnaby. There was a letter from Sœur Marguerite, saying *The Grace of Forgetting* was selling in Ypres. From England came news of the launching of the Duke of Edinburgh's Award Scheme, influenced by Kurt Hahn and to be run by John Hunt, further extending the reach of the Outward Bound idea. From the mountain school in Eskdale the news was not so good. The warden, Eric Shipton, had caused a scandal by having an affair with the bursar's wife, refusing to give her up, and refusing, too, to resign. He had been dismissed and was being divorced.

The long holiday in the south came to an end in March. Geoffrey had written to Jocelin: "This has been a *great* rest, and both are years younger, we think . . . L. is in great heart. On the whole, I haven't been physically so normal for years, wolfing down wine and pastas!" They returned home by train, to find England under a blizzard. They resumed their house-hunting, concentrating their attention on Kent and inspecting dozens of places. It was not until May that they found what they had been looking for – Grovehurst at Horsmonden.

Geoffrey described it in a letter to Jocelin:

It was a 14th-century manor house. It was recast by the Austens (Jane's ancestors) about 1640. The chief rooms are all of the "land" measure i.e. 16 feet 4 square. It lies up a gentle hill, on a quiet lane. Stands with dignity, among lawns under old Scotch pines, against a rising garden . . . Kentish gables, and stone, and roughcast, and small old brick; vast red slopes of tiled roof. Leaded casements. L. approves the kitchen provision. There's electricity and water . . . Three absurd staircases, one of them Jacobean, one from Noah's Ark. At least one "Hide" . . . Ideal for children! as you take hours to find where you are. Terrific cellars. Unusable huge attic spaces. *Lots* of inconveniences. *Much* charm. Garden gorgeous for children. That decided it; we saw them there.

The place was totally unsuitable for an aging couple with little money to spare, one of them seriously disabled, managing on their own. There was no heating system. It was full of low beams and awkward corners. There was not a straight line or level surface to be seen. The garden was far too big, and much of the house and many of the outbuildings were in serious disrepair.

Both were aware of all the disadvantages, but the great history of the house, its very oddness and character, appealed to their romantic natures. The garden, and the thought of the grandchildren playing there and exploring the whole estate, clinched it. The asking–price had been £5,000. Geoffrey offered £4,500, and it was promptly accepted. He bought it in Len's name "for reasons of probable life length".

They had been together nearly forty years and now, for the first time, they had a home that was their own.

22

Conclusions: 1955–8

THEY HAD TO WAIT SEVERAL months before they could move into Grovehurst, and they spent the time travelling the country and staying with friends. They saw Spencer Chapman, whom Geoffrey described as "Just the same, with every noble quality except humour". At Cambridge, guest of the Adrians, he presided over the allotment of £300 from the Donald Robertson Trust. They had nine sun-blessed days at the Old Dungeon Ghyll Hotel, seeing countless friends. He visited the mountain school at Eskdale, now settling down again, and the new one on the shores of Ullswater that was just beginning. He was principal speaker at the Climbers' Club Ladies' Evening, and then they drove southwards to stay with the Newbolts and see the grandchildren. In London they were the guests, as often before, of Geoffrey's cousin Robert Stopford, and there were meetings with Kurt Hahn and with Humphrey Trevelyan, who had just been appointed ambassador to Egypt. Geoffrey returned to the Alpine Club and read a paper on the history of mountaineering, citing Alexander the Great as the first successful Himalayan explorer.

The great occasion, however, was the fortieth anniversary dinner of the Friends' Ambulance Unit in Italy. Len had spent months tracing old members and persuading them to attend. More than fifty people turned up: "The Metcalfes with a handsome younger son, "Daddy" Dyne, Gerald Marriage, the Geoff. Thompsons, Bas Meyer who made the pictures for *Bolts from the Blues* . . ." Philip and Irene Noel-Baker were there, and G. M. Trevelyan – "his effective staccato remarks they all love".

Geoffrey spoke too: "I gave them a good uplift, with the meaning of it all, and a jolly good poem to finish!" It was a serious poem. Here is its closing verse:

> Compassion cannot die:
> it runs, a silver ripple out of the past

along the face of time and memory
while time and memory last.
For us, it is our Youth the ripple bears
mirrored in kindness, silvered with the years,
to meet us – in each other; a work, a self more generous
– still with us,
still with us – to remember.

His diary description of the party ended: "A terrific evening, with my songs; and they all stayed on talking till after midnight. After forty years!"

In the course of their travels about England, Len and Geoffrey spent much time exploring the Yorkshire Dales, particularly the region where she had spent her happy childhood. He had been working on the genealogy of the Slingsbys, tracing them back for many centuries. He was also studying the papers of his mother's family, the Kennedys of Ireland. He found letters descriptive of the potato famines of the 1840s and sent them to the historian Cecil Woodham-Smith, then researching for her book *The Great Hunger*.

In mid-August 1955 they moved into Grovehurst, helped by Jocelin who was on leave from Greece. They bought carpets and beds at Tunbridge Wells, filled the house with carpet-fitters and carpenters, and hired a charlady and a gardener. That summer's heat wave continued, and Geoffrey saw it as an encouraging omen: "We are finding it every day and early morning sunrise a more and more lovely home-like house and garden. I made my first walk round the pond – where I hear the moorhens every morning – and through the copse . . . It is a friendly, helpful neighbourhood, of good and conscientious workmen, and we face the immense drain on strength and pockets with far greater readiness and content." In September he wrote: "Still a lovely month; and we grow every day and night fonder of this charming old house and garden. A sudden solution, and a noble and unexpected harbour for age, after so many years of colour, movement, adventure and unrest."

The deaths of old friends nearly always moved Geoffrey to compose obituary tributes in his diary. In September, when he heard that Leo Amery had died at the age of eighty-one, he wrote:

Perhaps the last of the great men and mountaineers with whom I grew up through the years of adventure. A friend of some 60 years. A man of iron; small, ruthless, enormously able, and of a wide humanity and sense of poetry and romance. His services to the state are historic . . .

I feel perhaps he is the last of the men who shared with me the great romance of mountain exploration, in the widest sense; the poetry and the adventure, and the intellectual aspect.

When he wrote this he had clearly forgotten that an even earlier climbing companion of his was still alive. In November 1955 he noted: "Dear Sandy Mackay, Lord Mackay of the Scottish Sessions and the senior judge, has died at eighty. The last of those who climbed with me in my great days. The best mountaineer, the most equable, charming, reliable comrade that ever I had with me."

Geoffrey was writing his chapter for *Snowdon Biography* at this time, so his head was full of his Pen-y-Pass gatherings before and after the First World War. The more he recalled them, and contrasted them with what had happened to the sport subsequently, the stronger grew his feelings. He wrote in the diary: "I find very little contact now with the new 'Greasy Pole' school. They are so infernally *dull*!" But a few weeks later, at an Alpine Club dinner, when he was introduced to the leading man of the new school, he was entirely won over and referred, in his diary, to "that attractive phenomenon Joe Brown, the plumber and climber of Kangchenjunga".

The year's run of good weather held into October, bringing a stream of visitors to Grovehurst. Marcia came with her three boys to spend a week there, and Geoffrey played the proud grandfather: "Harry is a potential genius, or demon! Thomas sensitive and 'one of us'. Barnaby so far just infinitely amiable. Marcia ghastly overworked."

After Christmas and into the new year, they were more than happy with the new house: "Age, except as it touches arthritic joints, still holding kindly off me. We can't warm this house with heating; so we fight in detail for warm rooms, and I grow more content each day that we bought it, and that there is a chance of ending days here with dignity, and with pleasure for the eye and ease of mind. L. likes it as much. And does wonders in the keeping it going." Geoffrey enjoyed the nest-building. On January 22, 1956 he wrote to Jocelin: "We grow fonder and fonder of this place . . . Every corner is a pleasure to come round, and see the next . . . I've made curtains, and stuck up rods on the Parlour staircase . . . Rather fun, as an evening job."

The beginning of February, though, brought a steady north-east wind and blizzards and heavy frost. The charwoman could not get to the house. The water cisterns froze solid, and for a week they had no hot water at all. Then came a rapid thaw. Pipes burst; water leaked everywhere; some ceilings collapsed: "Feb. 6: The snow has gone. The house looks like an after-battle field on the Isonzo. Even at 79 I find it all makes me laugh, as it used to at 18, and again in the war! I was born obviously for an emergency sort of life, and react best to sudden disasters . . . It's hard on L., who has different likings, and hates mess and collapses of ceilings and chars." He told Jocelin: "Len manages wonderfully. It's just like life in an Alpine hut."

February 15 was G. M. Trevelyan's eightieth birthday, and Geoffrey sent him some celebratory lines:

> You were, and are, the Poet: now as then:
> You felt the poetry of moors and hills:
> You found it in the fate, and feats, of men,
> in movements of great hearts, and passionate wills.
> You *live* the poetry, that never ends
> for those with faith in Freedom, and in Friends.

Two days later, at St Martin-in-the-Fields in London, Geoffrey spoke movingly at the memorial service for Irene Noel-Baker. As he was being driven back to Kent, the snow was falling again, heralding another period of intense cold, frozen pipes and collapsing ceilings. Geoffrey commented: "It is grim luck that the worst winter for half a century should tackle us before we have got this place in order. The birds, fed with porridge, are our consolation. Baths and hot water, of a remote past!"

But spring came at last and he set to work in the garden, despite the increasing arthritic pain in his right hip. He was never heard to complain about this or any of his other ailments and disabilities. In the diary he wrote: "I will *not* let the hip rule life!"

He had been asked to deliver the W. P. Ker Memorial Lecture at Glasgow University, and decided to develop and expound the idea that had come to him in Greece. Len drove him north and he gave the lecture on May 2, describing it in his diary as ". . . some bold theorising. Very well received."

It was later published as a booklet, *The Influence of Mountains upon the Development of Human Intelligence*. It is a remarkable, original and polished piece of work. The core of his argument can be conveyed in two paragraphs:

Greece, however, the Peloponnese and Attica, is the one wholly mountainous land of racial antiquity and of a long and recorded culture. Mountainous, it is also the land with the most pellucid atmosphere, the clearest

lighting. It was the definiteness of Grecian sunlight, and its positive shadow, which gave to the Greek eye, and so to the mental realisation the first detached vision of natural beauty, the first perception of the relationship of form to colour, of a human being to his environment. It impelled the Greek to express this discovery in the first faultless artistic forms . . .

But the revealing light upon that mountainous, sympathetic, and therefore formative environment did more than create the artistic vision; it, first, taught the human mind to reason. In Greece occurred a simultaneous miracle, or, as we may term it, break-through, in the evolution of mankind. This small people not only first acquired detached artistic vision; it achieved coincidentally the sudden break-through of the intelligence into abstract thought and logical reasoning. For this, the cause, the influence exerted through numberless ages upon the succeeding human generations, is to be found, as we ourselves can still see it, in the unique balance, the perfect proportioning, of the landscape – which encircles us, no matter which way we turn, with an absolute harmony of relationship between hills and plain and sea and sky.

Geoffrey's theory was widely criticised, but his conviction was never undermined. He sent a copy of the booklet to Jocelin, and said in the accompanying letter: "It is at least audacious . . . I'm inclined to think it is the most original thinking I've contrived."

In July Jocelin and his family arrived for a holiday at Grovehurst. Jocelin was on his way to Norway to climb Skagastolstind on the eightieth anniversary of its first ascent by his grandfather Cecil Slingsby.

There was another eightieth anniversary that year – Geoffrey's birthday. On October 25 he noted:

Dear L. had stirred up friends a bit; and all day the postmaster staggered up with telegrams of greeting and parcels and the like. Over 60 wires, and from some half dozen different countries . . . The best excitement locally was one from Philip of Edinburgh, from Buckingham Palace. All the great mountain clubs wire or write, Italy, Swiss, English, Scottish, and all my schools, Outward Bound and so on. Most moving – for a quiet and very retired man . . . Kurt Hahn dashed down, with present of a chair, Phyllis Edwards worked the great surprise, by having a television set fixed up. Such a generous thought, for our aged fireside.

A little later he reflected : "I've long wanted to get past this age, and be done with it! The 70s were boring . . ."

This was not the end of the birthday celebrations. A few weeks later he and Len went to Eton where he was guest of honour at a select party for old Pen-y-Pass friends in the Provost's Lodge.

Claude Elliott, their host, presented Geoffrey with a large album, bound in red leather, which contained messages of congratulation from the Duke of Edinburgh, the British Mountaineering Council, many climbing clubs, Gordonstoun and Salem, and the Bourgmestre of Ypres. It also contained photographs of Geoffrey's favourite mountains, and the signatures of 250 mountaineers – 100 British, 10 American, 30 French, 20 New Zealanders including Sir Edmund Hillary and George Howe, Italians and Germans and Austrians, and almost 60 Swiss, including Josef Knubel. Geoffrey wrote in his diary: "Everything contributed to delightful and carefree talk and reminiscence, and long happy hours of evening company; such as now is rare, in such noble setting . . . As he ran downstairs at parting next day, Claude looked back, gleaming – 'Old men do *not* forget!' "

The television set proved a blessing. Despite his disability, Geoffrey had never lost his admiration for graceful, athletic movement of all kinds, and he spent many happy hours watching sports programmes – rugger and soccer, gymnastics and athletics, tennis and boxing. He and Len enjoyed *The Good Old Days*, a re-creation of Victorian/Edwardian music hall, and plays, and dancing. The popular maestro of strict-tempo ballroom dancing, Victor Sylvester, had served briefly with the ambulance unit in Italy and been wounded the day after Geoffrey lost his leg. In his diary Geoffrey said: "TV has made a real difference."

He still took an anxious interest in national affairs. When the Suez crisis exploded he was at first in support of Eden's interventionist moves, though he soon came to see them as a blunder. The continuing struggle with the Greeks over Cyprus remained a worry to him, partly because he loved Greece, partly because of its possible effects on Jocelin's position and work.

In October 1956 the Alpine Club at last made him an honorary member. He was writing an article – *Clubs and Climbers*, covering the years from 1880 to 1900 – for the special centenary issue of the *Alpine Journal*, to be published the following year.

As usual, he went in November to the Rucksack Club's annual dinner, and commented: "A very fair level of speaking. No vulgarities, thank goodness. My protest and Wilding's influence have cleared the air there. But up at the Fell and Rock Jubilee Dinner, L. reports some bad blots. The aftermath of war still, and the barrack-room. It lets down the whole level of speaking, if men play for these easy, pre-school sniggers."

Later that month Marcia had a baby girl, named Catherine Eacy. Geoffrey noted: "Colossally welcome after the troop of tough boys . . . Eacy to make the fifth generation of that name, that I've known."

The year's end found him planting roses in the garden and contented: "Somehow, now, my mind is happy, resting on that kind of beauty and its growth."

Things were not so good for Len. For weeks on end the house was full of workmen, installing the much-needed heating system. Jocelin contributed £400 to the cost.

The appearance of a book by Ronald Clark, *Six Great Mountaineers*, which included a chapter in praise of Geoffrey, prompted some modest self-assessment:

> He is most kind to me; and it still gives me an amused puzzlement to read of myself as "a legendary figure in his lifetime", and that sort of estimate. Honestly, I have never seen myself as the least "great", or deserving of half the sort of reception that has now caught up with me in age. I've enjoyed doing things, and later enjoyed writing things. And I never saw myself as "good-looking" in youth, and seemed to self half a failure, without good brains, and half a fraud. However, it's nice that anyone should think nice things . . .

Perhaps there were some intimations of mortality. He does not say so specifically in the diary, but in one passage he recalls that both his mother and his brother Georis died after thrombosis and says: "I know that now I am very vulnerable . . . May it come to me as suddenly, is my one deep anxiety." He was putting his affairs in order:

> I'm altering the disposal of what I leave. Now that I'm living so long, Eleanor will need all that's there, to cover her own age, of working these years, unaided, for mine. And the two children are launched, and have their own families; no longer needing that outside help useful in the starting of life and family. Also, this house, if kept going, may make the best retreat for any of them.

The winter of 1956–7 was much milder than its predecessor, so much so that the new heating was hardly needed: "The last adjustments made to heating and to lighting," Geoffrey noted in February 1957: "A comfortable warm house. George L. Trevelyan just identified it as a medieval double hall, from its structure etc. A clever piece of detection that pleases us. I like to think of the Grosgerts sitting in armour where I do! – who took their name from the Hall in 1200–1300."

Dr Janos Plesch died in March: "He looked after me free for some ten or more years. In return L. carried off his manuscript autobiography and got Gollancz to publish, which was a huge success . . . I never met anything like his marvellous diagnoses; or his hands. He knew, he said – and it was true – every inch of my anatomy, even below the surface, and did marvels for me during the bad 60s to 70s."

Although petrol was rationed, in the wake of the Suez crisis, Geoffrey managed to get to London to chair meetings of the Gordonstoun Council – "They treat me now as a venerable great-uncle" – and in May they were in North Wales for the Alpine Club's centenary meet:

> The Pen-Y-Gwryd and crowds. Arnold Lunn and Geoffrey Bartrum of the old school. The Hunts also, and the Olympic runners Brasher and Disley, nice boys. We drove about, and to the coast. I made up my mind at last about the immense change to the new climbing world. No use bridging any gap. It is a new and different mind, as well as approach. Joe Brown and the colossal new "tigers" doing their rock tricks for television. I was kept a whole morning to record a three-minute introduction. And I had to repeat it, owing to a camera break.

There was a prolonged drought that year, from March to July, and the garden at Grovehurst withered in the dry north-easterly wind. The drought ended with a ferocious hailstorm that smashed plants and the greenhouse. In addition, Geoffrey was increasingly worried about Jocelin's future in Greece, where things were getting difficult. Geoffrey and Len had planned to go to the Alps for another centenary meet of the Alpine Club, but they cancelled the trip: "Too laborious, for too little return. Yet I must get out and see J. K. again soon . . ." But he never did see Knubel again.

In September 1957 Geoffrey wrote the final entry in his diary:

> Monsignor Ronald – 'Ronnie' – Knox has died. The wittiest clergyman since Sydney Smith, they call him. He did essays for me at Eton, before his scholarship, like Keynes, Eustace Percy, Laurence Jones and other famous men and writers. I never saw him again afterwards. Oddly enough, his portrait is very like that other but very different and agnostic bishop, E. W. Barnes, who was also my close friend, at Cambridge. What a lot of remarkable and much abler men have at some time been my friends.

It was the last of the many thousands of diary paragraphs that Geoffrey had written since he started keeping a journal when he took up his post at Eton in January 1902.

He had committed himself to give a lecture at the Alpine Club centenary celebrations in London in December, but was having a struggle getting it finished. He felt tired and listless, and sometimes had to give up and go to bed, running a high temperature. Even so, he went on writing lively, newsy letters to Jocelin. He was at the Rucksack Club dinner in Manchester, and enjoyed Eustace Thomas's hospitality for the last time. And he went to London, on November 22, to attend an important meeting of the Friends of Gordonstoun.

The meeting was to launch plans for the expansion of the school, to be financed by ICI. The chief of the company, Sir Alex Fleck, was there, and Kurt Hahn, and the Duke of Edinburgh and Lord Louis Mountbatten, and many other dignitaries. There were speeches: "Then we circulated," Geoffrey reported to Jocelin:

> Philip by the by was observed only to take tonic water – and I chatted endlessly, with ex-admirals with high minds . . . With Fleck too, and congratulated a flushed Hahn. Mountbatten faded, not having the first place, but the other Sea Lords swam about . . . As the Select and Great thinned out, Philip stayed on, still flashing away with everyone in turn. He spotted me across the room, and came over for a good five minutes, about Outward Bound etc.

By early December the doctors knew that Geoffrey had stomach cancer. They told Len, and warned her that although he might well survive for some time, it was possible also that his heart might suddenly collapse under the strain. She had to decide whether Geoffrey should be told, and it did not take her long. He took the news with his customary courage, determined to go on living life at the full – as far as his condition would allow.

He and Len were in London to help the Alpine Club celebrate its 100th birthday. Sir John Hunt, now President of the Club, officiated and there was a grand reception attended by the Queen. Geoffrey wrote to Jocelin on December 14:

> The Shows were great fun. Hunt a magnificent man for the job. At the Reception, L. had a lovely gown, and the small turquoises; she looked 35, and made the best curtsey of the evening . . . The Queen had been given a glass of that horrible Bouvier – the only drink! – of course, couldn't drink it, and nobody took her glass, so she waved it about agreeably

through our talk. I made her throw back her head and laugh, about Philip . . . Everyone pursues me now with arm–chairs and affection, and it is quite moving. The lecture went with a bang. I let them have a bit of fire, and emotion. A swan–song. And dashed hard to hammer out, during this dragging autumn . . .

His lecture made a powerful impression. He took the opportunity of criticising some modern trends in mountaineering, but most of the talk was devoted to expressing what the mountains had meant to him. Wilfrid Noyce wrote: "Those who heard it will remember it always for the fire that still sparkled, the tones that continued to ring clear." And Arnold Lunn was so moved that he sent Geoffrey a long letter a few days later, thanking him for the lecture: ". . . I felt that it was, perhaps, the last that you would read to the AC, and I wanted to say something about your immense influence on generation after generation of young climbers." Lunn described his own debt to Geoffrey and added: "It is surely evidence of the strength of the mountain bond that you and I, whose interpretation of this funny universe is so very different and who are in many ways so very different, should yet have been such close and intimate friends."

In the same letter in which he described events at the Alpine Club, Geoffrey also told Jocelin: "And now, on clever little Rhodes' [his doctor's] decided advice, I retire to University College Hospital once more, where all are friendly. For inspection and probable radio action. These temperatures, and the coughy windpipe, were becoming a long nuisance. Glad to think it will relieve L. at last of the heavy burden of nursing, plus administration."

They were at Marcia's that Christmas, and she remembers it: "We had one wonderfully happy Christmas together at Wheathampstead, not long before he died because they were looking forward to their ruby wedding, and he put his arm round her as they sat on the sofa and sang 'My Old Dutch'. My mother, for once, didn't know what to say! but they were very much at peace with each other, after all the storms."

Jocelin managed to be with them as well before Geoffrey went into hospital. By mid-January he was home again at Grovehurst and writing to Jocelin:

That was a marvel of a visit. Like two or three other good surprise appearances, which I recall in your life. Did wonders for your mother. And relieved my mind, plus the pleasure . . . Our return marvellously organised, and went well. Nurse Juniper fills the bill. House warm, and all in order. Phones still popping away, with inquiries. One absurdity: my beloved fountain-pen entirely vanished on the last day, in my bare cell of a room. No search availed, with all the hospital hopping. A strange click, two days later, down here, and it turned up *in the artificial leg*! Must have slipped out of a front breast-pocket, while I was in the chair, and made its way down, and past the stump, into the leg, while I was wearing it. Sounds incredible! But a relief.

Geoffrey was suffering little pain from the cancer, and his letters continued chirpy. In February he wrote: "The mild weather recovers, and recovers. We may yet get through unsnowed and ungelidated . . . Crocus, snowdrop and starting daffodils colour the optimistic garden . . . I seem to get fewer set-backs, and to be climbing up near a 'normal' feeling." He was reading the diaries of Sir Alan Brooke – "most valuable of all the war diaries" – and rereading, with undiminished joy, the stories of Somerville and Ross. He was reading Kipling too: "Kipling was a genius. I never forget the explosive effect in the end-'80s of his thunderclap beginnings . . . And that they were compared to the sudden beginning of Macbeth. He gets under way faster than any successor."

April 25, 1958 was their Ruby Wedding. Two months before Geoffrey was searching for some agent in London "to find me some nice surprise of ruby glasses for L.". He must have known that this, the 40th anniversary of their wedding in the final year of the First World War, was probably the last one they would celebrate together. He honoured his tradition of writing her a love poem.

> Eleanor
> Our every day is new
> for me – for you – a new
> Pearl of day opening.
> Since that first April day,
> the while the years colour, and fade, and fall:
> colour, and fade, and fall,
> touching it not at all.
> Forty years wed; this is no sunset red
> colouring to the Fall!
> A ruby glow floods upon Spring:
> And Ruby links with Pearl, festivating –
> Around Time's Ring!

A few days after the anniversary he was very moved to receive this letter:

My dearest Commandant,

Just a few words to let you know how pleased I am you are at home at Grovehurst, with your dear and courageous wife Eleanor Winthrop Young.

I so often think of you and all the good you did at Ypres.

Last week the 25th April I prayed specially for you, and your dear family, for was it not 40 years you were married? A big "Proficiat" and a "Hip! Hip! Hoorah!" for you and dear Eleanor Winthrop Young.

Your ever grateful,

Sister Marguerite of Ypres.

In June Prince Philip wrote to Len: "Thank you very much for your letter. I was most distressed to hear of your husband's serious illness and I only hope that his apparently unlimited resources of courage will help him during these critical days. I shall always remember him as one of those pioneers of Gordonstoun who combined devotion to the School with action."

Geoffrey's last letter to Jocelin was handwritten, from his sick-bed, on June 3. The writing is clumsy but legible, and he continued to put up a bright, interested, cheerful front. He was still persuading friends to send their boys to Gordonstoun; still concerned about Jocelin's future. Kurt Hahn had visited him – ". . . delightful and full of optimistic *facts*". Most of the letter is about the garden at Grovehurst, showing he had lost none of his lifelong relish for bright colours: "Garden this year really gorgeous! I can see from the window succession of superlative shrubs, many in heavenly shades (azaleas), and on the left a blazing yellow azalea, bluebells still, and my two dwarf *pure scarlet* rhodos . . . Mostly, lovely sun. Wildfowl nesting . . . Mummy reads me aloud, extremely well." At the foot of the page, Len added: "We are well away with *Emma* now. Finished *Mansfield Park* . . . Written on a fairly bad day, with bouts of leg shoots, temperature, heavy sleeps. He is quite marvellous but very weak in body."

Geoffrey had always loved the Jane Austen novels, often reading them aloud to the children when they were growing up, but now they were too gentle and slow-moving for him. "I must have more action!" he said, so Len read *Lorna Doone* instead and then *Rupert of Hentzau*.

When the end approached, Geoffrey was moved to a nursing home in Holland Park, London. Apart from Len, Kurt Hahn was the last person to see him. There was a violent thunderstorm over-night and

Geoffrey died on September 6, 1958, a few weeks short of his 82nd birthday.

He was cremated, and Len and Jocelin took his ashes, in obedience to his wishes, and scattered them on the "little tops" above Pen-y-Pass, where he had loved to walk when he could no longer stump his way to the summits.

Geoffrey left everything to Len, and it was enough to keep her in modest comfort for a further thirty-five years. Grovehurst was sold. She lived in various places – Wooden Walls near Carlisle, flats in London, in Yorkshire and in Marlborough. It was an active widowhood, visiting family and friends, attending club dinners, giving her talks on the Brontës, and taking – until the very last years – an enthusiastic interest in everything that was going on. She attended the annual reunions of the Italian ambulance unit, and a fifty-years-on reunion in Ypres. She maintained the Slingsby Norwegian connection, visited her relations in Australia and her brother Will in Africa. She loved to reminisce about Geoffrey and their life together, almost always concluding with the words: "He was a *marvellous* man!" She never stopped missing him and in the last months, when she grew confused and frequently failed to recognise her visitors, her conversations were with Geoffrey or with her brother Laurence who was killed in the First World War. She died in a nursing home in Norfolk at the end of January 1994.

Much of Geoffrey's life's work survives and flourishes. His books and poems, although long out of print, are still read and enjoyed, especially by mountain lovers. British rock climbers approach the crags armed with the pocket-sized guidebooks that he inaugurated. The British Mountaineering Council speaks for the mountaineers, and works to protect their interests. The Alpine Club has shed its old exclusivity and stuffiness to such an extent that women have been admitted to membership. Gordonstoun goes on, and so does the Outward Bound idea. Trevelyans and Trinity-men still meet at Seatoller each year to hunt each other across the fells. In 1998 they will be celebrating their centenary. The Donald Robertson Travel Fund, which Geoffrey set up in 1911 to commemorate his lost friend, still gives financial help to students who want to go on adventurous holidays in the summer vacation.

A year or so before he died Geoffrey, together with Len and Jocelin, was in Cookham church and took the opportunity of looking at the memorial tablet to his brother Georis. It read: "Artist Author Diplomat Reformer 'Fight the good fight'". It set him wondering what should be the wording of the memorial tablet to him and Len. He noted in his diary: "I should like a tablet for us, under his. With just 'Poet Mountaineer Educator' and perhaps 'Live life at the full. Blend dream with the deed', with Eleanor and her chosen Yorkshire motto *'Dieu donne le bon aventure'*."

BIBLIOGRAPHY

Abraham, George and Ashley, *Rock Climbing in North Wales*, G. P. Abraham, 1906.

Brereton, H. L., *Gordonstoun: Ancient Estate and Modern School*, Gordonstoun School, 1982.

Carr H. R. C. (and Lister, G. A.), *The Mountains of Snowdonia*, Crosby Lockwood, 1948.

Graves, Robert, *Goodbye to All That*, Jonathan Cape, 1929.

Hankinson, Alan, *The Mountain Men*, Heinemann Educational Books, 1977.

Jones, L. E., *A Victorian Boyhood*, Macmillan, 1955.

Lunn, Arnold (ed.), *Oxford Mountaineering Essays*, Edward Arnold, 1912.

——*A Century of Mountaineering*, Allen and Unwin, 1957.

Murray, W. H., *Mountaineering in Scotland*, J. M. Dent, 1947, reissued in one volume with *Undiscovered Scotland*, Diadem 1979.

Pye, David, *George Leigh Mallory*, Oxford University Press, 1927.

Robertson, David, *George Mallory*, Faber and Faber, 1969.

Russell, Scott, *Mountain Prospect*, Chatto and Windus, 1946.

Slingsby, Cecil, *Norway: the Northern Playground* (edited by Eleanor Young, with foreword by Geoffrey Young), Blackwells, 1941.

Thomson, J. M. A., *The Climbs on Lliwedd*, Climbers' Club, 1909.

Trevelyan, G. M., *An Autobiography*, Longmans, 1949.

Young, G. W., *The Roof-Climber's Guide to Trinity*, Spalding, Cambridge, 1900.

——*Wall and Roof Climbing*, Spottiswoode, 1905.

——*From the Trenches*, T. Fisher Unwin, 1914.

——*Mountain Craft*, Methuen, 1920.

——*On High Hills*, Methuen, 1927.

——*Collected Poems*, Methuen, 1936.

——*Mountains with a Difference*, Eyre and Spottiswoode, 1951.

——*The Grace of Forgetting*, Country Life, 1953.

Young, G. W., with Sutton, G. and Noyce, W., *Snowdon Biography*, Dent, 1957.

See also *The Alpine Journal*, *The Climbers' Club Journal*, *The Pinnacle Club Journal*.

INDEX

("G" denotes Geoffrey throughout; Len is Eleanor. The relationships indicated inside brackets are to Geoffrey.)